AFFECTIVE AND SCHIZOPHRENIC DISORDERS:
New Approaches to Diagnosis and Treatment

AMERICAN COLLEGE OF PSYCHIATRISTS

Officers (at the time of 1982 Annual Meeting)
JOHN C. NEMIAH, M.D., *President*

ROBERT L. WILLIAMS, M.D.
President-Elect
HAROLD M. VISOTSKY, M.D.
First Vice-President
ROBERT O. PASNAU, M.D.
Second Vice-President

HENRY H. WORK, M.D.
Secretary-General
CHARLES E. SMITH, M.D.
Treasurer
SIDNEY MALITZ, M.D.
Archivist-Historian

Program Committee for 1982 Annual Meeting
ALLAN BEIGEL, M.D., *Chairperson*

JACK W. BONNER, M.D.
PIETRO CASTELNUOVO-TEDESCO, M.D.
ROBERT O. PASNAU, M.D.
RICHARD T. RADA, M.D.

KENNETH Z. ALTSHULER, M.D.
JOHN M. DAVIS, M.D.
JAMES S. EATON, M.D.
GEORGE L. ADAMS, M.D.

Publications Committee
MICHAEL R. ZALES, M.D., *Chairperson*

JERRY M. LEWIS, M.D.
JOE YAMAMOTO, M.D.
CARL EISDORFER, M.D.
BENJAMIN BRAUZER, M.D.
ROBERT E. JONES, M.D.

GEORGE SASLOW, M.D.
JOHN S. TAMERIN, M.D.
JOE P. TUPIN, M.D.
CHARLES E. WELLS, M.D.
HENRY H. WORK, M.D.

Affective and Schizophrenic Disorders:

New Approaches to Diagnosis and Treatment

Edited by

Michael R. Zales, M.D.

Associate Clinical Professor of Psychiatry
Yale University

BRUNNER/MAZEL, *Publishers* ● New York

Library of Congress Cataloging in Publication Data

Main entry under title:

Affective and schizophrenic disorders.

   Papers presented at the annual meeting of the
American College of Psychiatrists, held in 1982 in
Orlando, Fla.
   Includes index.
   1. Affective disorders—Congresses. 2. Schizophrenia
—Congresses. I. Zales, Michael R., 1937-
II. American College of Psychiatrists.
RC537.A3 1983   616.89   82-20698
ISBN 0-87630-324-6

Copyright © 1983 by The American College of Psychiatrists

Published by
BRUNNER/MAZEL, INC.
19 Union Square West
New York, New York 10003

MANUFACTURED IN THE UNITED STATES OF AMERICA

Contributors

NANCY C. ANDREASEN, M.D., Ph.D.

Professor of Psychiatry, University of Iowa, Iowa City, Iowa

ROBERT CANCRO, M.D.

Professor and Chairman of the Department of Psychiatry, New York University Medical Center, New York City, New York

JONATHAN O. COLE, M.D.

Lecturer in Psychiatry, Harvard Medical School; Psychiatrist, McLean Hospital, Belmont, Massachusetts

WILLIAM E. FANN, M.D.

Professor of Psychiatry and Associate Professor of Pharmacology, Baylor College of Medicine: Chief, Psychiatry Service, Veterans Administration Medical Center, Houston, Texas

JOHN P. F FEIGHNER, M.D.

Associate Clinical Professor of Psychiatry, University of California at San Diego Medical School, La Jolla, California; Director of Research, Feighner Research Institute, La Mesa, California

JON E. GUDEMAN, M.D.

Associate Professor of Psychiatry, Harvard Medical School; Center Director, Massachusetts Mental Health Center, Boston, Massachusetts

JOHN GUNDERSON, M.D.

Associate Professor of Psychiatry, Harvard Medical School, Boston, Massachusetts

DAVID J. KUPFER, M.D.

Professor of Psychiatry and Director of Research, Western Psychiatric Institute and Clinic, University of Pittsburgh School of Medicine, Pittsburgh, Pennsylvania

MORRIS A. LIPTON, Ph.D., M.D.

Sarah Graham Kenan Distinguished Professor of Psychiatry, Professor of Biochemistry, Director of the Biological Sciences Research Center, Child Development Research Institute, University of North Carolina School of Medicine, Chapel Hill, North Carolina

STEPHEN R. MARDER, M.D.

Assistant Professor of Psychiatry, UCLA School of Medicine, Los Angeles, California

JOHN J. MOONEY, M.D.

Instructor in Psychiatry, Harvard Medical School; Co-Director, Affective Disease Program, McLean Hospital, Belmont, Massachusetts

PAUL J. ORSULAK, Ph.D.

Assistant Professor of Psychiatry, Harvard Medical School; Associate Director, Neuropsychopharmacology Laboratory, Massachusetts Mental Health Center; Technical Director, Psychiatric Chemistry, New England Deaconess Hospital, Boston, Massachusetts

ALAN H. ROSENBAUM, M.D.

Director of Inpatient Services, Henry Ford Hospital, Detroit, Michigan

ROBERT T. RUBIN, M.D., Ph.D.

Professor of Psychiatry, Harbor-UCLA Medical Center, Torrance, California

A. JOHN RUSH, M.D.

Associate Professor, Department of Psychiatry, University of Texas Health Science Center, Dallas, Texas

ALAN F. SCHATZBERG, M.D.

Assistant Professor of Psychiatry, Harvard Medical School; Staff Psychiatrist, Massachusetts Mental Health Center, Boston, Massachusetts

JOSEPH J. SCHILDKRAUT, M.D.

Professor of Psychiatry, Harvard Medical School; Director, Neuropsychopharmacology Laboratory, Massachusetts Mental Health Center; Director, Psychiatric Chemistry Laboratory, New England Deaconess Hospital, Boston, Massachusetts

JOHN S. STRAUSS, M.D.

Professor of Psychiatry, Yale University School of Medicine, New Haven, Connecticut

Contents

Preface

It is not often that a man has the privilege of seeing his dreams come to fruition during his lifetime. The American College of Psychiatrists is a striking exception to that general rule. Founded nearly 20 years ago by Dr. Henry P. Laughlin, the College is now one of the major North American psychiatric professional organizations. The phrase "North American" is used advisedly, for the College draws its members from Canada, Mexico, and the United States in a spirit of truly international collegiality.

For several years before its formal founding in 1963, Dr. Laughlin had been laying the groundwork for a professional college designed to honor distinguished psychiatrists, to recognize younger men and women of promise, and to bring them together regularly in the pursuit of self-education. After its birth the College followed the course set by its founder and for a number of years met annually at the time of the American Psychiatric Association meetings for a day-long symposium of papers and discussions focused on a topic chosen by the Program Committee. In February of 1968, the first separate Post-Graduate Education Program seminar was held in New Orleans; in 1973, by which time the membership had grown to over 400 persons, the mid-winter P.G.E.P. seminar was expanded to a four-day Annual Meeting with a full program of scientific papers, discussion groups, self-assessment examination, business meeting, and the proper leaven of conviviality. The College, though a mere lad of 10, had come of age as a fully autonomous professional body.

The Annual Meeting has since remained the highlight of the College's activities, but over the years a number of important additional programs have taken firm root. The Stanley R. Dean Award for Research in Schizophrenia (created in honor of one of the College's Fellows) is bestowed each year at the Annual Meeting on a world-renowned investigator, who graces the membership with a lecture on work in progress. The papers comprising the scientific program are published in an annual volume, of which this, ably edited by Dr. Michael Zales and his Publications Committee, is the latest issue. Post-graduate education for a wider professional audience is further addressed in a series of regional scientific meetings held under the aegis of the College, as well as in the distribution of specially prepared audiotapes that record discussions of selected clinical topics by college members and invited guests. In recent years, the College has spearheaded the development of the annual Residents-in-Training Assessment Examination, which has now been adopted by a large number of residency programs as a means both of evaluating the progress of their residents and of providing the residents themselves with an experience in self-assessment. And last, but by no means least, the Laughlin Fellowship Program (named in honor of the founder of the College) enables a small group of carefully selected psychiatric residents to attend the Annual Meeting as guests of the membership. Highly prized and sought after by North American residents, the Laughlin Fellowships ensure the continued life and work of the College.

Now nearing 20, the College is chronologically in late adolescence. Its youthfulness belies its true maturity and vigor as it approaches its third decade of service to its members and to the psychiatric profession at large. *Crescat et floreat!*

JOHN C. NEMIAH, M.D.
President, 1981-1982
American College of Psychiatrists

Introduction

Since its inception, the American College of Psychiatrists has sought to provide through its annual meeting a forum for the discussion of new and synthesized material, leading to the best application of psychiatric knowledge, principles, and therapy (1).

This volume is the product of the annual scientific meeting held in 1982 in Orlando, Florida. Credit for developing the program and assembling the outstanding experts whose essays follow is due the Program Committee whose very able Chairperson was Allan Beigel.

This, the thirteenth publication of the College, is unique in that the College until now has not chosen to return to a subject previously touched upon. It has done so because the material contained herein is reflective of one of the major concerns of psychiatry today. In 1975 (2) the biological and psychological perspectives of schizophrenia were examined and, in 1976 (3), the clinical, biological, and psychological aspects of depression. Those volumes were excellent mirrors of the state of the art at that time, and yet we have only now, as this year's contributors repeatedly remind us, scratched the surface in our knowledge.

We are becoming increasingly aware of the interrelated ideas of multifactorial etiologies and multiple approaches to therapy. This volume gives due consideration to those aspects best comprehended in somatic and in psychological terms. There is not an emphasis here on the psychogenic theories of schizophrenic and affective disorders—and I think rightly so—as the purpose of this year's program was to focus on "new dimensions." The speakers were chosen with an unwavering eye toward recency, and it is thus the timely significance of the essays that comprises the substance of this work.

The chapters in this book fall rather naturally into an order of presentation. Part I is devoted to the evolution of our understanding of the affective and schizophrenic disorders, as well as diagnostic considerations. Lipton's chapter leads the way and proves to be as eclectic in approach as is the author. He guides the reader through the origins of biological psychiatry—clinical psychiatry, genetics, psychopharmacology, and neurobiology—moving from history to the laboratory to clinical practice with equal agility. As an oustanding teacher and scholar, he is able to make understandable and enlightening what might otherwise be difficult and mysterious. He attempts to return psychiatry to that place in science which he feels it has abdicated through the years, but, nevertheless, deserves.

For those of us who "saw" all 48 chromosomes, only to discover that there were 46, there was a tendency to sit back and allow genetics to catch up with us. For those who greeted DSM-III (4) with alarm, Andreasen's chapter soothes and calms. In a most thoughtful manner she moves from Kraepelin to Bleuler to Meyer and then discusses at length the changes in diagnostic concepts during the past 10 years, as well as their rationale through research and clinical observation. Always mindful of the practitioner, she then turns to the nature of these changes in diagnostic practice, the narrowing of the concept of schizophrenia, the broadening of the concept of affective disorder. Finally, Andreasen foretells the major nosological changes which will occur secondary to research during the next 10 years and thus provides an enticing preview of DSM-IV.

Completing Part I is a marvelously thorough chapter on biological markers in affective and schizophrenic disorders. Rubin and Marder carefully review the research and bring the reader into 1982 in this complex area. Beginning with the affective disorders, they examine the neurochemical, neurophysiological, neuroendocrine, and genetic markers. In the schizophrenic disorders, they present the biological markers related to the dopamine theory; the question as to whether schizophrenic patients have altered dopamine systems; the response of the dopamine system to neuroleptics; platelet monoamine oxidase activity; creatine phosphokinase; endorphins and enkephalins; anatomical abnormalities; EEG activity; evoked potentials; and, finally, they discuss the possible biological heterogeneity of schizophrenia. The chapter deserves rereading, and the 144 references provide an extraordinary opportunity for further study.

Part II is concerned with psychopharmacological advances. Schildkraut et al. discuss the discrimination of subtypes of depressive disorders through clinical laboratory testing and the prediction of responses to antidepressant drugs based on measurements of catecholamine metabolism. To those familiar with the literature, Schildkraut is an old friend, able to synthesize previous research swiftly, taking the reader into his laboratory to share today's results with him.* Particularly challenging and beguiling is the Depression-type (D-type) score developed in his laboratory. After presenting multiple studies of monoaminergic receptors and related measures in depressed patients, the chapter ends with a discussion of possible animal models of subtypes of depressive disorders and the practical

---

* Throughout this volume the generic "he" shall be used unless otherwise indicated.

clinical applications of the results of the first-rate research which Schildkraut's laboratory has consistently produced.

Fann's thoughtful chapter on recent advances in the pharmacological treatment of psychoses is dedicated to an exhaustive examination of three compounds: loxapine, molindone, and clozapine. He begins by discussing the failure to improve with neuroleptic therapy, then examines the aforementioned compounds, and, finally, comes to his own interesting but guarded conclusions. Feighner then presents the second and third generation of antidepressants which truly represent incremental improvements over the existing chemotherapy of major depressive disorders—especially if taken in overdose—as well as in terms of decreased side effects and rapidity of onset of action. Fann's and Feighner's chapters provide the practitioner with the most up-to-date reviews yet available in pharmacological treatment.

Part III relates to psychotherapy. In attempting to trace the evolution of psychotherapeutic approaches to affective and schizophrenic disorders, Strauss responds to this Herculean assignment with grace. He delineates the five major themes (tendencies) in this evolution: 1) either/or reasoning; 2) psychotherapy's moving from the interpretive toward the reality-oriented; 3) therapeutic approaches' emphasizing their differences while ignoring commonalities; 4) different conclusions about the nature of disorders becoming associated with specific treatment approaches; and 5) conceptualizing pure forms of treatment and the present need for heterogeneous approaches.

Employing his current research, Strauss presents a clinical example of the schematic course of one patient to illustrate the importance of using an intensive multiaxial follow-up model in an attempt even to begin to identify the processes that may be involved in treatment impact. It is this section of his chapter which demands that clinicians better conceptualize their own therapeutic modality(ies), as well as what is happening to their patients in and out of their offices.

In Rush's illuminating chapter he examines cognitive therapy in its application to patients with major depressive episodes. He provides the philosophical basis for this approach, reviews cognitive theory, and describes the therapeutic technique. He includes specific indications, contraindications, and the possible adverse results of this type of treatment. After examining the existing studies of efficacy, and its specific, active ingredients. Rush approaches his subject in a most scientific manner. There is no proselytizing here, and he thus lends further credibility to his past and present research.

Closing Part III is Gunderson's chapter on the psychotherapeutic approaches to schizophrenic disorders. He gives special attention to three major areas: institutional and milieu treatment, which provided the most productive and informative body of research in the 1970s; family therapy, an area of most interesting research today; and individual therapy, which continues to be of high theoretical and clinical interest while, at the same time, stimulating ongoing controversy. His conclusion that the therapy must always be tailored to the patient is a message repeated throughout the volume and is well to be remembered.

Part IV contains two chapters. The first is Kupfer's response to a request to present a unified view of the affective disorders. He begins by dealing with classification and a thorough clinical description of affective syndromes, thus clearing up the major source of confusion which has arisen secondary to the imprecise use of the term "depression." He follows with a balanced description of various etiological theories of depression and then turns to treatment per se. Kupfer covers pharmacotherapy, tricyclic antidepressants and monoamine oxidase inhibitors, and electroconvulsive therapy. In psychotherapy he looks at interpersonal, marital, and group therapies. Of great interest is his brief section of psychotherapy plus pharmacotherapy and his conclusions regarding maintenance treatment. Finally, he attempts integration in a most thoughtful and clinically useful manner.

The final chapter is the written form of the Stanley R. Dean Award Lecture, given this year by Robert Cancro. In a letter in 1981 (5), Manfred Bleuler wrote that the

> Award provides a great opportunity to focus on such worldwide progress in research. For 19 years it has encouraged and invited scientists from different countries and schools of thought to present their theories and results to each other. . . . I am particularly impressed by the stimulus of the Dean Award for arriving at international cooperation in treating the schizophrenias.

In this chapter Cancro presents an historical view of what the term schizophrenia has meant, how the illness has been diagnosed, and what is known concerning etiology and pathogenesis. The final section, "Personal Note," is extraordinary, for it provides a unified view not of the schizophrenic disorders, as the author readily admits, but of the researcher and clinician. It is reflective of Cancro himself and truly poetic in nature.

Undoubtedly, as psychiatry's knowledge increases, the College will decide to return to a consideration of schizophrenic and affective disorders. However, it is the hope that this volume, through the topical contributions contained herein, will provide the reader with material useful for the present.

Finally, I would like to express my great personal appreciation to John C.

Nemiah, President of the College, for his continued support and encouragement, and to the members of the Publications Committee for their diligent efforts.

MICHAEL R. ZALES, M.D.
Greenwich, Connecticut

REFERENCES

1. ZALES, M. (Ed.): *Eating, Sleeping, and Sexuality: Treatment of Disorders in Basic Life Functions*. New York: Brunner/Mazel, 1982.
2. USDIN, G. (Ed.): *Schizophrenia: Biological and Psychological Perspectives*. New York: Brunner/Mazel, 1975.
3. USDIN, G. (Ed.): *Depression: Clinical, Biological and Psychological Perspectives*. New York: Brunner/Mazel, 1977.
4. *Diagnostic and Statistical Manual of Mental Disorders*, Third Edition. Washington, D.C.: American Psychiatric Association, 1980.
5. BLEULER, M.: Personal Communication.

AFFECTIVE AND SCHIZOPHRENIC DISORDERS:
New Approaches to Diagnosis and Treatment

Part I

PERSPECTIVES AND DIAGNOSIS

1

The Evolution of the Biological Understanding of Affective and Schizophrenic Disorders

Morris A. Lipton, Ph.D., M.D.

INTRODUCTION

This chapter will be followed by others dealing with the most important problems of contemporary psychiatry in the area of affective and schizophrenic disorders. These problems are: how to diagnose, how to treat with drugs and with psychotherapy, and finally, how to view these complex disorders in a unified way. My task, as I see it, is to discuss the origins of biological psychiatry, and, perhaps, where it is going. To do so it is obviously necessary to describe where we are.

It is not possible to pinpoint precisely where biological psychiatry began, because it seems always to have been with us in one guise or another. It is, after all, an expression of an investigative approach which states that psychiatric illnesses, detected by disordered thinking, feeling and behavior, may be due to biological disturbances of the central nervous system and are subject to biological understanding and treatment. The specific term "biological psychiatry," as contrasted to psychiatry alone, or dynamic or social psychiatry, is relatively new. It is a convenient term, because it describes an approach to understanding and treatment, but it is not meant to be a term which excludes the psychological and social domains. Biology, after all, is the science of life and psychological events, and social systems are a part of life.

I think that biological psychiatry has five origins which independently have made significant progress over the past 100 years, and collectively have led to

5

vast increases in understanding, treatment, and great prospects for continued rapid advance. These origins are, respectively: clinical psychiatry, genetics, psychopharmacology, neurobiology, and, most recently, psychoneuroendocrinology.

Clinical Psychiatry

Scientific clinical psychiatry had its origins in medicine and can be traced to the famous physician, Sydenham, who in the 17th century developed an approach to the study of arthritis. By studying the clustering of symptoms in patients with this illness and by tracing its natural history and pathology, he was able to separate gouty arthritis from rheumatoid arthritis and to demonstrate that they were two distinct diseases. This approach is traditional in medicine and is still used with great success. It is the method by which diabetes mellitus was distinguished from diabetes insipidus, the various forms of hypertension were discovered, and most recently Legionnaire's disease, Reye's syndrome, and the toxic shock syndrome have become understood. This approach was most successfully used by Kraepelin, who had many less distinguished antecedents. Among them must be considered Kahlbaum, Korsakoff, and Griesinger (1). Utilizing Sydenham's approach, Kraepelin identified a number of psychiatric illnesses that were caused by alterations in the anatomy and chemistry of the brain and body, such as those associated with toxins, endocrine disorders, and trauma. He also identified three clusters that fit together on the basis of common symptoms and common prognosis. Because no identifiable physical or metabolic causes could be found, he termed these "functional." Although I have found him unclear on this point, I am inclined to think that he used the term "functional" as a statement of ignorance rather than as a denial that physical or metabolic disease actually existed and might be found in the future. The three symptom clusters with common prognosis which he recognized were: dementia praecox, in which young patients became increasingly mad and disorganized and did not recover completely; manic-depressive psychoses with alternating mood swings and with ultimate recovery rather than deterioration; and the personality disorders or psychopathies. Kraepelin fully recognized that psychological and cultural influences could trigger and color psychiatric disturbances, but he was committed to biological etiology. Given the very limited biology of the times, he was unable to discover any pathology other than the behavioral for these ills or to offer specific biological treatment, and his influence waned in the early 20th century. It has, of course, come back vigorously in the past 20 years and is expressed in DSM-III and in the current biological investigations and treatments.

Nonetheless, it is worth noting that this approach did lead to the discovery and cure for pellagra and neurosyphilis, illnesses which if not entirely psychiatric nonetheless produced devastating psychiatric sequellae, leading often to hospitalization in the asylums of the day. The discovery that pellagra, at one time considered to be a genetic disease and later an infectious one, was nutritional in origin and could be cured by a vitamin eliminated the illness and must be considered among the great public health achievements of all times. The discovery that the fever of malaria could cure CNS syphilis earned Wagner Jauregg, a contemporary of Freud's, a Nobel Prize. Until the discovery of antibiotics in the 1940s, it was the treatment of choice.

Psychiatric empiricism continued despite the presence of a cohesive theory. In 1934 Meduna (2), noting that schizophrenic patients who had convulsions from any cause improved, operated on the wrong assumption that schizophrenia and epilepsy were incompatible and introduced metrazol, a convulsant drug. Cerlitti and Bini (3) introduced electroconvulsive therapy (ECT) in 1938 for similar reasons. Sakel (2) first used insulin to improve appetite in psychiatric patients and noted that some schizophrenics who slipped into coma improved. He introduced it as a treatment in 1936. These treatments apparently offered limited and transient benefit to some patients and continued to be used pragmatically by biologically minded psychiatrists until the discovery of the psychotropic drugs in the 1950s. ECT is, of course, still used for affective disorders. Lobotomy, whose theoretical basis was the observation of Fulton that aggressive monkeys, from whom the frontal cortex was surgically removed, retained their intellectual ability but lost their aggressive tendencies, was introduced by Moniz in 1936 (1). Its rationale was that schizophrenia was thought to be a frontal lobe disorder, but it was later shown to be unpredictable with frequent complications and very limited success. Premature large-scale trials of this procedure exposed about 70,000 patients to this treatment with damage to significant numbers. It is no longer used for treatment of schizophrenia. It represents a low point in the history of biological psychiatry.

During the 40-year period of these types of biological treatment, repeated attempts with the currently available anatomical, physiological, and biochemical methods failed to reveal a demonstrable pathology. Moreover, the treatments had very limited effectiveness and some serious side effects. Finally, the underlying theories were very weak. Small wonder then that psychiatrists turned to psychoanalytic and psychodynamic theory and practice.

Freud, a young neuropsychiatrist well trained in the neurobiology of the day, and traumatized at age 28 by the severe criticism of his strong advocacy of the virtues of cocaine in 1884, studied under Charcot in Paris in 1886 and became a vigorous proponent of hypnosis for the treatment of hysteria. Although he attempted to sketch a neurophysiological theory of consciousness and both normal and pathological behavior, this failed. He then turned completely to psychological considerations of drives, defenses against them, regression and, above all, the concept of a dynamic unconsciousness in which conflicts between instinctual drives and their prohibited expression were determinants of illness.

In Chapter 7, Dr. Strauss addresses the development of psychoanalytic thinking about the affective disorders and schizophrenia. Let me therefore say that Freud was, throughout his life, highly enthusiastic about psychoanalysis as a tool for investigating pathogenesis, but less so as a therapeutic agent. Although he achieved fame from his discoveries and the success of his school of thought and defended it vigorously, at the same time he remained skeptical. This is clearly shown in "Analysis Terminable and Interminable," where he stated his belief in the biological origins of deviant behavior (4). In that same volume he describes the limited power of psychoanalysis to change behavior that may be constitutionally based. In his final work in 1938 he speaks of the day when biochemists and endocrinologists might alter these clinically but states that, until that day, psychoanalysis is not to be despised (5).

I would attribute Freud's reservations about psychoanalysis to his early training in neurology and neurophysiology, to his later experience with the powerful but unpredictable effects of cocaine, and most of all, to his intellectual honesty. This combination was less prominent in his followers. Jung and Adler gave short shrift to biology. Ferenczi wrote on the psychodynamics of general paresis, and in this country psychoanalysis emerged as a method for understanding and treating the major psychoses. At the peak of psychoanalytic thinking, Sydenham's and Kraepelin's methods for seeking to identify syndromes were considered useless. There was only mental illness, created by experience and understandable only in terms of psychodynamics. The biology of the individual was considered immutable. Change, if it could be made to occur at all, could be brought about only by the corrective psychotherapeutic experience. This remained true until the great revolution in psychopharmacology in the 1950s. The manifest successes following the introduction of drugs for the treatment of specific types of illness revived a great interest in classification. Biological psychiatry requires rigorous classification systems for measuring symptom clusters, symptom intensity, and symptom change. New sophisticated methods now using computers are constantly being developed with collaborative efforts among clinicians, psychometricians, statisticians, and biologists.

GENETIC ORIGINS

The use of genetic methods for the study of schizophrenia was initiated by Rudin in 1916 and further developed by Kallman in 1938 (6). Both investigators studied the relatives of more than 1,000 schizophrenic patients and found that, while schizophrenia had an expectancy rate of 1-2% in the population, it was about 9% for siblings of schizophrenics. Schizophrenia was also higher in the parents, and conversely, if both parents were schizophrenic, the expectancy range in children was between 35 and 68%. Nature and nuture were not separable in this type of research, and so the evidence was suggestive but not conclusive.

The strongest strategy for investigating a genetic contribution to schizophrenia involves separating nature from nurture. The other approach is to try to keep nurture constant. The former involves adoption studies in which the children of schizophrenic patients are adopted early in infancy and raised away from the biological parents. The latter compares concordance rates between monozygotic twins having identical genes and dizygotic twins who have genes only as similar as siblings with the same parents might have. This method assumes that the nurturing environment of fraternal twins is very similar to that of identical twins. Both types of studies yielded similar results. The adoption studies first conducted by Heston (7) and later and more extensively in Denmark by Kety and his group (8) resulted in the finding that schizophrenia was found in 10-20% of the children of schizophrenic mothers rather than at the 1% level in the population at large. If both biological parents had schizophrenia, the expectancy was 45%. The children of nonschizophrenic mothers adopted away shortly after birth had the same rate as the population at large, even though some had been subjected to the trauma of changes in foster home living. Somewhat surprisingly, the Kety study also showed that children of schizophrenic parents raised by their biological parents were at no greater risk for diagnosable schizophrenia than those adopted away and raised in nonschizophrenic families. The converse study of adopting biologically normal children into families in which a parent has schizophrenia cannot be done, since such adoptions are not permitted and rarely take place.

The powerful evidence from adoption studies for the genetic transmission of schizophrenia is buttressed by the twin studies (9), which in the work of several investigators have shown that, if a fraternal twin has schizophrenia, the expectancy that his sibling will have it is about 10% or the same as that for any other sibling. But if he is monozygotic, the odds rise to 45%. This is clear evidence that a genetic factor is involved, but it is equally clear that it is not sufficient. If it were, then concordance would be 100%. Very similar figures are found for cleft palate and club foot, where the correspondence rate for monozygotic twins is about 45% and for dizygotic twins about 10%. Environmental factors must play a role, but what these are is not yet clear.

I should emphasize at this point that the environmental factors need not necessarily be psychological. Obstetrical complications leading to anoxia, slow viruses, dietary insufficiencies or sensitivities, season of birth, and exceptional stress during pregnancy have all been implicated in epidemiological studies (10). Whether these can generate phenocopies in biological normals or whether a genetic diathesis is required is not known. Nor is the question of whether transmission occurs through a single gene with incomplete penetrance, a few genes or many genes, like intelligence. Penetrance refers to the frequency with which a gene produces its effects in those persons possessing it. A gene with low penetrance is one which will show its effect or produce illness in 10-20% of those who have it. Genes, by definition, synthesize proteins which may be structurally functionally like enzymes. Biological markers for either the schizophrenic state or trait have been sought for some time but no unequivocal ones have yet been found.

The situation is somewhat similar with affective disorders. Gershon, in a recent review of this topic, shows that the concordance rate for the major affective disorder in identical twins is about 65%, while that in fraternal twins is 14% (11). This implies that genetic vulnerability plays a major role. Adoption studies of suicide in biological relatives of depressed adoptees have also given evidence for a prominent role for genetic vulnerability. Studies of the twins concordant for depression show that about 20% have different forms of mood disorder where one twin is unipolar and the other bipolar. This suggests that in some cases the two disorders may be manifestations of the same genetic vulnerability. Since one-third of the identical twins are not concordant for affective disorders, one may infer that either some illnesses are phenocopies, i.e., illness found in the absence of genetic vulnerability, or that there is variable penetrance. It should be emphasized that all genetic studies have been done with severely ill patients so that we may not be able to generalize this evidence for milder forms of depression.

Regarding the question of whether or not unipolar and bipolar illnesses are genetically distinct, the evidence is still equivocal. Gershon believes that there is a single underlying disorder producing both unipolar and bipolar illness and that bipolar illness is a more severe form of the common disorder. The finding that lithium is therapeutic for bipolar patients in either the manic or depressed state, while in the unipolars it is only prophylactic, suggests to Gershon that the genetic abnormality may be in ion transport across neuronal membranes. A recent report of decreased lithium transport into erythrocytes in the ill relatives of bipolar patients offers evidence for this view (12).

There have been repeated attempts to find a chromosomal linkage in affective disorders. Two genes are linked if they are close together on the same chromosome and tend to segregate or are transmitted together in families. Non-linked genes segregate independently. For these types of studies it is necessary to trace an illness through an extended family pedigree and observe whether the illness and the marker segregate together or independently. Results from studies of this type have generated the hypothesis that bipolar disorders are transmitted on a single gene located close to the gene for color blindness on the X chromosome. Gershon and Bunney (12) have been unable to confirm this. However, Baron and Risch (13) find such linkage. They also find that a subset of schizoaffective disordered patients is genetically related to the major affective disorders and that the locus for carrying the schizoaffective trait is located on the X chromosome. They emphasize the potential role of linkage data in sorting out genetic subtypes from heterogeneous psychiatric disorders like schizoaffective illness.

PHARMACOLOGICAL ORIGINS

The origins of psychopharmacology lie in the ethnopharmacological practices of remote cultures. The use of alcohol to alter mood and behavior goes back many thousands of years. Anthropologists have traced the use of hallucinogenic plants in religious practices among diverse cultures in Asia, Africa, and the Americas. The use of opium for relief of pain and for its euphoric properties goes back hundreds if not thousands of years. The Spaniards arriving in Peru and Chile found the chewing of the coca plant to be a privilege of royalty, but quickly democratized it when they found it to increase work and endurance among their slaves. Later they introduced the leaves into Europe. And, in the mid-19th century, when natural products chemists became more sophisticated so that the active material was isolated, the use of cocaine in Europe and the United States became very common.

It is worth reading Byck's book (14), which includes Freud's Cocaine Papers, to recognize how popular cocaine became. It is said that there were many prominent users, including Thomas Edison and Queen Victoria. Dr. Merck, the founder of the Merck industries in Europe, and Dr. Parke, the founder of Parke-Davis, both built their businesses with cocaine. Parke sold an elixir of cocaine which was touted to cure or alleviate almost everything. Coca-Cola contained cocaine for many years.

Freud was much taken with cocaine. He experimented on himself, gave it to many patients and to his fiancée, and published several papers on its beneficial properties. I find it interesting that the only experimental work which generated hard data that he ever published was with cocaine. In this he measured and recorded his muscle strength and endurance with and without cocaine and re-corded that it significantly increased them. For a time he and others thought it to be an effective cure for morphine addiction. When disastrous results occurred with his friend who was also his patient, and as it was gradually discovered that cocaine was readily subject to abuse and could also produce psychosis, he was severely criticized in the scientific literature for his previous enthusiastic en-dorsement. Two years later he visited Charcot and returned with a lifetime commitment to psychological investigation. Within the period of about 10 years the pendulum swung from cocaine as the universal panacea to that of the "third scourge of humanity" (15), the other two being alcohol and opium. There is good reason for believing that cocaine is dangerous; however, the recent explosion of the use of illegal cocaine by affluent middle class adults, who extol its virtues and complain only, as Freud did, of its high cost, makes one wonder what its status will be in the next decade.

All of these drugs were, of course, tried on psychiatric patients, and there are books and papers on such diverse topics as the therapeutic use of LSD in the treatment of alcoholism and psychosis and on the use of tincture of opium in depression and schizophrenia. By and large, these agents demonstrated little therapeutic value for psychiatric patients. Their abuse potential was very high because they produced pleasant effects in normal subjects, and neurobiology had not advanced to the state where their heuristic value as tools for exploring brain and neuronal function was significant. The consequences were that these agents were ignored except as social menaces.

The situation was quite different in the middle 1950s when psychopharmacology is said to have been born, or when the great psychopharmacological revolution is said to have occurred. It is certainly true that the mood-elevating properties of monoamine oxidase (MAO) inhibitors were discovered accidentally when they were used as adjuncts in the treatment of tuberculosis. It is equally true that chlorpromazine was discovered in the search for a hypothermic agent and imipramine in the search for a better chlorpromazine, but the intellectual climate for their clinical investigation and for the study of their mode of action had changed dramatically. Chemical transmission between neurons had been accepted for acetylcholine and norepinephrine, and methods for the study of the effects of these agents upon chemical transmission were available. Such studies were immediately undertaken, and major effects were found. The discovery of these possible modes of action contributed to neurobiology, and neurobiology contributed to biological psychiatry by permitting plausible theories about the mechanism of action of these drugs. From this came plausible and testable hypotheses about the pathogenesis of depression and schizophrenia.

I would attribute the pharmacological revolution in psychiatry to four factors. First, compared to what had been previously available, the newly discovered drugs were immensely effective. Second, they offered no pleasure to psychologically normal people and were not biologically addictive; hence they have no abuse potential. Third, they fitted into the rubric of chemical neurobiology, had great heuristic value, and were legitimatized by some knowledge of their mechanism of action. Fourth, they offered substantial profits to the drug industry.

The pharmacological revolution goes on. We are learning to use drugs with greater skill derived from more specific diagnosis and a knowledge of therapeutic blood levels and pharmacokinetics. New drugs are constantly being developed here and abroad. For a time it seemed that these drugs were all in the same mold, derived from the same *in vivo* tests on animals and *in vitro* tests on animal brain preparations, but now new drugs are being developed with different pharmacological profiles and yet similar clinical effects. They are not only permitting a larger choice for special patients but are also raising questions about our unitary concept of the pathogenesis of depression. It seems more and more clear that there are subtypes. We are also learning more about the use of drug combinations. In a recent publication, Canadian workers demonstrated a conversion of tricyclic non-responders to responders within 48 hours when lithium was added after several weeks of tricyclic antidepressant (TCA) treatment (16). A slower but still dramatic conversion of non-responders to responders was recently demonstrated when triiodothyroxine is added to a tricyclic regimen (17). The mechanism of action is not clear for either treatment, and it is curious that lithium, which has antithyroid activity, produces the same clinical results as the thyroid hormone. Both of these studies need replication. If such efforts are successful, we will have improved therapy and gained additional insights into the mechanisms involved in the pharmacotherapy and pathogenesis of depression.

Origins from Basic Neurobiology

The work of Cajal and Golgi (18) at the end of the 19th century demonstrated that neurons were discrete entities with cell bodies, dendrites to receive input, and axons with terminals to discharge them. They also showed that there were anatomical gaps and specialized contact zones between neurons. These zones were named synapses by Sherrington. The synapse can clearly be seen with electron microscopic techniques; it is about 200 angstrom units wide. Long before the synapse was discovered, electrical properties of the nervous system were discovered, and for a long period the transmission of information from one neuron to another was considered to be electrical. It was as if the neuronal wires in the brain were all soldered together or, alternatively, joined by what might be considered to be spark plugs in which the electrical discharge from one neuron jumped the gap to the second neuron, thus propagating the neuronal impulse. There was no positive evidence to support this view, but there was substantial evidence to demonstrate that propagation of a nerve impulse in a single neuron was electrical. Thus, if one inserted electrodes into a neuron and its axons, one could easily detect a current as the impulse traveled down the neuron. Chemical research has shown that this wave of depolarization is associated with the efflux of potassium outside the cell and the influx of sodium into it. Between impulses the metabolic machinery of the neuron repolarizes it (19). Thus, chemical energy, as one would find in a battery, is required to prepare the nerve cell for conduction.

Conduction in a single neuron is clearly electrical, but the electrical theory of transmission between two neurons received a major challenge from the work of Loewi (20), who performed a simple experiment with the frog heart. In this he stimulated the vagus and what followed was the well known slowing of the heart. With a small needle in the ventricle he collected the fluid contents of this chamber. When he transferred the fluid to another rapidly beating heart, he was able to slow the second heart. He could thus demonstrate that a substance was released into the frog heart by vagal stimulation. This substance was later identified as acetylcholine.

This simple experiment initiated an intellectual rivalry which went on for two decades between the proponents of electrical transmission (Eccles and others) and chemical transmission (Dale and others). It was only in the 1950s and 1960s that the problem was resolved. Both types occur, but chemical transmission is much more frequent. Electrical transmission is very rapid but is inflexible. It is thought to be responsible for interconnecting excitable cells responsible for stereotyped behavior such as rapid saccadic eye movements. Chemical synapses are slower, more plastic and account for more complex behavior. This may be why chemical transmission seems to predominate (19).

About 50 years ago, Sir Henry Dale (21) postulated that any single mature neuron could release only one transmitter. This rule has generally stood the test of time. However, on the receiving end, the dendrites of a neuron may have multiple receptors. A neuron, therefore, has multiple inputs and a single output. Whether or not a postsynaptic neuron responds is determined by the balance of its inhibitory and excitatory inputs.

Once the concept of neurotransmission was established, a burst of research ensued. Rigorous criteria for the identification of a neurotransmitter were established. These were as follows: 1) It is synthesized in the neuron; 2) it is present in the presynaptic terminal and is released in quantities sufficient to exert its action on the affected neuron or effector organ; 3) when applied exogenously as a drug, it mimics exactly the action of the endogenously released transmitter; and 4) a specific mechanism exists for removing it from its site of action.

With these criteria eight transmitters have been unequivocally identified. These are acetylcholine (ACH); the four biogenic amines, dopamine (DA), norepinephrine (NE), serotonin (5HT) and histamine (H); and three amino acids, glycine, glutamine, and gamma-aminobutyric acid (GABA). In addition, there are now about 20 neuroactive peptides which do not yet fully satisfy all of the rigorous criteria for neurotransmitters, but all are localized in neurons by immunocytochemical techniques and all are intensely active when applied to the cell surfaces of neurons. These include endorphins and enkephalins, pituitary peptides such as ACTH, gut brain peptides like substance P and neurotensin, and others like bradykinin and oxytocin (19). There will be more discussion about some of these later, but the topic is very "hot" and very fluid with almost daily new advances in information about their distribution, mode of action, and functions within the nervous system.

The intellectual feat of conceiving first that a substance like morphine which is so powerful in its actions and is also addictive must have a receptor, and then, after the receptor was found, reasoning that there must be an endogenous substance for which this receptor evolved because evolution probably did not make a receptor for morphine in animals that never encountered this alkaloid, was extraordinarily clever. The search for endogenous substances which could compete for the morphine receptor led to the discovery of the endorphins and enkephalins.

Turning back to the canonical neurotransmitters, the first questions asked were what they were made from, what are the chemical steps involved in their synthesis, what enzymes and coenzymes or other cofactors are involved, how are they stored and released, how are they inactivated chemically, and what enzymes are involved in that? All of these questions have been answered and are readily available in texts (19, 23-26). Attention for the past half decade has instead focused increasingly upon the question of how their rates of synthesis, release, and degradation are controlled and what the effects of drugs are upon these processes. This is a very active field with many incomplete answers. It involves, among other things, a consideration of receptors.

We owe the concept of receptors to Ehrlich (22) who, in the late 19th century, noted the high chemical specificity for therapeutic and toxic effects of a wide variety of synthetic organic drugs. Langley also contributed to this concept by studying curare. He found that it inhibited nerve-stimulated or chemically induced contraction of muscle but had no effect on electrically induced contraction. This led him to postulate the existence of an active site at the junction of the nerve and muscle which is now known to be the acetylcholine receptor.

In contrast to transmitters, which are small nonprotein molecules and whose specific chemical structure is known, receptors are large complex glyco-or lipoproteins. There is relatively little known about the specific chemical structure of receptors. The best known of these is the acetylcholine receptor of the electric organ of the electric eel. This is present in huge concentrations and could therefore be purified. It is a protein with a molecular weight of about 250,000 and is made of four polypeptide subunits. Bungarotoxin, a snake venom, binds specifically and irreversibly to the receptor, and from quantitative studies of this binding, it has been learned that the molecule has two binding sites located on polypeptide A. When acetylcholine binds with this receptor, it causes a change in the ion permeability of the cellular membrane. Accelerated degradation of the acetylcholine receptor in the presence of autoantibodies is associated with myasthenia gravis.

Since their chemical structure is not precisely known, receptors are classified by what transmitters they bind, the biological consequences of their binding and activation, and what the effects of drugs are upon them.

All neurotransmitter receptors are located on the surface of the cell membranes enveloping neuronal cells. These membranes are about 50 angstrom units thick. The receptors are appropriately located because it is their function to receive specific chemical messages transmitted across the synaptic gap from presynaptic neurons and to translate them into specific and appropriate postsynaptic intracellular neuronal responses. It is believed that the outer surface of a receptor serves to recognize and bind the chemical transmitter. The inner surface acts as a transducer to effect the intracellular changes. Every receptor thus has two components, a recognition part and an effector part. It is the receptor, rather than the transmitter, which determines what a transmitter will do when it impinges on a given cell. Thus acetylcholine may be excitatory across some synapses and inhibitory across others, and sometimes does both at the same time.

Receptors are identified and assayed in several ways. Until recently, bioassays measuring the response of organs like the guinea pig ileum or a skeletal muscle were used exclusively. The use of these methods led, for example, to the recognition of denervation supersensitivity; a denervated muscle responds to much lower concentrations of acetylcholine than does a normal muscle. The first research leading to the identification of the morphine receptor used a bioassay. Such methods do not elucidate mechanisms. More sophisticated bioassays are employed by investigators who study the effect of CNS-active drugs by treating animals *in vivo* and then studying the effects of presynaptic stimulation on electrical postsynaptic neuronal responses. This method has the advantage of directly measuring biological activity, but is slow and technically difficult. Another method is to study the activity of the enzymes to which the receptor is coupled. In those receptors coupled to adenyl cyclase, an increase in enzyme activity or an accumulation of cyclic AMP is evidence that receptor activity has changed. This method is limited to the study of receptors which are coupled to effectors whose activity can be measured.

In the past decade radioligand binding techniques have been extensively utilized. With this method a receptor preparation like nerve cell membranes is prepared by differential centrifugation and is then incubated with an isotopically labeled compound called a ligand which binds to the receptor at very low molar concentrations. Then the ligand receptor complex is separated from the free ligand by filtration, precipitation, or centrifugation. A more popular technique is to use equilibrium dialysis, where the receptor ligand complex is determined by subtracting the ligand concentration in the bath from that in the dialysis sac. The identification and measurement of receptors by radioligand binding assays are restricted to the recognition part. Moreover, this technique is subject to many experimental artifacts.

Radioligands can bind nonspecifically to all types of membranes and even to glass fibers and talcum powder. Because of this, it is generally agreed (24) that authentic receptors should have the three following properties:

1) *Saturability*. Dose response curves should show saturability. Specific receptor binding should show high affinity and low capacity, whereas the reverse is true for nonspecific binding.
2) *Specificity*. There should be a high correlation between the binding affinity for a series of ligands and their biological response.
3) *Reversibility*. Since most drug transmitters and hormones act in a reversible manner, binding should be reversible and upon reversal, the ligand should be recovered in its natural form.

The radioligand technique is quick and powerful for the study of new drugs. However, it measures only affinity binding sites and tells us little about the biological consequences of the drugs, because it does not measure the effector portion.

The proper utilization of these methods has led to a vast explosion of useful information. For example, it has been possible to determine the anatomical distribution of receptors for individual neurotransmitters in different brain areas. The old problem of denervation supersensitivity was solved with the finding of a measurable increase in the number of postsynaptic receptors after input was diminished by destroying presynaptic neurons. The endorphins were discovered when isotopically labeled morphine was used as a ligand. A receptor for morphine was found in the brain, and a search was undertaken for endogenous ligands which could compete with morphine for the receptor binding sites. A result of great importance, of course, was that it became possible to address the problem of the chronic effects of drugs such as those commonly used in psychiatric patients. With membrane preparations from animal brains, Snyder was able to demonstrate that there is a strong correlation between the clinical potency of neuroleptics and their capacity to bind dopamine receptors (27). It also became possible to show a great difference between the acute and chronic biological effects of the tricyclics.

Receptors have been found in the brain for all of the common neurotransmitters like norepinephrine, serotonin, dopamine, acetylcholine, and several amino acid neurotransmitters, and they have been found also for peripheral pituitary hormones and hypothalamic hormones. Multiple receptors for single neurotransmitters have been found as well, and this can account for the fact that a neurotransmitter applied to one neuron causes activation of a postsynaptic neuron in some brain areas, while elsewhere it causes inhibition.

The question of how a few specific molecules of a hormone or neurotransmitter could initiate a cascade of major metabolic events was addressed by Sutherland in the 1960s (28, 29). Specifically, he asked how a small quantity of norepinephrine applied to a live cell caused the cell to break down glycogen and initiate carbohydrate metabolism. His studies revealed that a beta receptor on the liver cell surface was coupled with an enzyme, adenyl cyclase, on its intracellular surface. Norepinephrine, activating this receptor, stimulated the formation of cyclic adenosine monophosphate (cAMP); this initiated a series of changes including phosphorylation of intracellular enzyme proteins which led to the metabolism of glycogen. Norepinephrine was thus the first messenger to the liver cell. Cyclic AMP was the second messenger. It offered an intracellular mechanism which converted and greatly amplified the first message delivered by norepinephrine at the cell surface to a sequence of intracellular metabolic reactions. Coupling of neurotransmitter receptors to adenyl cyclase also occurs in neurons, but it has since been found that not all receptors are so coupled. Others, acting in different ways, open membrane channels for ionic movement, other molecular movements, release of hormones and transmitters, and protein synthesis (19, 23).

Receptor sensitivity can be altered in three ways: 1) There can be an alteration in the number of receptors; 2) there can be an alteration in the physical configuration of the receptor which changes its affinity for the ligand; and 3) the coupling of the recognition and binding site with the effector site (the receptor-effector complex) can be changed.

There are chemical methods for determining which of these mechanisms accounts for the perceived alterations in receptor sensitivity. In almost all cases an alteration in receptor number seems to be the preferred mechanism. Since receptors are large proteins whose numbers can be increased or decreased only by synthesis or degradation, a time-consuming process, this may account for the slow therapeutic action of the antidepressant and other psychotropic drugs.

It is currently believed that the common tricyclics immediately inhibit the reuptake mechanism for norepinephrine and/or serotonin into the presynaptic neuron. This results in a higher concentration of transmitter at the receptors of the postsynaptic neuron. In response to this, the postsynaptic neuron reduces the number of its receptors and presumably also its activity. This has been called down-regulation. Since the postsynaptic neuron feeds back to an autoreceptor on the presynaptic neuron and this autoreceptor is inhibitory, there is diminution of inhibitory activity which results in stimulation of the presynaptic neuron and a still greater output of transmitter. On the other hand the increase in transmitter stimulates the inhibitory autoreceptor and this diminishes transmitter output. The ultimate consequences of these shifting equilibria between transmitter concentration and receptor sensitivity on both the presynaptic and postsynaptic neuron are confusing. It does not look as if binding studies nor even studies of transmitter turnover rates will answer the question of actual synaptic efficacy following chronic drug use.

Electrophysiological methods, involving direct chemical stimulation of presynaptic cells and electrophysiological recording of the postsynaptic cells like those of Aghajanian (30) and Huang (31) are needed to assess the functional state of amine transmitter systems. Such studies in rats show that animals chronically treated with antidepressants have functionally supersensitive aminergic systems. Such studies obviously cannot be done in man. It is therefore difficult at present to speculate on the behavioral significance of these receptor changes, especially in man, and the possible implications they have regarding the neurochemical deficit in depression.

There is some evidence from transmitter metabolite studies in the urine and CSF in man that the levels of neurotransmitters are low in depression, but without simultaneously knowing the state of the brain receptors we cannot know their functional state. There is evidence that a receptor which binds imipramine in human platelets is lower in depressed patients than in controls and one is tempted to say this reflects similar changes in the brain but this is far from certain.

It is now recognized that regulation of the activity of a single neuron or of transmission between neurons can occur in many ways. In a single neuron the rate at which a transmitter is synthesized will depend initially upon the availability of precursors and the activity of the synthetic enzymes and coenzymes. The synthetized transmitter is then transported down the axon and is stored in vesicles close to the synaptic membrane. When these receptors are activated, they initiate a chain of events in this neuron which causes it to fire. A transmitter which is not used for postsynaptic transmission is disposed of by three mechanisms: 1) It can parsimoniously reenter the cell and be used again (although some of the reentering transmitter may be destroyed by intracellular enzymes before it is packed in vesicles); 2) it can be destroyed by extracellular enzymes like monamine oxidase; or 3) it can be washed away into the extracellular fluids.

All of these regulatory mechanisms are constantly employed naturally and they can be manipulated pharmacologically. For example, Wurtman and his coworkers (32) have shown that increasing the quantity of tryptophan, the dietary precursor of serotonin, or of choline, the dietary precursor of acetylcholine, can lead to increases in neuronal synthesis of serotonin and acetylcholine, respectively. Under ordinary circumstances this is not true for tyrosine, the precursor of dopamine and norepinephrine, the two catecholamine neurotransmitters, because here the rate of synthesis is limited by the activity of tyrosine hydroxylase, the first enzyme involved in synthesis. This type of pharmacological manipulation through diet is under investigation with tryptophan for depression and with choline for tardive dyskinesia and Alzheimer's disease. It is the basis for the use of L-DOPA in Parkinson's disease.

Pharmacological manipulation of the synthetic and degrading enzymes can also be employed. Alpha-methyltyrosine blocks the tyrosine hydroxylase and lowers catecholamine synthesis. MAO inhibitors block the activity of an important degrading enzyme and increase catecholamine and serotonin levels. Reserpine has the property of destroying storage vesicles, making the synthesized transmitters more vulnerable to intracellular degradation.

Receptors play an important role in regulation of synthesis and transmission. In general, inadequate stimulation of receptors increases their sensitivity leading to hypersensitivity. Presynaptic neurons have autoreceptors for the transmitters they release. These are generally inhibitory and, therefore, when the quantity of transmitter in the cleft is excessive and the autoreceptors are stimulated, synthesis of the transmitter is diminished. Postsynaptic neurons may also feed back to receptors on the presynaptic neuron. If these are inhibitory, the presynaptic cell will diminish its output of transmitter. If excitatory, an increase will occur. Such changes alter synaptic efficacy.

Regulation of neuronal activity through changes in synaptic efficacy is now known to be involved in learning. Kandell (33) has studied this in the marine snail, aplysia Californica. This primitive creature, weighing perhaps half a pound, has only a few thousand neurons in its nervous system. A particular pattern of behavior, the withdrawal of its gills in the presence of noxious stimuli, is controlled by 24 sensory and six motor neurons. These are fortunately large, so they can be studied electrically and chemically.

This primitive animal can learn. When presented with a novel stimulus, it withdraws its gills. If the stimulus is innocuous and is repeated 10 times, the animal no longer withdraws its gills. Habituation in this experiment lasts minutes to hours. But if the innocuous stimulus is repeated 10 times a day for four consecutive days, the animal stays habituated for several weeks. This is unquestionably a primitive form of learning and memory. Electrical recordings from the sensory and the motor cells reveal that the previously functioning chemical synapse between the sensory neuron and the motor neuron has become nonfunctional in the habituated animal. Chemical analysis reveals that this is because less transmitter is released. Still further analysis reveals that the diminution in transmitter release is caused by a prolonged decrease in calcium influx. Quantitative analysis showed that in the naive animal 90% of the sensory neurons have detectable synapses with the motor cells. After habituation only 30% of the connections were functional, and they stayed that way for a week. At three weeks an additional 30% had been restored.

These data seem to show directly that learning and memory are associated with long-term changes in synaptic efficacy. Sensitization, whereby an animal increases a given response to a noxious stimulus, is the opposite of habituation—behaviorally, electrophysiologically, and chemically. Synaptic efficacy in the sensitized animal is higher than in the control animal, and, of course, much higher than in the habituated animal. Can a habituated, nonfunctional synapse be restored by sensitization stimuli? The answer is yes.

These types of experiments demonstrate clearly that learning and memory need not involve major rearrangements in the CNS. Neither neurons nor synapses are made or destroyed. Only the functional efficacy of existing synapses is altered, and this seems to be done by regulating calcium influx into presynaptic terminals. The existence of the synapse is genetically determined; its efficacy can be interrupted and also restored by experience. There is also reason to believe that it can be altered by drugs or hormones.

To illustrate, Pedersen and Prange (34) are doing some exciting studies on the development of maternal behavior. The experiments are simple, the interpretation much more complex. A new mother rat exhibits maternal behavior. It licks, retrieves, builds a nest, and permits the pups to suckle. These are instinctive behaviors. The animals' nervous system is hardwired for these patterns. With the birth of pups, the program comes into play. If an adult virgin female is brought into a cage of newborn pups, she will seldom exhibit maternal behavior. Instead, she will ignore, avoid, trample, and sometimes eat the pups. If such a virgin rat, in estrus or primed with estrogen, is given a single dose of about ½ μg of oxytocin intracisternally, she will almost invariably behave like a proper mother and will continue to do so until the pups are mature. This is a dramatic phenomenon. It seems to be quite specific for oxytocin and structurally related compounds. The chemical life of administered oxytocin in the brain is only a few hours, yet the behavioral effects of a single administration exist for weeks.

There is obviously much to be learned about the cellular biology of this phenomenon; however, at the moment it certainly appears that the animal is wired genetically for maternal behavior but that the synapses are not functional. Oxytocin seems to render them functional, and once they are, they seem to be maintained that way by the reinforcing properties of the demanding pups and the continued maternal behavior. The relevance of this for human behavior or pathology is far from clear, but given the importance of early mother-child bonding, any new information that might help to enhance or assure it is most welcome.

Hubel and Wiesel (35) received the Nobel Prize this year for their extensive work on the development of the visual cortex. Essentially they first showed that a young animal deprived of vision in one eye by eliminating visual stimuli to that eye for the first three months of life remains permanently blind in that eye. This is not true for the adult. The reason, demonstrated by radioautographic histology, is that the cortical connections between the lateral geniculate body and the cortex require stimulation at critical periods to become established. If there is sensory deprivation during that critical period, the connections are not made. The functional blindness demonstrated 15 years ago is now recognized to have a structural anatomical basis in the visual cortex. Such effects thus far seem to be irreversible and this may have serious implications, particularly for psychiatrists. The types of developmental disabilities demonstrated by Spitz following social deprivation in infants and by Harlow and Suomi in infant monkeys raised in isolation for the first six months of life may well have structural correlates. Whether or not these can be reversed by types of psychological or pharmacological intervention remains a subject for research.

THE PRESENT STATUS AND FUTURE OF BIOLOGICAL PSYCHIATRY

The greatest contribution of biological psychiatry is the unequivocal demonstration that the brain is, indeed, the organ of the mind. As the transducer of environmental stimuli, the brain is changed by these stimuli. Learning, memory, and thinking all produce changes in the structure and function of the brain at the synapse, or perhaps within the cell, by as yet unknown mechanisms. Similarly, changes in the function and structure of the brain produced by physical illness, toxicity, aging, or genetic illness produce changes in mental functioning in perception, mood, and cognition. Given the brain as the common end organ for environmental input, it is hardly surprising that emotional stress is so frequently a precipitant of an initial depression or of repeated schizophrenic breaks.

The question of how best to intervene in a psychiatric illness should now be a pragmatic rather than an ideological one. It should not matter, *in principle,* whether we use drugs, cognitive therapy, social skills training, supportive psychotherapy, etc. for the treatment of depression. Nor should it matter if we use drugs, family support, peer group assistance, corrective emotional experiences, etc. in intensive psychotherapy or some combination for schizophrenics. *In practice* we should use the procedure or combination of procedures that will be most cost effective and yield the most lasting results. I have previously commented elsewhere (36) that there are now 140 listed types of psychotherapy. This is more than the number of approved drugs. A major question currently and for the future is how to select the correct therapy for any individual patient—which drug, which psychotherapy, or which combination. Hopefully, the psychiatrist of the future will increasingly be committed to solving clinical problems pragmatically, rather than by ideological and methodological commitments.

Progress is being made rapidly in these areas. The studies of Klerman and Weissman on the additive beneficial effects of tricyclics and psychotherapy in the treatment of depression are a well known example (37). Drugs sustain mood and diminish relapses. Psychotherapy enhances interpersonal relationships and social functioning. Together they are better than either alone. Another example is the more recent work on drugs and family therapy in acute schizophrenia (38).

Despite the well recognized beneficial effects of neuroleptics on symptom reduction to the point where discharge from a hospital is possible within a few weeks, problems remain. Patients are left with residual symptoms, usually of a negative sort, and with a relapse rate of about 25% in three months and 50% in six months. In 1978 Goldstein and coworkers (38) demonstrated a remarkable increase in effectiveness when brief family therapy was added to neuroleptics. They studied consecutive first and second admission schizophrenic patients who were hospitalized in the Ventura Mental Health Center. One hundred and four patients were studied; 60% were first lifetime admissions.

In the hospital they were rapidly neurolepticized so that the mean hospital stay was 14 days. During this stay family members were brought in, and they, along with the patient, were advised of the possibility of participating in the proposed research. Those who consented were randomly assigned to one of four treatment programs. These were low phenothiazine, low phenothiazine plus family crisis therapy, high phenothiazine, and high phenothiazine plus family crisis therapy. The phenothiazine was the long-acting fluphenazine enanthate at ¼ ml or 1.0 ml injected on the day of discharge, two weeks later, and two weeks after that. Family therapy had four objectives: 1) to have everyone agree on two or three current stressful circumstances, especially those that might have instigated the psychotic break; 2) to develop strategies to avoid this stress or cope with it; 3) to get patients and families to implement these strategies; and 4) to anticipate and plan for future stressful experience. This simple, concrete problem-oriented therapy went on once a week for only six weeks.

At the end of this time, both drugs and the family therapy were discontinued. Neither the length of drug treatment nor of family therapy was considered optimal, but it was sufficient to produce dramatic effects. At six months none of the patients who had received the high phenothiazines and family therapy for only the six-week period had relapsed. Twenty percent who had received high phenothiazine but no family therapy and 25% who received low phenothiazine and family therapy had relapsed. Forty-eight percent of those receiving low phenothiazine and no family therapy had relapsed. Analysis of these data suggests that both drugs and family crisis therapy are effective and that their effects are additive. Analysis of symptoms in relation to treatment showed that family therapy attenuated affective symptoms and withdrawal. That is, it was most powerful on the negative symptoms for which drugs are least powerful.

There is an ongoing follow-up study which seems to show that the effects of the six-week drug and family therapy effects seem to dissipate over time. The authors emphasize that their experiment was not designed to attempt to produce effects over much longer periods of time. They suggest that extending the drug period and moving family therapy and crisis management to relationship restructuring might better promote sustained recovery. Research of this type is under way both here and abroad (39).

Other major developments in biological psychiatry include the recognition that illnesses with the same clinical behavioral picture may have different etiologies and may respond best to different types of treatment. Clustering of behavioral symptoms started by Kraepelin and vastly extended in DSM-III is helpful but not sufficient (Chapters 3 and 4 present further discussion of biochemical and endocrinological aids to clinical diagnosis and treatment). The converse is equally true. The study of the varied behavioral adaptations to a biochemical difference such as low MAO activity is also producing interesting results.

Another major breakthrough in biological psychiatry is the recognition that pituitary and hypothalamic polypeptides, long thought to be synthesized within the cranium and to act only on peripheral end organs like the adrenal, thyroid, and gonads, also have dramatic central effects. Whether these peptides act as neurotransmitters or only as modulators is not known for certain in many cases. But that they have dramatic effects upon the functioning of the nervous system and behavior seems unquestioned. These hormones offer a therapeutic challenge. When given peripherally, they are rapidly degraded and do not readily penetrate the blood brain barrier. But it is virtually certain that the chemist will be able to alter them so that they are more stable and penetrable. If this is done, a whole new class of therapeutic agents may be developed.

What are the major problems of biological psychiatry for the future? Each of us would choose his own, but I would submit that among the greatest is that of better understanding of the nature, potential, and limits of plasticity in the brain. By plasticity I mean the degree to which the brain and its neurons can change with growth, learning, life experiences, and aging. Among the retarded there is limited plasticity, and this has been shown anatomically by Purpura (40) in the limited arborization of neuronal dendrites in a retarded child. It has also been shown in the work of Hubel and Weisel (35) described earlier. Does limited plasticity result in the behavior of schizophrenics whom Shakow (41) has described psychologically as neophobic? Experimentally, schizophrenic patients can be conditioned to learn, but having learned, persist in the same pattern when circumstances require change. Clinically they do the same, and they become more and more resistive to change as their illness continues. Does this continued regression imply an ongoing endogenous process of brain deterioration, or does it imply that the repetitive use of an unsuccessful and unrewarding coping pattern leads to reinforcement of this behavior, the loss of potential alternates, and the assumption of the amotivational and anhedonic life they lead? Could early intervention with drugs or psychotherapy or both alter this pattern?

Plasticity, it seems to me, can be achieved in two ways. An existing system which has broken down may be repaired or alternative systems may be given a greater task. In thinking about why it is that in affective disorders we have generated information involving the NE, 5HT, ACh, and DA systems, and that we now have different antidepressants which seem to act with fair specificity with each of these and yet are generally effective in the treatment of most of the depressions we encounter, an analogy occurred to me. There are a limited number of major transmitters in our brains. There are also a limited number of communication devices with which we interact with the world. These are talk, writing, telephoning, radio, and television. If any single one breaks down, we become initially anxious and then compensate by using the others more. Although this is a nuisance, it works fairly well, and we make do until the broken-down system is repaired.

Is this what happens with the antidepressants which are generally helpful clinically, regardless of which neurotransmitter systems they most directly affect? Do they permit functioning systems to work harder to compensate for the one which is broken down until it is repaired by mechanisms which we don't understand, or do they repair the nonfunctional system more directly? Similarly, there is now evidence to implicate DA, NE, phenylethylamine, GABA, ACh, and endorphins in schizophrenia (42). Yet the neuroleptics, which at the moment seem to act primarily by blocking DA receptors, work. Is it because they do more than block these receptors, or do other compensatory devices come into play? Are we trying to come to closure in theory with inadequate information? By doing so, do we throw out meaningful information that somehow doesn't fit? Do we need more solid bricklaying in the form of sound clinical information rather than new theories? I am inclined to think so.

CONCLUSIONS

Neurobiology along with genetics is the most exciting and rapidly advancing area of biological research. Since 1904, 36 Nobel Prizes have been given for neurobiological research. Its dramatic growth can be seen by the increase in membership in the Society of Neuroscience from less than 1,000 a decade ago to more than 7,000 today. Many of the members are psychiatrists who are simultaneously clinicians and research scientists. Their productivity is prodigious. Established journals like *The American Journal of Psychiatry* and the *Archives of General Psychiatry* now devote more than a third of their space to biological psychiatry. Moreover, the work becomes more and more technical and sophisticated. Many senior psychiatrists have expressed distress, saying things like, "If you don't know what a V_{max}, B_{max}, or K_m is, you can't understand them." This, of course, calls for new systems of training for the emerging psychiatrists and retraining for the older ones. The former problem is less difficult, even though psychiatry departments as a whole still suffer from lack of research space, which was not wanted because of the dominance of psychoanalytic thinking in the 1950s and 1960s when such space was readily available. Similarly, they suffer from deficits in research manpower and support. But such facilities are gradually coming into existence, and psychiatry departments are less and less distinguished by their couches and interviewing chairs and more and more resemble other clinical departments in physical structure and their faculties. This is good, but I hasten to add that the new neurobiology must not be taught at the expense of sound clinical training in description, diagnosis, and psychotherapy. Because the time and energy of our students is limited, I suspect that some of the new will be at the partial expense of what was previously the dominant theme of psychiatry—psychoanalysis. Whether or not this is good must await future scrutiny.

Let me end with a parable and a dream. We all know of the parable of the seven blind men and the elephant. Each insisted that his description of the elephant was proper, so they argued and fought and never described the elephant. Suppose they had listened to each other thoughtfully? Might they have synthesized a composite description of the elephant?

I use the parable because it seems highly applicable to what is still going on in psychiatry. There is a great need for critical examination and learning the information generated by such varied disciplines as molecular biology and social psychiatry. We must be interdisciplinary. That is our task, and if we succeed, I think we will have regenerated models like Sherrington, Charcot, Janet, and Freud—in other words, neuropsychiatrists. There will be students, researchers, and clinicians who understand both the brain and its behavioral output. That is a highly desirable goal.

REFERENCES

1. MORA, G.: Historical and theoretical trends in psychiatry. In: A.M. Freedman, H.I. Kaplan, and B.J. Sadock (Eds.), *Comparative Text of Psychiatry, Vol. II,* Baltimore: Williams and Wilkins, 1975.
2. BECK, A.T., BRADY, J.P., and QUEN, J.M. (consultants & advisor): *The History of Depression.* New York: Psychiatric Annals, Pfizer Laboratories, 1977, p. 46.
3. CERLITTI, U., and BINI, L.: Electroschok. *Arch. Gen. Neur. & Psychiat. & Psychoanalysis,* 19:266, 1938.
4. FREUD, S.: Analysis terminable and interminable. In: J. Strachey (Ed.), *The Standard Edition of the Complete Psychological Works of Sigmund Freud,* Vol. 23. London: Hogarth Press, 1953, p. 209.
5. FREUD, S.: An outline of psycho-analysis. In: J. Strachey (Ed.), *The Standard Edition of the Complete Psychological Works of Sigmund Freud,* Vol. 23. London: Hogarth Press, 1953, p. 182.
6. KALLMAN, F.J.: *Heredity in Health and Mental Disorder.* New York: W.W. Norton, 1953.
7. HESTON, L.L.: Psychiatric disorders in foster home reared children of schizophrenic mothers. *Br. J. Psychiat.,* 112:819-825, 1966.
8. KETY, S.S., ROSENTHAL, D., WENDER, P.H., and SCHULSINGER, F.: Mental illness in the biological and adoptive families of adopted schizophrenics. *Am. J. Psychiat.,* 128:302-306, 1971.

9. GOTTESMAN, I.I., and SHIELDS, J.: *Schizophrenia and Genetics: A Twin Study Vantage Point*. New York: Academic Press, 1972.
10. KETY, S.S., and KINNEY, D.K.: Biological risk factors in schizophrenia. Unpublished.
11. GERSHON, E.S.: Genetic factors from the clinical perspective, In: E.S. Gershon (Ed.), *The Psychobiology of Affective Disorders*. Basel: Karger, 1980, pp. 25-39.
12. GERSHON, E.S., and BUNNEY, W.E.: The question of X-linkage in bipolar manic-depressive illness. *J. Psychiat. Res.*, 15:99-117, 1977.
13. BARON, M., and RISCH, N.: X-linkage in affective and schizoaffective disorders, genetic and diagnostic implications. *Am. J. Psychiat.*, submitted, 1982.
14. BYCK, R.: *Cocaine Papers—Sigmund Freud*. New York: Meridian Press, 1974.
15. BYCK, R.Q., and VAN DYKE, C.: What are the effects of cocaine in man? *Natl. Inst. Drug Abuse Res.*, Monograph Series, 13:97-117, 1977.
16. DeMONTIGNY, C., GREENBERG, F., MAYER, A., and DESCHENNES, J.P.: Lithium induces rapid relief of depression in tricyclic antidepressant drug nonresponders. *Br. J. Psychiat.*, 138:252-256, 1981.
17. GOODWIN, F.K., PRANGE, A.J., Jr., POST, R.M., et al.: Reversal of tricyclic resistant depression with triiodothyronine. *Am. J. Psychiat.* 139: 34-38, 1982.
18. KANDELL, E.R.: Brain and behavior. In: E.R. Kandell, J.H. Schwartz, (Eds.), *Principles of Neural Science*. New York: Elsevier/North Holland, 1981, p. 4.
19. KANDELL, E.R., and SCHWARTZ, S.H.: *Principles of Neural Science* (Chaps. 3-7, 10). New York: Elsevier/North Holland, 1981.
20. LOEWI, O: Über humorale übertragbarkeit der herznerven werkung pflügers. *Arch. Ges. Physiol.,* 189:239-242, 1921.
21. DALE, H.: Pharmacology and nerve endings. *Proc. R. Soc. Med.,* 28:319-332, 1935.
22. EHRLICH, P.: Chemotherapeutics: Scientific principle, methods and results. *Lancet,* 2:445-451, 1913.
23. SIEGEL, G.J., ALBERS, R.W., AGRANOFF, B.W., and KATZMAN, R.: *Basic Neurochemistry*. Boston: Little, Brown and Co., 1981.
24. COOPER, J.R., BLOOM, F.E., and ROTH, R.H.: *The Biochemical Basis of Neuropharmacology*. New York: Oxford University Press, 1978.
25. GREEN, A.R., and COSTAIN, D.W.: *Pharmacology and Biochemistry of Psychiatric Disorders*. New York: John Wiley, 1981.
26. BARCHAS, J.D., BERGER, P.A., CIARANELLO, R.D., and ELLIOTT, G.D.: *Psychopharmacology from Theory to Practice,* New York: Oxford University Press, 1977.
27. SNYDER, S.H., CREESE, I., and BURT, D.R.: Dopamine receptor binding in mammalian brain: Relevance to psychiatry. In: E. Usdin, D.A. Hamburg, and S.D. Barchas (Eds.), *Neuroregulators and Psychiatric Disorders*. New York: Oxford University Press, 1977, p. 526.
28. GREEGARD, P.: *Cyclic Nucleotides, Phosphorylated Proteins and Neuronal Function*. New York: Raven Press, 1978.
29. ROBISON, G.A., BATCHER, R.W., and SUTHERLAND, E.W.: *Cyclic AMP*. New York: Academic Press, 1971.
30. DeMONTIGNY, C., and AGHAJANIAN, G.K.: Tricyclic antidepressants: Long-term increases in responsivity of rat forebrain neurons to serotonin. *Science,* 202:1303-1305, 1978.
31. HUANG, Y.H.: Chronic desipramine treatment increases the activity of post synaptic adrenergic cells. *Life Sciences,* 25:709-716, 1979.
32. WURTMAN, R., and FERNSTROM, S.: Control of brain neurotransmitter synthesis by

precursor availability and food conscription. In: E. Usdin, D.A. Hamburg, and J.B. Barchas (Eds.), *Neuroregulators and Psychiatric Disorders*. New York: Oxford University Press, 1977.

33. KANDELL, E.R.: Cellular insights into behavior and learning. *Harvey Lectures,* 73:19-72.

34. PEDERSEN, C.A., and PRANGE, A.J., Jr.: Induction of maternal behavior in virgin rats after intracerebroventricular administration of oxytocin. *Proc. Natl. Acad. Sci.,* 76:6661-6665, 1979.

35. HUBEL, D.H., and WIESEL, T.N.: Functional architecture, macaque monkey visual cortex. *Proc. Royal Soc.* (London), 198:1-59, 1977.

36. LIPTON, M.A.: Depression research excluding NE, 5HT, neuroendocrinology, cholinergic systems and genetics. In: E.S. Gershon (Ed.), *The Psychobiology of Affective Disorders*. Basel: Karger, 1980.

37. WEISSMAN, M.M.: Psychotherapy and its relevance to the pharmacotherapy of affective disorders: From ideology to. . . . In: M.A. Lipton, A. DiMascio, and K.F. Killam (Eds.), *Psychopharmacology: A Generation of Progress*. New York: Raven Press, 1978, pp. 1313-1321.

38. GOLDSTEIN, M.J., RODNICK, E.H., EVANS, J.R., MAY, P.R., and STEINBERG, M.P.: Drug and family therapy in the aftercare of acute schizophrenics. *Arch. Gen. Psychiat.,* 35 (10): 1169-77, 1978.

39. HOGARTY, G.E., SCHOOLER, N.R., ULRICH, R., et al.: Fluphenazine therapy and social therapy in the aftercare of schizophrenic patients. *Arch. Gen. Psychiat.,* 36:1283-1294, 1979.

40. PURPURA, D.P.: Dendrite spine "dysgenesis" and mental retardation. *Science,* 186:1126-1128, 1974.

41. SHAKOW, D.: *Adaptation in Schizophrenia: The Theory of Segmental Set*. New York: John Wiley & Sons, 1979, pp. 148-156.

42. BERGER, P.A.: Biochemistry and the schizophrenics. *J. Nerv. Ment. Dis.,* 169:90-99, 1981.

2

The Clinical Differentiation
of Affective and
Schizophrenic Disorders

Nancy C. Andreasen, M.D., Ph.D.

The credit for making the original clinical differentiation between the affective and schizophrenic disorders is usually given to Emil Kraepelin. Kraepelin brought remarkable order to the chaos of 19th century psychiatry by emphasizing the value of empirical description. Most of Kraepelin's contemporaries, such as Kleist, Meynert, or Freud, were preoccupied with developing theoretical models, whether of brain function or psychological mechanisms. Kraepelin bypassed theoretical systems and the search for etiology, observed many patients directly, and grouped together patients whose symptoms and course suggested that they fell into natural clusters. By and large, Kraepelin's basic classificatory system is still universally accepted, a convincing tribute to the value of empirical clinical observation.

The Kraepelinian synthesis coined two new terms: manic-depressive illness and dementia praecox (1,2). Manic-depressive illness was distinguished from the other major psychotic disorder occurring in younger patients, dementia praecox, on the basis of age and type of onset, course of illness, and clinical symptoms. Patients now referred to as having affective disorder were grouped together under a single heading, manic-depressive psychosis. Kraepelin recognized that many depressed patients were prone to cycle into mania and thus unified mania and depression into a single disorder. This was considered to represent a discrete illness, which tended to be relatively severe, episodic, and recurrent, with a good prognosis and a full restitutio ad integrum. On the other hand, dementia

29

praecox, as the name implies, was a severe illness which tended to begin at an early age, to be chronic, to have a poor prognosis, to lead to eventual deterioration, and to be characterized by severe cognitive symptoms that suggested a relationship to the dementias.

Although the basic Kraepelinian synthesis continues to be widely accepted, over the years a number of modifications have been added. The principal modification of dementia praecox was of course made by Bleuler (3). Bleuler rejected the term dementia praecox and substituted schizophrenia in its place, having observed that many patients at the Burgholzli developed symptoms at a later age and did not necessarily deteriorate. Bleuler was also more preoccupied than Kraepelin with theoretical issues and basic mechanisms. As a consequence, he renamed the disorder to describe what he considered to be the fundamental defect in these severely psychotic patients: their confused thinking and speech. Writing in an era when association psychology was popular, he appealed to the notion that the "associative threads" were somehow split or torn. By deemphasizing course and placing greater emphasis on fundamental psychological and cognitive deficits, Bleuler made his schizophrenia a much broader and more inclusive disorder than was Kraepelin's dementia praecox. Over the years, particularly in America, Bleulerian schizophrenia has come to mean any illness characterized by mild confusion in thinking and slightly impaired reality testing.

As time progressed, clinicians also began to suggest that the relatively narrow concept of manic-depressive illness could be broadened and renamed in order to include milder or more chronic depressive syndromes. Adolf Meyer, for example, developed a more dimensional and dynamic approach to the description of depression and other psychiatric disorders (4). He believed that each patient should be described individually in terms of a group of dimensions that included inheritance, physical status, personality, environmental factors, and symptoms. A depressive syndrome was best described as a *reaction* that occurred between these dimensions when other types of adaptation had failed. He used the dimensions to describe various forms of depression that ranged from mild (mergasias) to severe (holergasias and thymergasias).

Until very recently, the Meyerian point of view had more influence on the concept of schizophrenia than it did on the concept of affective disorders. Until approximately 10 years ago, psychiatry in the United States tended to use a relatively broad concept of schizophrenia and a relatively narrow concept of affective disorder. When confronted with a difficult differential diagnosis between these two disorders, the tendency was usually to consider the patient to have schizophrenia. As long as differential treatments, not to mention laboratory tests or biological markers, did not exist, diagnosis often did not even seem very important.

Changes in Diagnostic Concepts During the Past Ten Years

During the past 10 years, dramatic changes have occurred in psychiatry. The study of biological factors has assumed new importance, and the introduction of many kinds of specific treatments for different disorders has made diagnosis a serious undertaking. Clinicians and researchers have begun to review our nosological systems critically and to attempt to reformulate them so that they are more reliable, coherent, and clinically useful. This has led recently to a radical revision of the American diagnostic nomenclature in the *Third Diagnostic and Statistical Manual* of the American Psychiatric Association, or *DSM-III* (5). One important aspect of *DSM-III* is a reconceptualization of the relationship between affective and schizophrenic disorders, resulting in a narrowing of the concept of schizophrenia and a broadening of the concept of affective disorder.

Rationale for Recent Changes

In some respects, *DSM-III* simply formalized changes in diagnostic habits that had been developing for several years. These changes occurred as a consequence of two different lines of evidence, one from research investigations, and the other from clinical practice. Both lines of evidence converged to suggest that the concepts of affective disorder and schizophrenia needed revision.

Research Investigations

Cross-national studies. In the late 1960s and early 1970s several major investigations were undertaken to compare diagnostic practice in the United States and in the remainder of the world. These were the International Pilot Study of Schizophrenia (IPSS) and the US/UK study (6,7). The IPSS compared the way clinicians diagnosed schizophrenia in nine different countries, reflecting various geographic regions and levels of socioeconomic development, such as the United States, the USSR, the United Kingdom, Taiwan, and Colombia. The Present State Examination (PSE), a structured interview developed in order to standardize the evaluation of patients, stressed the importance of careful definition of symptoms and put Schneiderian first-rank symptoms (I shall return to these later) in a prominent position (8). In the IPSS, after joint training and reliability sessions, psychiatrists evaluated patients in their own countries using the PSE, and the rates for diagnosing schizophrenia and the nature of the symptoms were compared.

In the US/UK study, American and British psychiatrists made comparative evaluations of patients interviewed on videotape. From these studies, it soon became apparent that American psychiatrists tended to have a much broader concept of schizophrenia and a narrower concept of affective disorder than psychiatrists from other countries. American psychiatry appeared to be out of step with the rest of the world, and a concern developed about drawing closer to our international colleagues in our diagnostic practices.

Emphasis on the importance of reliability. Partly as a result of these cross-national studies, and partly as a consequence of a resurgence of interest in biological research, psychiatrists have also become increasingly aware of a need to improve the reliability of diagnosis. Reliability refers to the ability of observers to agree (interrater reliability) or for observations to remain consistent over time (test-retest reliability). It is axiomatic in nosological research that reliability places a ceiling on validity; that is, a diagnostic system will be of little use in making predictions about such important matters as outcome or response to treatment if observers cannot agree among themselves on whether or not the condition is actually present.

While the cross-national studies and other research initially created some pessimism about the possibility of achieving adequate reliability, a number of different investigators set to work to improve reliability. Alternative sets of diagnostic criteria were written, such as the St. Louis Criteria or the Research Diagnostic Criteria (RDC) (9,10). In addition to the PSE, new structured interviews were also developed, such as the Schedule for Affective Disorders and Schizophrenia (SADS) and the Diagnostic Interview Schedule (DIS) (11,12). Many investigators have now documented that good to excellent diagnostic reliability can be achieved through the use of criteria and structured interviews (13-18). The emphasis on the importance of reliability has had a major impact on American diagnosis, leading to the incorporation of diagnostic criteria in DSM-III.

The emphasis on the importance of reliability has also had an important impact on the symptoms used to define illness. As investigators became concerned about reliability, they tended to base diagnosis on those symptoms that were easier to define reliably. In the case of schizophrenia, this led to an emphasis on the use of delusions and hallucinations rather than the "softer" more subtle Bleulerian four As (usually defined as associations, affect, autism, and ambivalence). Delusions and hallucinations tend to be all-or-none phenomena; that is, they are either present or absent. Further, they are relatively striking and obvious when present. On the other hand, symptoms such as affective flattening or ambivalence tend to be on a continuum with normality and to be strongly influenced by a variety of social and cultural norms. As a consequence, they are more difficult to define in a way that will lead to high interrater agreement, because it is difficult to demarcate abnormality precisely.

Schneiderian first-rank symptoms. Partly because they were given a prominent position in the PSE, and partly because of an increased interest in German nosology, Schneiderian first-rank symptoms achieved prominence during the late 1960s and early 1970s (19). Schneiderian first-rank symptoms are specific types of delusions or hallucinations that have been considered pathognomonic of schizophrenia, e.g., hearing voices arguing or delusional experiences such as thought insertion or thought withdrawal. Early work indicated that the symptoms were very useful in discriminating between schizophrenia and mania. Consequently, they were introduced into widely used diagnostic criteria such as the RDC and also assumed an important position in *DSM-III*. On the other hand, more recently several studies have questioned whether they are actually pathognomonic of schizophrenia and have indicated that at least some patients who would be considered manic by most criteria may have first-rank symptoms (20,21). These latter findings have had an important impact on *DSM-III* by suggesting that many patients once considered to be schizophrenic or schizoaffective may in fact have a severe psychotic mania instead.

Studies of thinking and affect. Formal thought disorder and affective blunting are perhaps the most important among the Bleulerian symptoms. In fact, for many years formal thought disorder was considered to be the pathognomonic symptom of schizophrenia. However, recent investigations have also suggested that most types of formal thought disorder occur with considerable frequency in mania as well, thereby reducing their significance as totally characteristic symptoms (22,23). Likewise, affective blunting has been observed to be quite common in patients suffering from depression (24). Thus, although both of these symptoms may ultimately be quite useful in defining schizophrenia, particularly when patterns or groups of symptoms are studied, neither can be considered to occur solely in schizophrenia. Taken together with the studies indicating that Schneiderian first-rank symptoms are not pathognomonic, these studies suggest that schizophrenia cannot be defined monothetically (that is, on the basis of a single pathognomonic symptom), but instead must be treated as a polythetic construct.

Studies of good prognosis schizophrenia. For many years clinicians and researchers have recognized that some patients diagnosed as schizophrenic tend to improve markedly or even to recover fully. On the other hand, some tend to have a chronic and deteriorating course. This observation led a number of investigators to examine which symptoms tend to predict a good outcome (25,26). These studies have yielded a remarkable consensus concerning those symptoms that predict a good prognosis. Good prognosis indicators include a family history of affective disorder, an acute onset, presence of precipitating factors, prominent affective symptoms such as depression or elation, and a good premorbid personality. Indicators of poor outcome include a positive family history of schizophrenia, an insidious onset, absence of precipitants, absence of affective features, and a poor premorbid personality. The features that indicate a good prognosis are in fact also features that tend to characterize affective disorder. This recognition has led a number of investigators to suggest that good prognosis schizophrenia is not schizophrenia at all, but rather a severe form of affective disorder (27).

Clinical Observations

Strategies of clinical care. Practical aspects of patient care have also suggested that it might be useful to narrow the concept of schizophrenia and to broaden the concept of affective disorder. Basic clinical common sense dictates that one should err in the direction of overdiagnosing treatable illnesses and underdiagnosing untreatable illnesses. Obviously, this strategy minimizes the risks involved in diagnostic mistakes. The availability of effective treatments, such as tricyclic antidepressants or electroconvulsive therapy, has made affective disorder an illness with a good prognosis and a relatively rapid rate of recovery. Clinicians have come to realize that they do their patients a better service by diagnosing affective disorder when in doubt than by diagnosing schizophrenia, since they are at worst overdiagnosing treatable illness.

Further, the specific characteristics of available treatments make it even more desirable to overdiagnose affective disorder rather than schizophrenia. The patient who has a depressive disorder and is treated with phenothiazines will not improve and will in fact begin to resemble a schizophrenic quite closely, because of the apparent changes in affect induced by Parkinsonian side effects of phenothiazines. Thus, the clinican who misdiagnoses affective disorder as schizophrenia will not only not discover that he is wrong, but may have his erroneous diagnosis *confirmed* by his treatment. Again, if he must make a diagnostic error, he will do better to underdiagnose schizophenia rather than overdiagnose it. Almost no price is paid for misdiagnosing a patient who in fact has schizophrenia as having affective disorder, since the error is usually discovered through poor treatment response, and the diagnosis is changed.

Introduction of lithium. Lithium was introduced to clinical use in the United States in the late 1960s and early 1970s. The introduction of lithium gave clinicians an effective means for treating mania that was burdened with few side effects. Since tricyclic antidepressants had become available somewhat earlier, clinicians now had specific treatments for both poles of bipolar affective disorder. The availability of such specific treatments gave clinicians additional impetus for taking a more careful interest in diagnosis in general and for looking for affective disorder in particular. A specific diagnosis now dictated a specific pharmacological treatment.

The risk of tardive dyskinesia. The discovery of tardive dyskinesia is a third factor that has led many clinicians to pause cautiously and think before making a diagnosis of schizophrenia. A patient diagnosed as schizophrenic is likely to have long-term treatment with neuroleptics, which may place him at high risk for eventually developing tardive dyskinesia. Since tardive dyskinesia adds an unpleasant physical deformity to severe emotional incapacity, no clinician wants to place his patients under this risk unnecessarily. Although there is some risk associated with taking lithium or tricyclics, it is less than the risk associated with taking neuroleptics. Consequently, the clinician has been given yet another motivation for diagnosing affective disorder whenever in doubt.

THE NATURE OF THE CHANGES IN DIAGNOSTIC PRACTICE

Thus, during the past 10 years our conceptualization of the nature and significance of psychiatric diagnosis has undergone major changes. Diagnosis is now closely tied to treatment, as well as prediction of outcome. Both researchers and clinicians have come to realize the importance of using specified diagnostic criteria in order to improve reliability, and they now make diagnoses confident that a given diagnosis will carry a relatively consistent meaning to their colleagues. They have grown cautious about overdiagnosing schizophrenia and more aggressive in diagnosing affective disorder. While many of these changes became standard in research during the 1970s, in the 1980s they have also been given official recognition for clinical practice through their incorporation in our standardized nomenclature, DSM-III. In this new nomenclature, the clinical differentiation of affective disorders and schizophrenia has changed markedly.

Narrowing of the Concept of Schizophrenia

The narrowing of the concept of schizophrenia is tied to the narrowing of a concept of psychosis. "Psychosis" is a word that has often been used imprecisely. Sometimes it has been used to mean severe illness, sometimes to refer to impairment or incapacitation, sometimes to refer to disorganized cognition or impaired reality testing, and sometimes to indicate the presence of particular symptoms such as delusions or hallucinations. The definition of psychosis in DSM-II probably contributed to an imprecise conceptualization of psychosis by defining it very broadly; it was applied to individuals whose "mental functional [was] sufficiently impaired to interfere grossly with their capacity to meet the ordinary demands of life.'' The DSM-III definition requires gross impairment in reality testing, manifested by such direct evidence as delusions, hallucinations, severely disorganized behavior, or incoherent speech. Thus the definition is tied to objective manifestations that can be defined with reasonable reliability. Given this new definition of psychosis, some disorders that were classified among the psychosies in DSM-II, such as the affective disorders, are now classified separately, since they are not invariably characterized by the presence of psychotic features.

Table 1 illustrates visually the way the definition of schizophrenia has been narrowed. In DSM-II this rather broad category included patients who were severely disorganized and chronically ill, as well as patients who had acute psychotic breaks and also who were able to lead relatively normal lives. In DSM-III, schizophrenia can only be diagnosed when the disorder is relatively severe and chronic. This narrow conceptualization makes American diagnostic practices more like those of other countries such as Great Britain. Milder or more acute illnesses that were formerly considered to be forms of schizophrenia are now referred to as Psychoses Not Elsewhere Classified. Schizoaffective disorder now appears under this heading, rather than under schizophrenia. Acute schizophrenia is now brief reactive psychosis, if precipitating factors have played an important

TABLE 1

DSM-II	DSM-III
SCHIZOPHRENIA	SCHIZOPHRENIA
Paranoid	Paranoid
Hebephrenic	Disorganized
Catatonic	Catatonic
Chronic undifferentiated	Undifferentiated
	PSYCHOSES NOT ELSEWHERE CLASSIFIED
Acute	Brief reactive psychosis
Schizoaffective	Schizophreniform disorder
	Schizoaffective disorder
	Atypical psychotic disorder
	PERSONALITY DISORDERS
Simple	Schizoid
Latent	Schizotypal

role and symptoms are present for less than two weeks, or schizophreniform disorder, if symptoms have been present for two weeks to six months. Nonpsychotic forms of schizophrenia, such as latent or simple, reappear under the heading of Personality Disorders as either schizotypal or schizoid. Although epidemiological comparisons have not been completed as yet, it seems likely that this reconceptualization will reduce the number of patients diagnosed as schizophrenic by a substantial amount. This narrowing has been achieved by tightening the definition of schizophrenia in several different ways.

Course and duration. Longitudinal observation of patients is perhaps the single most powerful tool available to the diagnostician or nosologist if laboratory tests or anatomic data are not available. Thus course and duration are important defining features of any illness. The course of the illness was an important aspect of Kraepelinian dementia praecox. Although DSM-III schizophrenia is still considerably broader than Kraepelin's dementia praecox, nevertheless it has returned to Kraepelinian concepts in several respects. First of all, the diagnosis is restricted to those patients who have become ill prior to age 45. Although an onset prior to 45 is hardly "praecox," nevertheless persons who become ill for the first time in late middle age are no longer considered to have schizophrenia. In some systems, these patients would be considered to have an involutional paraphrenia or other involutional psychosis. In DSM-III they will be classified as atypical psychotic disorder.

Another important aspect of the definition is the requirement that patients manifest some symptoms of the illness for at least six months. During this six-month period they may have had any combination of prodromal and overtly psychotic symptoms. Clinicians have recognized for years that many schizophrenic patients experience an insidious onset of symptoms, with the earliest signs being social withdrawal, loss of interest in usual activities, eccentric behavior, odd speech, or peculiar thinking. This clinical awareness has been objectified as a list of common prodromal symptoms that may antedate the overt psychotic symptoms specified in the diagnostic criteria for schizophrenia. The requirement that patients be ill for at least six months with some combination of prodromal and overt psychotic features further serves to narrow the concept of schizophrenia. While the disorder so defined is not necessarily severely chronic, nevertheless it is also not acute. Although the six-month criterion may seem somewhat arbitrary, it was selected because research by Astrup (shown in Table 2) has indicated that six months of illness provides a useful cutting point for predicting prognosis (28). Patients who have been ill for at least six months tend to have a much poorer outcome than those who have been ill for less than six months.

TABLE 2
Duration of Illness Before Admission

Outcome	½ Year	½ to 1 Years	1 to 2 Years	2 to 5 Years	5 to 10 Years	> 10 Years	Total
Recovered	93	12	10	4	2	0	121
Improved	138	35	18	22	9	9	231
Schizophrenic personality change	34	10	10	28	11	1	100
Slight schizophrenic deterioration	24	21	37	57	22	16	177
Severe schizophrenic deterioration	9	10	14	23	13	8	77
TOTAL	298	88	95	134	57	34	706

Clinical symptoms. The clinical symptoms used to define schizophrenia have also changed markedly. These changes reflect many of the concerns discussed above. In particular, the Bleulerian four As have been deemphasized because of a concern about poor reliability. Two of the As, affective flattening and disorganized thinking, are included in the criteria. Although both these symptoms have also been observed in the affective disorders, the DSM-III definition of schizophrenia minimizes confusion or overlap by requiring that schizophrenia cannot be diagnosed when prominent affective symptoms are present. The symptoms of schizophrenia are specified in six separate criteria. The Bleulerian As appear only in criterion 6. The remaining five criteria describe various types of delusions and hallucinations, both Schneiderian and non-Schneiderian. Thus these more objective psychotic symptoms are given great prominence in the current definition and conceptualization. The diagnosis of schizophrenia cannot be made if the patient has not had psychotic symptoms at some time. Thus, the clinical description is used to exclude various non-psychotic forms of schizophrenia such as simple or latent.

Broadening of the Concept of Affective Disorder

While our current nosology has restricted the concept of schizophrenia by *excluding* what some might consider mild forms, it has broadened the concept of affective disorders by *including* mild forms. Table 1 showed how DSM-II schizophrenia was subdivided and moved to various parts of the new DSM-III nomenclature. Table 3 shows how precisely the opposite has occurred in the case of the affective disorders.

In DSM-II affective disorders are not included as a major heading. The affective disorders appeared under three different main headings: Psychoses, Neuroses, and Personality Disorders. The psychoses included manic-depressive illness, psychotic depressive reaction, and involutional depression. Less severe depressions were classified as depressive neuroses, while very mild bipolar illness was classified as cyclothymic personality disorder. In DSM-III these various disorders are grouped under a single main heading, Major Affective Disorders. The illnesses listed under this heading range from very severe (e.g., bipolar disorder, with mood incongruent psychotic features) to relatively mild (e.g., cyclothymic disorder). This grouping reflects a recent consensus that the various affective disorders may form a continuum of severity but are linked together by a single major symptom, a disorder of mood or affect.

Use of the bipolar/unipolar distinction. During the past several decades, the subdivision of affective disorders into bipolar and unipolar has become widely

TABLE 3

DSM-II	DSM-III
PSYCHOSES	MAJOR AFFECTIVE DISORDERS
Manic-depressive	Bipolar
Manic	Manic
Depressed	Depressed
Circular	Mixed
Psychotic depressive reaction	Major depression
Involutional depression	Single episode
	Recurrent
NEUROSES	Other specific affective disorders
Depressive	Dysthymic
	Cyclothymic
PERSONALITY DISORDERS	Atypical affective disorders
Cyclothymic	Bipolar
	Depression

accepted both in clinical practice and in research. The availability of lithium as a specific treatment for bipolar disorder has been an important contributing factor. In addition, the distinction has been supported by a large amount of research evidence, which is summarized in Table 4. Bipolar and unipolar affective disorders have been found to differ in terms of genetics and familial prevalence (29-36), various kinds of biological markers (37-45), response to treatment (46-51), and course and prognosis (30,34, 51,52). Although the term bipolar disorder has been widely used throughout the world, it has only been given official recognition in a standard nosological system for the first time in DSM-III. It provides a useful replacement for the older Kraepelinian term, manic-depressive psychosis, which tended to be much less precise. The term manic-depressive was used interchangeably to mean either bipolar disorder or very severe recurrent depressive disorder, thereby leading to considerable confusion.

Use of chronicity and course. Chronicity and course are also important defining features for the various subtypes of affective disorders. These disorders are broken down into two main groups. One group consists of bipolar disorder and major depression, while the other group is the Other Specific Affective Disorders, cyclothymic disorder and dysthymic disorder. In addition to being more severe, the first grouping also tends to be more episodic. On the other hand, the Other Specific Affective Disorders are by definition chronic. That is, they are disorders in which the symptoms have persisted for at least two years. Thus they are similar to some types of depressive neurosis or to personality disorder.

TABLE 4
Validation of the Bipolar-Unipolar Distinction

Genetic and Family Studies	Increased familial prevalence in bipolar Is and IIs (29-34) Increased Mz:Dz ratio for bipolars in twin studies (35) Transmission and linkage studies (34,36)
Biological Studies	Decreased MHPG in bipolar depression (37-40) Augmentation of average evoked response in bipolars (41) Low platelet MAO in bipolars (42) Neuroendocrine response in bipolars (43-44) Red cell membrane and intracellular lithium concentration in bipolars (45)
Response to Treatment	Increased response to lithium in bipolar depressives (46-49) Lithium decreases hypomanic episodes but not depression in bipolar IIs (50)
Course and Prognosis	Earlier onset in bipolar Is and IIs (30,51) More episodes and more social impairment in bipolars (51,52) Higher suicide rate in bipolar Is and IIs (30,34)

Inclusion of very severe affective disorder. In DSM-III the concept of affective disorder has been broadened at both ends. It includes both patients who have very severe illnesses and those who have very mild illnesses. Not only does it include some patients who would have been considered psychotic according to DSM-II, but it even includes some who would have been considered schizophrenic. This broadening at the more severe end occurred in response to increasing evidence that schizoaffective disorder was closely allied with affective disorder. Schizoaffective patients tend to resemble those with affective disorder more than those with schizophrenia in terms of family history, clinical symptoms, and response to treatment (27). Because of this evidence and the various clinical rationales discussed above, the concept of mood-incongruent psychotic features was introduced in DSM-III. Patients with Schneiderian first-rank symptoms, once considered pathognomonic of schizophrenia, are now diagnosed as having affective disorder if they have a predominantly affective syndrome. The concept of pathognomonic symptoms has been dropped altogether and the concept of schizoaffective disorder minimized markedly.

Inclusion of relatively mild disorders. Affective disorders have also been broadened at the less severe end of the continuum in a variety of ways. Disorders once classified as personality disorders or neuroses, such as cyclothymic disorder or dysthymic disorder, are now included under this broad concept. Mild bipolar disorders, such as bipolar-II (included under Atypical Bipolar Disorder), are also given some recognition.

Perhaps the most striking innovation, however, is the fact that major depression has been defined very broadly. Although a minimal duration requirement is included (two weeks), the symptom list is relatively inclusive. The symptoms listed in the criteria would be regarded by many clinicians as relatively mild (or neurotic) depressive symptoms, such as eating excessively, sleeping excessively, fatigue, or feelings of worthlessness. Since only four symptoms are required, the diagnosis of major depression can be made in patients with a relatively mild syndrome. Thus, while some patients with neurotic depression will be classified as dysthymic disorder, many will be classified as having major depressive disorder.

Major Changes During the Next Ten Years

The developments just discussed were once a frontier. Now they are past history. During the coming 10 years we can anticipate that innovations are likely to occur in clinical treatment and in research that will be at least as great as those just described. Thus we can anticipate that 10 years from now the conceptualization and classification of schizophrenia and the affective disorders will differ substantially. Further, since the Diagnostic and Statistical Manual has traditionally been revised in approximately 10-year cycles, a decade from now we will probably all be trying to familiarize ourselves with the contents of DSM-IV. It is interesting to speculate about what the nosology of *fin de siècle* America will be like.

The Schizophrenias in the Future

The next 10 years should be exciting ones for research in schizophrenia. During the past two or three years (primarily during the interval since DSM-III went to press), several new areas have opened up in schizophrenia research which are likely to be very influential.

Schizophrenia and Models of Brain Function

Because the cognitive incapacity in schizophrenia is so severe, clinicians and researchers for a number of years have suspected that this might be due to some type of specific brain abnormality. Kraepelin appears to have recognized a prominent organic component in schizophrenia when he named the disorder dementia praecox, highlighting the fact that the illness might somehow be related to other dementias.

The search for brain abnormalities in schizophrenia has been handicapped by a variety of factors, such as poor definition of the illness, but one major problem has been the difficulties inherent in studying the human brain. Very few autopsy studies have been conducted because specimens are difficult to obtain. Consequently, nearly everything that we know about possible brain abnormalities in schizophrenia is inferential—based on neuropsychological testing, investigation of the peripheral metabolites, EEG data, or sampling of cerebrospinal fluid.

In 1973 a powerful new technology for studying brain structure in living human beings was developed. This technique, computerized tomography, permits visualization and three-dimensional reconstruction of many brain structures. Since its original development, the technology has improved steadily, permitting increasingly improved resolution and visualization.

During very recent years, this technique has been used to study structural brain abnormalities in schizophrenia and has demonstrated that a substantial number of schizophrenic patients have various types of structural brain abnormalities. These abnormalities include ventricular enlargement, sulcal enlargement or cortical atrophy, and reversals of cerebral asymmetry (53-63). While not all of these findings have been equally strong, it appears almost certain that some type of structural brain abnormality occurs in schizophrenia. The results of a number of recent studies of one finding, ventricular enlargement, are summarized in Table 5. As Table 5 indicates, with only one exception (63), all investigations have found significant differences in ventricular size between schizophrenic patients and controls.

TABLE 5
Studies of Ventricular Enlargement in Schizophrenia

Investigators	Schizophrenics		Controls		p
	N	VBR	N	VBR	
Johnstone et al. (57)	18	— *	10	— *	.01
Weinberger et al. (53)	58	8.7 ± 3.9	56	3.5 ± 2.3	.0001
Golden et al. (67)	42	12 ± 5	—	— —	—
Andreasen et al. (59)	52	6.0 ± 3.9	47	4.5 ± 3.1	.03
Nasrallah et al. (68)	55	8.7 ± 4.0	27	4.5 ± 2.6	.00001
Jernigan et al. (63)	30	— *	35	— *	NS

* Mean and SD not reported.

The significance of these results will be explored intensively during the coming years. Investigators will be examining the relationship between structural brain abnormalities and clinical symptoms, course, premorbid adjustment, response to treatment, and indices of cognitive function. Several investigators have proposed that ventricular enlargement may define a particular subtype of schizophrenia, referred to as negative or defect schizophrenia. This type of schizophrenia is contrasted with positive or florid schizophrenia, a type in which the patients do not have ventricular enlargement. The original formulation of this hypothesized classification, developed by Crow (58), is summarized in Table 6.

Negative or defect schizophrenia is characterized by a more insidious onset, prominent negative symptoms such as affective flattening or poverty of speech, markedly impaired cognitive function manifested by symptoms such as poor memory, and a poor response to treatment with neuroleptics. This disorder is hypothesized to be due to neuronal loss, is manifested by ventricular enlargement or cortical atrophy, and is likely to be irreversible. Positive or florid schizophrenia is characterized by a more acute onset and more episodic course, prominent positive symptoms such as delusions or hallucinations, a normal sensorium, and at least a partial response to neurleptics. Its hypothesized mechanism is neurochemical, and therefore it is more likely to be reversible.

While this is an interesting heuristic model and has been partially supported by recent research, the investigation of structural brain abnormalities will no doubt also involve other approaches. For example, to date the use of CT scanning has emphasized the search for various types of diffuse abnormalities, as manifested by cortical atrophy and ventricular enlargement. The emphasis should soon shift to a search for more focal abnormalities, particularly in areas of the brain that appear to be dysfunctional, either because of the nature of schizophrenic symptoms or data from neurochemical research. The clinical symptoms of schizophrenia suggest possible abnormalities in the frontal lobes or the left temporal lobe. Neurochemical research implicates areas rich in dopaminergic transmitters such as the mesolimbic system. One could speculate that the classification of schizophrenia in DSM-IV might be based on various subtypes of structural and neurochemical brain abnormalities.

Return of Interest in Bleulerian Approaches

The neo-Kraepelinian revival of the 1970s has probably nearly run its course. During the next 10 years investigators are likely to return to Kraepelin's great rival, Eugen Bleuler, for a renewal of insights concerning the nature of schizophrenia. Two of Bleuler's insights may be particularly useful.

One of Bleuler's major points, stressed in the subtitle of his book (3), was

TABLE 6
Two Types of Schizophrenia

	Positive (Delusions, Hallucinations)	Negative (Poverty of Speech, Flat Affect)
Onset	Variable, sometimes acute	Insidious
Outcome	Variable, sometimes good	Poor
Characteristic symptoms	Positive	Negative
Sensorium and cognition	Normal	Impaired
Response to treatment	Good	Poor
Pathological process	Reversible	Irreversible
Etiology and mechanism	Focal—neurochemical	Diffuse—structural

that the schizophrenias were a heterogeneous grouping of disorders. During the past 10 years, nosological research on the subtyping of depressive disorders has been a hot but not very illuminating area, while the subtyping of schizophrenia has been virtually ignored. In spite of this, nearly everyone who treats schizophrenic patients or does research on schizophrenia is impressed with the great variety and probable heterogeneity of the disorder. Many competing systems for subtyping schizophrenia exist, including good *versus* poor premorbid, good *versus* poor prognosis, paranoid *versus* non-paranoid, and the traditional Kraepelinian subtypes. If the good prognosis subtype is removed from the concept of schizophrenia, the remaining subtypes appear to have little predictive validity. During the next 10 years, researchers should and will explore various new approaches to subtyping schizophrenia. Some of these will emphasize a search for structural or neurochemical brain abnormalities and biological markers. Others will stress the use of characteristic clinical symptoms to define subtypes, such as prominent positive or negative symptoms, or prominent delusions or hallucinations or disorganized speech.

A second important Bleulerian insight concerns the nature of characteristic or core schizophrenic symptoms. While Bleuler may not have been right in conceptualizing associative loosening as the pathognomonic symptom, he was undoubtedly right that delusions or hallucinations are not pathognomonic symptoms either. During the coming years, clinicians and researchers will return again to exploring the significance of those symptoms that Bleuler regarded as important, such as disorganized thinking and speech, affective flattening, inattention, avolition, and anhedonia. Some research completed to date has indicated that these symptoms can be defined reliably if tied to various objective phenomena, thereby alleviating one major concern about their usefulness. Treatment research and CT scan research have recently indicated that these symptoms may be very useful prognostically, both in predicting outcome and in predicting response to treatment. We can anticipate that in DSM-IV various types of Bleulerian symptoms will enjoy a more prominent place than they did in DSM-III.

Return of Interest in Milder or Spectrum Schizophrenia

The resurgence of interest in Bleulerian symptoms is also likely to lead to a resurgence of interest in mild or spectrum schizophrenia. Many Bleulerian symptoms are similar to those occurring in the disorders sometimes referred to as schizoid, schizotypal, or latent schizophrenia. Genetic research has given some support to the possibility that these milder non-psychotic, but schizophrenic-like, disorders may in fact be mild forms of schizophrenia (64). This tantalizing possibility will almost certainly be pursued further during the coming years. It is quite possible that in DSM-IV these mild or non-psychotic disorders will be returned again to the schizophrenic fold.

Conceptualizations concerning affective disorders should also change radically during the 1980s, although less radically than those of the schizophrenic disorders. Clinical and nosological research of the affective disorders has already made major advances during the 1970s, and the changes during the 1980s are likely to involve a variety of refinements.

Narrowing of the Concept of Affective Disorders

The concept of the affective disorders was broadened for several reasons outlined above. One set of reasons was clinical. Because of the effective treatments available for affective disorders, it is strategically better for patients if clinicians make affective diagnoses as frequently as possible. The second reason was the recognition that at least some patients called schizophrenic had been misclassified. The inclusion of relatively mild forms has helped to alert the public and the federal government to the high rate of psychiatric illness in our society and the importance of supporting mental health services and research. Now that these useful correctives have been made, clinicians and researchers are likely to begin to look critically at the negative consequences of a broad definition.

This close look is likely to lead to a narrowing of the concept. As mentioned earlier, the definition of major depression, widely used both in research and clinical practice, delineates a very broadly defined syndrome. As such, it is probably composed of several different types of depression that are etiologically heterogeneous. Although research studies often divide patients into those with or without endogenous depression (or melancholia), even the definition of endogenous depression in the Research Diagnostic Criteria (RDC) or melancholia in DSM-III is quite broad. Studies are beginning to indicate that these syndromal definitions are not useful in distinguishing patients on the basis of validators that are currently widely used, such as familial patterns of illness or response to dexamethasone suppression (65,66). Consequently, we can anticipate that in DSM-IV both major depression and depression with melancholia will be more tightly defined. The relationship of other mild forms, such as dysthymic disorder, will also be explored. It seems possible that they may even be removed from the broad heading of Affective Disorders and into another heading, such as Situational or Adjustment Disorders.

The implications of deemphasizing the concept of schizoaffective disorder will also be evaluated critically. The inclusion of patients with mood-incongruent psychotic features in manic disorder or major depressive disorder has also increased the heterogeneity of the concept. During the next 10 years, more refined research may indicate that patients with such severe psychotic features do indeed have a different course, response to treatment, and familial pattern of inheritance. Much of the research leading to the decision to group schizoaffective patients within affective disorder was based on poorly defined samples (27). As the samples are defined more carefully, significant differences may well be noted in those patients with such severe affective disorder.

Emphasis on biological approaches. The emphasis on a search for biological correlates of affective disorder will continue. During the next 10 years there will be a closer interaction between biological psychiatrists and nosologists, which may lead to the development of classification systems couched in more biological terms. Neuroendocrine and neurochemical research, already a well explored if not heavily populated frontier, will no doubt be supplemented with research involving various techniques for studying brain structure of cognition. Promising new areas, in which research is only beginning, include the use of CT and PET scanning, the exploration of asymmetries, and the examination of the relationship between depressive pseudodementia and the degenerative or cerebrovascular dementias. It is conceivable that a classification developed in the 1980s or '90s might subdivide biological depression into those due to neurochemical, those due to neuroendocrine, and those due to structural brain abnormalities.

Study of social factors in depression. Studies of social factors have to date been primitive and embryonic in comparison with studies of biological factors. This is largely because of the difficulties inherent in developing techniques for measuring social factors or social change. The recent interest in developing reliable techniques for making diagnoses is likely to spill over into research on social factors during the next decade. Any clinician who works with patients experiencing depressive symptoms cannot fail to be aware of the importance of social factors. During the 1980s this promises to be a rich and productive area of investigation for clinicians and researchers interested in exploring milder forms of depression.

REFERENCES

1. KRAEPELIN, E.: *Manic-Depressive Insanity and Paranoia.* Edinburgh: E. and S. Livingstone, 1921.

2. KRAEPELIN, E.: *Dementia Praecox and Paraphrenia*. Edinburgh: E. and S. Livingstone, 1921.

3. BLEULER, E.: *Dementia Praecox or the Group of Schizophrenias*. New York: International Universities Press, 1950.

4. MEYER, A.: The problems of mental reaction types, mental causes, and diseases. *Psychol. Bull.*, 5:245, 1908.

5. *Diagnostic and Statistical Manual of Mental Disorders (DSM-III)*, 3rd ed. Washington, D.C.: American Psychiatric Association, 1980.

6. World Health Organization.: *The International Pilot Study of Schizophrenia*, Volume I. Geneva: World Health Organization, 1973.

7. KENDELL, R.E., COOPER, J.E., GOURLAY, A.J., and COPELAND, J.R.M.: Diagnostic criteria of American and British psychiatrists. *Arch. Gen. Psychiat.*, 25:123-130, 1971.

8. WING, J.K.: A standard form of psychiatric Present State Examination and a method for standardizing the classification of symptoms. In: E.H. Hare and J.K. Wing (Eds.), *Psychiatric Epidemiology: An International Symposium*, London: Oxford University Press, 1970.

9. FEIGHNER, J.P., ROBINS, E., GUZE, S.B., WOODRUFF, R.A., WINOKUR, G., and MUNOZ, R.: Diagnostic criteria for use in psychiatric research. *Arch. Gen. Psychiat.*, 26:57-63, 1972.

10. SPITZER, R.L., ENDICOTT, J., and ROBINS, E.: Research Diagnostic Criteria: Rationale and reliability. *Arch. Gen. Psychiat.*, 35:773-782, 1978.

11. ENDICOTT, J., and SPITZER, R.L.: A diagnostic interview: The Schedule for Affective Disorders and Schizophrenia. *Arch. Gen. Psychiat.*, 35:837-844, 1978.

12. ROBINS, L.N., HELZER, J.E., CROUGHAN, J., and RATCLIFF, K.S.: National Institute of Mental Health Diagnostic Interview Schedule. *Arch. Gen. Psychiat.*, 38:381-389, 1981.

13. ANDREASEN, N.C., McDONALD-SCOTT, P., GROVE, W.M., KELLER, M.B., SHAPIRO, R.W., and HIRSCHFELD, R.M.A.: Assessment of reliability in multi-center collaborative research using a videotape approach. *Am. J. Psychiat.*, 139:876-882, 1982.

14. ANDREASEN, N.C., GROVE, W.M., SHAPIRO, R.W., KELLER, M.B., HIRSCHFELD, R.M.A., and McDONALD-SCOTT, P.: Reliability of lifetime diagnosis: A multi-center collaborative perspective. *Arch. of Gen. Psychiat.*, 38:400-405, 1981.

15. GROVE, W.M., ANDREASEN, N.C., McDONALD-SCOTT, P., KELLER, M.B., and SHAPIRO, R.W.: Reliability studies of psychiatric diagnosis: Theory and practice. *Arch. Gen. Psychiat.*, 38:408-413, 1981.

16. HELZER, J.E., ROBINS, L.N., TAIBLESON, M., WOODRUFF, R.A., REICH, T., and WISH, E.D.: Reliability of psychiatric diagnosis: I. A methodological review. *Arch. Gen. Psychiat.*, 34:129-133, 1977.

17. HELZER, J.E., CLAYTON, P.J., PAMBAKIAN, R., REICH, T., WOODRUFF, R.A., and REVELEY, M.A.: Reliability of psychiatric diagnosis: II. The test-retest reliability of diagnostic classification. *Arch. Gen. Psychiat.*, 34:136-141, 1977.

18. WING, J.K., BEBBINGTON, P., and ROBINS, L.N.: *What is a Case?* London: Grant McIntyre, Ltd., 1981.

19. MELLOR, C.S.: First-rank symptoms of schizophrenia. *Br. J. Psych.*, 117:15-23, 1970.

20. CARPENTER, W.T., STRAUSS, J.S., and MULEH, S.: Are there pathognomonic symptoms of schizophrenia? *Arc. Gen. Psychiat.*, 28:847-852, 1973.

21. TAYLOR, M.A., and ABRAMS, R.: The phenomenology of mania: A new look at some old patients. *Arch. Gen. Psychiat.*, 29:520-522, 1973.
22. ANDREASEN, N.C.: The clinical assessment of thought, language, and communication disorders: I. The definition of terms and evaluation of their reliability. *Arch. Gen. Psychiat.*, 36:1315-1321, 1979.
23. ANDREASEN, N.C.: The clinical assessment of thought, language and communication disorders: II. Diagnostic significance. *Arch. Gen. Psychiat.*, 36:1325-1330, 1979.
24. ANDREASEN, N.C.: Affective flattening and the criteria for schizophrenia. *Am. J. Psychiat.*, 136:944-946, 1979.
25. VAILLANT, G.E.: Prospective prediction of schizophrenic remission. *Arch. Gen. Psychiat.*, 11:509-518, 1964.
26. STEPHENS, J.H., et al.: Prognostic factors in recovered and deteriorated schizophrenics. *Am. J. Psychiat.*, 122:1116-1120, 1966.
27. POPE, H., and LIPINSKY, J.: Diagnosis in schizophrenia and manic-depressive illness. *Arch. Gen. Psychiat.*, 35:811-828, 1978.
28. ASTRUP, C., and NOREIK, K.: *Functional Psychoses: Diagnostic and Prognostic Models.* Springfield, IL: Charles C Thomas, 1966.
29. ANGST, J.: Zur Ätiologie und Nosologie endogener depressiver Psychosen. In: *Monographen aus der Neurologie und Psychiatrie*, No. 112. Berlin: Springer-Verlag, 1966.
30. DUNNER, D.L., GERSHON, E.S., and GOODWIN, F.K.: Heritable factors in the severity of affective illness. *Biol. Psychiat.*, 11:31-42, 1976.
31. GERSHON, E.S., BUNNEY, W.E., LECKMAN, J.F., van ERDEWEGH, M., and DE BAUCHE, B.A.: The inheritance of affective disorders: A review of data and hypotheses. *Behav. Gen.*, 6:227-261, 1976.
32. PERRIS, C.: Genetic transmission of depressive psychoses. *Acta Psychiat.* (Scand. Suppl. 203, 1968.
33. TRZEBIATOWSKA-TRZECIAK, O.: Genetical analysis of unipolar and bipolar endogenous affective psychoses. *Br. J. Psychiat.*, 131:478-485, 1977.
34. WINOKUR, G., CLAYTON, P.J., and REICH, T.: *Manic-Depressive Illness.* St. Louis: C.V. Mosby Company, 1969.
35. ALLEN, M.D.: Twin studies of affective illness. *Arch. Gen. Psychiat.*, 33:1476-1478, 1976.
36. MENDLEWICZ, J., and FLEISS, J.L.: Linkage studies with X-chromosome markers in bipolar (manic-depressive) and unipolar (depressive) illnesses. *Biolog. Psychiat.*, 9:261-294, 1974.
37. GOODWIN, F.K., MUSCETTOLA, G., GOLD, P.W., and WEHR, T.: Biochemical and pharmacological differentiation of affective disorder: An overview. In: H.S. Akiskal and W.L. Webb (Eds)., *Psychiatric Diagnosis: Exploration of Biological Predictors.* New York and London: Spectrum Publications, 1978.
38. GARFINKEL, P.E., WALSH, J.J., and STANCER, H.C.: Depression: New evidence in support of biological differentiation. *Am. J. Psychiat.*, 136:535-539, 1979.
39. SCHILDKRAUT, J.J., ORSULAK, P.J., SCHATZBERG, A.F., GUDEMAN, J.E., COLE, J.O., ROHDE, W.A., and LaBRIE, R.A.: Toward a biochemical classification of depressive disorders: I. Differences in urinary excretion of MHPG and other catecholamine metabolites in clinically defined subtypes of depression. *Arch. Gen. Psychiat.*, 35:1427-1433, 1978.

40. SCHILDKRAUT, J.J., ORSULAK, P.J., LABRIE, R.A., SCHATZBERG, A.F., GUDEMAN, J.E., COLE, J.O., and ROHDE, W.A.: Toward a biochemical classification of depressive disorders: II. Application of multivariate discriminant function analysis to data on urinary catecholamines and metabolites. *Arch. Gen. Psychiat.*, 35:1436-1439, 1978.

41. BUCHSBAUM, M.S.: The average evoked response technique in the differentiation of bipolar, unipolar, and schizophrenic disorders. In: H.S. Akiskal and W.L. Webb (Eds.), *Psychiatric Diagnosis: Exploration of Biological Predictors*. New York and London: Spectrum Publications, 1978.

42. MURPHY, D.L., and WEISS, R.: Reduced monamine oxidase activity in blood platelets from bipolar depressed patients. *Am. J. Psychiat.*, 128:1351-1357, 1972.

43. CARROLL, B., CURTIS, C.G., and MENDELS, J.: Neuroendocrine regulation in depression. *Arch. Gen. Psychiat.*, 33:1039-1044, 1976.

44. BROWN, W.A., JOHNSTONE, R., and MAYFIELD, D.: The 24-hour dexamethasone suppression test in a clinical setting: Relationship to diagnosis, symptoms, and response to treatment. *Am. J. Psychiat.*, 136:543-547, 1979.

45. MENDELS, J., and FRAZER, A.: Reduced central serotonergic activity in mania: Implications for the relationship between depression and mania. *Br. J. Psychiat.*, 126:241-248, 1975.

46. GOODWIN, F.K., MURPHY, D.L., and BUNNEY, W.E.: Lithium response in unipolar vs. bipolar depression. *Am. J. Psychiat.*, 129:44-47, 1972.

47. FIEVE, R.R., KUMBARACI, T., and DUNNER, D.L.: Lithium prophylaxis of depression in bipolar I, bipolar II, and unipolar patients. *Am. J. Psychiat.*, 133:925-929, 1976.

48. MENDELS, J.: Lithium in the treatment of depression. *Am. J. Psychiat.*, 133:373-378, 1976.

49. QUITKIN, F., RIFKIN, A., and KLEIN, D.F.: Prophylaxis of affective disorders: Current status of knowledge. *Arch. Gen. Psychiat.*, 33:337-341, 1976.

50. DUNNER, D.L., STALLONE, F., and FIEVE, R.R.: Lithium carbonate and affective disorders. *Arch. Gen. Psychiat.*, 33:117-120, 1976.

51. ANGST, J., BASTRUP, P., GROF, H., HIPPIUS, H., POLDINGER, W., and WEIS, P.: The course of monopolar depression and bipolar psychoses. *Psychiatrica Neurologica et Neurochirurgia* 76:489-500, 1973.

52. BRODIE, H.K.H., and LEFF, M.J.: A comparative study of patient characteristics. *Am. J. Psychiat.*, 127:1086-1090, 1971.

53. WEINBERGER, D.R., TORREY, E.F., NEOPHYTIDES, A.N., and WYATT, R.J.: Lateral cerebral ventricular enlargement in chronic schizophrenia. *Arch. Gen. Psychiat.*, 36:735-739, 1979.

54. WEINBERGER, D.R., TORREY, E.F., NEOPHYTIDES, A.N., and WYATT, R.J.: Structural abnormalities in the cerebral cortex of chronic schizophrenic patients. *Arch. Gen. Psychiat.*, 336:935-939, 1979.

55. LUCHINS, D.J., WEINBERGER, D.R., TORREY, E.F., JOHNSON, A., ROGENTINE, N., and WYATT, R.J.: HLA-A2 antigen in schiozphrenic patients with reversed cerebral asymmetry. *Br. J. Psychiat.*, 138:240-243, 1981.

56. LUCHINS, D.J., WEINBERGER, D.R., and WYATT, R.J.: Schizophrenia: Evidence of a subgroup with reversed cerebral asymmetry. *Arch. Gen. Psychiat.*, 36:1309-1311, 1979.

57. JOHNSTONE, E.C., CROW, T.J., FRITH, C.D., HUSBAND, J., and KREEL, L.: Cerebral ventricular size and cognitive impairment in chronic schizophrenia. *Lancet*, 2:924-926, 1976.

58. CROW, T.J.: Molecular pathology of schizophrenia: More than one disease process? *Brit. Med. J.*, 280:1-9, 1980.

59. ANDREASEN, N.C., OLSEN, S.A., DENNERT, J.W., and SMITH, M.R.: Ventricular enlargement in schizophrenia: Relationship to positive and negative symptoms. *Am. J. Psychiat.*, 139:297-302, 1982.

60. ANDREASEN, N.C., SMITH, M.R., JACOBY, C.G., DENNERT, J.W., and OLSEN, S.A.: Ventricular enlargement in schizophrenia: Definition and prevalence. *Am. J. Psychiat.*, 139:292-296, 1982.

61. ANDREASEN, N.C., DENNERT, J.W., OLSEN, S.A., and DAMASIO, A.R.: Hemispheric asymmetries and schizophrenia. *Am. J. Psychiat.*, 139:427-430, 1982.

62. NAESER, M.A., LEVINE, H.L., BENSON, D.F., STRUSS, D.T., and WEIR, W.S.: Frontal leukotomy size and hemispheric asymmetries on computerized tomographic scans of schizophrenics with variable recovery. *Arch. Neurol.*, 38:30-37, 1981.

63. JERNIGAN, T.L., ZATZ, L.M., MOSES, J.A., and BERGER, P.A.: Computerized measurements of cerebral atrophy in schizophrenics and normal volunteers. *Arch. Gen. Psychiat.*, in press.

64. KETY, S.S., ROSENTHAL, D., WENDER, P.H., and SCHULSINGER, F. The types and prevalence of mental illness in the biological and adoptive families of adopted schizophrenics. In: D. Rosenthal and S.S. Kety (Eds.), *The Transmission of Schizophrenia*. Oxford: Pergamon Press, 1968, pp. 345-362.

65. CORYELL, W., GAFFNEY, G., and BURKHARDT, P.E.: DSM-III melancholia and the primary-secondary distinction: A comparison of diagnostic validity using the dexamethasone suppression test. *Am. J. Psychiat.*, in press.

66. HIRSCHFELD, R.M.A.: Clinical and familial aspects of endogenous depression. Presented at the annual meeting of the American Psychiatric Association, New Orleans, 1981.

67. GOLDEN, C.J. MOSES, J.A., ZELAZOWSKI, M.A., GRABER, B., ZATZ, L.M., HORVATH, T.V., and BERGER, T.A. Cerebral ventricular size and neuropsychological impairment in young chronic schizophrenics. *Arch. Gen. Psychiat.*, 37:619-623, 1980.

68. NASRALLAH, H.A., JACOBY, C.G., McCALLEY-WHITTERS, M., and KUPERMAN, S. Cerebral ventricular enlargement in subtypes of chronic schizophrenia. *Arch. Gen. Psychiat.*, 39:774-777, 1982.

3

Biological Markers in Affective and Schizophrenic Disorders: A Review of Contemporary Research

Robert T. Rubin, M.D., Ph. D.
and Stephen R. Marder, M.D.

AFFECTIVE DISORDERS

Affective disorders, particularly depression, have been the focus of psychiatric investigations because depression is a prominent illness. Its lifetime incidence in the United States is around 10% for men and 20% for women (1), and it is an illness with a significant, and often preventable, mortality. Frequently, affective disorders are episodically recurring, so that patients may be at risk for much of their lives. Some affective disorders respond well to somatic therapies, including antidepressants of several classes, antimanic agents such as lithium, and electroconvulsive treatment. For these reasons the search for biologic markers in depressive illness, as clinical aids to diagnosis and prediction of treatment response, has special importance.

Depressive illness is a heterogeneous group of disorders with dissimilar clinical symptomatology and response to treatment, as well as, undoubtedly, variable etiology. Although many individuals suffer self-limited depressions, often precipitated by some identifiable major life stress, these must be distinguished from

Supported by NIMH Grants MH 28380 and MH 30911, by NIMH Research Scientist Development Award MH 47363 (to R.T.R.), and by N.I.H. Clinical Research Center Grant RR 00425.

a type of depression, called endogenous (2,3), endogenomorphic (4), or melancholic (5). The latter is characterized by a specific cluster of symptoms, a prolonged course, often a family history of similar illness, and generally a responsiveness only to somatic therapies. While this type of depression also may follow an identifiable precipitating stress, the particular symptom cluster and requirement for somatic therapy are the primary factors that characterize such a depression as endogenous. The signs and symptoms of endogenous depression have been codified in the Research Diagnostic Criteria (3) and in the DSM-III of the American Psychiatric Association (5). They include anhedonia (inability to experience pleasure), lack of energy, fatigability, reduced sexual drive, anorexia, weight loss, sleep disturbance (especially early morning awakening), depression worse in the morning, self-reproach, excessive guilt, psychomotor agitation or retardation, and lack of reactivity to the environment. Delusions (often of a depressive or somatic nature) or hallucinations also may be present, giving an additional, psychotic dimension to the illness.

These newer diagnostic schemes permit the detailed description of affectively disordered patients along several overlapping dimensions: bipolar versus unipolar, primary versus secondary, endogenous versus non-endogenous, psychotic versus non-psychotic, agitated versus retarded, etc. Thus, it now becomes possible to describe in specific detail the group of patients for whom certain biologic markers are being investigated. For example, the bipolar versus unipolar distinction has been made in many studies of the neurochemistry of affective disorders; and the endogenous versus non-endogenous distinction has been made in many studies of the neuroendocrinology of these disorders. In Chapter 2, Andreasen traces the historical development of current diagnostic schemes.

Neurochemical Markers

The biological variables that have been studied in affective disorders include neurochemical, neurophysiological, neuroendocrine, and genetic markers. Neurochemical measures include the concentrations of catecholamines and indoleamines, and their metabolites in urine, cerebrospinal fluid (CSF), and serum or plasma (6-8). Catecholamines, including norepinephrine and dopamine, and the indoleamine, serotonin, are in high concentration in the limbic system, hypothalamus, and brain stem—the phylogenetically older areas of the brain that have been implicated as likely neuroanatomical sites for whatever neurochemical disturbances may underlie the affective disorders.

The catecholamine and indoleamine hypotheses of affective illness have been present in the psychiatric literature for over a decade. In their simplest forms, they postulate a functional underactivity of norepinephrine or serotonin, or both, in the central nervous system in depression, and a functional overactivity of these neurotransmitters in mania or hypomania. While most investigators acknowledge that the actual interplay of neurotransmitters, including their synthesis, metabolic degradation, and influence on receptor regulation, is exceedingly complex (9), these monoamine theories have provided a beginning rationale for neurochemical investigations in depression and mania. Although many of the resultant data are inconsistent, some investigators believe there is clinical utility in certain measures of monoamines and their metabolites, such as urinary methoxy-hydroxy-phenylglycol (MHPG) and other metabolites of norepinephrine (6). In Chapter 4 Schildkraut et al. elaborate on the development of a discriminant function equation, based on urinary norepinephrine and epinephrine metabolites, that may distinguish unipolar depressive patients from bipolar depressives and patients with schizoaffective depressions.

Neurophysiological Markers

The neurophysiological measures studied in affective disorders include sleep recordings, with quantification of time spent in the various sleep stages and the timing of the shifts among them. The sleep-wake cycle and shifts between the stages of sleep are regularly occurring phenomena. The sleep-wake cycle in humans normally has a circadian rhythm, occurring once every 24 hours. Electrophysiologic (electroencephalographic, electromyographic, and electrooculographic) recordings of normal nocturnal sleep have shown that sleep is not a unitary state but consists of two distinct phases—rapid eye movement (REM) and non-REM sleep. Non-REM sleep can be subdivided further into four numbered stages (10,11).

Sleep staging within the hours of sleep demonstrates an ultradian rhythm of 80 to 110 minutes. Figure 1 illustrates the "architecture" of sleep—the regular alternation between REM episodes and non-REM sleep, including slow-wave or delta sleep (SWS) (12). Normally, individuals pass through stages 1 to 4 in the first one or two hours of sleep. A short REM episode then appears, and throughout the rest of the night REM and non-REM sleep alternate rhythmically. As sleep progresses, SWS occurs less and less, while REM sleep becomes more prominent. Under normal conditions, the amount of time spent in each of the stages of sleep is relatively constant from night to night and from subject to subject. Also, the relative amount of time of each of these stages is fairly constant throughout the decades of adult life, except for SWS sleep, which declines, being occasionally absent in the elderly, as indicated in Figure 1.

One of the prominent symptoms of depression is sleep disturbance. Studies have shown that endogenous depression almost always is accompanied by alterations in sleep staging, including increased sleep discontinuity (disruption of sleep architecture), reduced SWS, shortened REM latency (the interval from the

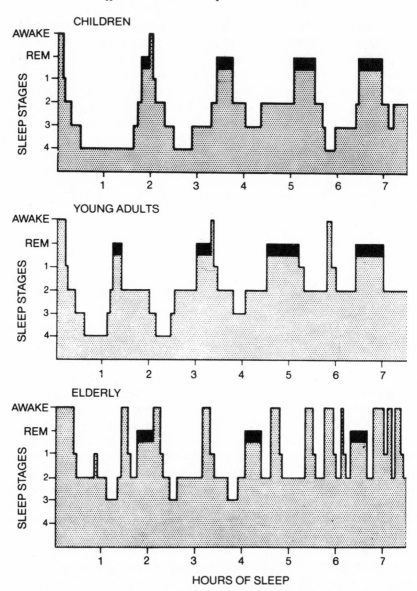

FIGURE 1. Sleep cycles of normal subjects. Young adults have early appearance of stages 3 and 4 (slow-wave) sleep, progressive lengthening of the first few rapid eye movement (REM) episodes, and infrequent awakenings. Elderly persons have reduced slow-wave sleep, more uniform REM episodes, and frequent awakenings. Figure reproduced, with permission, from Kales (12).

onset of sleep until the onset of the first REM period), and increased REM density (the ratio of the sum of eye movements to the length of time in REM sleep), compared to control subjects (13,14). The most prominent finding in depression is the decrease in REM latency. In normal subjects, the first REM period occurs 70 to 90 minutes after sleep onset, while in depressed patients the first REM period occurs in about half that time. A positive correlation has been found between the severity of depression and the shortening of REM sleep latency (15). These changes in sleep stage patterns occurring in endogenously depressed patients are not transient; they can persist for weeks in untreated patients and for months in patients who do not respond to treatment (13,16,17).

Based on sleep electrophysiology, endogenously depressed patients can be differentiated easily from normal control subjects. Of greater clinical relevance is whether endogenously depressed patients can be discriminated from other psychiatric patients, such as those with secondary depressions, schizophrenia, alcoholism, or drug addiction, and from patients with other medical disorders without psychiatric symptoms. While thorough sleep electrophysiology studies for these various groups of patients have not yet been performed, recent studies indicate that endogenously depressed patients do have unique sleep abnormalities that distinguish them from some of the other patient populations.

In a series of studies, Kupfer et al. (13,14) found that primary depressives differed significantly from secondary depressives on a number of sleep measures. With discriminant function analysis, these investigators were able to distinguish a group of approximately 50 primary depressives from a similar number of secondary depressives with an 81% accuracy. The primary depressives had significantly reduced REM latency and significantly increased REM density; these two variables made the greatest contribution to the analysis (Figure 2). Further discriminant function analysis indicated that psychotic and non-psychotic subgroups of the primary depressives could be distinguished with 75% accuracy, using the variables of sleep efficiency (the ratio of time of sleep to total recording time), REM sleep percentage, and SWS (delta) sleep percentage (Figure 2). The psychotically depressed patients had significantly lower values on all three of these measures. Also, a similar analysis, using the variables of REM activity and intermittent nocturnal awakenings, discriminated two subgroups of the secondary depressives, those with and without major medical illness, with an 81% accuracy (Figure 2). The secondary depressives with medical disease had significantly decreased REM activity and significantly increased wakefulness throughout the night. These findings have been confirmed by other investigators (18,19).

Sleep studies in depression also may be useful for the prediction of clinical response to various treatment regimens. In several studies, Kupfer et al.

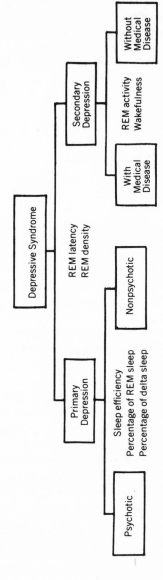

FIGURE 2. EEG sleep measures discriminating between groups of depressed patients. Primary depressives have reduced REM latency and increased REM density compared to secondary depressives. Psychotic primary depressives have reduced sleep efficiency (ratio of time of sleep to total recording time), reduced REM sleep percent, and reduced slow-wave sleep, compared to non-psychotic primary depressives. Secondary depressives with medical disease have reduced REM activity and increased wakefulness compared to secondary depressives without medical disease. Figure reproduced, with permission, from Kupfer et al. (14).

(14,20,21) showed that endogenously depressed patients who ultimately re-sponded well to tricyclic antidepressant (amitriptyline) treatment generally could not be distinguished from those patients who were treatment non-responders by their pre-drug baseline sleep measures. However, the responders could be dis-criminated from the non-responders with an 80% accuracy after the first two nights of drug treatment. The treatment responders showed a significantly re-duced sleep latency (the time from lights out to sleep onset), a significant pro-longation in REM latency, and a significant reduction in REM activity within 48 hours after the beginning of antidepressant therapy. These sleep variables were more powerful predictors of treatment response than were dimensions of the depressive symptomatology. Since it normally takes one to two weeks for antidepressant medication to effect a reduction in core clinical symptoms, a test to predict eventual responders to treatment clearly will have considerable practical importance.

Neuroendocrine Markers

The presence of normally occurring hormone rhythms, some of which are closely linked to the sleep-wake cycle or to specific sleep stages; their alteration by experimental neurochemical and neuroanatomic manipulations of the central nervous system (CNS), such as hypothalamic deafferentation of experimental animals; and the responsiveness of many of these hormones to psychological stress all provide supporting evidence for the importance of the CNS in endocrine function. They highlight the role of open-loop mechanisms (CNS driving) in the control of pituitary hormone release, in addition to the more classical closed-loop mechanisms (negative and positive feedback between target organ hormones and the hypothalamo-pituitary unit and between the pituitary itself and the hy-pothalamus). The hypothalamus is in many respects a final common pathway for limbic system neural circuits. It contains the neurosecretory cells that produce the pituitary hormone-releasing and -inhibiting factors, secreted into the portal circulation to the anterior pituitary, as well as the posterior pituitary hormones that are released directly from these cells. Figure 3 portrays these neuroanatomical relationships, along with the major anterior and posterior pituitary hormones and their effects on peripheral target endocrine glands.

Severe endogenous depression frequently has concomitant neuroendocrine disturbances (22-29). These include abnormalities in the secretion patterns of the anterior pituitary polypeptide hormones and their peripheral target endocrine gland steroid hormones. The most clearly delineated to date are the hypersecretion of ACTH and cortisol and their resistance to suppression by the synthetic glu-cocorticoid, dexamethasone; the reduced responsiveness of pituitary thyrotropin (TSH) secretion to thyrotropin-releasing hormone (TRH) stimulation; and the

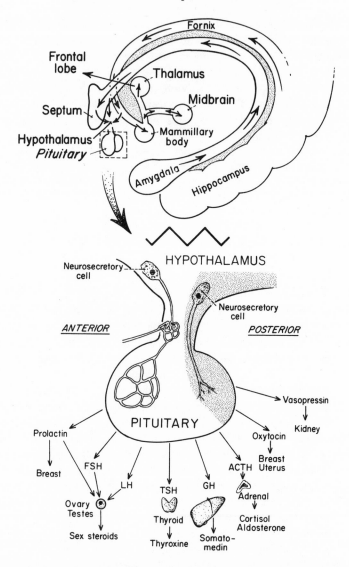

FIGURE 3. Limbic brain circuits and their relationship to the hypothalamo-pituitary unit (top); the anterior and posterior pituitary, their functional relationships to the median eminence of the hypothalamus, their pituitary hormones, and their target organ effects (bottom). Figure reproduced, with permission, from Rubin and Kendler (23).

reduced responsiveness of growth hormone (GH) secretion to several challenges, including amphetamine, desmethylimipramine, clonidine, and insulin-induced hypoglycemia (Table 1). Changes in other endocrine axes, such as the hypothalamo-pituitary-gonadal axis, also have been identified (Table 1), but the data as yet are sparse. The regularity of some of the endocrine changes and their specificity to endogenous depression have led to the proposal of endocrine testing as a laboratory adjunct to the differential diagnosis of this illness (30) and the prediction of treatment response.

ACTH/cortisol. Circulating ACTH and cortisol normally have a prominent circadian variation, with lowest levels occurring in the first few hours of sleep, and peak levels occurring in the morning around the time of awakening (31). Because of the impetus given to psychoendocrine research by Selye's formulation of the general adaptation syndrome (32), and because colorimetric blood and urine corticosteroid measurement techniques were available 25 years ago, early endocrine studies of depression focused on this endocrine axis (33,34).

Many studies showed that adrenocortical activity was increased in depression compared to mania or normalcy. Some investigators believed that the subjectively experienced anxiety and dysphoria of the depressed patient resulted in an adrenocortical stress response according to the Selye model (35), while others postulated that both the depressed affect and the increased corticosteroid secretion could be secondary to an underlying disturbance of brain function (33,36). Studies of the circadian patterns of corticosteroid secretion and its response to pharmacologic suppression by dexamethasone support the latter hypothesis, that a CNS mechanism more fundamental than subjectively felt anxiety appears to underlie the increased corticosteroid production in endogenous depression. A noradrenergic inhibitory mechanism for ACTH secretion has been identified

TABLE 1

Identified Anterior Pituitary and Target Gland Hormone Abnormalities in Endogenous Depression

1. ACTH/cortisol: increased nocturnal and diurnal secretion; early escape from dexamethasone suppression.
2. TRH/TSH: blunted TSH response to exogenous TRH; possibly increased endogenous TRH in CSF.
3. GH: reduced slow-wave sleep-related secretion; reduced response to insulin hypoglycemia, amphetamine, clonidine, and desmethylimipramine; possibly abnormal response to TRH.
4. LH/gonadal steroids: reduced nocturnal and diurnal secretion.
5. PRL: reduced sleep-related secretion; possibly decreased response to TRH.

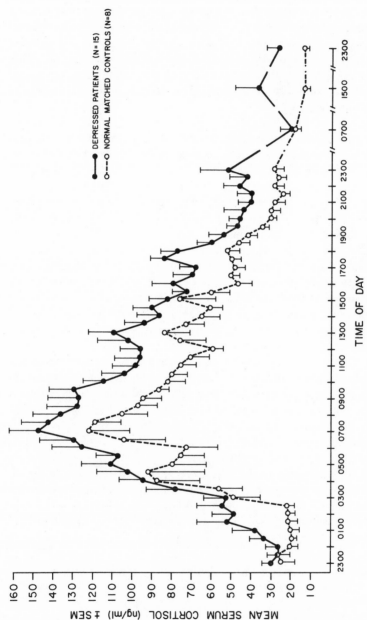

FIGURE 4. Mean serum cortisol concentrations (ng/ml) ± 1 SEM, for 15 primary endogenously depressed patients and 8 normal age, sex, race, and menstrual status-matched control subjects. At 2300 on the second night, dexamethasone (1 mg p.o.) was given. The patients showed cortisol escape following dexamethasone, whereas the normal controls showed cortisol suppression. Figure reproduced, with permission, from Rubin et al. (40).

(37), and an imbalance in monoamine as well as other neurotransmitters in the limbic system and hypothalamus may underlie this and other endocrine disturbances in depression.

Increased adrenocortical activity occurs in apathetic as well as in anxious depressives, and it occurs throughout the entire 24 hours, especially during the sleep period (38-40). Figure 4 portrays mean half-hourly serum cortisol determinations over a 24-hour period in 15 primary, endogenously depressed patients (six men and nine women) and eight normal age-, sex-, race-, and menstrual-status-matched control subjects studied by our research group (40). The patients had higher serum cortisol levels during both the night and the day.

A specific indicator of the hyperactivity of the ACTH/cortisol axis in endogenous depression is the early escape of these hormones from dexamethasone (DEX) suppression. DEX (1.0 or 2.0 mg p.o.) given at midnight normally suppresses ACTH and cortisol for a full 24 hours. However, endogenously depressed patients often show an early increase in serum cortisol, between 16 and 24 hours post-DEX. Both the normal controls and the depressed patients shown in Figure 4 were given DEX (1.0 mg p.o.) at 2300 on the second night, and serum cortisol was measured every eight hours for the next 24 hours. The control subjects suppressed normally, whereas the depressed patients showed a typical pattern of cortisol escape at 16 and 24 hours post-DEX.

The DEX suppression test has an approximately 90-95% specificity for endogenous depression (few false positives in non-endogenously depressed patients and other types of psychiatric disorders), but its sensitivity is only about 50% (about 50% false negatives in definitely endogenous depressives) (30). While most investigators have confirmed these percentages (41), some have found both a lower specificity and a lower sensitivity (42,43) and have suggested that cortisol escape may correlate better with the severity of depressive symptomatology than with the diagnosis of endogenous subtype per se. Nevertheless, it is generally agreed that the DEX suppression test has a high construct validity: It is more frequently positive in definitely endogenous compared to probably endogenous depressives and in suicidal compared to non-suicidal depressives; it normalizes with a switch from depression to mania; and it normalizes gradually with treatment (30,39).

Figure 5 depicts typical DEX suppression responses during illness and recovery in a 49-year-old agitated, unipolar depressed woman with a strong family history of depression (39). The first test (April 2) was carried out three days after hospital admission, and the second (April 9) was carried out a week later, when the patient was receiving placebo medication. High midnight pre-DEX plasma cortisols and obvious cortisol escape from DEX suppression characterized the first two tests. The patient then was treated with antidepressant medication, and over

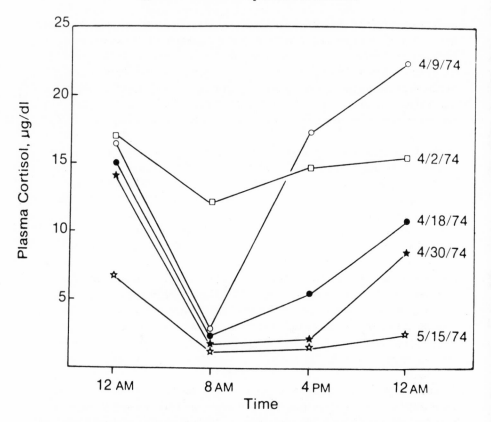

FIGURE 5. Midnight pre-dexamethasone and 8, 16, and 24 hour post-dexamethasone (2 mg p.o.) plasma cortisol concentrations (ug/dl) in a depressed woman before (April 2 and 9) and during pharmacotherapy. The initially abnormal dexamethasone suppression test gradually reverted to normal with clinical improvement. Figure reproduced, with permission, from Carroll et al. (39). Copyright 1976 by the American Medical Association.

the next five weeks her DEX suppression tests gradually normalized as her illness remitted. At the time of her last DEX test, which showed a complete 24-hour cortisol suppression, her pre-DEX midnight cortisol level had decreased to the normal range.

The cortisol escape from DEX suppression in endogenously depressed patients does not appear to be a result of altered pharmacokinetics of DEX metabolism (40,44) and most likely reflects enhanced limbic-hypothalamic driving of the pituitary-adrenocortical axis. Nocturnal hypersecretion of cortisol and cortisol escape from DEX suppression generally occur together in endogenously depressed patients (Figure 4), raising the question of whether a single nocturnal blood sample for cortisol might serve the same purpose as a DEX suppression test. While the sensitivities of both measures generally are the same, the specificity of an elevated pre-DEX plasma cortisol has been found to be much less than that of the DEX test, i.e., an elevated nocturnal cortisol occurred in 45% of non-endogenously depressed patients (30,45). Thus, from a diagnostic standpoint, the DEX suppression test appears to be the better of the two measures of cortisol hypersecretion.

A positive DEX suppression test also may be associated with certain familial types of depression. Winokur et al. (46) subdivided primary unipolar depressive illness into three groups based on family history data: pure depressive disease (history of depression but not of mania, alcoholism, or sociopathy in a first-degree relative): sporadic depressive disease (no psychiatric illness history in any first-degree relative); and depression spectrum disease (history of alcoholism, sociopathy, or both in a first-degree relative). Schlesser et al. (47) performed DEX suppression tests on 221 depressed patients, subdivided as shown in Figure 6, and on 109 control patients. Figure 6 indicates the specificity of the DEX test for primary depression—only those patients showed abnormal tests. Similar findings have been reported by several other groups of investigators (41). Bipolar depressed patients as a group had a higher incidence of abnormal tests than did unipolar depressed patients. When the primary unipolar depressives were subdivided according to the familial classification described above (46), there were clear differences among the percentages of patients in each category showing cortisol non-suppression.

These data are provocative in that they suggest a possible genetic influence on at least one neuroendocrine aspect of depression—the DEX suppression test. The data are even more intriguing, since Schlesser et al. (47) measured cortisol in only a single 0800 blood sample, taken nine hours after DEX administration at 2300. As indicated in Figures 4 and 5, the 16- and 24-hour post-DEX blood samples often yield a much better sensitivity for cortisol escape (30). Using the full 3×8 hour post-DEX sampling schedule, other investigators have found a considerably higher incidence of abnormal DEX tests in patients with depression spectrum disease (48-50). Further attempts to resolve this question need to be undertaken.

Some investigators are attempting to use the DEX test as an aid to the choice of treatment for endogenously depressed patients and in the prediction of treatment response. In a small group of patients, those with positive DEX tests tended to have a better treatment response to imipramine or desipramine than to amitriptyline or clomipramine, while the converse was true for the cortisol suppressors (51,52). These data support the hypothesis that patients with a positive DEX test had a norepinephrine-deficiency type of depression. As mentioned above, norepinephrine normally inhibits the hypothalamo-pituitary-adrenocor-

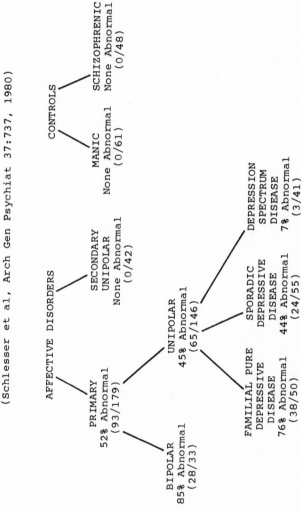

ABNORMAL DEXAMETHASONE SUPPRESSION TEST RESULTS IN SUBTYPES OF DEPRESSION

(Schlesser et al, Arch Gen Psychiat 37:737, 1980)

AFFECTIVE DISORDERS

PRIMARY
52% Abnormal
(93/179)

SECONDARY
UNIPOLAR
None Abnormal
(0/42)

CONTROLS

MANIC
None Abnormal
(0/61)

SCHIZOPHRENIC
None Abnormal
(0/48)

BIPOLAR
85% Abnormal
(28/33)

UNIPOLAR
45% Abnormal
(65/146)

FAMILIAL PURE
DEPRESSIVE
DISEASE
76% Abnormal
(38/50)

SPORADIC
DEPRESSIVE
DISEASE
44% Abnormal
(24/55)

DEPRESSION
SPECTRUM
DISEASE
7% Abnormal
(3/41)

Dexamethasone (1.0 mg p.o.) given at 2300 hrs.; serum cortisol determined at 0800 hrs. (competitive protein binding); criterion for abnormal test = cortisol >50 ng/ml.

FIGURE 6. Differential incidences of abnormal dexamethasone suppression tests in subtypes of depression. Dexamethasone (1 mg p.o.) was given at 2300, and serum cortisol was determined nine hours later, at 0800. The criterion for an abnormal test was cortisol >50 ng/ml. Figure adapted from Schlesser et al. (47).

tical axis, so that such patients should have responded best to drugs like imipramine or desipramine, which are strong norepinephrine reuptake inhibitors, whereas patients who showed normal cortisol suppression had a serotonin-deficiency type of depression and thus would have responded best to predominantly serotonin reuptake inhibitors, like amitriptyline or clomipramine. In another small study, it was found that an abnormal DEX test predicted a poor clinical response to the antidepressant mianserin, primarily a serotonin reuptake inhibitor, whereas normal cortisol suppression following DEX predicted a good clinical response to this drug (53). Thus, neuroendocrine testing in depression may be useful for predicting treatment response, just as the sleep measures discussed earlier may be useful. This is an obviously fruitful area for future large-scale studies.

As mentioned, the DEX suppression test generally normalizes with successful treatment of the depressive episode, whether the treatment is by medication (39) or electroconvulsive therapy (54,55). In two small studies it was found that patients who do not normalize their DEX tests after treatment are at higher risk for early relapse than those patients who show a normal cortisol suppression after treatment (56,57). Here, too, further studies should be undertaken to verify the utility of the DEX test as a treatment prognosticator.

Finally, two methodologic aspects of the DEX test should be mentioned. First, Carroll et al. (30) found that 215 endogenously depressed (melancholic) patients segregated into two groups based on their 16-hour post-DEX plasma cortisol values: a group of suppressors, whose values distributed identically to those of non-endogenously depressed patients; and a second group of non-suppressors, with higher values. The cortisol value dividing these two groups was 50 ng/ml (Figure 7), which was the criterion value that gave the best combination of sensitivity and specificity (30). However, cortisol was measured in these patients by competitive protein-binding assay, whereas most laboratories now use more specific radioimmunoassay techniques. Thus, the criterion value for cortisol non-suppression may need to be revised downward, depending upon the specific laboratory technique used to measure this hormone. In our laboratory, cortisol values by radioimmunoassay average approximately 40% lower than values determined on the same samples by competitive protein-binding assay, so that we now use a criterion for non-suppression of 35 ng/ml.

Second, we have found that the profiles of saliva cortisol in endogenously depressed patients closely reflect their serum cortisol values (Figure 8) and thus appear to be an equally useful discriminator of suppressors versus non-suppressors (58). The use of saliva cortisol in the DEX suppression test has obvious advantages in that it is a non-invasive technique. With saliva collections, the DEX test can be done on patients entirely at home, and samples can be taken

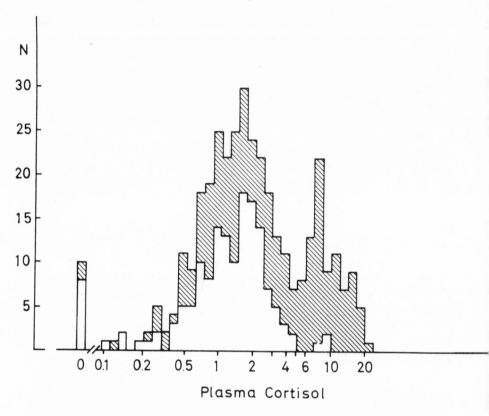

FIGURE 7. Distribution of 1600 post-dexamethasone plasma cortisol concentrations (ug/dl, log-transformed) in 215 patients with endogenous (melancholic) depression (shaded area) and 153 patients with other diagnoses (white area). These data represent combined results for both outpatients and inpatients and for both 1 and 2 mg doses of dexamethasone. Figure reproduced, with permission, from Carroll et al. (30). Copyright 1981 by the American Medical Association.

at those times of the day and night when it is difficult to obtain a blood sample. Also, the test becomes much easier to perform on special groups of patients, such as young children. Here again, more subjects need to be studied to validate the utility of saliva cortisol measures in the DEX suppression test.

TRH/TSH. A second neuroendocrine abnormality that has been confirmed in many studies of endogenously depressed patients is a blunted thyrotropin (thyroid-stimulating hormone—TSH) response to thyrotropin-releasing hormone (TRH) stimulation (59-62). TRH is the hypothalamic hormone that promotes

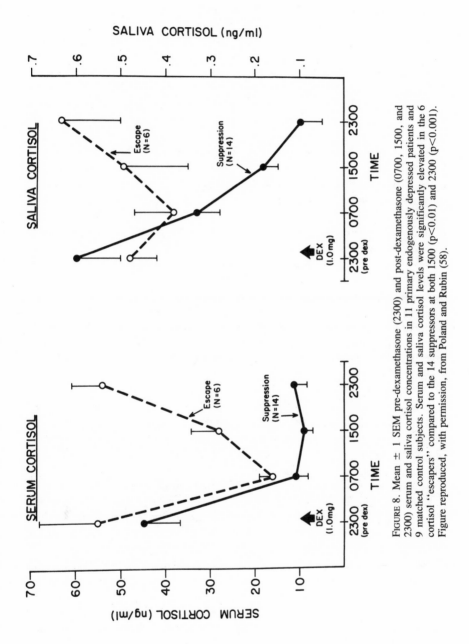

FIGURE 8. Mean ± 1 SEM pre-dexamethasone (2300) and post-dexamethasone (0700, 1500, and 2300) serum and saliva cortisol concentrations in 11 primary endogenously depressed patients and 9 matched control subjects. Serum and saliva cortisol levels were significantly elevated in the 6 cortisol "escapers" compared to the 14 suppressors at both 1500 (p<0.01) and 2300 (p<0.001). Figure reproduced, with permission, from Poland and Rubin (58).

TSH secretion from the anterior pituitary, and it now is available synthetically for administration as an endocrine test. This test has not been as well validated in affective disorders as the DEX suppression test, because different doses of TRH and different blood sampling schedules for TSH have been used (59,62). Also, the TRH stimulation test is not as specific as the DEX suppression test, since a certain percentage of non-endogenously depressed patients as well as normal subjects have blunted TSH responses (Figure 9). On the average, only about 20% of endogenously depressed patients have shown TSH responses below the normal range.

Because of its rather low sensitivity and specificity, the TRH test appears to be of little value in the differential diagnosis of endogenous depression. However, when administered in a test-retest fashion, it may have some utility as a predictor of which successfully treated patients are likely to remain in remission following treatment, versus those patients likely to have an early relapse. In a series of studies, Kirkegaard et al. (62) have shown a good correlation between the normalization (increase) in the TSH response, following the institution of antidepressant therapy and the maintenance of remission following its discontinuance. That is, in a group of patients who showed a clinical "cure" on antidepressant treatment, about 40% showed normalization of their TSH responses after about a month of treatment. Most of these patients remained symptom-free for up to six months after cessation of therapy. The other group of patients, who continued to have blunted TSH responses, generally relapsed within a few months after medication was stopped. As mentioned earlier, similar findings have been reported for the DEX suppression test when used on a test-retest basis.

The reduced TSH response to TRH in depression is not easily explained, as it occurs at the pituitary level, and there is no clear disturbance of overall thyroid function in this illness (63-65). One possibility is that CSF TRH may be elevated in depression (62,66), leading to down-regulation of the TRH receptors on the pituitary thyrotrophs. However, the failure of CSF TRH levels to decline in treated patients, in the face of clinical improvement and normalization of the TSH response to administered TRH (66), argues against this explanation.

Attempts now are being made to develop combinations of neuroendocrine and neurophysiologic tests to improve the overall sensitivity of these diagnostic aids in endogenous depression. For example, a combination of the DEX suppression and TRH stimulation tests has yielded an abnormality on one or the other test in about four-fifths of endogenously depressed patients (Figure 10 and Table 2) (67,68). However, as mentioned above, the TRH stimulation test has a low sensitivity and specificity compared to the DEX suppression test, and it remains to be determined just what the overall diagnostic confidence will be for the combination of these two tests, as well as for the addition of other tests, such as sleep recordings.

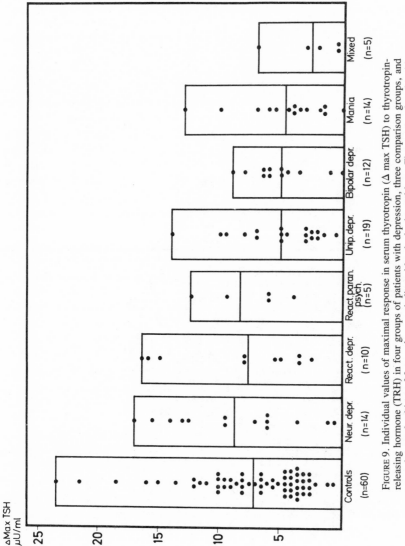

FIGURE 9. Individual values of maximal response in serum thyrotropin (Δ max TSH) to thyrotropin-releasing hormone (TRH) in four groups of patients with depression, three comparison groups, and normal control subjects. Mean values are indicated by the horizontal bars. Figure reproduced, with permission, from Kirkegaard et al. (60). Copyright 1978 by the American Medical Association.

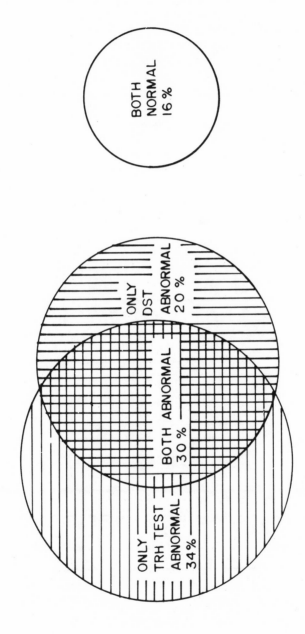

FIGURE 10. Relationship between TRH stimulation test and dexamethasone suppression test (DST) abnormalities in 50 patients with unipolar depression. Figure reproduced, with permission, from Extein et al. (67).

TABLE 2

Relationship of Abnormal Dexamethasone Suppression and TRH Stimulation
Tests in 19 Primary Endogenously Depressed Patients.

Abnormal DEX test = 10/19 = 53%
Abnormal TRH test = 8/19 = 42%
Abnormal DEX *and* TRH tests = 2/19 = 11%
Abnormal DEX *or* TRH tests = 16/19 = 84%

GH. In endogenous depression, the growth hormone (GH) response to several challenges also has been shown to be blunted. The stimuli used have included insulin-induced hypoglycemia, amphetamine, the alpha-adrenergic agonist clonidine, and the acute administration of the antidepressant desmethylimipramine (DMI) (23-26, 69-71). Insulin-induced hypoglycemia was the earliest stimulus to be studied, and therefore has been used in the largest number of patients. However, this has not proved to be a reproducible stimulus, since the decrease in blood sugar has been variable. The other stimuli mentioned appear to be more reproducible. Furthermore, estrogen potentiates the GH response to these various stimuli, so that the response normally is reduced in postmenopausal women, whether or not they are depressed (71). Therefore, the GH response may be a useful additional neuroendocrine test only in certain subgroups of endogenous depressive patients. Here, too, the sensitivity and specificity with a standard stimulus to GH secretion need to be worked out in larger groups of subjects, before the ultimate clinical utility of this test can be determined.

Genetic Markers

Many studies suggest that the phenotypic expression of affective disorders is familial (72,73); a review of these data is beyond the scope of this chapter. A number of biological measures have been investigated in family studies of affective disorders; an example discussed earlier is the relationship of the DEX suppression test to familial subtypes of unipolar depression (47). Other studies have included the enzymes catecholamine-O-methyltransferase, monoamine oxidase, and dopamine-beta-hydroxylase. Altered levels of these enzymes have been noted in some patients with affective disturbances, and the serum levels of these enzymes (high, medium, or low) also seem to follow a familial pattern. However, for the most part, these patterns appear to be independent of the presence or absence of affective illness in different family members; they also appear to be trait rather than state markers (not changing with presence or absence of clinical illness within individuals). Thus, the utility of circulating enzyme levels as biological markers of familial predisposition to affective illness remains uncertain.

In the last several years, three specific genetic markers have been proposed as having some linkage to affective disturbance. Both the Xg blood group and protan/deutan (red/green) color blindness initially were thought to show a close linkage with bipolar illness, but the data now are controversial (74-76). The human leukocyte antigen (HLA) locus also may be linked to depression, since pairs of siblings with affective disturbance appear to have a significant sharing of HLA haplotypes (77,78). Replication studies will be required to confirm the strength of this association (79).

SCHIZOPHRENIC DISORDERS

Certain symptoms of schizophrenia have long convinced researchers that there must be biological differences between schizophrenic patients and normals. For example, hallucinations and delusions are experienced by normal individuals only when they have been exposed to certain drugs or profound sensory deprivation. In addition, considerable evidence indicates that schizophrenic individuals may inherit a genetic predisposition to the development of their illness (80).

Early research on the biochemistry of schizophrenia focused on isolating endogenous substances in the blood and urine of patients. For example, Heath et al. (81) claimed to have identified the endogenous, blood-borne psychotogen taraxein. Other researchers noted a chromatographic abnormality in urine, the so-called "pink spot" (82). These and other findings initially were welcomed with enthusiasm, which turned to disappointment when the findings could not be confirmed. Nevertheless, in performing these studies, biological psychiatrists gained a greater appreciation for the methodologic problems and sources of error inherent in attempting to identify biological markers in schizophrenia.

Kety's early description of such sources of error is still relevant (83). First, schizophrenia may be a group of disorders rather than a single disease entity. The illness can only be defined presently by the clinical variables of signs, symptoms, and course. It is not unusual in medicine for very different disease processes to have similar clinical presentations; an obvious example in psychiatry is dementia. Similarly, several biochemical anomalies could be responsible for similar clusters of signs and symptoms in schizophrenia. If this is so, and schizophrenia indeed is a heterogenous disorder, the task of locating biological markers becomes considerably more complex. Second, Kety observed that a number of variables unrelated to the etiology of schizophrenia could cause schizophrenic patients to appear biochemically different from normals. These include institutional overcrowding, diet, drugs, sanitary conditions, and the general emotional distress which schizophrenic patients often suffer.

This next section will focus on the current search for useful biological markers in schizophrenia, omitting references largely of historical interest. A major focus will be on the biological markers related to the dopamine hypothesis, the most important contemporary approach to the understanding of this illness.

Biological Markers Related to the Dopamine Theory

The discovery of drugs with clearly demonstrable anti-schizophrenic effects has resulted in a shift away from the search for endogenous psychotogens, toward understanding the neurochemical effects of these drugs on the behavior of schizophrenic patients. And, in place of the rather unstructured search for a particular substance, biologists have turned their attention to developing working hypotheses, the most important of which is the dopamine (DA) hypothesis.

In its simplest form the DA hypothesis states that schizophrenia is related to an overactivity of CNS DA. The major support for this theory comes from the related observations that: 1) drugs which increase DA activity tend to make schizophrenic patients worse and can cause schizophrenic-like symptoms in normals; and 2) drugs which decrease DA activity improve schizophrenic symptoms. Although this form of the DA hypothesis has inspired a considerable amount of research, there is only limited evidence to support excess CNS DA activity as the cause of schizophrenia (84).

There is, however, considerable evidence to support the hypothesis that neuroleptic drugs improve schizophrenia by blocking DA receptors. New techniques now permit direct studies of the properties of DA receptors (85,86). Homogenates are prepared from areas of animal CNS, such as caudate, that are rich in DA receptors. Substances such as haloperidol, spiroperidol, or DA itself are radiolabeled and added to the homogenate. Specialized techniques permit the separation of specific binding of the radiolabeled substance with the receptor from nonspecific binding. Figure 11 depicts the ability of various neuroleptics to compete with labeled spiroperidol for DA receptors, versus the average clinical daily dose of each drug (87). The impressive correlation between the clinical potency of the drugs and their affinity for DA receptors suggests that the two are related. Figure 11 also depicts the relationships between clinical potency and the affinity of these drugs for serotonergic, alpha-adrenergic, and histaminergic receptors. Although the neuroleptics do bind weakly to these other receptors, their clinical potencies correlate only with their affinities for DA receptors.

Acknowledging the lack of evidence for an impaired DA system in schizophrenia, Davis (84) proposed a two-factor theory to explain the convincing

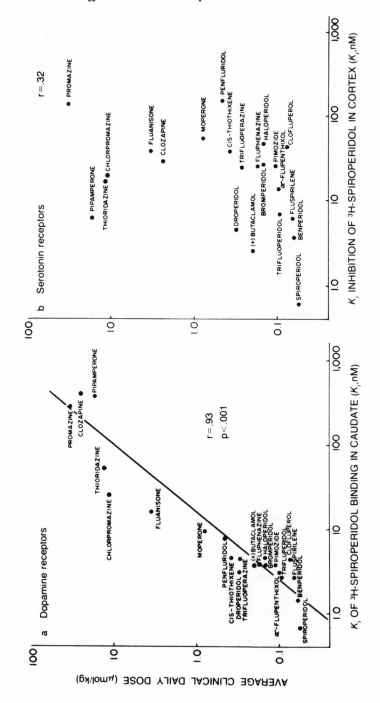

FIGURE 11. Correlation between average clinical doses of neuroleptics with their affinity for dopamine receptors (a), serotonin receptors (b), α-adrenergic receptors (c), and histamine H₁ receptors (d). Only the correlation between dose and dopamine receptor affinity is significant. Figure reproduced, with permission, from Peroutka and Snyder (87). Copyright 1980 by the American Psychiatric Association.

evidence that neuroleptics work by blocking DA receptors. Whereas DA dysfunction may not be the basic cause of schizophrenia, increasing or decreasing DA activity can modulate schizophrenic symptoms, similar to the volume control on a radio. This can be compared to hypertension, in which some drugs regulate blood pressure by mechanisms unrelated to the cause of the disease.

The two variants of the DA hypothesis will be discussed separately, since they would be associated with different kinds of biological markers. That is, the original hypothesis initiated a search for differences in DA systems between normals and schizophrenic patients, whereas the alternative hypothesis has led to a search for biological changes in DA systems which may be associated with drug responses.

Do Schizophrenic Patients Have Altered Dopamine Systems?

DA acts as a neurotransmitter in several discrete CNS pathways (Figure 12). The cell bodies of the nigrostriatal system are located in the substantia nigra of the brainstem, and their nerve terminals end in the corpus striatum (caudate and putamen). Parkinson's disease is associated with a deficiency of DA in this system. When neuroleptic drugs block the receptors for these terminals in the striatum, the symptoms of Parkinsonism can be reproduced.

The tuberoinfundibular system consists of cell bodies in the arcuate nucleus of the hypothalamus, with their axons terminating in the median eminence. DA in these terminals has important effects on the secretion of some pituitary hormones, particularly prolactin and growth hormone. This system will be discussed later in relation to prolactin secretion.

Much less is understood about the functioning of the mesolimbic and mesocortical DA pathways, although they have been proposed as being related to schizophrenia. Mesolimbic DA cell bodies are located in the ventral tegmental area, and their axons ascend to the nucleus accumbens, nucleus of the stria terminalis, and portions of the olfactory tubercle. These limbic structures are believed to mediate memory, learning, affects, and behavior. Stevens (88) proposed that these limbic structures act as a gating mechanism which prevents consciousness from being inundated by various internal and external sensory signals; schizophrenia may be the result of a failure of these systems. Mesocortical DA cell bodies are adjacent to mesolimbic cell bodies, but their axons ascend to various cortical structures. The function of this DA system also is unclear.

Although the mesolimbic and mesocortical DA tracts may be the most relevant to schizophrenia, they also are the most difficult to study. However, recent investigations of postmortem human brains are promising. Mackay et al. (89) compared brains of patients dying with a hospital diagnosis of schizophrenia to those of non-schizophrenic patients. In the schizophrenic patients, DA concentrations were elevated in the nucleus accumbens and anterior perforated substance, both limbic areas. Using radio-receptor techniques, these investigators also found that the schizophrenic brains had a higher number of DA receptors in both nucleus accumbens and caudate. Lee and Seeman (90) found a similar

Major dopamine pathways.

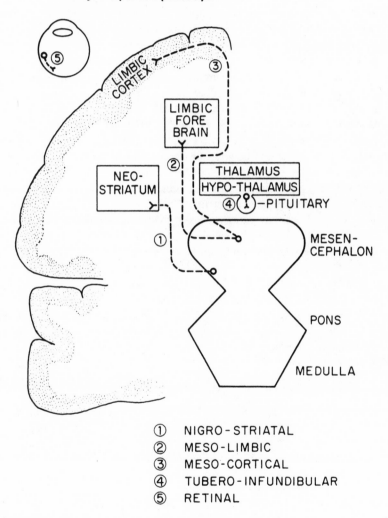

① NIGRO-STRIATAL
② MESO-LIMBIC
③ MESO-CORTICAL
④ TUBERO-INFUNDIBULAR
⑤ RETINAL

FIGURE 12. Major dopaminergic pathways in mammalian brain. Figure reproduced, with permission, from Meltzer (94).

increase in DA binding sites in nucleus accumbens, as well as in two striatal areas, the caudate and putamen, for schizophrenic patients compared to controls. Before concluding that these differences are related to the diagnoses of the patients, it is important to rule out the possibility that they are an artifact related to neuroleptic drug treatment of the schizophrenic patients. Neuroleptics have been shown to increase ligand binding to DA receptors in animals (91). Although Mackay et al. (89) found that the number of DA receptors was increased only in patients who had received neuroleptics, Lee and Seeman (90) found greater numbers of receptors in schizophrenic patients who had never been treated with drugs. This remains a controversial area of research.

Another strategy for studying DA activity in schizophrenia involves measuring the levels of DA metabolites in cerebrospinal fluid (CSF). Homovanillic acid (HVA) is the most commonly studied metabolite, although dihydroxyphenyl-acetic acid (DOPAC) also is important. CSF HVA probably reflects DA turnover in the corpus striatum rather than in those limbic structures presumed to be important in schizophrenia. In most studies, probenecid was administered to patients prior to the lumbar puncture in order to block the efflux of HVA from CSF. This technique abolishes the concentration gradient that normally exists between the ventricles and the puncture site.

Several investigators have compared CSF HVA in schizophrenic patients, normals, and patients with other illnesses. Post et al. (92) found no difference in CSF HVA concentrations between schizophrenic and normal patients. Interestingly, when the schizophrenic patients improved, their CSF HVA concentrations decreased, suggesting a relationship between DA turnover and clinical state. Both Post et al. (92) and Bowers (93) found that schizophrenic patients with poor prognoses actually had reduced, rather than elevated, CSF HVA levels. These studies do not support CSF HVA as a biological marker in schizophrenia.

The responses of schizophrenic patients to different drugs also have been used to support the DA hypothesis. Amphetamine and methylphenidate promote cate-cholamine release and inhibit catecholamine reuptake. Although norepinephrine also is affected by these drugs, their effects on psychotic symptoms are probably related to DA (94). Janowsky et al. (95) found that intravenously administered methylphenidate led to a worsening of a variety of psychotic symptoms in clinically ill schizophrenic patients, whereas remitted schizophrenic patients and normals did not have this reaction. Although most studies of amphetamine responses indicate that a significant proportion of schizophrenic patients worsen after receiving the drug, it certainly is not a reliable response. Kornetsky (96) found that none of the 25 schizophrenic patients he studied worsened after receiving amphetamine. Van Kammen et al. (97) reported that 13 of 45 schizophrenic patients actually improved after receiving amphetamine intravenously, while 18 worsened. In this study, improvers on amphetamine were the most psychotic at the time the study was done. Taken together, these studies do not suggest that a patient's response to enhancers of CNS catecholamine activity can be a useful diagnostic tool.

Prolactin secretion by the anterior pituitary is inhibited, and growth hormone secretion is enhanced, by DA released from the tuberoinfundibular tract. Evidence suggests that DA itself may reach the pituitary via the portal circulation and directly stimulate inhibitory receptors on prolactin-secreting cells. Serum prolactin levels therefore provide a means for monitoring DA activity in the hypothalamus (98). If there is DA overactivity in the tuberoinfundibular tract of schizophrenic patients, they might be expected to have lower serum prolactin levels than normals. In fact, serum prolactin levels in unmedicated schizophrenic patients appear to be normal or even slightly elevated (99,100).

Supersensitivity of postsynaptic DA receptors has been proposed as a defect which might be related to schizophrenia (101). One method of investigating receptor sensitivity is to administer drugs with known effects on DA receptors

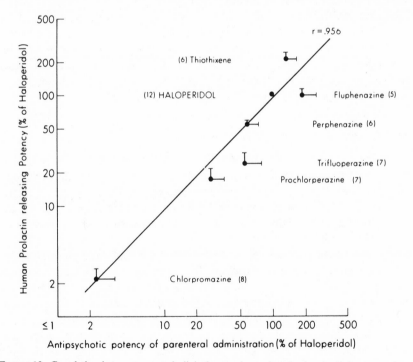

FIGURE 13. Correlation between reported clinical potencies and prolactin-stimulating potencies of seven neuroleptic drugs administered intramuscularly to normal men. Values are expressed relative to the clinical and prolactin-stimulating potencies of haloperidol. Figure reproduced, with permission, from Sachar (107).

to patients. Pandey et al. (102) administered apomorphine, a DA agonist, to schizophrenic patients and controls and monitored the extent to which growth hormone was elevated. Acute schizophrenic patients had increased growth hormone responses, while chronic schizophrenic patients had the same responses as normals. On the other hand, Rotrosen et al. (103) and Ettigi et al. (104) found decreased growth hormone responses to apomorphine in chronic schizophrenic patients. Rotrosen et al. (105) also found a decrease in schizophrenic patients in the normal prolactin suppression which occurs with apomorphine administration.

Experiences with neuroendocrine stimulation tests in affective disorders, particularly the dexamethasone suppression test, suggest that similar strategies deserve further study in schizophrenia. As yet, it is unclear whether a schizophrenic patient's neuroendocrine response to a DA agonist is an enduring trait that remains stable regardless of clinical condition, or whether it changes along with clinical state. Furthermore, it remains unclear whether or not prior neuroleptic treatment can affect these responses.

In summary, there is no direct evidence of a functional difference in the CNS DA systems of schizophrenic patients and normals. However, this does not mean that such a difference does not exist. Most studies have evaluated the functioning of only the nigrostriatal and tuberoinfundibular DA tracts. As mentioned above, information regarding the mesolimbic and mesocortical tracts is scanty, even though these appear to be most closely related to schizophrenia.

Response of the DA System to Neuroleptics

A more conservative DA hypothesis states that neuroleptic drugs lead to improvement in schizophrenia by blocking DA receptors, a link in the pathologic chain of events that is removed from the unknown etiologic first step. With this in mind, investigators have studied whether a measurable response of the DA system to neuroleptics can be used as a biological marker for monitoring the effects of these drugs.

Patients who receive neuroleptics have increases in CSF HVA during the first weeks of treatment. These increases are thought to result from a feedback mechanism whereby DA turnover is increased when DA receptors are blocked. Van Praag and Korf (106) measured CSF HVA after probenecid in schizophrenic patients before and one week after neuroleptic treatment was started, and found that the percentage increase in HVA correlated with improvement in the psychosis. Furthermore, the HVA increase was greatest in patients with the most severe extrapyramidal reactions. If confirmed, these findings suggest that CSF HVA measurement may be a useful method for monitoring a patient's neuroleptic response.

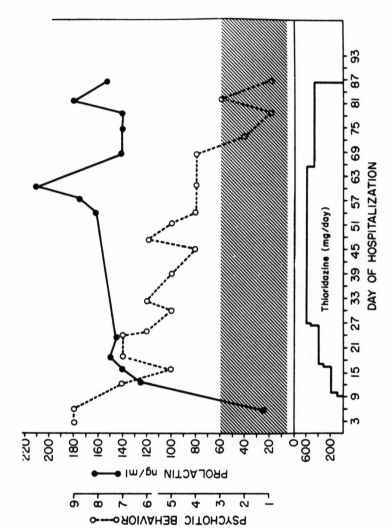

FIGURE 14. Longitudinal serum prolactin concentrations (ng/ml) and psychotic behavior ratings in a chronic schizophrenic woman treated with thioridazine. Figure reproduced, with permission, from Meltzer and Fang (111). Copyright 1976 by the American Medical Association.

Considerable attention has focused on the prolactin increase associated with neuroleptic drugs. Galactorrhea, the discharge of milk from the breasts of non-nursing women and men, is a side effect of neuroleptics which results from elevated prolactin levels. Prolactin measurements can be made on peripheral blood samples, thus providing perhaps the simplest method for monitoring a DA tract. Proposed applications include using prolactin response to measure clinical response, predicting response to drug treatment on the basis of prolactin response, and utilizing prolactin levels to monitor compliance with neuroleptics (98).

The antipsychotic potencies of neuroleptic drugs correlate well with their prolactin-stimulating potencies (Figure 13) (107). This suggests a relationship

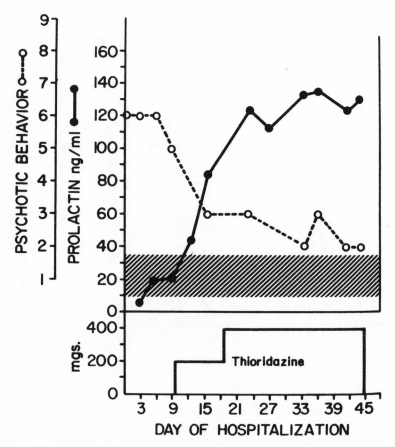

FIGURE 15. Longitudinal serum prolactin concentrations (ng/ml) and psychotic behavior ratings in an acutely schizophrenic man treated with thioridazine. Figure reproduced, with permission, from Meltzer and Fang (111). Copyright 1976 by the American Medical Association.

between the activities of these drugs in the tuberoinfundibular DA tract and the DA tracts involved in schizophrenia. A possible exception is clozapine, which may selectively block mesocortical and mesolimbic DA receptors and thus have little effect on pituitary prolactin secretion (108).

Prolactin levels are elevated within 30 minutes after a patient receives a parenteral dose of neuroleptic drug. Following oral medication, as noted in Figures 14 and 15, prolactin levels rise during the first days of treatment as the neuroleptic dose is increased. Because estrogen potentiates the prolactin response in premenopausal women, serum hormone concentrations increase faster in women (Figure 14) than they do in men on comparable doses of neuroleptics (Figure 15). Figure 16 indicates that at doses of neuroleptic up to 600 mg of chlorpromazine or its equivalent, there is a correlation between drug dose and prolactin level, with higher levels in women. Above this dose, patients show no additional prolactin elevation.

Although intuitively it would appear helpful to measure blood levels of neuroleptic drugs, research does not justify their use in routine clinical practice (109). The measurement of prolactin levels has been suggested as an alternative. If prolactin concentrations provided information about an individual's clinical response to pharmacotherapy, their measurement might be a significant aid to clinicians. Unfortunately, there are some serious limitations to the use of the prolactin response. Commonly prescribed doses of neuroleptic drugs maximally stimulate prolactin (110). Since prolactin secretion is potentiated by estrogen levels, differences found in female patients might reflect estrogen status rather than neuroleptic treatment (98). Indeed, Meltzer and Fang (111) found a significant correlation between prolactin level and clinical response in men, but not in women. However, Gruen et al. (112) did not find such a relationship in either men or women. This lack of agreement may be due to Meltzer and Fang's having prescribed lower dose equivalents of neuroleptics. Further studies will be necessary to determine whether prolactin levels ultimately will be clinically useful in patients treated within certain neuroleptic dose ranges.

The utility of prolactin measurements in monitoring drug compliance is probably limited. Patients on chronic neuroleptics may show elevated prolactin levels for months after they discontinue drugs (113). Furthermore, patients who are not compliant could elevate their prolactin levels by simply taking a dose of medication the day before blood sampling (98).

The prolactin response to low doses of neuroleptic has been proposed as a predictor of eventual clinical response (98). Utilizing a test-dose procedure elaborated by May et al. (114), patients are administered a small parenteral dose of neuroleptic, and prolactin levels are measured during the next six to eight hours. This strategy might improve a clinician's ability to predict a patient's ultimate drug response by providing information about individual differences in drug

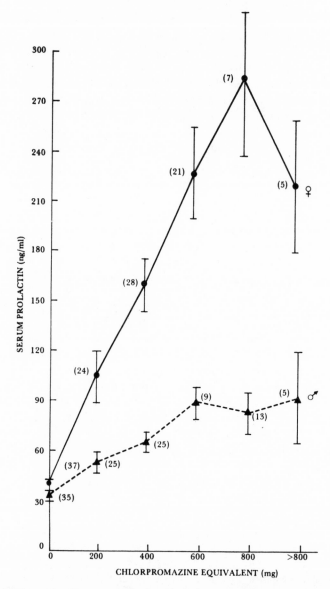

FIGURE 16. Effect of neuroleptic treatment on serum prolactin concentrations (ng/ml). Schizophrenic patients (numbers in parentheses) were treated with several different neuroleptics on a twice-a-day dosing schedule. Blood samples were obtained after at least one week at each dose level, 12 hours after the last dose. All dosages were converted to chlorpromazine equivalents. Figure reproduced, with permission, from Meltzer (94).

metabolism, receptor sensitivity, or other variables. However, even normal men demonstrate considerable variability in the magnitude and time course of their prolactin responses to parenteral neuroleptics (115), so that the test-dose model might not prove to be applicable to the prolactin system.

Platelet Monoamine Oxidase Activity

In 1972, Murphy and Wyatt (116) reported that platelet monoamine oxidase (MAO) activity was reduced in chronic schizophrenic patients. This initial observation has led to considerable research on the biology of MAO and its clinical significance. MAO is important in the enzymatic breakdown of amine neurotransmitters including dopamine, norepinephrine, and serotonin. If the reported decreases of this enzyme in platelets were paralleled in the CNS, there could be an increase in the availability of any or all of these neurotransmitters in schizophrenia. Considerable attention has focused on issues such as the relationship between platelet MAO activity and CNS MAO activity and the functional significance of altered MAO activity in man.

Murphy and Wyatt's original study (116) has been replicated by several groups of investigators. Wyatt et al. (117) reviewed 31 studies in which platelet MAO activity was compared in normals and chronic schizophrenic patients. In all but six studies, the schizophrenic patients had reduced platelet MAO activity. Buchsbaum and colleagues (118) concluded that this is the most widely replicated neurochemical finding in schizophrenia.

Despite the convincing evidence of a decrease in platelet MAO activity in schizophrenic patients, it may have only limited usefulness to the clinician. Not all individuals demonstrate this characteristic; a substantial proportion of chronic schizophrenic patients have normal or even elevated platelet MAO activity. Conversely, a number of normal controls have reduced activity. Furthermore, MAO activity may be reduced in some patients with affective disorders and alcoholism (119). One interesting study of normal college students found that individuals with low platelet MAO activity needed more psychiatric and psychological counseling than individuals with high activity (120). Bowers (121) has suggested that low platelet MAO activity may be a biochemical marker for vulnerability to a number of psychiatric illnesses.

Although platelet MAO activity is unlikely to be of help in diagnosing schizophrenia, it may be useful for defining biologically homogeneous subgroups. Groups of acute schizophrenic patients have much greater variability of MAO activity than groups of chronic schizophrenic patients. Schildkraut et al. (122) reported that schizophrenic patients with low platelet MAO activity tend to suffer from auditory hallucinations, whereas patients with normal activity do not. Others

(123) have reported an association between low platelet MAO activity and paranoid symptoms in chronic schizophrenia, and elevated MAO activity may be associated with "schizophrenia-related depression" (124).

Thus, although platelet MAO activity appears to be reduced in chronic schizophrenic patients, this should not imply that a causal relationship has been established. This "abnormality" also exists both in normals and in individuals with other illnesses and therefore is unlikely to be of help in diagnosing schizophrenia.

Creatine Phosphokinase (CPK)

Meltzer et al. (125) have studied the relationship between neuromuscular dysfunction and schizophrenia. Serum creatine phosphokinase (CPK) is elevated in a substantial proportion of acutely psychotic patients with schizophrenia and affective illness. The significance of this is uncertain, since most CPK comes from skeletal muscle rather than from brain. However, Meltzer also has reported abnormalities in skeletal muscle fibers and subterminal motor nerves in schizophrenia.

Endorphins and Enkephalins

Endorphins and enkephalins are endogenous peptides with opiate-like activity. Whereas the enkephalins are small peptides which may act as neurotransmitters, the endorphins are larger, have a longer duration of action, and are thought to act as hormones. Some circumstantial evidence suggests that an excess of CNS endorphins might be associated with schizophrenia. Beta endorphin produces a state of muscular rigidity in rats, which has been likened to catatonia (126). Increased levels of an endorphin fraction have been found in the CSF of chronic schizophrenic patients. Two groups of investigators (127,128) have found that naloxone, a drug which competes for opiate receptors, decreases auditory hallucinations in some schizophrenic patients, but other investigators (129) could not confirm these results. Studies of the effects of intravenous beta-endorphin on schizophrenia are conflicting (130,131). A nonopiate-like peptide, des-tyr-gamma-endorphin, has been reported to have antipsychotic activity (132), although this effect has not been replicated in other studies (133,134).

Palmour et al. (135) reported that the initial hemodialysates of schizophrenic patients who improved with hemodialysis contained elevated levels of an abnormal endorphin. Here, too, subsequent studies have not replicated this finding (136). Additionally, double-blind studies have failed to support the efficacy of hemodialysis as a treatment for schizophrenia (137).

Anatomical Abnormalities in Schizophrenia

Early studies using pneumoencephalography pointed to enlarged cerebral ventricles as being common in schizophrenia. The present availability of computerized tomography (CT) scans has permitted the study of ventricular morphology using a method which is both safe and reliable. Weinberger et al. (138) found a significant difference in ventricular size between chronic schizophrenic patients and controls, with 53% of those with chronic schizophrenia having ventricular sizes more than two standard deviations larger than the mean of the controls. This very interesting finding has been confirmed by others (139).

Additional studies have suggested that chronic schizophrenic patients with enlarged ventricles may form a biologically homogeneous subgroup. Such patients had a poorer response to drug treatment than a matched group of chronic schizophrenic patients with normal-sized ventricles (140). Enlarged ventricles appear to be more common in those patients who perform poorly on cognitive and neuropsychological tests (139). On CT scans, some schizophrenic patients also showed evidence of cortical abnormalities, and some had reverses in cortical asymmetry (141). Taken together, these studies suggest that structural brain abnormalities also could be useful in forming meaningful clinical subtypes of schizophrenic patients.

Electroencephalographic Activity

Studies two or three decades ago suggested that schizophrenic patients have abnormal EEGs. These early reports are difficult to interpret, since they relied on visual analysis and therefore are highly subjective. More recently, investigators have used computerized "power spectral" analysis, in which the amount of activity in various frequencies is studied. Although there is considerable overlap in EEG patterns between schizophrenic patients and control subjects, patients have been shown to have somewhat less alpha activity (8 to 13 Hz) and more beta activity (14 to 25 Hz) than controls (Figure 17). This EEG pattern in resting schizophrenic patients is akin to that in normal individuals when they are given sensory stimulation, suggesting that schizophrenic patients have impaired filtering of normal sensory input (142). As mentioned above, mesolimbic DA may be the gating mechanism for this filtering.

Other studies suggest that a schizophrenic patient's EEG profile may be helpful in predicting treatment response. Itil et al. (143) reported that patients with low alpha and high beta activity showed the best responses to neuroleptic treatment. In these patients, neuroleptic treatment appears to normalize their EEG pattern.

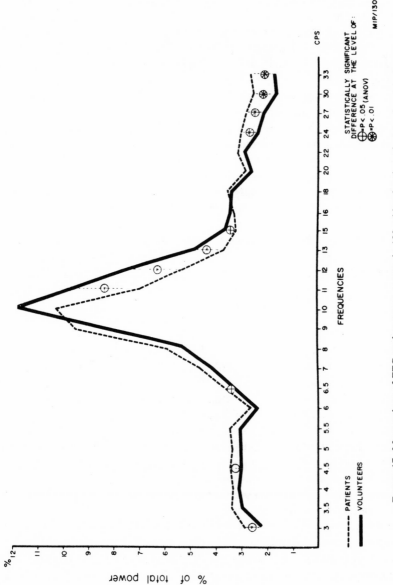

FIGURE 17. Mean values of EEG analog power spectra in 100 schizophrenic patients and matched normal control subjects. Twenty-four frequency bands are represented on the abscissa, and the percentage of the total power spent in each of these bands is indicated on the ordinate. The schizophrenic patients showed more voltage in the delta, theta, and fast beta frequency bands and less voltage in the fast alpha and beta bands. Figure reproduced, with permission, from Itil (143).

Evoked Potentials

In evoked potential (EP) studies, the EEG is measured while a subject is presented a series of visual, somatosensory, or auditory stimuli. Computer-averaging techniques are used to analyze the EEG responses. Various components of the EP are differentiated according to the time elapsed following the stimulus; these components appear to reflect different stages of information processing.

As with virtually all other proposed biological markers, there is no EP pattern pathognomonic for schizophrenia. When groups of subjects were compared, the schizophrenic patients tended to have lower EP amplitudes than the normals (142). As the stimulus became more intense, the patients failed to show the increase in EP amplitude that normals demonstrated. Conversely, when the groups were given information about stimulus arrival, the normal subjects were more likely to show a reduction in EP amplitude. These data suggest that some schizophrenic patients have a deficit that renders them unable to modulate stimulus input normally.

Biological Heterogeneity of Schizophrenia

It is apparent from the above review that there is little evidence for any single biological marker that is associated only with schizophrenia. The relentless search for a unitary biological explanation and the failure to find it have convinced many investigators that the most useful strategy is to acknowledge the heterogeneity of schizophrenia. This should relieve researchers of the need to explain a large body of data by a single unitary etiology (142). Crow (144) adopted such an approach in proposing two different disease processes in schizophrenia. The Type I syndrome is characterized by a relatively acute course and positive symptoms of schizophrenia such as hallucinations, delusions, and thought disorder. The Type II syndrome consists of a chronic course and negative symptoms such as flattened affect and impoverished speech. Patients with the Type I syndrome respond well to neuroleptics and are postulated to have increased numbers of CNS DA receptors. On the other hand, patients with the Type II syndrome respond poorly to neuroleptics and are more likely to show intellectual impairment as well as structural brain abnormalities on CT scan. Some patients may have characteristics of both syndromes. Crow's theory (144) explains a considerable amount of the data presented here and is more consistent with the view of most clinicians that multiple biological and psychological processes underlie schizophrenia. It will be of great interest to see if the Type I/Type II hypothesis endures the test of future research.

REFERENCES

1. BOYD, J.H., and WEISSMAN, M.M.: Epidemology of affective disorders: a re-examination and future directions. *Arch. Gen. Psychiat.*, 38:1039-1046, 1981.
2. KENDELL, R.E.: The classification of depressions: a review of contemporary confusion. *Br. J. Psychiat.*, 129:15-28, 1976.
3. SPITZER, R.L., ENDICOTT, J., and ROBINS, E.: Research diagnostic criteria: Rationale and reliability. *Arch. Gen. Psychiat.*, 35:773-782, 1978.
4. KLEIN, D.F.: Endogenomorphic depression: A conceptual and terminological revision. *Arch. Gen. Psychiat.*, 31:447-454, 1974.
5. *Diagnostic and Statistical Manual of Mental Disorders* (Third Edition). Washington, D.C.: American Psychiatric Association. 1980.
6. SCHILDKRAUT, J.J., ORSULAK, P.J., SCHATZBERG, A.F., and ROSENBAUM, A.H.: Urinary MHPG in affective disorders. In: R.M. Post and J.C. Ballenger (Eds.), *The Neurobiology of Mood Disorders*. Baltimore: Williams and Wilkins, 1982, in press.
7. DeMET, E.M., and HALARIS, A.E.: Origin and distribution of 3-methoxy-4-hydroxyphenylglycol in body fluids. *Biochem. Pharmacol.*, 28:3043-3050, 1979.
8. MURPHY, D.L., CAMPBELL, I., and COSTA, J.L.: Current status of the indoleamine hypothesis of the affective disorders. In: M.A. Lipton, A. DiMascio, and K.F. Killam (Eds.), *Psychopharmacology: A Generation of Progress*. New York: Raven, 1978, pp. 1235-1247.
9. WALDMEIER, P.C.: Noradrenergic transmission in depression: Under- or over-function? *Pharmakopsychiat.*, 14:3-9, 1981.
10. RECHTSCHAFFEN, A., and KALES, A. (Eds.): *A Manual of Standardized Terminology, Techniques, and Scoring System for Sleep Stages of Human Subjects*. Washington, D.C.: Public Health Service, U.S. Government Printing Office, 1968.
11. ANDERS, T., EMDE, R., and PARMELEE, A. (Eds.): *A Manual of Standardized Terminology, Techniques and Criteria for Scoring of States of Sleep and Wakefulness in Newborn Infants*. Los Angeles: UCLA Brain Information Service, NINDS Neurological Information Network, 1971.
12. KALES, A.: Sleep and dreams. *Ann. Intern. Med.*, 68:1078-1104, 1968.
13. KUPFER, D.J., and FOSTER, F.G.: EEG sleep and depression. In: R.L. Williams and I. Karacan (Eds.), *Sleep Disorders: Diagnosis and Treatment*. New York: Wiley, 1978, pp. 163-204.
14. KUPFER, D.J., FOSTER, F.G., COBLE, P., McPARTLAND, R.J., and ULRICH, R.F.: The application of EEG sleep for the differential diagnosis of affective disorders. *Am. J. Psychiat.*, 135:69-74, 1978.
15. SPIKER, D.G., COBLE, P., COFSKY, J., FOSTER, F.G., and KUPFER, D.J.: EEG sleep and severity of depression. *Biol. Psychiat.*, 13:485-488, 1978.
16. COBLE, P.A., KUPFER, D.J., SPIKER, D.G., NEIL, J.F., and McPARTLAND, R.J.: EEG sleep in primary depression. *J. Affect. Dis.*, 1:131-138, 1979.
17. COBLE, P.A., KUPFER, D.J., and SHAW, D.H.: Distribution of REM latency in depression. *Biol. Psychiat.*, 16:453-466, 1981.
18. GILLIN, J.C., DUNCAN, W.C., PETTIGREW, K.D., FRANKEL, B.L., and SNYDER, F.: Successful separation of depressed, normal, and insomniac subjects by EEG sleep data. *Arch. Gen. Psychiat.*, 36:85-89, 1979.
19. GILLIN, J.C., DUNCAN, W.C., MURPHY, D.L., POST, R.M., WEHR, T.A., GOODWIN,

F.K., WYATT, R.J., and BUNNEY, W.E.: Age-related changes in sleep in depressed and normal subjects. *Psychiat. Res.*, 4:73-78, 1981.

20. KUPFER, D.J., SPIKER, D.G., COBLE, P.A., NEIL, J.F., ULRICH, R., and SHAW, D.H.: Sleep and treatment prediction in endogenous depression. *Am. J. Psychiat.*, 138:429-434, 1981.

21. KUPFER, D.J., SPIKER, D.G., ROSSI, A., COBLE, P.A., ULRICH, R., and SHAW, D.H.: Recent diagnostic and treatment advances in REM sleep and depression. In: P. Clayton and J. Barrett (Eds.), *Treatment of Depression: Old Controversies and New Approaches*. New York: Raven, 1982, in press.

22. RUBIN, R.T., GOUIN, P.R., and POLAND, R.E.,: Biogenic amine metabolism and neuroendocrine function in affective disorders. In: R. de la Fuente and M.N. Weisman (Eds.), *Psychiatry: Proceedings of the V World Congress of Psychiatry*. Amsterdam: Excerpta Medica, 1973, pp. 1036-1039.

23. RUBIN, R.T., and KENDLER, K.S.: Psychoneuroendocrinology: Fundamental concepts and correlates in depression. In: G. Usdin (Ed.), *Depression: Clinical, Biological, and Psychological Perspectives*. New York: Brunner/Mazel, 1977, pp. 122-138.

24. CARROLL, B.J.: Neuroendocrine dysfunction in psychiatric disorders. In: M.A. Lipton, A. DiMascio, and K.F. Killam (Eds.): *Psychopharmacology: A Generation of Progress*. New York: Raven, 1978, pp. 487-497.

25. RUBIN, R.T., POLAND, R.E., and HAYS, S.E.: Psychoneuroendocrine research in endogenous depression: A review. In: J. Obiols, C. Ballus, E. Gonzales Monclus, and J. Pujol (Eds.), *Biological Psychiatry Today*. Amsterdam: Elsevier-North Holland, 1979, pp. 684-688.

26. CHECKLEY, S.A.: Neuroendocrine tests of monoamine function in man: A review of basic theory and its application to the study of depressive illness. *Psychol. Med.*, 10:35-53, 1980.

27. RUBIN, R.T., and POLAND, R.E.: The chronoendocrinology of endogenous depression. In: R.M. MacLeod and E.E. Müller (Eds.): *Neuroendocrine Perspectives, Volume 1*. Amsterdam: Elsevier/North Holland, 1982, in press.

28. RUBIN, R.T., and POLAND, R.E.: Pituitary-adrenocortical and pituitary-gonadal function in affective disorder. In: G.M. Brown and S.H. Koslow (Eds.): *Proceedings of NIMH Psychoneuroendocrinology Symposium*, New York: Raven, 1982, in press.

29. RUBIN, R.T.: Sex steroid hormone dynamics in endogenous depression: A review. *Int. J. Ment. Health*, 1982, in press.

30. CARROLL, B.J., FEINBERG, M., GREDEN, J.F., TARIKA, J., ALBALA, A.A., HASKETT, R.F., JAMES, N.McI., KRONFOL, Z., LOHR, N., STEINER, M., DE VIGNE, J.P., and YOUNG, E.: A specific laboratory test for the diagnosis of melancholia: Standardization, validation, and clinical utility. *Arc. Gen. Psychiat.*, 38:15-22, 1981.

31. KRIEGER, D.T.: Rhythms in CRF, ACTH, and corticosteroids. In: D.T. Krieger (Ed.), *Endocrine Rhythms*. New York: Raven, 1979, pp. 123-142.

32. SELYE, H.: The evolution of the stress concept. *Amer. Scientist*, 61:692-699, 1973.

33. RUBIN, R.T., and MANDELL, A.J.: Adrenal cortical activity in pathological emotional states: A review. *Am. J. Psychiat.*, 123:387-400, 1966.

34. MASON, J.W.: A review of psychoendocrine research on the pituitary-adrenal cortical system. *Psychosom. Med.*, 30:576-607, 1968.

35. SACHAR, E.J., HELLMAN, L., FUKUSHIMA, D.K., and GALLAGHER, T.F.: Cortisol production in depressive illness. *Arch. Gen. Psychiat.*, 23:289-298, 1970.
36. CARROLL, B.J.: Limbic system-adrenal cortex regulation in depression and schizophrenia. *Psychosom. Med.*, 38:106-121, 1976.
37. VAN LOON, G.R.: Brain catecholamines and ACTH secretion. In: W.F. Ganong and L. Martini (Eds.), *Frontiers in Neuroendocrinology*, 1973. New York: Oxford, 1973, pp. 209-247.
38. SACHAR, E.J., HELLMAN, L., ROFFWARG, H.P., HALPERN, F.S., FUKUSHIMA, D.K., and GALLAGHER, T.F.: Disrupted 24-hour patterns of cortisol secretion in psychotic depression. *Arch. Gen. Psychiat.*, 28:19-24, 1973.
39. CARROLL, B.J., CURTIS, G.C., and MENDELS, J.: Neuroendocrine regulation in depression I. Limbic system-adrenocortical dysfunction. *Arch. Gen. Psychiat.*, 33:1039-1044, 1976.
40. RUBIN, R.T., POLAND, R.E., BLODGETT, A.L.N., WINSTON, R.A., FORSTER, B., and CARROLL, B.J.: Cortisol dynamics and dexamethasone pharmacokinetics in primary endogenous depression: Preliminary findings. In F. Brambilla, G. Racagni, and D. deWied (Eds.), *Progress in Psychoneuroendocrinology*. Amsterdam, Elsevier/North Holland, 1980, pp. 223-234.
41. CARROLL, B.J.: The dexamethasone suppression test for melancholia. *Br. J. Psychiat.*, 1982, in press.
42. HOLSBOER, F., BENDER, W., BENKERT, O., KLEIN, H.E., and SCHMAUS, M.: Diagnostic value of dexamethasone suppression test in depression. *Lancet*, ii:706, 1980.
43. SHULMAN, R.: The dexamethasone test and depression. *Lancet*, ii: 1085, 1980.
44. CARROLL, B.J., SCHROEDER, K., MUKHOPADHYAY, S., GREDEN, J.F., FEINBERG, M., RITCHIE, J., and TARIKA, J.: Plasma dexamethasone concentrations and cortisol suppression response in patients with endogenous depression. *J. Clin. Endocrinol. Metab.*, 51:433-437, 1980.
45. PAPAKOSTAS, Y., FINK, M., LEE, J., IRWIN, P., and JOHNSON, L.: Neuroendocrine measures in psychiatric patients: Course and outcome with ECT. *Psychiat. Res.*, 4:55-64, 1981.
46. WINOKUR, G., BEHAR, D., VAN VALKENBURG, C., and LOWRY, M.: Is a familial definition of depression both feasible and valid? *J. Nerv. Ment. Dis.*, 166:764-768, 1978.
47. SCHLESSER, M.A., WINOKUR, G., and SHERMAN, B.M.: Hypothalamic-pituitary-adrenal axis activity in depressive illness: Its relationship to classification. *Arch. Gen. Psychiat.*, 37:737-743, 1980.
48. CARROLL, B.J., GREDEN, J.F., FEINBERG, M., JAMES, N.McI., HASKETT, R.F., STEINER, M., and TARIKA, J.: Neuroendocrine dysfunction in genetic subtypes of primary unipolar depression. *Psychiat. Res.*, 2:251-258, 1980.
49. HWU, H-G., RUDORFER, M.V., and CLAYTON, P.J.: Dexamethasone suppression test and subtypes of depression. *Arch. Gen. Psychiat.*, 38:363, 1981.
50. SCHLESSER, M.A., WINOKUR, G., and SHERMAN, B.M.: Dexamethasone suppression test and subtypes of depression. *Arch. Gen. Psychiat.*, 38:363, 1981.
51. BROWN, W.A., HAIER, R.J., and QUALLS, C.B.: Dexamethasone suppression test identifies subtypes of depression which respond to different antidepressants. *Lancet*, i:928-929, 1980.

52. BROWN, W.A., and QUALLS, C.B.: Pituitary-adrenal disinhibition in depression: Marker of a subtype with characteristic clinical features and response to treatment? *Psychiat. Res.*, 4:115-128, 1981.
53. COBBIN, D.M., CAIRNCROSS, K.D., JURD, S., VELTMAN, D.G., and POHLEN, G.H.: Urinary MHPG levels and the dexamethasone test predict clinical response to the antidepressant drug mianserin. *Neuroendocrinol. Lett.*, 3:133-138, 1981.
54. DYSKEN, M.W., PANDEY, G.N., CHANG, S.S., HICKS, R., and DAVIS, J.M.: Serial post-dexamethasone cortisol levels in a patient undergoing ECT. *Am. J. Psychiat.*, 136:1328-1329, 1979.
55. ALBALA, A.A., and GREDEN, J.F.: Serial dexamethasone suppression tests in affective disorders. *Am. J. Psychiat.*, 137:383, 1980.
56. GOLDBERG, I.K.: Dexamethasone suppression test as an indicator of safe withdrawal of antidepressant therapy. *Lancet*, i:376, 1980.
57. GREDEN, J.F., ALBALA, A.A., HASKETT, R.F., JAMES, N.McI., GOODMAN, L., STEINER, M., and CARROLL, B.J.: Normalization of dexamethasone suppression test: A laboratory index of recovery from endogenous depression. *Biol. Psychiat.*, 15:449-458, 1980.
58. POLAND, R.E., and RUBIN, R.T.: Saliva cortisol levels following dexamethasone administration in endogenously depressed patients. *Life Sci.*, 1982, in press.
59. HOLLISTER, L.E., DAVIS, K.L., and BERGER, P.A.: Thyrotropin-releasing hormone and psychiatric disorders. In: E. Usdin, D.A. Hamburg, and J.D. Barchas (Eds.), *Neuroregulators and Psychiatric Disorders*. New York: Oxford University Press, 1977, pp. 250-257.
60. KIRKEGAARD, C., BJØRUM, N., COHN D., and LAURIDSEN, U.B.: Thyrotropin-releasing hormone (TRH) stimulation test in manic-depressive illness. *Arch. Gen. Psychiat.*, 35:1017-1021, 1978.
61. LOOSEN, P.T., and PRANGE, A.J.: Thyrotropin releasing hormone (TRH): A useful tool for psychoneuroendocrine investigation. *Psychoneuroendocrinol.*, 5:63-80, 1980.
62. KIRKEGAARD, C.: The thyrotropin response to thyrotropin-releasing hormone in endogenous depression. *Psychoneuroendocrinol.*, 6:189-212, 1981.
63. DEWHURST, K.E., EL KABIR, D.J., HARRIS, G.W., and MANDELBROTE, B.M.: Observations on the blood concentration of thyrotrophic hormone (TSH) in schizophrenia and the affective states. *Br. J. Psychiat.*, 155:1003-1011, 1969.
64. KOLAKOWSKA, T., and SWIGAR, M.E.: Thyroid function in depression and alcohol abuse. *Arch. Gen. Psychiat.*, 34:984-988, 1977.
65. RINIERIS, P.M., CHRISTODOULOU, G.N., SOUVATZOGLOU, A.M., KOUTRAS, D.A., and STEFANIS, C.N.: Free-thyroxine index in psychotic and neurotic depression. *Acta Psychiat. (Scand.)*, 58:56-60, 1978.
66. KIRKEGAARD, C., FABER, J., HUMMER, L., and ROGOWSKI, P.: Increased levels of TRH in cerebrospinal fluid from patients with endogenous depression. *Psychoneuroendocrinol.*, 4:227-235, 1979.
67. EXTEIN, I., POTTASH, A.L.C., and GOLD, M.S.: Relationship of thyrotropin-releasing hormone test and dexamethasone suppression test abnormalities in unipolar depression. *Psychiat. Res.*, 4:49-53, 1981.
68. RUBIN, R.T., POLAND, R.E., BLODGETT, A.L.N., WINSTON, R.A., FORSTER, B., and HART, P.J.: Endocrine responses to perturbation tests in primary endogenous

depression: Preliminary findings. In: B. Jansson, C. Perris, and G. Struwe (Eds.), *Proceedings of the III World Congress on Biological Psychiatry*. Amsterdam: Elsevier/North Holland, 1982, in press.

69. BROWN, G.M., SEGGIE, J.A., CHAMBERS, J.W., and ETTIGI, P.G.: Psychoendocrinology and growth hormone: A review. *Psychoneuroendocrinol.*, 3:131-153, 1978.

70. MATUSSEK, N., ACKENHEIL, M., HIPPIUS, H., MÜLLER, F., SCHRÖDER, H-Th., SCHULTES, H., and WASILEWSKI, B.: Effect of clonidine on growth hormone release in psychiatric patients and controls. *Psychiat. Res.*, 2:25-36, 1980.

71. LAAKMANN, G.: Beeinflussung der Hypophysenvorderlappen-Hormonsekretion durch Antidepressiva bei gesunden Probanden, neurotische und endogen depressiven Patienten. *Nervenarzt*, 51:725-732, 1980.

72. GERSHON, E.S.: The search for genetic markers in affective disorders. In: M.A. Lipton, A. DiMascio, and K.F. Killam (Eds.), *Psychopharmacology: A Generation of Progress*. New York: Raven, 1978, pp. 1197-1212.

73. PERRIS, C.: Recent perspectives in the genetics of affective disorders. In: J. Mendlewicz and B. Shopsin (Eds.), *Genetic Aspects of Affective Illness*. New York: SP Books, 1979, pp. 7-19.

74. MENDLEWICZ, J., LINKOWSKI, P., GUROFF, J.J., and VAN PRAAG, H.M.: Color blindness linkage to bipolar manic-depressive illness: New evidence. *Arch. Gen. Psychiat.*, 36:1442-1447, 1979.

75. LECKMAN, J.F., GERSHON, E.S., McGINNISS, M.H., TARGUM, S.D., and DIBBLE, E.D.: New data do not suggest linkage between the Xg blood group and bipolar illness. *Arch. Gen. Psychiat.*, 36:1435-1441, 1979.

76. GERSHON, E.S., TARGUM, S.D., MATTHYSSE, S., and BUNNEY, W.E.: Color blindness not closely linked to bipolar illness: Report of a new pedigree series. *Arch. Gen. Psychiat.*, 36:1423-1430, 1979.

77. SMERALDI, E., NEGRI, F., MELICA, A.M., and SCORZA-SMERALDI, R.: HLA system and affective disorders: A sibship genetic study. *Tissue Antigens*, 12:270-274, 1978.

78. WEITKAMP, L.R., STANCER, H.C., PERSAD, E., FLOOD, C., and GUTTORMSEN, S.: Depressive disorders and HLA: A gene on chromosome 6 that can affect behavior. *New Engl. J. Med.*, 305:1301-1306, 1981.

79. MATTHYSSE, S., and KIDD, K.K.: Evidence of HLA linkage in depressive disorders. *New Engl. J. Med.*, 305:1340-1341, 1981.

80. KESSLER, S.: The genetics of schizophrenia: A review. *Schiz. Bull.*, 6:404-416, 1980.

81. HEATH, R.G., GUSHMAN, A.F., and COFFEY, J.W.: Relation of taraxein to schizophrenia. *Dis. Nerv. Syst.*, 31:391-395, 1970.

82. FRIEDHOFF, A.J., and VAN WINKLE, E.: Isolation and characterization of a compound from the urine of schizophrenics. *Nature*, 194:897-898, 1962.

83. KETY, S.S.: Biochemical theories of schizophrenia. Part I. *Science*, 129:1528-1532, 1959.

84. DAVIS, J.M.: Dopamine theory of schizophrenia: A two-factor theory. In L.C. Wynne, R.L. Cromwell, and S. Matthysse, (Eds.), *The Nature of Schizophrenia: New Approaches to Research and Treatment*. New York: Wiley, 1978, pp. 105-115.

85. CREESE, I., BURT, D.R., and SNYDER, S.H.: Dopamine receptor binding predicts

clinical and pharmacological potencies of antischizophrenic drugs. *Science,* 192:481-483, 1976.

86. SEEMAN, P., CHAU-WONG, M., TEDESCO, J., and WONG, K.: Brain receptors for antipsychotic drugs and dopamine: Direct binding assays. *Proc. Natl. Acad. Sci. USA,* 72:4376-4380, 1975.
87. PEROUTKA, S.J., and SNYDER, S.H.: Relationship of neuroleptic drug effects at brain dopamine, serotonin, alpha-adrenergic, and histamine receptors to clinical potency. *Am. J. Psychiat.,* 137:1518-1522, 1980.
88. STEVENS, J.R.: An anatomy of schizophrenia? *Arch. Gen. Psychiat.,* 29:177-189, 1973.
89. MACKAY, A.V.P., BIRD, E.D., IVERSON, L.L., SPOKES, E.G., CREESE, I., and SNYDER, S.H.: Dopaminergic abnormalities in postmortem schizophrenic brain. In: F. Cattabeni, G. Racagni, P.F. Spano and E. Costa (Eds.), *Long-term Effects of Neuroleptics.* New York: Raven, 1980, pp. 325-334.
90. LEE, T., and SEEMAN, P.: Elevation of brain neuroleptic/dopamine receptors in schizophrenia. *Am. J. Psychiat.,* 137:191-197, 1980.
91. BURT, D.R., CREESE, I., and SNYDER, S.H.: Antischizophrenic drugs: Chronic treatment elevates dopamine receptor binding in brain. *Science,* 196:326-328, 1977.
92. POST, R.M., FINK, E., CARPENTER, W.T. Jr., and GOODWIN, F.K.: Cerebrospinal fluid amine metabolites in acute schizophrenia. *Arch. Gen. Psychiat.,* 32:1063-1069, 1975.
93. BOWERS, M.B.: Central dopamine turnover in schizophrenic syndromes. *Arch. Gen. Psychiat.,* 31:50-57, 1974.
94. MELTZER, H.Y.: Biochemical studies in schizophrenia. In: L. Bellak (Ed.), *Disorders of the Schizophrenic Syndrome.* New York: Basic Books, 1979, pp. 45-135.
95. JANOWSKY, D.S., EL-YOUSEF, M.K., DAVIS, J.M., and SEKERKE, H.J.: Provocation of schizophrenic symptoms by intravenous administration of methylphenidate. *Arch. Gen. Psychiat.,* 28:185-191, 1973.
96. KORNETSKY, C.: Hyporesponsivity of chronic schizophrenic patients to dextroamphetamine. *Arch. Gen. Psychiat.,* 33:1425-1428, 1976.
97. VAN KAMMEN, D.P., BUNNEY, W.E. Jr., DOCHERTY, J.P., MARDER, S.R., EBERT, M.H., ROSENBLATT, J.E., and RAYNER, J.N.: d-Amphetamine induces heterogeneous changes in psychotic behavior in schizophrenia. *Am. J. Psychiat.,* in press.
98. RUBIN, R.T., and HAYS, S.E.: The prolactin secretory response to neuroleptic drugs: mechanisms, applications and limitations. *Psychoneuroendocrinol.,* 5:121-137, 1980.
99. JOHNSTONE, E.C., CROW, T.J., and MASHITER, K.: Anterior pituitary hormone secretion in chronic schizophrenia—An approach to neuro-humoral mechanisms. *Psychol. Med.,* 7:223-228, 1977.
100. MELTZER, H.Y., SACHAR, E.J., and FRANTZ, A.A.: Serum prolactin levels in unmedicated schizophrenic patients. *Arch. Gen. Psychiat.,* 31:564-569, 1974.
101. SNYDER, S.H.: The dopamine hypothesis of schizophrenia: Focus on the dopamine receptor. *Am. J. Psychiat.,* 133:197-202, 1976.
102. PANDEY, G.W., GARVER, D.L., TAMMINGA, C., ERICKSEN, S., ALI, S.I., and DAVIS, J.M.: Postsynaptic supersensitivity in schizophrenia. *Am. J. Psychiat.,* 134:518-521, 1977.

103. ROTROSEN, J., ANGRIST, B.M., GERSHON, S., SACHAR, E.J., and HALPERN, F.S.: Dopamine receptor alteration in schizophrenia: Neuroendocrine evidence. *Psychopharmacol.*, 51:1-7, 1976.

104. ETTIGI, P., NAIR, N.P.V., LAL, S., CERVANTES, P., and GUYDA, H.: Effect of apomorphine on growth hormone and prolactin secretion in schizophrenic patients, with or without oral dyskinesia, withdrawn from chronic neuroleptic therapy. *J. Neurol. Neurosurg. Psychiat.*, 39:870-876, 1976.

105. ROTROSEN, J., ANGRIST, B.M., CLARK, C., GERSHON, S., HALPERN, F.S., and SACHAR, E.J.: Suppression of prolactin by dopamine agonists in schizophrenics and controls. *Am. J. Psychiat.*, 135:949-951, 1978.

106. VAN PRAAG, H.M., and KORF, J.: Importance of dopamine metabolism for clinical effects and side effects of neuroleptics. *Am. J. Psychiat.*, 133:1171-1177, 1976.

107. SACHAR, E.J.: Neuroendocrine responses to psychotropic drugs. In M.A. Lipton, A. DiMascio, and K.F. Killam (Eds.), *Psychopharmacology: A Generation of Progress*. New York, Raven, 1978, pp. 499-507.

108. MELTZER, H.Y., GOODE, D.J., and FANG, V.S.: The effect of psychotropic drugs on endocrine function. I. neuroleptics, precursors and agonists. In M.A. Lipton, A. DiMascio, and K.F. Killam (Eds.), *Psychopharmacology: A Generation of Progress*. New York: Raven, 1978, pp. 509-529.

109. COOPER, T.B.: Plasma level monitoring of antipsychotic drugs. *Clin. Pharmacokinet.*, 3:14-38, 1978.

110. RUBIN, R.T., POLAND, R.E., O'CONNOR, D., GOUIN, P.R., and TOWER, B.B.: Selective neuroendocrine effects of low-dose haloperidol in normal adult men. *Psychopharmacol.*, 47:135-140, 1976.

111. MELTZER, H.Y., and FANG, V.: The effect of neuroleptics on serum prolactin in schizophrenic patients. *Arch. Gen. Psychiat.*, 33:279-286, 1976.

112. GRUEN, P.H., SACHAR, E.J., ALTMAN, N., LANGER, G., TABRIZI, M.A., and HALPERN, F.S.: Relation of plasma prolactin to clinical response in schizophrenic patients. *Arch. Gen. Psychiat.*, 35: 1222-1227, 1978.

113. WISTEDT, B., WILES, D., and KOLAKOWSKA, T.: Slow decline of plasma drug and prolactin levels after discontinuation of chronic treatment with depot neuroleptics. *Lancet*, i:1163, 1981.

114. MAY, P.R.A., VAN PUTTEN, T., YALE, C., POTEPAN, P., JENDEN, D.J., FAIRCHILD, M.D., GOLDSTEIN, M.J., and DIXON, W.J.: Predicting individual responses to drug treatment in schizophrenia: A test dose model. *J. Nerv. Ment. Dis.*, 162:177-183, 1976.

115. HAYS, S.E., and RUBIN, R.T.: Variability of prolactin response to intravenous and intramuscular haloperidol in normal adult men. *Psychopharmacol.*, 61:17-24, 1979.

116. MURPHY, D.L., and WYATT, R.J.: Reduced monoamine oxidase activity in blood platelets from schizophrenic patients. *Nature*, 238:225-226, 1972.

117. WYATT, R.J., POTKIN, S.G., and MURPHY, D.L.: Platelet monoamine oxidase activity in schizophrenia: A review of the data. *Am. J. Psychiat.*, 136:377-385, 1979.

118. BUCHSBAUM, M.S., COURSEY, R.D., and MURPHY, D.L.: Schizophrenia and platelet monoamine oxidase: Research strategies. *Schiz. Bull.*, 6:375-384, 1980.

119. BELMAKER, R.H., BRACHA, H.S., and EBSTEIN, R.P.: Platelet monoamine oxidase in affective illness and alcoholism. *Schiz. Bull.*, 6: 320-323, 1980.

120. BUCHSBAUM, M.S., COURSEY, R.D., and MURPHY, D.L.: The biochemical high risk paradigm: Behavioral and familial correlates of low platelet monoamine oxidase activity. *Science*, 194:339-341, 1976.

121. BOWERS, M.B.: Biochemical processes in schizophrenia: An update. *Schiz. Bull.*, 6:393-403, 1980.

122. SCHILDKRAUT, J.J., HERZOG, J.M., and ORSULAK, P.J.: Reduced platelet MAO activity in a subgroup of schizophrenic patients. *Am. J. Psychiat.*, 133:438-440, 1976.

123. POTKIN, S.G., CANNON, H.E., MURPHY, D.L., and WYATT, R.J.: Are paranoid schizophrenics biologically different from other schizophrenics? *New Engl. J. Med.*, 298:61-66, 1978.

124. ORSULAK, P.J., SCHILDKRAUT, J.J., SCHATZBERG, A.F., and HERZOG, J.M.: Differences in platelet MAO activity in subgroups of schizophrenic and depressive disorders. *Biol. Psychiat.*, 13:637-647, 1978.

125. MELTZER, H.Y.: Serum creatine phosphokinase in schizophrenia. *Am. J. Psychiat.*, 133:192-196, 1976.

126. BLOOM, F., SEGAL, D., LING, N., and GUILLEMIN, R.: Endorphins: Profound behavioral effects in rats suggest new etiological factors in mental illness. *Science*, 195:630-632, 1976.

127. GUNNE, L.M., LINDSTROM, L., and TERENIUS, L.: Naloxone-induced reversal of schizophrenic hallucinations. *J. Neural Trans.*, 40:13-19, 1977.

128. WATSON, S.J., BERGER, P.A., and AKIL, H.: Effects of naloxone on schizophrenia: Reduction in hallucinations in a subpopulation of schizophrenics. *Science*, 201:73-76, 1978.

129. DAVIS, G.C., BUNNEY, W.E., and DEFRAITES, E.G.: Intravenous naloxone administration in schizophrenia and affective illness. *Science*, 197:74-77, 1977.

130. GERNER, R.H., CATLIN, D.H., GORELICK, D.A., HUI, K.K., and LI, C.H.: Beta-endorphin: Intravenous infusion causes behavioral change in psychiatric inpatients. *Arch. Gen. Psychiat.*, 37:642-647, 1980.

131. BERGER, P.A., WATSON, S.J., AKIL, H., ELLIOT, G.R., RUBIN, R.T., PFEFFERBAUM, A., DAVIS, K.L., BARCHAS, J.L., and LI, C.H.: Beta-endorphin and schizophrenia. *Arch. Gen. Psychiat.*, 37:635-640, 1980.

132. VERHOEVEN, W.M.A., VAN PRAAG, H.M., VAN REE, J.M., and DE WIED, D.: Improvement of schizophrenic patients treated with [Des-Tyr[1]]-γ-endorphin (DT-γE). *Arch. Gen. Psychiat.*, 36:294-298, 1979.

133. CASEY, D.E., KORSGAARD, S., GERLACH, J., JØRGENSEN, A., and SIMMELSGAARD, H.: Effect of des-tyrosine-γ-endorphin in tardive dyskinesia. *Arch. Gen. Psychiat.*, 38:158-160, 1981.

134. TAMMINGA, C.A., TIGHE, P.J., CHASE, T.N., DEFRAITES, E.G., and SCHAFFER, M.H.: Des-tyrosine-γ-endorphin administration in chronic schizophrenics: A preliminary report. *Arch. Gen. Psychiat.*, 38:167-168, 1981.

135. PALMOUR, R.M., ERVIN, F.R., and WAGEMAKER, H.: Characterization of a peptide from the serum of psychiatric patients. In E. Usdin, W.E. Bunney, and N.S. Kline (Eds.), *Endorphins in Mental Health Research*. New York: Oxford University Press, 1979, pp. 581-593.

136. LEWIS, R.V., GERBER, L.D., STEIN, S., STEPHEN, R.L., GROSSER, B.I., VELICK, S.F., and UDENFRIEND, S.: On β_H-leu[5]-endorphin and schizophrenia. *Arch. Gen. Psychiat.*, 36:237-239, 1979.

137. SCHULZ, S.C., VAN KAMMEN, D.P., BALOW, J.E., FLYE, M.W., and BUNNEY, W.E. Jr.: Dialysis in schizophrenia: A double-blind evaluation. *Science*, 211:1066-1068, 1981.

138. WEINBERGER, D.R., TORREY, E.F., NEOPHYTIDES, A.N., and WYATT, R.J.: Lateral cerebral ventricular enlargement in chronic schizophrenia. *Arch. Gen. Psychiat.*, 36:735-739, 1979.

139. GOLDEN, C.J., MOSES, J.A., ZELAZOWSKI, R., GRABER, B., ZATZ, L.M., HORVATH, T.B., and BERGER, P.A.: Cerebral ventricular size and neuropsychological impairment in young chronic schizophrenics: Measurement by the standardized Luria-Nebraska neuropsychological battery. *Arch. Gen. Psychiat.*, 37:619-623, 1980.

140. WEINBERGER, D.R., BIGELOW, L.B., KLIENMAN, J.E., KLEIN, S.T., ROSENBLATT, J.E., and WYATT, R.J.: Cerebral ventricular enlargement in chronic schizophrenia: An association with poor response to treatment. *Arch. Gen. Psychiat.*, 37:11-13, 1980.

141. WEINBERGER, D.R., TORREY, E.F., NEOPHYTIDES, A.N., and WYATT, R.J.: Structural abnormalities in the cerebral cortex of chronic schizophrenic patients. *Arch. Gen. Psychiat.*, 36:935-939, 1979.

142. BUCHSBAUM, M.S.: Neurophysiological aspects of the schizophrenic syndrome. In L. Bellak (Ed.), *Disorders of the Schizophrenic Syndrome*. New York, Basic Books, 1979, pp. 152-180.

143. ITIL, T.M.: Qualitative and quantitative EEG findings in schizophrenia. *Schiz. Bull.*, 3:61-79, 1977.

144. CROW, T.J.: Molecular pathology of schizophrenia: More than one disease process? *Br. Med. J.*, 280:66-68, 1980.

Part II

PSYCHOPHARMACOLOGICAL ADVANCES

4

Laboratory Tests for Discriminating Subtypes of Depressive Disorders Based on Measurements of Catecholamine Metabolism

Joseph J. Schildkraut, M.D., Paul J. Orsulak, Ph.D., Alan F. Schatzberg, M.D., John J. Mooney, M.D., Alan H. Rosenbaum, M.D., Jon E. Gudeman, M.D., and Jonathan O. Cole, M.D.

The biological heterogeneity of depressive disorders was discussed in an early review of the catecholamine hypothesis of affective disorders (1), where it was noted that various alterations in catecholamine metabolism might be of importance in the pathophysiology of certain types of depressions. From the outset, it was recognized that this focus on catecholamine metabolism was, at best, a reductionistic oversimplification of an extremely complex biological state (which undoubtedly involved abnormalities in many other neurotransmitter or neuromodulator systems, as well as endocrine changes and other biochemical abnormalities). Nonetheless, the possibility that different subgroups of patients with depressive disorders might be characterized by differences in the metabolism of norepinephrine and the physiology of noradrenergic neuronal systems, including alterations in noradrenergic receptor sensitivity, was suggested more than 15

This work was supported in part by Grant No. MH15413 from the National Institute of Mental Health.

years ago (1). Since that time, studies by our research group (2-8), as well as by other investigators, have provided data supporting this possibility, and this literature has been reviewed recently (9).

Since the late 1960s, it has been acknowledged that urinary 3-methoxy-4-hydroxyphenylglycol (MHPG) is a major metabolite of norepinephrine (NE) originating in the brain (10-12). While urinary MHPG may also derive in part from the peripheral sympathetic nervous system, and the fraction of urinary MHPG deriving from norepinephrine originating in the brain remains uncertain (13-15), it has been noted that even if most urinary MHPG were derived from peripheral sources, MHPG levels might nonetheless be of value in exploring the pathophysiology of depressions, in defining subgroups of depressive disorders, and in predicting differential responses to various antidepressant drugs.

URINARY MHPG LEVELS IN BIPOLAR MANIC-DEPRESSIVE DISORDERS

In longitudinal studies of patients with naturally occurring or amphetamine-induced bipolar manic-depressive episodes, many investigators have found that levels of urinary MHPG were lower during periods of depression and higher during periods of mania or hypomania than during periods of remission (16-23). All depressed patients, however, do not excrete comparably low levels of MHPG (24,25). Consequently, a number of investigators have explored the possibility that urinary levels of MHPG as well as other catecholamine metabolites might provide a biochemical basis for differentiating among the depressive disorders.

Our research group initially reported that urinary MHPG levels were significantly lower in bipolar manic-depressive depressions than in patients with unipolar nonendogenous chronic characterological depressions (26,27), and the finding of reduced urinary MHPG levels in patients with bipolar manic-depressive depressions has been confirmed by a number of laboratories in addition to ours (2,3,28-34). Of particular interest is the finding of one of these studies (31) which showed that when the peripheral contribution to urinary MHPG was reduced with carbidopa (a decarboxylase inhibitor that does not cross the blood/brain barrier), the differences in urinary MHPG levels in bipolar manic-depressive depressions and control subjects became more pronounced and statistically significant.

In contrast to the reduction in urinary MHPG levels in patients with bipolar manic-depressive depressions when compared with values in unipolar depressions, there were no differences in urinary 3-methoxy-4-hydroxymandelic acid (VMA) levels (2,6). This is of importance, since reports that circulating MHPG may be converted to VMA (14,15) raised questions concerning the specific value of urinary MHPG (e.g., in contrast to VMA) as an index of norepinephrine metabolism in the brain or as a biochemical marker in studies of depressed patients.

URINARY MHPG LEVELS IN
UNIPOLAR DEPRESSIVE DISORDERS

In contrast to the relatively consistent findings showing that patients with bipolar manic-depressive depressions have low urinary MHPG levels, consistent findings have not been obtained in studies of patients with unipolar depressions in whom low (29,35-37), normal (30,32,33), or high (38) urinary MHPG levels have been reported. Diagnostic heterogeneity may account for these discrepancies, since previously reported findings from our laboratory (2) revealed a wide range of urinary MHPG levels in patients with unipolar depressive disorders, and these findings have been confirmed and extended in our more recent investigations. In that previously reported series of 16 patients with unipolar endogenous depressions, the mean value of urinary MHPG was 1950 μg/24 hours (2). And in a subsequent study of an enlarged sample of 70 patients (6), 26 of the 50 patients with unipolar depressions had urinary MHPG levels > 1950 μg/24 hours, while only three of the 20 patients with bipolar manic-depressive or schizoaffective depressions (identified according to clinical criteria described in reference 2) had MHPG levels > 1950 μg/24 hours (chi square = 6.6; p < .025).

A scatter plot of MHPG levels in this series of 70 depressed patients revealed a natural break in MHPG levels around 2500 μg/24 hours, suggesting the possible existence of a subgroup of unipolar depressions with MHPG levels > 2500 μg/24 hours. For example, in this series, 17 of 50 patients with unipolar depressions had urinary MHPG levels > 2500 μg/24 hours, while only one of the 20 patients with bipolar manic-depressive or schizoaffective depressions had MHPG levels > 2500 μg/24 hours (chi square = 4.9; p < .05).

Thus, the data from this series of patients with unipolar depressive disorders further substantiate the biochemical heterogeneity of unipolar depressions, demonstrating that some patients have low MHPG levels (comparable to values seen in the bipolar manic-depressive or schizoaffective depressions), while others have high MHPG levels (sometimes higher than control values), and still others have MHPG levels in an intermediate range. However, it should be stressed that urinary MHPG levels in most depressed patients (including unipolar, bipolar, and schizoaffective depressions) fall within the broad range of values observed in normal control subjects (6,39). Thus, while urinary MHPG levels may help to differentiate among subtypes of depressive disorders once a clinical diagnosis of depression has been made, urinary MHPG levels cannot be used to make a diagnosis of depression per se.

In support of these findings, data on the distribution of urinary MHPG levels in a series of 102 patients with unipolar major depressive disorders revealed a clustering of patients with urinary MHPG levels above 2500 μg/24 hours, in addition to clusters occurring at lower MHPG levels (40). Moreover, the distribution of pretreatment urinary MHPG levels in an independent series of more than 200 patients with unipolar major depressive disorders, included in a collaborative multicenter study of urinary MHPG levels as predictors of responses to oxaprotiline (BA49802), amitriptyline or placebo (coordinated by Mark Roffman, Ph.D. of Ciba-Geigy in conjunction with our laboratory), revealed a similar pattern with a clustering of depressed patients having urinary MHPG levels > 2500 μg/24 hours. In contrast, a comparable discrete clustering (i.e., peaking) of values > 2500 μg/24 hours, with relatively few values between 2300 and 2500 μg/24 hours, was not observed when urinary MHPG levels were examined in a comparison series of more than 100 control subjects.

The existence of a biologically meaningful subgroup of unipolar depressions with elevated urinary MHPG levels is also supported by our findings in a study of patients with very severe unipolar depressions (8), which revealed a subgroup of patients with very high urinary MHPG levels (> 2500 μg/24 hours) who also had very high levels of urinary-free cortisol (UFC > 200 μg/24 hours). To rule out the possibility that the high UFC and urinary MHPG levels observed in this series of severely depressed patients might be secondary to anxiety, we studied urinary MHPG and UFC levels in patients with moderate to severe anxiety states, and did not observe comparably elevated MHPG levels or markedly elevated UFC levels (> 200 μg/24 hours) in these patients with anxiety disorders. However, the very high UFC levels observed in our series of severely depressed patients might be related to the severity of the depression, since preliminary data from a study of UFC levels in patients with less severe depressions revealed few patients with markedly elevated UFC levels (41).

One possibility that might explain our finding of a subgroup of severely depressed patients with high urinary MHPG levels and markedly elevated UFC levels is that in these patients high urinary MHPG and UFC levels may occur as a secondary response to an increase in cholinergic activity. This possibility is consistent with the hypothesis that central cholinergic factors may play a role in the etiology of depressive disorders (42-44), and is particularly intriguing in view of the findings of other investigators that:

1) physostigmine, an anticholinesterase, and other pharmacological agents which increase brain cholinergic activity exacerbate depressive symptoms in depressed patients (42,45) and induce depressive symptoms in normal controls (46);

2) physostigmine produces an increase in plasma cortisol levels in normal controls (46);

3) physostigmine can overcome suppression of the hypothalamic-pituitary-adrenocortical axis by dexamethasone in normal subjects, thereby mimicking the abnormal escape from dexamethasone suppression seen in some patients who show cortisol hypersecretion (47); and

4) physostigmine produces an increase in cerebrospinal fluid levels of MHPG in normal subjects (48).

Thus, the markedly elevated UFC levels that we have observed in some patients with severe unipolar depressive disorders could result from an increase in cholinergic activity, and the elevated urinary MHPG levels in these patients could represent a secondary noradrenergic response to such cholinergic hyperactivity. This formulation suggests the possibility that the anticholinergic effects of certain antidepressant drugs may contribute to their antidepressant effects in patients with this subtype of depressive disorder.

Thus, the findings of our recent studies further substantiate the biochemical heterogeneity of the unipolar depressive disorders, and suggest that there may be at least three subtypes of unipolar depressions that can be discriminated on the basis of differences in urinary MHPG levels. Subtype I, with low pretreatment urinary MHPG levels, may have low norepinephrine output as the result of a decrease in norepinephrine synthesis or a decrease in its release from noradrenergic neurons. In contrast, Subtype II, with intermediate urinary MHPG levels, may have normal norepinephrine output but abnormalities in other biochemical systems. And Subtype III, with high urinary MHPG levels, may have high norepinephrine output in response to alterations in noradrenergic receptors and/or to an increase in cholinergic activity as described above. Further studies will be required and are currently in progress to confirm these findings and to explore the possible pathophysiological abnormalities that may be associated with these subtypes of unipolar depressive disorders.

Urinary MHPG Levels as Predictors of Differential Responses to Antidepressant Drugs

Studies from a number of laboratories have indicated that pretreatment levels of urinary MHPG may aid in predicting responses to certain tricyclic and tetracyclic antidepressant drugs. Specifically, depressed patients with "low" pretreatment urinary MHPG levels have been found to respond more favorably to treatment with imipramine (5,25,49-53), desipramine (25), nortriptyline (54), or maprotiline (4,53), than do patients with "high" MHPG levels. In contrast, some studies (49,51,55,56) have found that depressed patients with "high" pretreatment levels of urinary MHPG respond more favorably to treatment with amitriptyline than do patients with lower MHPG levels, but this has not been observed in all studies (57-60). Further research will clearly be required to account for these differences in findings. Nevertheless, it should be stressed that the findings of these studies do point to differences between amitriptyline and imipramine, in that low pretreatment urinary MHPG levels have been shown to predict more favorable responses to imipramine in many studies, whereas this has not been found in any of the studies of amitriptyline.

Our recently published prospective studies have confirmed that patients with relatively low urinary MHPG levels ($\leq$ 1950 μg/24 hours) respond more favorably to treatment with imipramine or maprotiline than do patients with higher MHPG levels (4,5). Since our findings (described above) suggested that there may be at least three subtypes of unipolar depressive disorders that could be discriminated on the basis of differences in pretreatment urinary MHPG levels (6), data from these two studies of pretreatment urinary MHPG levels as predictors of responses to imipramine and maprotiline were combined in order to provide us with a large enough series of patients to compare treatment responses in these three subtypes. While further studies in a larger series of patients will be required for confirmation (and are currently in progress), our findings suggest that depressed patients with elevated MHPG levels (> 2500 μg/24 hours) may be more responsive to treatment with imipramine or maprotiline than are patients with intermediate MHPG levels (1951-2500 μg/24 hours), though neither group is as responsive to these drugs as are patients with low pretreatment urinary MHPG levels ($\leq$ 1950 μg/24 hours). Moreover, as described in a recently published paper (4), we observed that patients with low pretreatment urinary MHPG levels responded rapidly to relatively low doses of maprotiline, whereas those patients with higher MHPG levels, who responded to maprotiline, required significantly higher doses and longer periods of drug administration.

The complex effects on noradrenergic, dopaminergic, and other neurotransmitter systems, including alterations in various indices of presynaptic and postsynaptic receptor functions that are observed after chronic administration of various antidepressant drugs (61-70), suggest that specific empirical trials will be required to assess the value of urinary MHPG levels, or any other biochemical measure, as clinically useful predictors of responses to a specific antidepressant drug. For example, it has recently been reported that patients with normal or high urinary MHPG levels who show suppression of cortisol in response to dexamethasone respond favorably to treatment with mianserin, whereas patients with low urinary MHPG levels whose cortisol secretion is not suppressed by dexamethasone do not respond to mianserin (71).

APPLICATION OF MULTIVARIATE DISCRIMINANT
FUNCTION ANALYSIS TO DATA
ON URINARY CATECHOLAMINES AND
METABOLITES IN DEPRESSED PATIENTS

Although MHPG was the only catecholamine metabolite that showed a pronounced difference when values in bipolar manic-depressive depressions and unipolar nonendogenous chronic characterological depressions were compared in our early studies (2), multivariate discriminant function analysis was used to explore the possibility that other catecholamine metabolites—including VMA, normetanephrine (NMN) and metanephrine (MN)—might provide further information that would aid in differentiating among subtypes of depressions (3). By applying stepwise multivariate discriminant function analysis to data on urinary catecholamines and metabolites, we generated an empirically derived equation that provided an even more precise discrimination between bipolar manic-depressive and unipolar nonendogenous chronic characterological depressions than did urinary MHPG alone. In generating this equation, a metric was established so that low scores were related to patients with bipolar manic-depressive depressions, whereas high scores were related to patients with unipolar nonendogenous depressions. Preliminary validation of this equation was then obtained in a sample of patients whose data had not been used in the derivation of the equation (3). This discrimination equation for computing the Depression-type (D-type) score was of the form:

$$\text{D-type score} = C_1(\text{MHPG}) - C_2(\text{VMA}) + C_3(\text{NE}) - C_4\frac{(\text{NMN} + \text{MN})}{\text{VMA}} + C_0$$

While this discrimination equation was generated mathematically to provide the best least squares fit of the data (and the terms were not selected by the investigators), the inclusion of VMA as well as other urinary catecholamines and metabolites (of peripheral origin) in this empirically derived equation may be correcting for that fraction of urinary MHPG that comes from peripheral sources rather than from the brain (3).

As described in a paper published several years ago (3), to evaluate the contribution of each of the terms in this 4-term discrimination equation, we derived discrimination equations based on 1-, 2-, and 3-, as well as on 4-, terms using the biochemical data obtained from the initial series of patients with bipolar manic-depressive and unipolar nonendogenous depressions which had been used to derive the 4-term discrimination equation. D-type scores based on these equations were then generated for a series of depressed patients in the validation sample whose biochemical data had not been used to derive the equations.

D-type scores in the patients with bipolar manic-depressive and schizoaffective depressions were then compared to the scores in patients with unipolar nonendogenous depressions using the 1-, 2-, 3-, and 4-term discrimination equations. The 1-term equation based on MHPG alone tended to separate these groups with some overlap; the 2-term equation based on MHPG and VMA provided a better discrimination between the groups but some overlap remained; the 3-term equation based on MHPG, VMA and NE removed all overlap between the two groups; and the 4-term equation based on MHPG, VMA, NE, and (NMN + MN)/VMA improved on the discrimination by providing a very wide separation of the D-type scores in these two groups without any overlap. It should be reemphasized that these groups were composed only of patients from the validation sample whose biochemical data had not been used to derive these equations (3).

We have subsequently obtained D-type scores on more than 80 additional depressed patients whose data were not used in the original derivation of this equation (i.e., in selecting the terms and determining the coefficients and constant) or in its preliminary validation (as described above). In the light of our finding that patients with unipolar depressive disorders appear to be biochemically heterogeneous with respect to urinary MHPG levels, we were particularly interested in the distribution of D-type scores in the newly studied patients with unipolar depressions diagnosed according to our system of classification on the basis of clinical histories and presenting signs and symptoms (2). Recent analyses of these data showed that the D-type scores (computed using the original D-type equation with the previously derived coefficients and constant) segregated these newly studied patients with unipolar depressions into two widely separated groupings—one with D-type scores < 0.5—i.e., in the range of values comparable to that previously observed in bipolar manic-depressive depressions (3), and another with considerably higher D-type scores.

A similar separation of depressed patients with D-type scores <0.5 was observed in patients with non-schizotypal unipolar major depressive disorders diagnosed according to the Research Diagnostic Criteria (RDC) (72). Analysis of these data showed that this separation was not evident when MHPG levels alone (or scores on the 1-term D-type equation that is based solely on MHPG levels) were examined, whereas scores on the 4-term D-type equation clearly delineated a clustering of patients with low D-type scores (<0.5). These analyses also showed that all but one of the patients with urinary MHPG levels >2500 μg/24 hours had D-type scores >0.9.

On the basis of earlier findings, we had hypothesized that low D type scores in patients with so-called "unipolar" depressions might aid in the identification of those patients having latent bipolar disorders even prior to the first clinical episode of mania or hypomania. Consistent with this hypothesis, pilot follow-up data from our studies have shown that a number of the patients with an initial diagnosis of "unipolar" depression who had low D-type scores (in the range usually seen in bipolar manic-depressive depressions), when they were initially studied, went on to develop their first manic, hypomanic, or schizoaffective psychotic episode several months to several years after their biochemical studies were completed. Thus, our findings suggest that low D-type scores can predict subsequent occurrences of manic or manic-like episodes even in the absence of a history of prior manic episodes.

Relatively few patients with typical bipolar manic-depressive depressions could be included in our recent studies, since most patients with this diagnosis now receive maintenance lithium treatment, which ethically could not be discontinued to study such patients biochemically. However, many of the patients in this newly studied series had depressive disorders that could not be assigned unambiguously to one of the diagnostic categories in our classification system, usually due to the presence of clinical features suggesting the possibility of a bipolar disorder or a schizophrenia-related disorder (with chronic asocial, eccentric, or bizarre behavior). The distribution of D-type scores in a series of 37 patients with such diagnostically unclassifiable depressions was significantly different from that observed in patients with unipolar depressions. Moreover, in contrast to the findings in patients with unipolar depressions, the D-type scores in these diagnostically unclassifiable depressions were not separated into discrete clusters.

In this series of patients with diagnostically unclassifiable depressive disorders, we were particularly interested in exploring the hypothesis that patients with low D-type scores would show clinical features suggestive of a bipolar disorder even though the clinical diagnosis of a definite bipolar disorder could not be made in these patients. In support of this hypothesis, we found that of the eight diagnostically unclassifiable depressed patients with lowest D-type scores, seven met the criteria for at least a probable bipolar disorder in our classification system, and at least a probable bipolar I or bipolar II diagnosis according to the RDC. In contrast, of the 29 remaining patients with diagnostically unclassifiable depressions, only seven showed comparable evidence for bipolarity (chi square = 8.2; p < .01).

To evaluate the contributions of each of the terms in this 4-term discrimination equation, in separating out the subgroup of patients with probable bipolar disorders who had low D-type scores from the larger group of unclassifiable depressions, we used the discrimination equations, based on 1-term (MHPG), 2-term (MHPG and VMA), 3-term (MHPG, VMA, and NE), as well as the 4-term, discrimination equation, all of which had been previously generated using a separate body of data, as described above. A graphic plot revealed that the D-type scores of patients who did not meet the criteria for probable bipolar disorders gradually shifted upward with the addition of each successive term. However, identification of a discrete subgroup of patients with low D-type scores having probable bipolar disorders was only achieved by the 4-term D-type equation.

Preliminary data from our ongoing studies also suggest that D-type scores may provide even more accurate predictors of responses to treatment with imipramine or maprotiline than do urinary MHPG levels. For example, several patients in our studies who had urinary MHPG levels ≤ 1950 μg/24 hours, but who failed to respond to imipramine or maprotiline, were found to have high D-type scores (despite their relatively low levels of urinary MHPG). Further studies are currently in progress to elucidate the pathophysiological implications of the D-type equation and to explore its practical clinical applications.

In regard to the possible pathophysiological implications, several years ago we suggested that the fourth term—the ratio (NMN + MN)/VMA—might be inversely related to MAO activity, since the O-methylated metabolites, NMN and MN, could be converted to VMA by deamination (3). Indeed, such an inverse correlation has recently been documented between this ratio—(NMN + MN)/VMA—and platelet MAO activity, in a series of 90 patients in whom we obtained concurrent measurements ($r = -.29$; $p < .005$). In addition to confirming that this fourth term of the D-type equation is related to platelet MAO activity, this correlation (although modest) also suggests that measurement of platelet MAO activity may provide functionally relevant information with respect to monoamine metabolism, in that it relates in a logical way to a ratio of levels of nondeaminated:deaminated urinary catecholamine metabolites.

STUDIES OF MONOAMINERGIC RECEPTORS
AND RELATED MEASURES IN
DEPRESSED PATIENTS

It has been proposed that patients with affective disorders may show alterations in the sensitivity of one or another type of monoaminergic receptor (1,73,74). Many antidepressant drugs have been found to alter the sensitivity of various neurotransmitter or neuromodulator receptors in brain after chronic treatment (61-70,75-78), and the changes in receptor function coincide with the time course of clinical improvement during antidepressant therapy. Pharmacological challenges producing peripheral effects (such as changes in blood pressure) and neuroendocrine responses (such as release of cortisol or growth hormone), which are under central control mechanisms, have been undertaken to clarify both the central noradrenergic receptor function (62,79) and relationships between central cholinergic, noradrenergic, and other neurotransmitter or neuromodulator systems (44,80,81). These results suggest that alterations in receptor sensitivity may play a role in both the pathophysiology of the depressive disorders and the mechanisms of action of various antidepressant drugs.

Adrenergic receptors on human blood cells have been suggested as a readily available source of material for the study of adrenergic receptors in psychiatric patients (82). β-adrenergic receptors have been identified on leukocytes (83,84), and one group of investigators (85) found the specific binding of the β-adrenergic antagonist, ^{3}H-dihydroalprenolol to lymphocytes, was decreased in depressed and manic patients when compared to control subjects and euthymic patients. Moreover, β-adrenergic-receptor-mediated stimulation of cAMP production by isoproteronol was reduced in leukocytes (86) and lymphocytes (85) from depressed patients. While it has been cautioned that the decreased β-adrenergic receptor function in lymphocytes from depressed patients may reflect homeostatic regulation of peripheral β-adrenergic receptors in response to increases in plasma catecholamines (85), β-adrenergic stimulants (e.g., salbutamol) have been reported to be rapidly effective in the treatment of depressed patients (87).

Human platelets possess α_2-adrenergic receptors (88,89) which suppress the activity of platelet adenylate cyclase (90,91). Neither basal (92) nor α-adrenergic-receptor-mediated suppression of prostaglandin-stimulated cAMP production (93,94) has been found to be altered in platelets in depressed patients. However, depressed patients have been reported to have greater platelet α_2-receptor numbers than control subjects in several recent studies (95-98), but not in all (99). This discrepancy could possibly reflect differences in platelet α_2-adrenergic receptors across subgroups of depressed patients.

^{3}H-imipramine binds to high affinity sites in brain (100-102), and platelets (102-105), and cellular uptake regulation sites for serotonin have been labeled with ^{3}H-imipramine (100,104,106). A highly significant decrease in the number of ^{3}H-imipramine binding sites with no significant change in the apparent affinity constant was observed in platelets from depressed patients compared with those from control subjects (102,107,108). Decreased platelet serotonin uptake has been observed in patients with depressive disorders (109-111), and it has been proposed that decreased platelet ^{3}H-imipramine binding observed in depressed patients may reflect a deficiency in the platelet serotonin transport mechanism in these patients (108).

Research ongoing in our laboratory during the past several years has enabled us to develop and refine a blood fractionation and platelet homogenization procedure which provides high yields of platelet membrane vesicles as well as free intact platelet mitochondria from relatively small clinically obtainable blood samples (112-114). Using this procedure, we have isolated partially purified platelet membrane vesicles containing both α_2-adrenergic receptors and membrane-bound adenylate cyclase, which is coupled to prostaglandin receptors and receptors for α_2-adrenergic agonists (114). We have examined and compared the binding of adrenergic agonists, partial agonists, and antagonists using this membrane preparation, and we have also studied the regulation by monovalent cations and guanine neucleotides of 1) α_2-adrenergic agonists (both high and low affinity) and antagonist binding to platelet membranes, and 2) platelet membrane adenylate cyclase activity (114). This preparative procedure also enables us to isolate leukocytes and measure β-adrenergic receptor binding for agonist and antagonist ligands, as well as β-adrenergic-stimulated adenylate cyclase activity in the leukocytes from these same blood specimens.

We are currently beginning to apply these procedures to studies of adrenergic receptor functions in patients with various subtypes of depressive disorders examined before and after treatment with antidepressant drugs. In particular, we shall be testing the hypothesis that there will be differences in the properties of platelet α_2-adrenergic receptors and/or leukocyte β-adrenergic receptors when groups of depressed patients with low and high urinary MHPG levels (or low and high D-type scores) are compared.

STUDIES OF POSSIBLE ANIMAL MODELS OF SUBTYPES OF DEPRESSIVE DISORDERS

For many years our laboratory has been interested in the development of possible biochemical models of various subtypes of depressive disorders (115). Recent findings from our laboratory now suggest that two specific paradigms in the rat may be biochemically analogous to two of the biochemical subgroups of depressive disorders identified in our clinical studies (116). The amphetamine withdrawal state in the rat, which we have found to be associated with decreases in the sensitivity to intracranial reinforcement (117) and decreases in brain levels of MHPG (118), may provide an animal model for the subgroup of depressive disorders characterized biochemically by low levels of urinary MHPG or low D-type scores (e.g., bipolar manic-depressive or schizoaffective depressions as well as one of the subtypes of unipolar depressions, as described above). In contrast, the "learned helplessness" or "inactivity" state in the rat, which we have found to be associated with high brain levels of MHPG (119,120), may provide an animal model for the subtype of unipolar depression, described above, that is characterized by high levels of urinary MHPG or high D-type scores. In regard to this environmentally induced animal model, it is of interest that preliminary analysis of our clinical data shows patients with high D-type scores to have a higher incidence of situational or secondary depressions than patients with low D-type scores.

Such animal models will permit us and other investigators to undertake essential biochemical, physiological, and neuropharmacological studies that could not possibly be performed in human subjects. Moreover, these studies in animals

(119, 120) suggest the possibility that changes in norepinephrine metabolism, resulting from stressful environmental experiences during the course of development, may interact with genetically determined biological systems within the brain to alter the sensitivity of the organism to stress-related events, its ability to cope with stresses, and its vulnerability to stress-related medical or psychiatric disorders—including specific subtypes of depressions.

PRACTICAL CLINICAL APPLICATIONS OF THIS RESEARCH AND THE DEVELOPMENT OF THE PSYCHIATRIC CHEMISTRY LABORATORY

For several years our research laboratory provided collaborating physicians with determinations of urinary MHPG levels, as well as other relevant biochemical measurements, for use in their clinical practices. However, the number of requests soon became overwhelming, and in 1977, in cooperation with the Department of Pathology at the New England Deaconess Hospital, our group established the Psychiatric Chemistry Laboratory as a model academic clinical laboratory facility for the integration and translation of biochemical research into clinical psychiatric practice (121). In addition to providing specialized clinical laboratory tests for use in psychiatry, an explicit aim of the Psychiatric Chemistry Laboratory has been to provide consultation and educational services to assist physicians in using and interpreting these tests.

In summary, we have now reached a point where the clinical laboratory can be used in psychiatry, as it is in other fields of medicine, both to assist in making more specific diagnoses and to aid in prescribing more effective forms of treatment. For example, one may draw an analogy between the pneumonias and the depressions, in that both are disorders diagnosed on the basis of clinical data. In the case of pneumonias, the physician makes a diagnosis on the basis of history and physical examination (including the chest X-ray). Having made the diagnosis, sputum cultures can then be obtained from the clinical laboratory to aid in determining the specific type of pneumonia that the patient may have, and the specific antibiotic or other forms of treatment that may be most effective. Similarly in the case of depressions, the physician diagnoses depression on the basis of clinical history coupled with physical and mental status examinations. Having made a diagnosis of depression, a physician can then use clinical laboratory tests to obtain further information to assist in determining the type of depression the patient may have, and the forms of treatment most likely to be effective in the care of that patient.

While none of the biochemical tests we have today will insure that the physician can select a clinically effective treatment on the first trial, the use of these clinical laboratory tests can increase the probability of doing so. Considering the time it takes for antidepressant drugs to exert their clinical effects, even a small increase in the percentage of patients who receive an effective drug on the first clinical trial would represent a major advance in the treatment of patients with depressive disorders.

REFERENCES

1. SCHILDKRAUT, J.J.: The catecholamine hypothesis of affective disorders: A review of supporting evidence. *Am. J. Psychiat.*, 122:509-522, 1965.
2. SCHILDKRAUT, J.J., ORSULAK, P.J., SCHATZBERG, A.F., GUDEMAN, J.E., COLE, J.O., ROHDE, W.A., and LaBRIE, R.A.: Toward a biochemical classification of depressive disorders I: Differences in urinary MHPG and other catecholamine metabolites in clinically defined subtypes of depressions. *Arch. Gen. Psychiat.*, 35:1427-1433, 1978.
3. SCHILDKRAUT, J.J., ORSULAK, P.J., LaBRIE, R.A., SCHATZBERG, A.F., GUDEMAN, J.E., COLE, J.O., and ROHDE, W.A.: Toward a biochemical classification of depressive disorders II: Application of multivariate discriminant function analysis to data on urinary catecholamines and metabolites. *Arch. Gen. Psychiat.*, 35:1436-1439, 1978.
4. SCHATZBERG, A.F., ROSENBAUM, A.H., ORSULAK, P.J., ROHDE, W.A., MARUTA, T., KRUGER, E.R., COLE, J.O., and SCHILDKRAUT, J.J.: Toward a biochemical classification of depressive disorders III: Pretreatment of urinary MHPG levels as predictors of response to treatment with maprotiline. *Psychopharmacol.*, 75:34-38, 1981.
5. SCHATZBERG, A.F., ORSULAK, P.J., ROSENBAUM, A.H., MARUTA, T., KRUGER, E., COLE, J.O., and SCHILDKRAUT, J.J.: Toward a biochemical classification of depressive disorders IV: Pretreatment urinary MHPG levels as predictors of antidepressant response to imipramine. *Commun. Psychopharmacol.*, 4:441-445, 1890-1981.
6. SCHATZBERG, A.F., ORSULAK, P.J., ROSENBAUM, A.H., MARUTA, T., KRUGER, E.R., COLE, J.O., and SCHILDKRAUT, J.J.: Toward a biochemical classification of depressive disorders V: Heterogeneity of unipolar depressions. *Am. J. Psychiat.*, 139:471-475, 1982.
7. GUDEMAN, J.E., SCHATZBERG, A.F., SAMSON, J.A., ORSULAK, P.J., COLE, J.O., and SCHILDKRAUT, J.J.: Toward a biochemical classification of depressive disorders VI: Platelet MAO activity and clinical symptoms in depressed patients. *Am. J. Psychiat.*, 139:630-633, 1982.
8. ROSENBAUM, A.H., MARUTA, T., SCHATZBERG, A.F., ORSULAK, P.J., JIANG, N-S., COLE, J.O., and SCHILDKRAUT, J.J.: Toward a biochemical classification of depressive disorders VII: Urinary free cortisol and urinary MHPG in depressions. *Am. J. Psychiat.*, in press.
9. SCHILDKRAUT, J.J., ORSULAK, P.J., SCHATZBERG, A.F., and ROSENBAUM, A.H.: The role of norepinephrine in depressive disorders. In: E. Friedman (Ed.), *Depression and Antidepressants*. New York: Raven Press, in press.
10. MAAS, J.W., and LANDIS, D.H.: *In vivo* studies of metabolism of norepinephrine in central nervous system. *J. Pharmacol. Exper. Ther.*, 163:147-162, 1968.

11. SCHANBERG, S.M., BREESE, G.R., SCHILDKRAUT, J.J., GORDON, E.K., and KOPIN, I.J.: 3-Methoxy-4-hydroxyphenylglycol sulfate in brain and cerebrospinal fluid. *Biochem. Pharmacol.*, 17:2006-2008, 1968.

12. SCHANBERG, S.M., SCHILDKRAUT, J.J., BREESE, G.R., and KOPIN, I.J.: Metabolism of normetanephrine-H³ in rat brain—identification of conjugated 3-methoxy-4-hydroxyphenylglycol as major metabolite. *Biochem. Pharmacol.*, 17:247-254, 1968.

13. MAAS, J.W., HATTOX, S.E., GREENE, N.M., and LANDIS, D.H.: 3-Methoxy-4-hydroxyphenethyleneglycol production by human brain *in vivo*. *Science*, 205:1025-1027, 1979.

14. BLOMBERY, P.A., KOPIN, I.J., GORDON, E.K., MARKEY, S.P., and EBERT, M.H. Conversion of MHPG to vanillylmandelic acid. *Arch. Gen. Psychiat.*, 1095-1098, 1980.

15. MARDH, G., SJOQUIST, B., and ANGGARD, E.: Norepinephrine metabolism in man using deuterium labelling: The conversion of 4-hydroxy-3-methoxyphenylglycol to 4-hydroxy-3-methoxy-mandelic acid. *J. Neurochem.*, 36: 1181-1185, 1981.

16. GREENSPAN, K., SCHILDKRAUT, J.J., GORDON, E.K., BAER, L., ARONOFF, M.S., and DURELL, J.: Catecholamine metabolism in affective disorders III. MHPG and other catecholamine metabolites in patients treated with lithium carbonate. *J. Psychiat. Res.*, 7:171-183, 1970.

17. SCHILDKRAUT, J.J., WATSON, R., DRASKOCZY, P.R., and HARTMANN, E.: Amphetamine withdrawal: Depression and MHPG excretion. *Lancet*, II:485-486, 1971.

18. SCHILDKRAUT, J.J., KEELER, B.A., ROGERS, M.P., and DRASKOCZY, P.R.: Catecholamine metabolism in affective disorders: A longitudinal study of a patient treated with amitriptyline and ECT. *Psychosomatic Med.*, 34:470, 1972; plus erratum *Psychosomatic Med.*, 35:274, 1973.

19. WATSON, R., HARTMANN, E., and SCHILDKRAUT, J.J.: Amphetamine withdrawal: Affective state, sleep patterns and MHPG excretion. *Am. J. Psychiat.*, 129:263-269, 1972.

20. BOND, P.A., JENNER, F.A., and SAMPSON, G.A.: Daily variations of the urine content of 3-methoxy-4-hydroxyphenylglycol in two manic-depressive patients. *Psychol. Med.*, 2:81-85, 1972.

21. BOND, P.A., DIMITRAKOUDI, M., HOWLETT, D.R., and JENNER, F.A.: Urinary excretion of the sulfate and glucuronide of 3-methoxy-4-hydroxyphenylethyleneglycol in a manic-depressive patient. *Psychol. Med.*, 5:279-285, 1975.

22. DELEON-JONES, F.D., MAAS, J.W., DEKIRMENJIAN, H., and FAWCETT, J.A.: Urinary catecholamine metabolites during behavioral changes in a patient with manic-depressive cycles. *Science*, 179:300-302, 1973.

23. POST, R.M., STODDARD, F.J., GILLIN, C., BUCHSBAUM, M.S., RUNKLE, D.C., BLACK, K.E., and BUNNEY, W.E., Jr.: Alterations in motor activity, sleep and biochemistry in a cycling manic-depressive patient. *Arch. Gen. Psychiat.*, 34:470-477, 1977.

24. MAAS, J.W., FAWCETT, J.A. and DEKIRMENJIAN, H.: 3-Methoxy-4-hydroxyphenylglycol (MHPG) excretion in depressive states. *Arch. Gen. Psychiat.*, 19:129-134, 1968.

25. MAAS, J.W., FAWCETT, J.A., and DEKIRMENJIAN, H.: Catecholamine metabolism, depressive illness and drug response. *Arch. Gen. Psychiat.*, 26:252-262, 1972.

26. SCHILDKRAUT, J.J., KEELER, B.A., GRAB, E.L., KANTROWICH, J., and HARTMANN,

E.: MHPG excretion and clinical classification in depressive disorders. *Lancet,* I:1251-1252, 1973.

27. SCHILDKRAUT, J.J., KEELER, B.A., PAPOUSEK, M., and HARTMANN, E.: MHPG excretion in depressive disorders: Relation to clinical subtypes and desynchronized sleep. *Science,* 181:762-764, 1973.

28. MAAS, J.W., DEKIRMENJIAN, H., and DELEON-JONES, F.: The identification of depressed patients who have a disorder of norepinephrine metabolism and/or disposition. In: E. Usdin and S. Snyder (Eds.), *Frontiers in Catecholamine Research—Third International Catecholamine Symposium.* New York: Pergamon Press, 1973, pp. 1091-1096.

29. DELEON-JONES, F., MAAS, J.W., DEKIRMENJIAN, H., and SANCHEZ, J.: Diagnostic subgroups of affective disorders and their urinary excretion of catecholamine metabolites. *Am. J. Psychiat.,* 132:1141-1148, 1975.

30. GOODWIN, F.K., and POST, R.M.: Studies of amine metabolites in affective illness and in schizophrenia: A comparative analysis. In: D.X. Freedman (Ed.), *Biology of Major Psychoses.* New York: Raven Press, 1975, pp. 299-332.

31. GARFINKEL, P.E., WARSH, J.H., STANCER, H.C., and GODSE, D.D. CNS monoamine metabolism in bipolar affective disorders. *Arch. Gen. Psychiat.,* 34:735-739, 1977.

32. GOODWIN, F.K., and POTTER, W.Z.: Norepinephrine metabolite studies in affective illness. In: E. Usdin, I. Kopin, and J. Barchas (Eds.), *Catecholamines: Basic and Clinical Frontiers,* Volume Two. New York: Pergamon Press, 1979, pp. 1863-1865.

33. BECKMANN, H., and GOODWIN, F.K.: Urinary MHPG in subgroups of depressed patients and normal controls. *Neuropsychobiol.,* 6:91-100, 1980.

34. EDWARDS, D.J., SPIKER, D.G., NEIL, J.F., KUPFER, D.J., and RIZK, M.: MHPG excretion in depression. *Psychiat. Res.,* 2:295-305, 1980.

35. MAAS, J.W.: Clinical and biochemical heterogeneity of depressive disorders. *Ann. Int. Med.,* 88:556-663, 1978.

36. TAUBE, S.L., KIRSTEIN, L.S., SWEENEY, D.R., HENINGER, G.R., and MAAS, J.W.: Urinary 3-methoxy-4-hydroxyphenylglycol and psychiatric diagnosis. *Am. J. Psychiat.,* 135; 78-82, 1978.

37. CASPER, R.C., DAVIS, J.M., PANDEY, G.N., GARVER, D.L., and DEKIRMENJIAN, H.: Neuroendocrine and amine studies in affective illness. *Psychoneuroendocrinol.,* 2:105-113, 1977.

38. GARFINKEL, P.E., WARSH, J.J., and STANCER, H.C.: Depression: New evidence in support of biological differentiation. *Am. J. Psychiat.,* 136:535-539, 1979.

39. HOLLISTER, L.E., DAVIS, K.L., OVERALL, J.E., and ANDERSON, T.: Excretion of MHPG in normal subjects. Implications for biological classification of affective disorders. *Arch. Gen. Psychiat.,* 35:1410-1415, 1978.

40. SCHILDKRAUT, J.J., ORSULAK, P.J., SCHATZBERG, A.F., COLE, J.O., and ROSENBAUM, A.H.: Biochemical discrimination of depressive disorders based on differences in catecholamine metabolism. In: I. Hanin and E. Usdin (Eds.), *Biological Markers in Psychiatry and Neurology.* New York: Pergamon Press, 1982, pp. 23-33.

41. ROSENBAUM, A.H., MARUTA, T., SCHATZBERG, A.F., ORSULAK, P.J., and SCHILDKRAUT, J.J.: Urinary free cortisol and MHPG levels in anxious patients and normal controls. Paper presented at Society of Biological Psychiatry Annual Meeting, New Orleans, May, 1981.

42. JANOWSKY, D.S., EL-YOUSEF, M., DAVIS, J.M., and SEKERKE, H.J.: A cholinergic-adrenergic hypothesis of mania and depression. *Lancet,* II:632-635, 1972.
43. SITARAM, N., and GILLIN, C.: Development and use of pharmacological probes of the CNS in man: Evidence of cholinergic abnormality in primary affective illness. *Biol. Psychiat.,* 15:925-955, 1980.
44. RISCH, S.C., KALIN, N.H., and JANOWSKY, D.S.: Cholinergic challenges in affective illness: Behavioral and neuroendocrine correlates. *J. Clin. Psychopharmacol.,* 1:186-192, 1981.
45. GARVER, D.L., and DAVIS, J.M.: Biogenic amine hypothesis of affective disorders. *Life Sci.,* 24:383-394, 1979.
46. RISCH, S.C., COHEN, R.M., JANOWSKY, D.S., KALIN, N.H., and MURPHY, D.L.: Mood and behavioral effects of physostigmine on humans are accompanied by elevations in plasma β-endorphin and cortisol. *Science,* 209:1545-1546, 1980.
47. CARROLL, B.J., GREDEN, J.F., HASKETT, R., FEINBERG, M., ALBALA, A.A., MARTIN, F.I.R., RUBIN, R.T., HEATH, B., SHARP, P.T., McLEOD, W.L., and McLEOD, M.F.: Neurotransmitter studies of neuroendocrine pathology in depression. *Acta Psychiatr. Scand.,* 61:183-199, 1980.
48. DAVIS, K.L., HOLLISTER, L.E., GOODWIN, F.K., and GORDON, E.K.: Neurotransmitter metabolites in cerebrospinal fluid of man following physostigmine. *Life Sci.,* 21:933-936, 1977.
49. BECKMANN, H., and GOODWIN, F.K. Antidepressant response to tricyclics and urinary MHPG in unipolar patients. *Arch. Gen. Psychiat.,* 32:17-21, 1975.
50. STEINBOOK, R.M., JACOBSON, A.F., WEISS, B.L., and GOLDSTEIN, B.J.: Amoxapine, imipramine and placebo: A double-blind study with pretherapy urinary 3-methoxy-4-hydroxyphenylglycol levels. *Curr. Ther. Res.,* 26:490-496, 1979.
51. COBBIN, D.M., REQUIN-BLOW, B., WILLIAMS, L.R., and WILLIAM, W.O.: Urinary MHPG levels and tricyclic antidepressant drug-selection. *Arch. Gen. Psychiat.,* 36:1111-1115, 1979.
52. MAAS, J., BOWDEN, C., MENDELS, J., and KOSCIS, J.H.: Neurotransmitter metabolites and the therapeutic response to antidepressant drugs. Paper presented at the 12th Congress of the College Internationale Neuropsychopharmacologicum, Goteborg, Sweden, June 22-26, 1980.
53. ROSENBAUM, A.H., SCHATZBERG, A., MARUTA, T., ORSULAK, P.J., COLE, J.O., GRAB, E.L., and SCHILDKRAUT, J.J.: MHPG as a predictor of antidepressant response to imipramine and maprotiline. *Am. J. Psychiat.,* 137:1090-1092, 1980.
54. HOLLISTER, L.E., DAVIS, K.L., and BERGER, P.A.: Subtypes of depression based on excretion of MHPG and response to nortriptyline. *Arch. Gen. Psychiat.,* 37:1107-1110, 1980.
55. SCHILDKRAUT, J.J.: Norepinephrine metabolites as biochemical criteria for classifying depressive disorders and predicting responses to treatment. Preliminary findings. *Am. J. Psychiat.,* 130:696-699, 1973.
56. MODAI, I., APTER, A., GOLOMB, M., and WIJSENBEEK, H.: Response to amitriptyline and urinary MHPG in bipolar depressive patients. *Neuropsychobiol.,* 5:181-184, 1979.
57. SACCHETTI, E., ALLARIA, E., NEGRI, F., BIONDI, P.A., SMERALDI, E., and CAZZULLO, C.L.: 3-Methoxy-4-hydroxyphenylglycol and primary depression: Clinical and pharmacological considerations. *Biol. Psychiat.,* 14:473-484, 1979.
58. COPPEN, A., RAMA RAO, V.A., RUTHVEN, C.R.J., GOODWIN, B.L., and SANDLER, M.: Urinary 4-hydroxy-3-methoxyphenylglycol is not a predictor for clinical

response to amitriptyline in depressive illness. *Psychopharmacol.*, 64:95-97, 1979.

59. SPIKER, D.G., EDWARDS, D., HANIN, I., NEIL, J.F., and KUPFER, D.J.: Urinary MHPG and clinical response to amitriptyline in depressed patients. *Am. J. Psychiat.*, 137:1183-1187, 1980.

60. ROFFMAN, M. Ciba-Geigy collaborative study, unpublished data—personal communication.

61. SULSER, F., VETULANI, J., and MOBLEY, P.K.: Mode of action of antidepressant drugs. *Biochem. Pharmacol.*, 27:257-261, 1978.

62. CHARNEY, D.S., MENKES, D.B., and HENINGER, G.R.: Receptor sensitivity and the mechanisms of action of antidepressant treatment. *Arch. Gen. Psychiat.*, 38:1160-1180, 1981.

63. WALDMEIER, P.C.: Noradrenergic transmission in depression: Under- or overfunction: *Pharmakopsychiat.*, 14:3-9, 1981.

64. HENINGER, G.R.: The monoamine receptor sensitivity hypothesis of antidepressant drug action. *Abstracts of ACNP Meeting*, December 1981, p. 39.

65. FRAZER, A., LUCKI, I., and HEYDORN, W.: Antidepressant drugs: Effects on monoamine receptors and monoamine responsiveness, *Abstracts of ACNP Meeting*, December 1981, p. 39.

66. DeMONTIGNY, C., and BLIER, P.: Pre- and postsynaptic effects of antidepressant treatments on monoaminergic systems. *Abstracts of ACNP Meeting*, December 1981, p. 39.

67. SVENSSON, T.H., and SCUVEE-MOREAU, J.: Sensitivity in vivo of central α_2- and opiate receptors after chronic treatment with various antidepressants. *Abstracts of ACNP Meeting*, December 1981, p. 39.

68. DAVIS, M.: Agonist induced changes in behavior as a measure of functional changes in receptor sensitivity following chronic administration of antidepressant drugs. *Abstracts of ACNP Meeting*, December 1981, p. 41.

69. PANDEY, G.N., DAVIS, J.M., CASPER, R., SUDARSHAN, P., DYSKEN, M., and CHANA, S.: Antidepressant treatment and central adrenergic histamine receptors. *Abstracts of ACNP Meeting*, December 1981, p. 41.

70. CHARNEY, D.S., and HENINGER, G.R.: Receptor sensitivity and the etiology and treatment of depressive illness. *Abstracts of ACNP Meeting*, December 1981, p. 42.

71. CAIRNCROSS, K.D., COBBIN, D.M. and POHLEN, G.J.: Letter to Editor. *Br. Med. J.*, 283:991, 1981.

72. SPITZER, R.L., ENDICOTT, J., and ROBINS, E.: Research diagnostic criteria. Rationale and reliability. *Arch. Gen. Psychiat.*, 35:773-782, 1978.

73. BUNNEY, W.E., POST, R.M., ANDERSEN, A.E., and KOPANDA, R.T.: A neuronal receptor sensitivity mechanism in affective illness (a review of evidence). *Commun. Psychopharmacol.*, 1:393-405, 1977.

74. COHEN, R.M., CAMPBELL, I.C., COHEN, M.R., TORDA, T., PICKAR, D., SIEVER, L.J., and MURPHY, D.L.: Presynaptic noradrenergic regulation during depressions and antidepressant drug treatment. *Psychiat. Res.*, 3:93-105, 1980.

75. SEGAWA, T., MIZUTA, T., and NOMURA, Z.: Modifications of central 5-hydroxy-tryptamine binding sites in synaptic membranes from rat brain after long-term administration of tricyclic antidepressants. *Eur. J. Pharmacol.*, 58:75-83, 1979.

76. MAGGI, A., U'PRITCHARD, D.C., and ENNA, S.J.: Differential effects of antide-

pressant treatment on brain monoaminergic receptors. *Eur. J. Pharmacol.*, 61:91-98, 1980.

77. PEROUTKA, S.J., and SNYDER, S.H.: Long-term antidepressant treatment decreases spiroperiodol-labeled serotonin receptor binding. *Science*, 210:88-90, 1980.

78. ENNA, S.J., and KENDALL, D.A.: Interactions of antidepressants with brain neurotransmitter receptors. *J. Clin. Psychopharmacol.*, 1 (Supplement): 125-175, 1981.

79. SIEVER, L., INSEL, T., and UHDE, T.: Noradrenergic challenges in the affective disorders. *J. Clin. Psychopharmacol.*, 1:193-206, 1981.

80. RISCH, S.C. KALIN, N.H., and MURPHY, D.L.: Neurochemical mechanisms in the affective disorders and neurochemical correlates. *J. Clin. Psychopharmacol.*, 1:180-185, 1981.

81. RISCH, S.C., KALIN, N.H., and MURPHY, D.L.: Pharmacological challenge strategies: Implications for neurochemical mechanisms in affective disorders and treatment approaches. *J. Clin. Psychopharmacol.*, 1:238-243, 1981.

82. BUNNEY, W.E., and MURPHY, D.L.: Strategies for the systematic study of neurotransmitter receptor function in man. In: E. Usdin and W.E. Bunney, (Eds.), *Pre- and Postsynaptic Receptors.* New York: Marcel Dekker, 1975, pp. 283-313.

83. SCOTT, R.E.: Effects of prostaglandins, epinephrine and NaF on human leukocyte, platelet and liver adenyl cyclase. *Blood*, 35:514-516, 1970.

84. WILLIAMS, L.T., SNYDERMAN, R., and LEFKOWITZ, R.J.: Identification of β-adrenergic receptors in human lymphocytes by (−)(^{3}H) alprenolol binding. *J. Clin. Invest.*, 57:149-155, 1976.

85. EXTEIN, I., TALLMAN, J., SMITH, C.C., and GOODWIN, F.K.: Changes in lymphocyte beta-adrenergic receptors in depression and mania. *Psychiat. Res.*, 1:191-197, 1979.

86. PANDEY, G.N., DYSKEN, M.W., GARVER, D.L., and DAVIS, J.M.: Beta-adrenergic receptor function in affective illness. *Am. J. Psychiat.*, 136:675-678, 1979.

87. LECRUBIER, Y., PUECH, A.J., JOUVENT, R., SIMON, P., and WIDLOCHER, D.: A beta-adrenergic stimulant (salbutamol) versus clomipramine in depression: A controlled study. *Br. J. Psychiat.*, 136:354-358, 1980.

88. HOFFMAN, B.B., DELEAN, A., WOOD, C.L., SCHOCKEN, D.D., and LEFKOWITZ, R.J.: Alpha-adrenergic receptor subtypes: Quantitative assessment by ligand binding. *Life Science*, 24:1739-1746, 1979.

89. WOOD, C.L., ARNETT, C.D., CLARKE, W.R., TSAI, B.S., and LEFKOWITZ, R.J.: Subclassification of alpha-adrenergic receptors by direct binding studies. *Biochem. Pharmacol.*, 28:1277-1282, 1979.

90. LEFKOWITZ, R.F.: Identification and regulation of alpha- and beta-adrenergic receptors. *Fed. Proc.*, 37:123-129, 1978.

91. FAIN, J.H., and GARCIA-SAINZ, J.A.: Role of phosphatidylinositol turnover in alpha$_1$ and of adenylate cyclase in alpha$_2$ effects of catecholamines. *Life Sci.*, 26:1183-1194, 1980.

92. SCOTT, M., READING, H.W., and LUDON, J.B.: Studies on human blood platelets in affective disorders. *Psychopharmacol.*, 60:131-135, 1979.

93. WANG, Y.-C., PANDEY, G.N., MENDELS, J., and FRAZER, A.: Platelet adenylate cyclase responses in depression: Implications for a receptor defect. *Psychopharmacologia (Berl.)*, 36:291-300, 1974.

94. MURPHY, D.L., DONNELLY, C., and MOSKOWITZ, J.: Inhibition by lithium of prostaglandin E_1 and norepinephrine effects on cyclic adenosine monophosphate production in human platelets. *Clin. Pharmacol. Ther.*, 14:810-814, 1973.

95. GARCIA-SEVILLA, J.A., ZIS, A.P., HOLLINGSWORTH, P.J., GREDEN, J.F., and SMITH, C.B.: Platelet α_2-adrenergic receptors in major depressive disorders. *Arch. Gen. Psychiat.*, 38:1327-1333, 1981.

96. GARCIA-SEVILLA, J.A., ZIS, A.P., HOLLINGSWORTH, P.J., GREDEN, J.F., and SMITH, C.B.: Platelet alpha$_2$-adrenoreceptors in major depressive disorders (MDD). *The Pharmacologist*, 23:216 (abstr. 536), 1981.

97. GARCIA-SEVILLA, J.A., ZIS, A.P., ZELNICK, T.C., and SMITH, C.B.: Tricyclic antidepressant drug treatment decreases α_2-adrenoreceptors on human platelet membranes. *Eur. J. Pharmacol.*, 69:121-123, 1981.

98. KAFKA, M.S., VAN KAMMEN, D.P., KLEINMAN, J.E., NURNBERGER, J.I., SIEVER, L.J., UHDE, T.W., and POLINSKY, R.J.: Alpha-adrenergic receptor function in schizophrenia, affective disorders, and some neurological diseases. *Commun. Psychopharmacol.*, 4:477-486, 1980.

99. U'PRITCHARD, D.C., DAIGUJI, M., TONG, C., MITRIUS, J.C., and MELTZER, H.Y.: α_2-Adrenergic receptors: Comparative biochemistry of neural and nonneural receptors, and *in vitro* analysis of psychiatric patients. In: I. Hanin and E. Usdin (Eds.), *Biological Markers in Psychiatry and Neurology*. New York: Pergamon Press, 1981, pp. 205-217.

100. LANGER, S.Z., MORET, C., RAISMAN, R., DUBOCOVICH, M.L., and BRILEY, M.: High affinity (^{3}H)-imipramine binding in rat hypothalamus: Association with uptake of serotonin but not of norepinephrine. *Science*, 210:1133-1135, 1980.

101. REHAVI, M., PAUL, S.M., SKOLNICH, P., and GOODWIN, F.K.: Demonstration of specific high affinity binding sites for (^{3}H) imipramine in human brain. *Life Sci.*, 26:2273-2279, 1980.

102. LANGER, S.Z., ZARIFIAN, E., BRILEY, M., RAISMAN, R., and SECHTER, D.: High-affinity binding of ^{3}H-imipramine in brain and platelets and its relevance to the biochemistry of affective disorders. *Life Sci.*, 29:211-220, 1981.

103. BRILEY, M.S., RAISMAN, R., and LANGER, S.A.: Human platelets possess high-affinity binding sites for ^{3}H-imipramine. *Eur. J. Pharmacol.*, 58:347-348, 1979.

104. TALVENHEIMO, J., NELSON, P.J., and RUDNICK, G.: Mechanism of imipramine inhibition of platelet 5-hydroxytryptamine transport. *J. Biol. Chem.*, 254:4631-4635, 1979.

105. PAUL, S.M., REHAVI, M., SKOLNICH, P., and GOODWIN, F.K.: Demonstration of specific "high affinity" binding sites for (^{3}H)-imipramine on human platelets. *Life Sci.*, 26:953-959, 1980.

106. PAUL, S.M., REHAVI, M., RICE, X.C., ITTAH, Y., and SKOLNICH, P.: Does high affinity (^{3}H)-imipramine binding label serotonin reuptake sites in brain and platelet? *Life Sci.*, 28:2753-2760, 1981.

107. BRILEY, M.S., LANGER, S.Z., RAISMAN, R., SECHTER, D., and ZARIFIAN, E.: Tritiated imipramine binding sites are decreased in platelets of untreated depressed patients. *Science*, 209:303-305, 1980.

108. PAUL, S.M., REHAVI, M., SKOLNICH, P., BALLENGER, J.C., and GOODWIN, F.K.: Depressed patients have decreased binding of tritiated imipramine to platelet serotonin "transporter." *Arch. Gen. Psychiat.*, 38:1315-1317, 1981.

109. COPPEN, A., SWADE, C., and WOOD, K.: Platelet 5-hydroxytryptamine accumulation in depressive illness. *Clin. Chim. Acta*, 87: 165-168, 1978.

110. TUOMISTO, J., TUKIAINEN, E., and AHLFORS, U.G.: Decreased uptake of 5-hydroxy-tryptamine in blood platelets from patients with endogenous depression. *Psychopharmacol.*, 65:141-147, 1979.

111. MELTZER, H.Y., ARORA, R.C., BABER, R., and TRICOU, B.J.: Serotonin uptake in blood platelets of psychiatric patients. *Arch. Gen. Psychiat.*, 38:1322-1326, 1981.

112. MOONEY, J.J., CHAO, F.C., ORSULAK, P.J., and SCHILDKRAUT, J.J.: An improved method for the recovery of mitochondrial monoamine oxidase from human platelets using colchicine and nitrogen decompression. *Biochem. Med.*, 26:156-166, 1981.

113. MOONEY, J.J., CHAO, F.C., ORSULAK, P.J., ADLER, S.A., and SCHILDKRAUT, J.J.: Platelet monoamine oxidase activity in psychiatric disorders: The application of a technique for the isolation of free platelet mitochondria from relatively small blood samples. *J. Psychiat. Res.*, 16:163-171, 1981.

114. MOONEY, J.J., HORNE, W.C., HANDIN, R.I., SCHILDKRAUT, J.J., and ALEXANDER, R.W.: Sodium inhibits both adenylate cyclase and high affinity (^{3}H) p-amino-clonidine binding to α_2-adrenergic receptors in purified human platelet membranes. *Molec. Pharmacol.*, 21:600-608, 1982.

115. SCHILDKRAUT, J.J.: Neuropharmacologically generated models of the affective disorders: Biochemical versus behavioral models. *Psychopharmacol. Bull.*, 8:61-62, 1972.

116. CASSENS, G., KURUC, A., ORSULAK, P.J., ROFFMAN, M., and SCHILDKRAUT, J.J.: Animal models of subgroups of depressions. Thirty-fifth Annual Convention and Scientific Program, Society of Biological Psychiatry, 1980, p. 89.

117. CASSENS, G., ACTOR, C., KLING, M., and SCHILDKRAUT, J.J.: Amphetamine withdrawal: Effects on intracranial reinforcement. *Psychopharmacol.*, 73:318-322, 1981.

118. CASSENS, G., KURUC, A., ORSULAK, P.J., and SCHILDKRAUT, J.J.: Amphetamine withdrawal: Effects on brain levels of MHPG-SO$_4$ in the rat. *Commun. Psychopharmacol.*, 3:217-233, 1979.

119. CASSENS, G., KURUC, A., ROFFMAN, M., ORSULAK, P., and SCHILDKRAUT, J.J.: Alterations in brain norepinephrine metabolism and behavior induced by environmental stimuli previously paired with inescapable shock. *Behav. Brain Res.*, 2:387-407, 1981.

120. CASSENS, G., KURUC, A., ROFFMAN, M., ORSULAK, P., and SCHILDKRAUT, J.J.: Alterations in brain norepinephrine induced by environmental stimuli previously paired with inescapable shock. *Science*, 209:1138-1140, 1980.

121. SCHILDKRAUT, J.J., ORSULAK, P.J., COPELAND, B.E., and LEGG, M.A.: *Clinical Laboratory Tests in Depressions and Schizophrenias*. (Offered by the Psychiatric Chemistry Laboratory, in cooperation with the New England Deaconess Hospital, Department of Pathology.) Boston, MA: New England Deaconess Hospital, 1978.

5

Recent Advances in the Pharmacological Treatment of Psychoses

William E. Fann, M.D.

Medication, especially the neuroleptics, is a very large part of the treatment approaches to the psychotic patient. However, it is readily apparent that many schizophrenic patients have difficulty tolerating the presently available neuroleptics and may be refractory to them, so that a change of therapy using a compound of another molecular structure may allow resumption of therapeutic benefit to a patient who develops tolerance to his original medication. All of the presently marketed neuroleptics are fraught in their use with side effects, including serious extrapyramidal and cardiovascular symptoms, and the unpleasantness of such side effects strongly influences the patients' compliance with the medication regimen. Such lack of compliance is particularly acute in outpatient populations among whom the medications have contributed heavily to satisfactory function outside the institution. Side effects, which occur in most patients, together with lack of significant therapeutic response in some patients, inhibit universal acceptance of neuroleptics as definitive cures for schizophrenia. It is known that cross-tolerance may develop to neuroleptics with similar chemical structures.

Which are the safest neuroleptics? Unfortunately no single compound can be recommended for every patient. All marketed neuroleptics share the same spectrum of side effects, differing only quantitatively, not qualitatively, from each other. Thus, all may produce orthostatic hypotension, extrapyramidal symptoms, or sedation, but some more likely than others for any particular one of such side

This work was supported in part by a grant from the Veterans Administration.

124

effects. The psychiatrist's familiarity with quantitative differences is important in matching the drug to the patient, taking into account, among other factors, individual susceptibility to the dominant side effect profile of the compound in prescription charts.

FAILURE TO IMPROVE WITH NEUROLEPTIC THERAPY

What factors underlie non-response to neuroleptic therapy? Inadequate dose or blood level of the drug is a clear consideration. There are studies which demonstrate that clinical response is correlated to blood level of the neuroleptic, particularly chlorpromazine. Presumably such correlative studies could be made for all of these existing neuroleptics, though methods are not available for all the neuroleptics (1). Where technology is available for the determination, complications such as the timing of the blood drawing (i.e., early in the course of therapy or after steady state levels have been achieved) add other variables for the clinician who is attempting to make an interpretation of the results. While accurate and standardized laboratory data would be of assistance to the clinician in determining the dose of neuroleptic given the patient, such standards have not been set for all of the neuroleptics, and reliability of commercial laboratories remains problematic. For these reasons, among others, blood level procedures have not gained the place they deserve in the clinical routine.

The question of inadequate blood levels of neuroleptics leads, of course, to its correlative: Might too high a blood level cause a poor response? In other words, does a "therapeutic window" exist for neuroleptics, as it does for certain tricyclic antidepressants? There is good evidence that, for some neuroleptics at least, such a "window" does exist. For these neuroleptics a certain blood level of the medication must be attained in order to achieve a therapeutic response, but increasing the dose above a certain level may well lead to a reversal of the therapeutic changes (2). In such cases, the drug blood level determination would be of paramount importance to the clinician. A poor response might lead the physician to increase the dose and thereby add to the problem, particularly in a patient who metabolizes a particular drug slowly. Such a patient may accumulate toxic levels of the drug even on relatively small doses. The small oral dose of the drug may lead to the false deduction that the neuroleptic dose is inadequate. The clinician may then increase the dose, which may result in further and perhaps serious complications. Because the neuroleptic blood level can give the clinican this added dimension to his assessment and care of his patient, it is recommended where it is available from a reliable laboratory with the capability for making the determination of the compound in question.

Another factor which might contribute to lack of response to medication is change in the structure of brain discovered in some schizophrenic patients through

TABLE 1
Comparative Side Effects of Classes of Neuroleptics*

	Sedation	Cardio-Vascular	Autonomic	Extra-Pyramidal	Appetite
PHENOTHIAZINES					
Aliphatic type (e.g., chlorpromazine, promazine, trifluopromazine)	3+	3+	3+	2-3+	↑
Piperazine type (e.g., fluphenazine, perphenazine, trifluoperazine)	2+	2+	2+	3+	↑
Piperadine type e.g., thioridazine, mesoridazine)	3+	4+	3-4+	1+	↑
THIOXANTHENES (e.g., chlorprothixene, thiothixene)	2+	2+	3+	2+	↑
BUTYROPHENONES (e.g., haloperidol)	2+	1+	2+	4+	↑
DIHYDROINDOLONES (e.g., molindone)	3+	2+	2+	2-3+	↓
DIBENZOXAZEPINES (e.g., loxapine)	3+	2+	2+	2+	↑

* Note that all classes have all side effects: The differences are quantitative, not qualitative. Numerical designation refers to probable severity as well as probable frequency of the side effect.

the use of new non-invasive techniques. Alterations in ventricular brain ratios, for instance, found in some schizophrenic patients, as compared to normals and other mentally ill controls, have been correlated with poor response to medication. Such brain alterations may be due to exposure to long-term medication regimens in the chronically hospitalized mentally ill, though the fact that such alterations have been discovered even in young schizophrenic patients not previously medicated (3) suggests that these abnormalities are part of the disease and not secondary to the medication. The implications these findings have for delineation of subpopulations of schizophrenic patients and for differentiating those persons who may be "constitutional non-responders" is exciting. Prediction of non-response would define those patients who should not be given the medication, since for them the risk/benefit ratio would be prohibitive.

The physician's therapeutic options in the use of presently marketed compounds are necessarily limited because of these side effects. In addition to this limitation, there is seldom a complete and unqualified remission of schizophrenia or of its symptoms which can be attributed to medication; in other patients there is no response or even a symptomatic worsening.

This chapter will review the two most prominent recently marketed new compounds, loxapine and molindone, and briefly examine a compound not marketed for clinical use in the United States, i.e., clozapine. Clozapine's clinical effects and pharmacology are outlined here for comparative purposes. Because of its side effects, it is no longer in use even experimentally in man in this country. However, it is of interest because of its close structural relationship to the compound loxapine (see Figure 1). In approximately 16 years of use in Europe, no cases of tardive dyskinesia have been reported secondary to administration of clozapine, so that it was felt to be not only an advance for the clinician and the patient, but also of heuristic value, because it did not seem to have the pharmacological profile of the other antipsychotics. However, there are reports now from mainland China, where the compound is being used extensively clinically, that tardive dyskinesia is being seen in association with its administration (4).

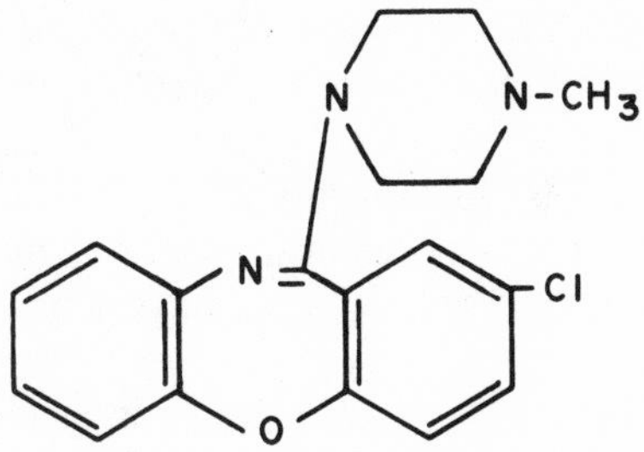

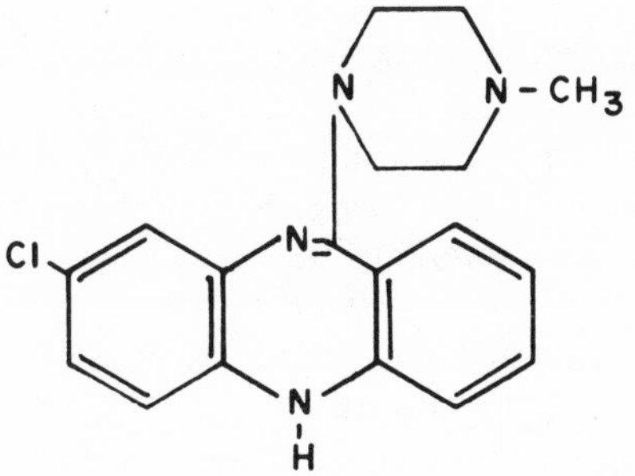

FIGURE 1. Note similarity in molecular structure of loxapine and clozapine.

LOXAPINE

Development of loxapine was an attempt to solve the problem of cross-tolerance: Where a phenothiazine compound has lost therapeutic benefit, an alternate drug with a similar structure will probably not be useful. In such cases, to provide symptomatic relief, pharmacologists formulated in loxapine a neuroleptic with chemical structures completely different from the phenothiazines, thioxanthenes, or butyrophenones, being a tricyclic dibenzoxazepine derivative. The pharmacological responses of loxapine are similar to the major tranquilizers—phenothiazines, thioxanthenes, butyrophenones, and molindone. Although the exact mode of action has not been established, it appears to reduce the firing thresholds of CNS neurons acting in polysynaptic pathways, particularly those in the reticular formation (5,6a). Changes in the level of excitability of subcortical inhibitory areas have been observed in several animal species in association with calmative effects and suppression of aggressive behavior, locomotor activity, and conditioned avoidance response (5,6c).

Although the drug appears to have potent antiemetic effects in dogs, antiemetic activity in humans has not been clinically evaluated (5,6b). The drug does not appear to have antidepressant or anticonvulsant activity, and may in fact lower the convulsive threshold (5,6c).

Absorption of loxapine from the gastrointestinal tract is virtually complete and clearance from plasma is rapid. Peak serum levels usually occur within two hours and generally range from 0.006 to 0.0013 mg per ml with a 25 mg oral dose. The major metabolite in serum is 8-hydroxyloxapine, which reaches maximum concentrations two to four hours after administration. Serum levels decline in a biphasic manner. The half-life of the first phase is five hours and of the second phase is 19 hours (5,6a,6b,8).

Radioactive drug assays indicate that loxapine and/or its metabolites are widely distributed in body tissues. Highest concentration of the drug occurs in brain, lungs, heart, liver, and pancreas, with lesser concentrations in spleen, fat, kidney, muscle, and blood. It also appears in cerebrospinal fluid (5,6a,6b,8).

Metabolism is extensive and excretion occurs in both urine and feces. About 50% of a single oral dose is excreted within the first 24 hours—17% within six hours, 21% within 12 hours, and 46% within 24 hours. The main route of excretion is renal. Within one week 60% to 70% is excreted through the kidney and 15% to 20% through the gastrointestinal tract (5,6a).

Loxapine is indicated in the management of the manifestations of schizophrenia. Initial response is evident within one to four weeks (6c), and maximum improvement is generally attained by the end of the third (9) or fourth (10) treatment month, followed by a therapeutic plateau. Symptoms such as insomnia, irritability, restlessness, excitation, hyperkinesia, anxiety, tension, and aggressiveness are generally affected first, followed by improvement in hallucinations, delusions, and depersonalization (9). Significant improvement in social competence and interest and in manageability may also occur (5). Schizophrenic patients are usually calmer and more manageable without being heavily drugged or drowsy (7). Sedation in schizophrenic patients is frequently more transient and decreases with continued treatment (6c).

Therapeutic dose range for loxapine is 50-200 mg. Although some schizophrenic patients have been effectively controlled with 20-60 mg/day, they usually require a minimum of 50 mg daily to respond therapeutically. The majority of patients with acute psychotic symptoms and chronic patients who have not received medication in the immediate past respond to 60-100 mg daily. The optimal dose range for severely ill schizophrenic patients appears to be between 100 and 200 mg, although some patients have been treated with as much as 250 mg/day (5,6c,9). Starting dose for mild psychotic symptoms is 10 mg twice a day; moderate symptoms may require 10 mg given three or four times a day; for severe symptoms, a starting dose of 25 mg twice a day is recommended (5,6c). As with all neuroleptics, it is generally advisable to begin prescription at relatively low doses and increase the dose until a therapeutic response is achieved or deleterious side effects intervene. Dosage may be increased fairly rapidly during the first seven to 10 days of therapy in accordance with response and tolerance of the patients. In schizophrenic patients with depression, loxapine can be safely prescribed with tricyclic antidepressants (9). Because loxapine potentiates the action of other CNS depressants (barbiturates and alcohol) or anticholinergic agents, caution should be used when prescribing these drugs concomitantly to prevent overdosage (5,6a,6c,9).

Loxapine has been prescribed concurrently with psychotropics, sedative hypnotics, anticonvulsants, and other drugs without serious adverse interaction other than additive potentiation of some drug effects (i.e., sedation). Loxapine also inhibits the vasopressor effect of epinephrine. If patients receiving loxapine require a vasopressor agent, phenylephrine or levarterenol should be used (5).

Loxapine has generally been more effective in treating young (under 40 years of age), short-term (hospitalized less than 10 years) patients who have been partially responsive to the usual therapeutic dose of a neuroleptic. The older the patient, the more impoverished the patient's affect, and the longer the duration of the psychosis, the poorer the therapeutic response to loxapine, although in more than half of these treatment resistant cases loxapine is reported to have antipsychotic effects as good as or superior to other neuroleptics (8-15). The patients whose duration of illness was less than two years showed the greatest improvement; the group who had been ill longer than 10 years was the most severely ill and showed little improvement (11).

Reluctance to prescribe recently marketed drugs because of unknown potential hazards and deleterious side effects is understandable. However, in the 15 years since loxapine was first clinically evaluated in Germany (10), available evidence indicates that the drug is a potent neuroleptic which is safe for use. Most of the side effects are minor-to-moderate and transient, disappearing as treatment continues or eliminated by reduction in dosage or concomitant prescription of another drug.

Side effects encountered with loxapine are quite similar to those occurring with other neuroleptics: most commonly, transient initial drowsiness and extrapyramidal reactions (5,6c,7,9,11,12). Extrapyramidal symptoms include tremor, rigidity, akathesia, dystonia, and the excessive salivation associated with parkinsonism. Patients who experienced extrapyramidal syndromes when prescribed other antipsychotic drugs in the past tend to react similarly to loxapine. These syndromes are usually controlled easily by administration of antiparkinsonian medications and/or the reduction in dosage or withdrawal of loxapine. Autonomic symptoms include dryness of the mouth, blurred vision, nasal congestion, and constipation. Like other neuroleptics, loxapine may cause weakness and fatigue, insomnia, headache, dizziness, and weight change. Dermatitis, pruritus, seborrhea, and facial edema have also been reported (5,6,9).

Evaluation of electrocardiograms, pulse rates, and blood pressures indicates no unusual or serious adverse effect from loxapine on the cardiovascular system (5,7-13), though significant changes in blood pressure and pulse were reported in a two-year trial. Blood pressure decreased and pulse rate increased, with changes reaching their maximum around the ninth month of treatment (13).

Ophthalmologic studies for effects of loxapine have revealed no definite pathological pigmentation in the refractive media or retina (8,9,11,13,15).

Loxapine appears to be a relatively nontoxic drug. Extensive liver and renal tests, urinalysis, and hematological studies have generally been within normal limits. Although clinical laboratory abnormalities were found in some studies, they were not clinically significant nor did they appear to be drug-related (8,9,11-16). Deviations from normal, when present, generally occurred in WBC, BUN concentrations, lymphocytes, and segmented neutrophils (8,9,12).

Currently, there has been no evidence of adverse effects or tolerance as a result of long-term administration of loxapine. Although cases of tardive dyskinesia have not been reported at this time, physicians should carefully monitor their long-term maintenance patients for the development of this often irreversible hyperkinetic syndrome (5,6). As with other potent neuroleptics, it is possible that protracted treatment with loxapine could cause tardive dyskinesia in susceptible individuals.

Loxapine is contraindicated in patients in comatose states or with severe CNS depression secondary to alcohol, barbiturates, and narcotics, or in patients hypersensitive to the drug. It may lower the convulsive threshold and should be prescribed with caution to patients with cardiovascular disorders. Because of the possible anticholinergic action of loxapine, it should be prescribed with caution to patients with glaucoma or a tendency for urinary retention (5,6b).

Antiemetic properties may mask signs of overdose of toxic drugs and may interfere with the diagnosis of conditions such as brain tumor and intestinal obstruction (5,6b).

Ambulatory patients should be warned against performing hazardous activities requiring mental alertness or physical coordination such as operating machinery or driving a car (5,6b).

Loxapine has been compared with a variety of neuroleptics, including chlorpromazine, thiothixene, and trifluoperazine. Clark et al. (15) compared loxapine and chlorpromazine in a 12-week, double-blind, placebo-controlled study. They reported that the antipsychotic effect of loxapine was at least as effective as, if not superior to, that of chlorpromazine. Furthermore, only about half as many side effects and laboratory abnormalities occurred in the loxapine group, and these were relatively mild, consisting primarily of extrapyramidal signs, drowsiness, and sinus tachycardia.

Investigators have found the effects of loxapine to be similar to trifluoperazine. Simpson and Cuculic (14) found no clinical difference between the two drugs. Ten of 18 BPRS items improved significantly in both groups. Additionally, loxapine patients showed significant improvement on grandiosity, hostility, and disorientation, while trifluoperazine patients showed significant improvement in motor retardation. Side effects, primarily extrapyramidal and minor laboratory abnormalities, were not significantly different between groups.

Investigators generally agree on the equivalent doses of loxapine and other neuroleptics. Loxapine is about half as potent as trifluoperazine, so a 2:1 ratio is recommended (6,8,14). Loxapine is about 10 times more potent than chlorpromazine, so 10 mg of the former would be equivalent to 100 mg of the latter (6,15,16,18). Although there has been some disagreement about the equivalent doses of loxapine and thiothixene, loxapine is about one-half to one-third as potent on a milligram-for-milligram basis as thiothixene (6). Charalampous et al. recommended the use of 25 mg of loxapine for 10 mg of thiothixene (17). Filho et al., however, prescribed 10 mg loxapine to 3 mg thiothixene (11).

MOLINDONE

Molindone, a dihydroindolone derivative, was synthesized in the search for related compounds with potential antipsychotic activity. It is similar in some respects to reserpine but otherwise unlike other currently available therapeutic agents (19) (Figure 2).

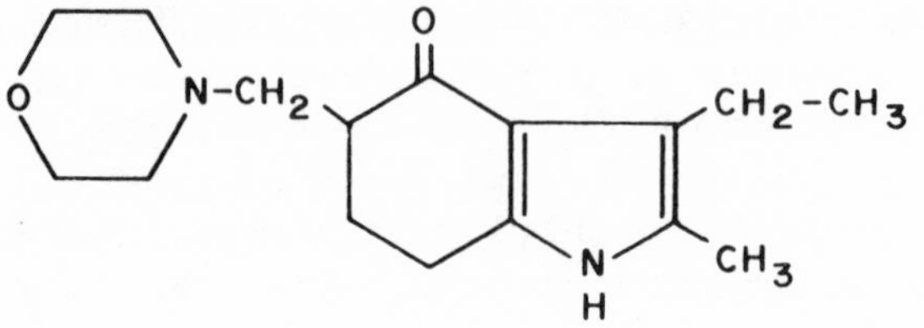

MOLINDONE

FIGURE 2.

Available evidence suggests that most psychotropic drugs alter mood or behavior by influencing the synthesis, disposition, and metabolism of norepinephrine, dopamine, serotonin, acetylcholine, and possibly other brain amines. Molindone shares with other antipsychotic agents the one characteristic common to all neuroleptics—an ability to affect central dopamine (DA) neurons (20). The "indole theory" of schizophrenia (that schizophrenia might be due to an abnormal metabolite of serotonin—5-hydroxytryptamine or 5-HT, an indole alkylamine) was partly responsible for stimulating some of the research into nonphenothiazine neuroleptics. Serotonin (5-HT) is found in many parts of the body and in brain, but particularly in the limbic system. Structurally, serotonin is characterized by the indole nucleus, which is also present in reserpine, LSD, molindone, and a wide variety of derivatives found in body fluids. The similarity between these substances suggests that they are capable of occupying the same receptor sites on nerve cell membranes, thereby preventing any other substance of like structure from exerting its action at those sites at the same time. For example, therapeutic doses of reserpine lead to striking decreases in the level of serotonin in the blood. Because serotonin affects the extent to which cholinergic nerve impulses are transmitted across the synapse, it is possible that reserpine achieves its tranquilizing effect by disrupting sympathetic nerve transmission.

It is thought that changes in brain levels of noradrenaline, dopamine, and 5-HT—amines which are presumed to function as transmitter agents across synapses—may be responsible for some of the signs and symptoms of psychiatric illness.

Molindone is absorbed rapidly into the gastrointestinal tract and, according to animal studies, is widely distributed in body tissues. Peak blood levels are reached approximately one hour after oral administration. Duration of action following a single dose is about 36 hours. Single daily doses do not cause more frequent or more severe side effects than the same total dosage divided throughout the day (21).

Molindone is rapidly metabolized, probably by the liver. More than 90% of a single dose is excreted within 24 hours in the feces and urine, and a small amount is excreted by the lungs as carbon dioxide. Thirty-six metabolites of molindone have been identified in urine and feces (22,23).

In humans, this drug produces tranquilization in the absence of muscle relaxation or incoordination. Acute and chronic schizophrenic patients responsive to the drug generally respond within two to four weeks, attaining maximum improvement by the end of the third treatment month. Symptoms such as insomnia, irritability, restlessness, retardation, paranoid belligerence, disorientation, and aggressiveness are generally affected first, followed by improvement in hallucinatory behavior, thinking and perceptual distortions, disorganization and social competence (21,24,25). Clinical data and experience indicate that different patients have a widely varying range of tolerance, and therapeutic dose may be as low as 1 mg (in some geriatric patients) or as high as 200 mg/day. Some patients have even been able to tolerate dosages as high as 300 and 400 mg/day (21). Most schizophrenic patients require at least 50 mg daily for therapeutic response to occur.

As with all neuroleptics, it is generally advisable to begin prescription at a low dose and to raise dosage gradually until either a therapeutic response is achieved or deleterious side effects intervene. For mild symptoms, 5 mg taken three or four times a day may be adequate, although an increase to 15 mg three or four times a day may be required. More moderate symptoms may require 10 mg taken three or four times daily raised to 25 mg taken on the same schedule. In cases of severe symptoms, daily doses of 225 mg may be prescribed (23).

When necessary, molindone can also be safely prescribed in conjunction with tricyclic antidepressants. Molindone has been prescribed concurrently with psychotropics, sedative hypnotics, anticonvulsants, and other drugs without serious adverse interaction other than some potentiation of the actions of the other drugs (21,23).

In the years since 1966, when molindone was first clinically evaluated by Sugarman and Hermann (24), available evidence indicates that this drug is a potent neuroleptic which is safe for use. Most of the side effects are minor to moderate and transient, disappearing as treatment continues or eliminated by reduction in dosage or concomitant prescription of another drug.

Thus far, the majority of patients treated with molindone have been schizophrenic patients. Practically all of them had been treated previously with various neuroleptics and were totally or partially non-responsive, so any drug-induced improvement is significant. In more than half of these treatment-resistant cases, molindone is reported to have antianxiety and antipsychotic effects as good as or superior to other neuroleptics (21,26-28). Psychiatrists experienced in treating severely ill patients who respond minimally to treatment with available neuroleptics will agree that any drug which improves the condition of these patients is a welcome addition to the armamentarium of psychotropic medications.

Side effects encountered with molindone are essentially those occurring with other neuroleptics, most commonly transient initial drowsiness. Extrapyramidal reactions, usually mild to moderate in severity and ranging from the various manifestations of akinesia to dyskinesia, akathesia, and parkinsonism, occur with about the same frequency as with other major tranquilizers. These extrapyramidal reactions are a neurophysiologic and not a toxic effect of the drug and can generally be controlled or eliminated by reduction of dose, mild sedation, or anti-parkinsonism medication. Drug-induced extrapyramidal reactions appear to be influenced by the age, sex, and physical condition of the patient. Young patients develop dystonia or oculogyric reactions more frequently, whereas middle-aged patients are more susceptible to akathesia, and the elderly tend to develop parkinsonian symptoms most often (21). Molindone, however, has not thus far demonstrated a greater propensity for causing extrapyramidal symptoms than other potent neuroleptics. One investigator has reported that these adverse symptoms occur somewhat less frequently with molindone (28).

Despite completely different chemical structures, molindone produces EEG changes similar to those of trifluoperazine and other major tranquilizers. In both molindone and trifluoperazine an increase in percentage of slow alpha, an increase in synchronization and rhythmical activity, and an increase of amplitude and burst activity along with decreased fast beta activity are evident. Particularly in low doses, molindone has a central stimulatory effect similar to that of other neuroleptics. It appears that molindone exerts its predominant effect on the ascending reticular activating system. Itil et al. report that marked EEG changes during molindone treatment were correlated with improvement of psychotic symptoms in acute schizophrenic patients, whereas minimal EEG changes were associated with limited improvement in chronic patients (29).

Like other neuroleptics, molindone may cause fatigue, insomnia, dizziness, blurred vision, nausea, mild hypotension, dry mouth, headache, restlessness, constipation, weight changes, and hyperactivity. Laboratory findings have generally been within normal limits and indicate that the drug is well tolerated in recommended doses (26,27). Allergic reactions, primarily nonspecific skin rash, have been extremely rare (21). Thus far, there has been no evidence of adverse effects or tolerance resulting from long-term administration of molindone, and no abstinence syndrome on abrupt withdrawal of molindone (23). As with other potent neuroleptics, it is possible that protracted treatment with molindone could cause tardive dyskinesia in certain individuals, although cases of tardive dyskinesia have not yet been reported.

The use of molindone is contraindicated in patients with severe central nervous system depression secondary to alcohol, barbiturates, or narcotics. Because it often causes some drowsiness initially, patients should be warned against engaging in activities which require alertness. The drug can also produce increased activity and consequently should be prescribed with caution to patients to whom activity would be harmful.

Nearly all the comparative studies to date have tested molindone against trifluoperazine. Although significant improvement in the symptoms of schizophrenia occurs with both drugs, the therapeutic effectiveness of molindone cannot be distinguished from that of trifluoperazine (19,26-29). Brauzer and Goldstein reported that, although the differences were not statistically significant, there was some indication of differential response to these two drugs. Psychotic target symptoms responded better to trifluoperazine, while symptoms of anxiety and depression were better relieved by molindone (26). Simpson et al. (28) found that molindone was less active after two weeks of treatment, but there was no significant difference between drug groups after four weeks of treatment. Side effects for both drugs were generally similar (19,26). Although one study reported that extrapyramidal symptoms were both less frequent and less severe in the molindone group (28), another reported that side effects were slightly more frequent in patients treated with molindone. Furthermore, molindone patients showed a somewhat greater tendency to relapse after discontinuation of medication (27).

There has been some disagreement regarding the equivalent doses of molindone and trifluoperazine. Claghorn reported that the two drugs are of about equal potency milligram for milligram and recommended a 1:1 ratio (19). Itil et al. reported that they found the therapeutic dose for molindone was approximately 25% higher than for trifluoperazine (29). Most investigators, however, report that molindone is about half as potent as trifluoperazine and recommend a 2:1 ratio (26-28).

Thus far there has not been enough published clinical experience with either molindone or loxapine to indicate their specific selection as the first-prescribed antipsychotic for individual patients. Because loxapine is not extensively metabolized in the liver, it may be useful in treating alcoholic patients and others with compromised liver function. Molindone's possible appetite suppressant features may suggest its use in obese psychotic patients or others on weight reduction diets; the other antipsychotics are well-known as appetite stimulants, and many patients who must be maintained on them experience undesirable large weight increases. For patients who fail to respond to the established phenothiazine, butyrophenone, and thioxanthene compounds, trials of loxapine or molidone are appropriate in the absence of other contraindications. These compounds have low milligram potency, and the physician who is transferring a patient from another neuroleptic to loxapine or molindone, with which he has probably had less clinical experience, should exercise more than usual caution in assessing cross-compound dose equivalents, starting molindone or loxapine at the same or lower dose equivalent.

CLOZAPINE

Until recently, it was assumed that the antipsychotic properties of the neuroleptics were correlated with disturbances in extrapyramidal function, that a compound which blocked dopamine receptors at one area would block these structures at all sites in brain. Anti-schizophrenic effects and extrapyramidal symptoms seemed to be inextricably linked. Pharmacological characteristics of the neuroleptics have included cataleptic effect and an ability to inhibit pharmacogenic stereotyped behavior in animals—effects which are due to the blockade of dopamine receptors in the brain, leading to enhanced turnover of dopamine. Blockade of mesolimbic dopamine receptors is antipsychotic, but this activity in the nigrostriatal area also causes extrapyramidal side effects (30). Enhanced turnover of dopamine is measurable by the detection of increased levels of homovanillic acid (HVA), the main metabolite of dopamine, and increased levels of HVA have been found both in the brain of animals and the cerebrospinal fluid (CSF) of patients treated with neuroleptics (31).

Clozapine is a dibenzodiazepine derivative similar to loxapine and possessing neuroleptic properties (Figure 1). Clozapine enhances the turnover of brain dopamine (although to a lesser extent than other neuroleptics), possibly more so in the limbic system than in the striatum (32). Additionally, it affects the central nonadrenergic system by blockade of noradrenaline receptors (31,32). Although clozapine reacts similarly in the body to other neuroleptics, it lacks cataleptic effects, fails to show antagonistic effects against apomorphine stereotypes, and has only slight antagonistic effect against amphetamine-induced stereotypies (31-34). It has marked anticholinergic, noradrenolytic, and sympatholytic effects peripherally (32). The most profound way in which clozapine differs from other neuroleptics, however, is that it rarely induces parkinson-type extrapyramidal side effects. This finding indicates that extrapyramidal side effects are not an absolutely necessary concomitant of antipsychotic effects (35,36).

Studies have been conducted on the effect of clozapine on homovanillic acid (HVA) and 5-hydroxyindoleacetic acid (5-HIAA), the main metabolite of serotonin, in the cerebrospinal fluid (CSF). One study of nine male patients treated with clozapine reported a significant increase in CSF HVA levels, a slight but insignificant increase in 5-HIAA, and a significant decrease in 3-methoxy-4-hydroxyphenylglycol (MHPG), the major metabolite of norepinephrine (31).

Another study, however, reported contradicting results. Eight male schizophrenic patients participated in a double-blind crossover study comparing extrapyramidal side effects as well as effects on HVA and 5-HIAA in CSF of patients treated with clozapine and haloperidol. Although increased HVA concentration occurred with haloperidol, decreased HVA and 5-HIAA concentration in CSF occurred with clozapine. Within four days of treatment with clozapine, concentration of HVA and 5-HIAA dropped significantly, 34% and 32%, respectively. At 21 days the decrease in concentration was 23% for HVA and 21% for 5-HIAA, insignificant drops (37).

It has been speculated that the anticholinergic actions of phenothiazines might, to varying degrees, attenuate extrapyramidal effects. Phenothiazines bear structural resemblance to drugs which block muscarinic cholinergic synapses, such as the major drugs in the treatment of Parkinson's disease. This structural similarity suggests that low extrapyramidal symptoms might be related to anticholinergic activity. By blocking muscarinic cholinergic receptors in the brain, it is speculated that phenothiazines might antagonize their own tendency to elicit extrapyramidal side effects through dopamine receptor blockade. Therefore, the potency as an antagonist of muscarinic cholinergic receptors in the brain would vary inversely with the tendency to evoke extrapyramidal side effects (30). 3-Quinuclidinyl benzilate (QNB) is a potent antagonist of muscarinic cholinergic receptors, and clozapine, which produces almost no acute extrapyramidal side effects, has the greatest affinity of all neuroleptics for QNB binding sites. Haloperidol has the least affinity for QNB binding sites, and it generally produces the most acute extrapyramidal disturbances of any neuroleptic (31). Clozapine seems to have six times more potent anticholinergic actions at central antimuscarinic receptors in mammalian brain tissue than does thioridazine; in fact, the potency of clozapine is similar to standard anticholinergic drugs such as benztropine mesylate and trihexyphenidyl (30,38). Furthermore, reports of central anticholinergic symptoms in patients on clozapine and the prompt reversal of these symptoms by physostigmine can be interpreted as clinical evidence for a central antimuscarinic action of clozapine (38).

Clozapine is used rather extensively in Europe and in China (4) but is not yet marketed in the United States. It is an active antipsychotic agent (32,34). It has a marked and rapid sedative effect, a pronounced inhibitory effect on aggression, agitation, and psychomotor hyperactivity, and is considered extremely useful in mitigating disturbed affect and behavior (32,33). Additionally, "anti-autistic" or resocializing effects have been noted (35,39).

Patients treated with clozapine showed a highly significant drop in production of schizophrenic symptoms such as somatic concern, conceptual disorganization, mannerisms and posturing, suspiciousness, hallucinatory behavior, unusual thought content, and disorientation. There was a corresponding drop in anxiety and tension, and clozapine also had a significant effect on emotional withdrawal and blunted affect (32).

In 34 patients given clozapine, the drug was most effective in relieving anxiety and fear, tension, delusions, hallucinations, hostility, disordered thought content, and disorientation. It was less effective in depressive moods, emotional shallowness, restlessness, thought disintegration and negativism. Ninety-one percent of the 34 hospitalized patients improved on clozapine—6% were judged "cured," 60% were substantially improved, and 25% were improved (41).

In another study, clozapine was prescribed to 10 acute and 10 chronic schizophrenic patients. Seventy-five percent, eight acute and seven chronic patients, improved. Therapeutic effect was better in acute cases. In these patients, clozapine initially influenced disintegration of thought, delusions of persecution, bizarre thought content and attitude to reality, and subsequently improved hallucinations and reduced hyperemotionality. In chronic patients, improvement was greatest in emotional contact. Inhibitory and anxiolytic effects occurred in chronic patients before psychotolytic effect (42).

Patients who had suffered from two to six exacerbations annually since the outbreak of their illness could be reintegrated into their social environment when treated with clozapine. Those treated with clozapine attended follow-up therapy sessions regularly in contrast to their previous irregular attendance, and they took their prescribed medications voluntarily as opposed to their previous frequent rejection of other major tranquilizers (35).

Improvement in schizophrenic symptoms is clearly apparent at 200 mg and above (34). Generally, initial dose of 25 mg tid is well tolerated. Subsequently, dosage can be raised in fairly high increments (50-75 mg/day) without marked adverse effects (33). The sedative-hypnotic effects of clozapine are more pronounced initially. Patients usually fall asleep within 20 minutes of their first dose; however, the sedative effect diminishes after one to four weeks and then almost disappears (32,39). It is a paradox that the overt therapeutic response should be pronounced and maintained without increasing dosage after tolerance to acute effects has developed and that alertness replaces sleepiness with normal sleep pattern (39). When needed, good hypnotic effect can be maintained by division of daily dose.

Quiet patients may react with pronounced sedation on 50-100 mg/day, while active patients may tolerate up to 800 mg/day without sedation. In nonhyperactive patients an initial single dose of 10-25 mg is recommended, with subsequent gradual increases. During maintenance, a single evening dose of 100-200 mg could be given (32,39,40). Patients may continue to improve until the 10th week, and a definite assessment of progress should not be made before that time (40).

The most common side effect associated with clozapine is sedation and tiredness. Most patients fall asleep within 20 minutes after being administered clozapine, but tolerance and normal sleep patterns are usually established within a week (32,33,39,40,42-44). Ninety six percent of 34 patients complained of fatigue and somnolence initially during the day (41).

Moderate pyrexia with a feeling of physical illness lasting from three to eight days upset some patients at first. Although the cause is unknown, it never lasted more than eight days. Of course, pyrexia must be distinguished from influenza and other febrile conditions (39-42).

Hypersalivation occurs in most patients. This effect seems to be dose-related and is often excessive. Some patients develop tolerance, although others do not. The mechanism is not known (33,38-40,42,43). Some patients were unable to sleep on their backs because of inhaling saliva.

Some patients complained of dizziness and vertigo for a maximum of three days (39). Dizziness was reported in 35% of 34 patients (41).

Although autonomic effects were not consistent (39), many patients complained of tachycardia, and hypotension and tachycardia were reported in all the patients in some studies (38,41,44). Increased heart rate sometimes lasted as long as 30 days (35). Postural hypotension was severe, and three of 13 patients in one study fainted (43). Twenty percent of the patients in one study (35) and 46% of the patients in another study (41) showed moderate and transient arterial hypotension.

The only extrapyramidal symptom reported with any frequency was mild tremor (34,44). No rigidity or coarse parkinsonian tremor was reported (34).

Confusion and delirium for 24 hours were noted in one chronic patient (39). A 25-year-old-woman developed signs of central anticholinergic toxicity and tachycardia, which were both fully reversed with 2 mg physostigmine (38).

Occasional facial vasoconstriction (pallor) has been reported during the first week (39,40). Seizures may be potentiated in epileptics (40).

Most patients gained about 1 kg/week for six weeks, and then weight stabilized. Weight gain seemed to be due primarily to increased appetite (39-41). In fact, the enormous and persistent increase in appetite was so dramatic that one author speculated that clozapine might be useful in the treatment of anorexia nervosa (43).

Characteristic EEG changes in patients on clozapine included a marked increase of slow activity, a decrease in basic frequency by one-half to 1½ Hz, and the incidence of paroxysmal abnormalities represented mostly by episodes of delta activity. After 20 days of treatment, all 16 patients had abnormal EEGs (44). Fifteen of 20 patients showed slight general changes or slight diffuse slowing of EEG during treatment. Three patients showed persisting slight general changes in EEG in the course of four to 10 months (45).

During June and July of 1975, 18 cases of severe blood disorder (nine fatal—eight agranulocytosis and one probable leukemia) were reported in Finland among patients receiving clozapine. Three possible explanations were cited:

(1) A myelotoxicity of the drug or allergic reaction to drug or drug-associated immunological reaction caused by clozapine itself or impurity of the product.
(2) Interaction between clozapine and other concomitant drugs.
(3) Special genetic characteristics of the patients involved (45).

The National Board of Health speculated that the first explanation was most likely and withdrew the use of clozapine until the possible causal link between the drug and the adverse reactions could be identified.

Following a washout period, 20 hospitalized schizophrenic patients were randomly assigned to either clozapine or haloperidol treatment for 82 days; after another drug-free period, during which symptoms returned, patients were prescribed the other drug for 82 days. Most patients could reach a suitable maintenance dose of clozapine within 10 days, but a longer period of dosage adjustment was needed for haloperidol. Approximately 25 mg of clozapine was equal to 1 mg of haloperidol in clinical effect. On BPRS parameters, clozapine appeared significantly superior to haloperidol generally and specifically on factors of somatic concern, conceptual disorganization, mannerisms and posturing, anxiety, tension, and emotional withdrawal. The therapeutic effect of clozapine was most pronounced in the more severe cases and when the patient simultaneously suffered from anxiety, tenseness, and psychomotor restlessness. The antipsychotic superiority of clozapine over haloperidol was more pronounced and significant in these patients (32).

Eight male schizophrenic patients participated in a double-blind crossover study of extrapyramidal side effects associated with clozapine and haloperidol. Haloperidol (9 mg/day) caused parkinsonism and reduced tardive dyskinesia. Clozapine (225 mg/day) had no effect on neurological parameters. During the discontinuation phase following administration of haloperidol, tardive dyskinesia (TD) occurred and was aggravated; TD did not occur after clozapine administration. The investigators suggest that clozapine does not induce dopaminergic hypersensitivity and therefore will not induce tardive dyskinesia (37).

One interesting but unexplained finding is an apparent increase in sensitivity to extrapyramidal disturbances when chlorpromazine is prescribed after termination of clozapine. Four of 21 patients in a study of clozapine exhibited marked extrapyramidal symptoms when chlorpromazine was instituted following discontinuance of clozapine therapy (33).

Because of its effect on sleep disturbances and anxiety, clozapine may be suitable in the treatment of neuroses. Neurotic symptomatology was favorably influenced in 89% of 38 neurotics treated with clozapine (36).

Clozapine was administered to 75 patients hospitalized for endogenous depression. Improvement was considered complete in 50% and partial in an additional 21%. Clozapine was especially effective in treating atypical depressive forms with paranoid hallucinatory elements and agitated depressions in which the sedative hypnotic action of the drug was beneficial during the first days (47).

Because of its apparent difference in pharmacological profile and the advantage to certain patients which such a compound offers, it might be desirable for clozapine to be reintroduced in this country for additional research. Qualified investigators could administer it to schizophrenic patients who benefit from no other available pharmacological agent. Unfortunately, the manufacturer of the compound does not wish to face the added medico-legal risks of further developing clozapine, and it appears that we will not see its application.

CONCLUSION

The advent of safe and effective novel neuroleptics may represent a significant advance in the pharmacotherapy of schizophrenia. Although it has not yet been demonstrated unequivocally that the new compounds are consistently more effective than the traditionally available antipsychotics, there is evidence that they are particularly useful in treating patients who have not shown satisfactory response to the phenothiazines, thioxanthenes, or butyrophenones. Side effects of the new compounds have not appeared to be extraordinary thus far, although the Finnish episode must be clearly resolved before clozapine can be made available for general use. It should furthermore be stated that the new neuroleptics have not been in use long enough to assess the incidence of such long-term side effects as tardive dyskinesia and cardiovascular abnormalities. Even with the standard antipsychotics, there has been consistent debate concerning specificity of action.

REFERENCES

1. VAN PUTTEN, T., MAY, P.R.A., and JENDEN, D.J.: Plasma levels of chlorpromazine and clinical response. *Psychopharm. Bull.*, 17:113-115, 1981.
2. EXTEIN, I. AUGUSTHY, K.A., GOLD, M.S., et al.: Plasma haloperidol levels and clinical response in acute schizophrenia. *Psychopharm. Bull.* In press, 1982.
3. SCHULZ, S. C., KOLLER, M., KISHORE, P., et al.: Abnormal CAT scans in young schizophrenic patients. *Psychopharm. Bull.* In press, 1982.
4. WYATT, R.J.: Personal communication, 1981.
5. American Hospital Formulary Services, Loxapine succinate.
6. Loxitane, loxapine succinate. Lederle Laboratories pamphlets: a) formulary information, b) pharmacology, c) product Q & A.

7. GERSHON, S., HEKIMIAN, L.J., BURDOCK, E.I., et al.: Antipsychotic properties of loxapine succinate. *Curr. Ther. Res.*, 12(5):280-285, 1970.
8. MOYANO, C.A.: A double-blind comparison of loxitane, loxapine succinate and trifluoperazine hydrochloride in chronic schizophrenic patients. *Dis. Ner. Sys.*, 36(6): 301-304, 1975.
9. GALLANT, D.M., BISHOP, G., STEEL, C.A., et al.: Loxapine: A six-month evaluation in severely ill schizophrenic patients. *Curr. Ther. Res.*, 15(4):205-209, 1973.
10. AYD, F. An appraisal of loxapine succinate. *Inter. Drug. Ther. Newsletter*, 11(7):25-28, 1976.
11. FILHO, U.V., CALDEIRA, M.V., and BUENO, J.R.: The efficacy and safety of loxapine succinate in the treatment of schizophrenia: A comparative study with thiothixene. *Curr. Ther. Res.*, 18(3):476-490, 1975.
12. SIMPSON, G.M., BRANCHEY, M.H., LEE, J.H., et al.: A two-year trial of loxapine succinate in chronic psychotic patients. *Dis. Nerv. Sys.*, 37(5):305-307, 1976.
13. SCHIELE, B.C.: Loxapine succinate: A controlled double-blind comparison in chronic schizophrenia. *Dis. Nerv. Sys.*, 36(7):361-364, 1975.
14. SIMPSON, P., and CUCULIC, Z.: A double-blind comparison of loxapine succinate and trifluoperazine in newly admitted schizophrenic patients. *Clin. Pharmacol.*, 16(1):783-791, 1976.
15. CLARK, M.L., HUBER, W.K., SULLIVAN, J. et al.: Evaluation of loxapine succinate in chronic schizophrenia. *Dis. Nerv. Sys.*, 33:783-791, 1972.
16. MOORE, D.F.: Treatment of acute schizophrenia with loxapine succinate (Loxitane) in a controlled study with chlorpromazine. *Curr. Ther. Res.*, 18(1): 172-180, 1975.
17. CHARALAMPOUS, K.D., FREEMESSER, G.F., MALEV, J., et al.: Loxapine succinate: A controlled double-blind study in schizophrenia. *Curr. Ther. Res.*, 16(8):829-837, 1974.
18. SHOPSIN, B., PEARSON, E. GERSHON, S., et al.: A controlled double-blind comparison between loxapine succinate and chlorpromazine in acute newly hospitalized schizophrenic patients. *Curr. Ther. Res.*, 14(11): 739-748, 1972.
19. CLAGHORN, J.: Psychopharmacologic characteristics of an indole compound—molindone. *Curr. Ther. Res.*, 11(8):524-527, 1969.
20. BUNNEY, B.S., ROTH, R.H., and AGHAJANIAN, G.K.: Effects of molindone on central dopaminergic neuronal activity and metabolism: Similarity to other neuroleptics. *Psychopharm. Comm.*, 1(4):349-358, 1975.
21. AYD, F.: A critical evaluation of molindone (Moban): A new indole derivative neuroleptic. *Dis. Nerv. Sys.*, 35(10):447-452, 1974.
22. American Hospital Formulary Service, Molindone.
23. Physicians' Desk Reference, 1976, Molindone.
24. SUGARMAN, A., and HERMANN, J.: Molindone: An indole derivative with antipsychotic activity. *Clin. Pharm. Therap.*, 8(2):261-265, 1967.
25. SIMPSON, G., and KRAKOV, L.: A preliminary study of molindone (EN-1733A) in chronic schizophrenia. *Curr. Ther. Res.*, 10(1):41-46, 1968.
26. BRAUZER, B., and GOLDSTEIN, B.: A clinical comparison of molindone hydrochloride with trifluoperazine in psychotic outpatients. *Curr. Ther. Res.*, 13(3):152-157, 1971.
27. FREEMAN, H., and FREDERICK, A.: Comparison of trifluoperazine and molindone in chronic schizophrenic patients. *Curr. Ther. Res.*, 11(11):670-676, 1969.

28. SIMPSON, G., AMIN, M., and EDWARDS, G.: A double-blind comparison of molindone and trifluoperazine in the treatment of acute schizophrenia. *J. Clin. Pharmacol.,* 11(3):227-236, 1971.

29. ITIL, T., POLVAN, N., UCOK, A., et al.: Comparison of the clinical and EEG effects of molindone and trifluoperazine in acute schizophrenic patients. *Physicians' Drug Manual,* 2:80-87, 1970.

30. SNYDER, S., GREENBERG, D., and YAMAMURA, H.: Antischizophrenic drugs and brain cholinergic receptors. *Arch. Gen. Psychiat.,* 31:58-61, 1974.

31. ACKENHEIL, M., BECKMANN, H., GRIEL, W., et al.: Antipsychotic efficacy of clozapine in correlation to changes in catecholamine metabolism in man. In I. Forrest, J. Carr, and E. Usdin (Eds.), *Advances in Biochemical Psychopharmacology, Phenothiazines and Structurally Related Drugs,* Vol. 9. New York: Raven Press, 1974.

32. GERLACH, J., KOPPELHUS, P., HELWEG, E., et al.: Clozapine and haloperidol in a single-blind cross-over trial: Therapeutic and biochemical aspects in the treatment of schizophrenia. *Acta Psychiat. (Scand.),* 50:410-424, 1974.

33. MATZ, R., RICK, W., OH, D., et al.: Clozapine—an antipsychotic agent without extrapyramidal manifestations. *Curr. Ther. Res.,* 16(7):687-695, 1974.

34. SIMPSON, G., and VARGA, E.: Clozapine—a new antipsychotic agent. *Curr. Ther. Res.,* 16(7):679-686, 1974.

35. DeMAIO, D.: Clozapine, a novel major tranquilizer. *Arzneim-Forsch,* 22(5), 919-921, 1972.

36. NICA, St., CIUREZU, T., and UDANGIU, L.: Results achieved with clozapine (Leponex) in the treatment of neuroses. *Act. Nerv. Super.* (Praha), 16(3): 201-202, 1974.

37. GERLACH, J., THORSEN, K., and FOG, R.: Extrapyramidal reactions and amine metabolites in cerebrospinal fluid during haloperidol and clozapine treatment of schizophrenic patients. *Psychopharmacologia,* 40:341-350, 1975.

38. SCHUSTER, P., GABRIEL, E., KUFFERLE, B., et al.: Reversal by physostigmine of clozapine-induced delirium. *Lancet,* January 3, 1976, pp. 37-38.

39. HEMPHILL, R., PASCOE, F., and ZABOW, T.: An investigation of clozapine in the treatment of acute and chronic schizophrenia and gross behavior disorders. *South African Med. J.,* November 29, 1975, pp. 2121-2125.

40. HEMPHILL, R., PASCOE, F., and ZABOW, T.: Clozapine (Leponex) in psychiatric treatment. *South African Med. J.,* October 26, 1974, p. 2168.

41. ZAPLETALEK, M., PAZDIREK, S., and HUBSCH, T.: Clinical experience with clozapine in psychoses. *Act. Nerv. Super.* (Praha), 16(3):203-204, 1974.

41. MOLCAN, J., NOVOTNY, V., and SCHLUPKOVA, L.: Our experience with clozapine treatment. *Act. Nerv. Super.* (Praha), 16(3):200-201, 1974.

43. NORRIS, D., and ISRAELSTAM, K.: Clozapine (Leponex) overdosage. *South African Med. J.,* March 15, 1975, p. 385.

44. NAHUNEK, K., SVESTKA, J., RODOVA, A., et al.: Further clinical and EEG experience with clozapine. *Act. Nerv. Super.* (Praha), 16(3):202-203, 1974.

45. PREININGEROVA, O., HANUS, H., and ZAPLETALEK, M.: Clozapine in outpatient practice. *Act. Nerv. Super.* (Praha), 16(3):204-205, 1974.

46. IDANPAAN-HEIKKILA, J., ALHAVA, E., OLKNUORA, M., et al.: Clozapine and agranulocytosis. *Lancet,* September 27, 1975, p. 611.

47. NAHUNEK, K., RODOVA, A., SVESTKA, J., et al. Clinical experience with clozapine in endogenous depression. *Act. Nerv. Super.* (Praha), 15(3):111, 1973.

6

Second- and Third-generation Antidepressants: A Clinical Overview

John P. Feighner, M.D.

THE NEW GENERATION OF ANTIDEPRESSANTS

Prognosis for patients with depressive disorders changed significantly for the better with the advent of psychotropic drugs in the 1950s. However, current treatment with the tricyclic antidepressants (TCAs) and the monoamine oxidase (MAO) inhibitors is problematic because of their slow onset of action, unpleasant side effects, and frequently lethal results when used in suicide attempts. The last few years have witnessed the further development of new, biologically more specific classes of drugs which are at least as effective in treating depression as the earlier compounds and have eliminated many of their negative aspects (1).

This chapter will review a number of the newer compounds* which our research institute has been investigating over the last few years and which have either already been released or should be clinically available within one to five years. They are the new tricyclics, tetracyclics, selective serotonin reuptake inhibitors, and dopaminergic compounds. Theoretical issues will be considered in the course of the discussion on specific drugs.

1) *The New Tricyclic Drugs*

Trimipramine (Surmontil) is one of the earliest tricyclic antidepressive drugs

---

* In an effort to summarize relevant similarities and differences between the newer antidepressants, Tables 1 and 2 and Figure 1 have been included at the end of this chapter.

in the new groups. It is an iminodibenzyl which has proved to be effective in more than 21 years of use (2). Unlike imipramine, it has a relatively short half-life that ranges from three to eight hours depending on which metabolites are examined. It is a tertiary amine with serotonergic activity, but its sedative effects are related to CNS H_1 receptor blockade, and like other TCAs, it has moderate atropine-like effect. Additional evidence indicates that trimipramine has considerable Histamine-H_2 receptor blockade, and early clinical trials indicate significant clinical effect in acid-peptic disease (3). Its spectrum of clinical application for depression is similar to imipramine and amitriptyline and it appears to have a somewhat lower side effect profile (4).

Amoxapine (Asendin) is a more recent tricyclic compound of the dibenzoxazepine family with noradrenergic and mild dopaminolytic effect. It is a demethylated derivative of loxapine succinate and, like other demethylated derivatives of some of the neuroleptics such as the thionxathenes and the piperazine phenothiazines, it has antidepressive effects (5). Its action has been examined in 108 studies utilizing over 2,000 patients in the United States. According to its manufacturers, the medication's onset of action is more rapid and its antidepressant effect greater than the standard tricyclics such as amitriptyline (Elavil) or imipramine (Tofranil). Maximum improvement on the Hamilton Depression Rating (HAM-D) Scale was greater at the end of the first week for patients on amoxapine than those on imipramine or amitriptyline, but at endpoint* the treatment groups were equal (6). The dosage range is generally from 200-400 mg, but it may at times be necessary to raise this to as high as 600 mg, particularly if the patient is in a hospital setting. Amoxapine has moderate atropine effect and antihistaminic activity. The major active antidepressant metabolite is 8-hydroxyamoxapine and it is a potent noradrenaline reuptake inhibitor with a 30-hour half-life. Thus, as with many tricyclics, the drug can be given in divided doses or as a single bedtime dose. The 7-hydroxyamoxapine metabolite which is a dopamine antagonist accounts for a small percentage (5-7) of the activity of the compound and has a short three-to-four-hour half-life. However, the presence of this antipsychotic metabolite raises the possibility of extrapyramidal side effects and, potentially, of tardive dyskinesia.

Another claim made for amoxapine by the manufacturers is that it has low cardiovascular toxicity even in cases of overdose. Both this and the earlier mentioned claim concerning the rapidity of onset of effectiveness in treatment of depression must be substantiated by further study.

Because of dopamine antagonist effect, the possibility of extrapyramidal side effects and tardive dyskinesia exists. However, because of the dopaminolytic action, amoxapine may be most effective in treatment of the agitated or psychotic

---

* Endpoint analysis refers to the last evaluable visit for each patient regardless of when this occurs during the study and includes all patients evaluated.

subtypes of depression. More systematic study of the effects of amoxapine on patients with psychotic depressions is therefore indicated.

2) *Tetracyclic Compounds*

Maprotiline (Ludiomil) is the first available tetracyclic compound in the United States, and it has been in use for several years as a prescription drug on a worldwide basis. It is a tetracyclic compound with potent noradrenergic and antihistaminic effect. It has moderate anticholinergic but no serotonergic effect. The dosage range is from 50-300 mg and may be given in divided doses or as a single bedtime dose. The compound has a relatively long half-life (40-50 hours) and is suitable for single dose maintenance therapy (7). Results from our own research clinic show it to be at least as effective in its antidepressive action as imipramine, with a moderately better therapeutic index due to reduced atropine effect (8). Because of this, the compound may be more useful in geriatric depression and in patients with cardiovascular disease (9). However, further clinical studies in these areas are warranted.

Oxaprotiline which is a hydroxyanalogue of maprotiline is a more potent norepinephrine reuptake inhibitor than its parent compound and has considerably less atropine effect (10). Animal studies indicate its potency to be five to 50 times greater than that of maprotiline; however, our own clinical studies using both open-label and double-blind trials on both inpatients and outpatients indicate a dosage range of 50-150 mg, usually given at bedtime (11).

Results from a large double-blind multicenter study comparing oxaprotiline with amitriptyline and placebo in 278 outpatients with major depressive disorder indicate equal efficacy for both drugs, and both are statistically superior to placebo (12). Oxaprotiline had a superior side effect profile with much lower sedative and anticholinergic effect. Fewer patients dropped out because of adverse effect, and overall, oxaprotiline was much better tolerated than amitriptyline. This is especially important for patient compliance and long-term maintenance therapy.

Mianserin is a tetracyclic compound which has been used extensively in Europe and most industrialized countries. It has been administered in excess of 100,000 patients and is considered a safe and effective antidepressant (13). The results of double-blind and open-label studies carried out on over 10,000 patients have shown it to be as effective as imipramine and amitriptyline but with few atropine side effects, minimal cardiovascular toxicity even with overdose, and little adverse drug-drug interaction with other psychotropic and cardiovascular drugs (14). Its dosage range is 30-150 mg given as a single dose at bedtime, and common side effects include weight gain, drowsiness, and lethargy.

Mianserin is theoretically interesting because it functions as an alpha-2 presynaptic blocker, thus enhancing the production and release of norepinephrine. On the other hand, its sedative properties appear to be related to its potent antihistaminic affect. It has no MAO inhibition and no effect on dopamine or serotonin (15).

We recently completed a six-week double-blind, parallel, random assignment study in which we compared mianserin with amitriptyline on 81 outpatients who fulfilled the Feighner criteria for primary depression and the Research Diagnostic Criteria (RDC) for Major Depressive Disorder and who evidenced moderate depression, exhibiting a minimum baseline score of 19 on the 21 item HAM-D Scale (16).

Patients were evaluated weekly with standard clinical and side effect scales. The demographic characteristics were comparable for both groups and consistent with depressed outpatient populations. The mean daily dose for mianserin was 105 mg bedtime and for amitriptyline, 154 mg bedtime. Both groups showed statistically significant improvement from baseline on all parameters, and both drugs were similar on all efficacy parameters. At endpoint, 57% of mianserin patients and 54% of amitriptyline patients achieved a 50% or greater reduction in symptoms as elicited by the HAM-D Scale.

The greatest difference between the drugs was on the side effect profile, as 26 of the 41 mianserin patients and 39 of the 40 amitriptyline patients reported drug-related side effects. The efficacy index demonstrated clear superiority of mianserin over amitriptyline. The most common side effects for amitriptyline were anticholinergic, whereas the most common side effect for mianserin was drowsiness. These findings support the results of international studies (17).

Because of its efficacy and low side effect profile, mianserin should be particularly suited for geriatric depression and in patients who cannot tolerate the anticholinergic side effects. Lack of placebo-controlled data has delayed the appearance of this important compound as a prescription drug in the United States.

3) *Triazolopyridine Derivatives*

Trazodone is the first of the triazolopyridine derivatives to be used clinically. Its pharmacologic profile is atypical of antidepressive drugs in use at present in that it has virtually no effect on dopamine or norepinephrine, no atropine effect, and no MAO inhibitor effect (18). Its antidepressant action appears to be associated with its inhibition of serotonin reuptake, and it potentiates 5-hydroxytryptophan. In addition, it has peripheral antiserotonin effect and is an alpha-adrenergic blocker (19).

It has been extensively investigated in Europe over the last 13 years and in the United States for the past six years (20). It has low cardiovascular toxicity and no atropine-like effect. The dosage range is 50-800 mg, and because of its sedative effects, the main dose is usually administered at bedtime. The hypnotic effect is therapeutically useful, and we have found the compound to be most effective in depressed patients with agitation, anxiety, and insomnia. Negative side effects are lethargy, drowsiness, headaches, nausea, and mild gastrointestinal distress (21).

In addition to its use in major depressive disorders, trazodone has demonstrated usefulness in schizophrenic patients who exhibit secondary depression (22). Trazodone does not appear to exacerbate psychotic symptoms and has no potentiating atropine effect to complicate neuroleptic therapy. In addition, since trazodone has minimal effects on the dopamine system, theoretically it would not exacerbate manic symptoms to the same extent as other antidepressants (23,24). A large multicenter trial with trazodone revealed no manic episodes and to date there are no reports in the scientific literature of trazodone-induced mania (25). Further study of trazodone and its role in bipolar major affective disorder, schizophrenia with secondary depression, and schizoaffective disorder is warranted.

We have carried out two double-blind studies, one on severely ill hospitalized depressive patients and the other on outpatients (21,26). The former compared the effects of trazodone with imipramine and a placebo over a period of one month. The latter, which was a long-term study with one year follow-up, was carried out with trazodone and imipramine only. Results from the inpatient study showed trazodone to have a more rapid onset of action than imipramine and to be clearly superior to placebo. A 50% reduction of depression between pretreatment level and endpoint scores, as measured by the HAM-D Scale and the CGIS (Clinical Global Impression Scale), was used as an index of significant improvement. At endpoint analysis, 53% of the trazodone patients had significantly improved, while only 28% showed improvement on imipramine and none on placebo.

The outpatient double-blind study was carried out on 79 patients, of whom roughly twice as many were on trazodone as those on imipramine. Virtually all parameters favored trazodone over imipramine, and both drugs were effective over the year-long study. At endpoint, 56% of trazodone patients showed significant improvement as opposed to 36% of those on imipramine. Common side effects for imipramine included the atropine-like effects and, for patients on trazodone, were drowsiness, lethargy, occasional headaches, and nausea. Fewer trazodone patients dropped out because of side effects than those on imipramine. This makes trazodone a useful drug for the long-term treatment of depression to prevent relapse, especially during the first year.

Because of its lack of anticholinergic effect, trazodone may be well suited for geriatric patients with major depressive disorders. Gerner et al. compared trazodone to imipramine in 60 geriatric depressed patients and found equal efficacy, but noted that trazodone had a lower side effect profile with fewer dropouts and overall was better tolerated than imipramine (27).

The above studies, and others summarized by Brogden et al., indicate a potential wide range of clinical application for this triazolopyridine derivative (19).

4) *Selective Serotonin Reuptake Inhibitors*

Zimelidine is a bicyclic compound which is a potent serotonin reuptake inhibitor. It is void of atropine, dopamine, norepinephrine, and antihistaminic effects (28). Its cardiovascular toxicity is low. Its dosage range is from 100-300 mg per day, given in a single or divided daytime dose as it has minimal sedative effect. Common side effects include hyperactivity, restlessness, tremulousness, nausea, diarrhea, and, occasionally, headaches (29,30).

Results of both national and international studies indicate that zimelidine has equal efficacy to amitriptyline, imipramine, and newer antidepressants such as maprotiline, nomifensine, and mianserin (31-33). Its major advantage is in a high therapeutic index with a low side effect profile, and it is generally well tolerated by most patients.

Despite its lack of sedation, zimelidine demonstrates stabilization of both anxiety symptoms and sleep disturbance that accompany the depressive syndrome (30). In addition, because of its lack of antihistaminic and anticholinergic effects, zimelidine is well suited for geriatric depression, obese patients, and inpatients who cannot tolerate the atropine-like side effects (32).

Fluoxetine is a high selective serotonin reuptake inhibitor (34). Its effect on dopamine and norepinephrine is not cliniclly significant and, unlike the tricyclic antidepressants, it is void of anticholinergic and antihistaminic side effects.

In man, the inhibition of serotonin uptake by fluoxetine has been investigated by Lemberger et al. (35). They demonstrated that fluoxetine caused a diminution of endogenous serotonin in platelets and had no effect on the noradrenergic responses as measured by the pressor effect to tyramine and noradrenaline, and thus, a highly specific serotonin effect for both fluoxetine and its primary desmethyl metabolite.

Results of initial open-label studies in patients with major depressive disorder were positive and suggested potent antidepressant effect with minimal side effects in a dosage range of 20-80 mg per day (35).

We recently completed a double-blind, random assignment comparison of fluoxetine and amitriptyline on 44 outpatients with primary major depressive disorder (36). The study included one week of single-blind placebo washout to eliminate apparent placebo responders, and then was followed by five weeks of active medication. Standard rating scales for efficacy and safety were performed weekly, and appropriate laboratory data including blood count, urinalysis, chemistry panel, EKG, and opthalmological exams were obtained pre- and post-drug study.

The demography of the patients was consistent for outpatient depressive patients, and there were no significant differences between the two treatment groups. The baseline 21 item HAM-D Scale score had to be at least 20, with a minimum Raskin Depression Scale score of 8. (Outpatients manifesting this level of symptomatology are usually thought of as experiencing depression of moderate severity.)

Results from the study showed that both treatment groups demonstrated statistically significant improvement from baseline to endpoint. Fluoxetine patients demonstrated greater improvement with overall fewer side effects than the amitriptyline patients. Only three out of 22 fluoxetine patients discontinued the study because of adverse effects, whereas nine out of 22 amitriptyline patients did. The most common side effects for amitriptyline were related to sedation and anticholinergic effects. The most common side effects for fluoxetine were nausea, diarrhea, and restlessness. No significant drug-related laboratory abnormalities were noted. One drug-related minor arrhythmia was noted in the amitriptyline group. Of interest was the fact that there was a nonsignificant weight gain in the amitriptyline group, whereas in the fluoxetine group there was an average weight loss of three pounds. This was significant between the two groups and suggests that fluoxetine may be useful in obese depressed patients. In addition, because of its lack of anticholinergic and antihistamine effects, fluoxetine may be well suited for geriatric depressed patients, patients with cardiovascular disease, and those who are intolerant of the atropine-like side effects.

Fluvoxamine is chemically different but pharmacologically similar to both zimelidine and fluoxetine. It is a highly selective serotonin reuptake inhibitor with no anticholinergic, antihistamine, noradrenergic, or dopaminergic effects (37). It has remarkably few active metabolites and the kidney is the sole excretory organ with 95% of an oral dose recovered in the urine within 48 hours after a single dose.

Early clinical trials indicate antidepressant activity with a low side effect profile and a dosage range of 100-300 mg per day given in a single or divided dose (38). Common side effects are similar to zimelidine and include nausea, diarrhea, and restlessness. Further study is in progress on a national and international basis with all three drugs, as well as a structurally similar compound, clovoxamine (39).

4) *New Drugs of Other Classes*

Nomifensine is a tetrahydroisoquinoline compound of particular interest, because it is both a norepinephrine and a dopamine reuptake inhibitor (40). In addition, nomifensine has essentially no anticholinergic or antihistaminic effects and, in therapeutic doses, may have anticonvulsant properties (41). Burrows et al. have demonstrated lower cardiovascular toxicity for nomifensine as opposed to the tricyclic antidepressants (42). Nomifensine is readily absorbed and conjugated to the glucuronide metabolite with a plasma half-life of two to four hours and is excreted predominantly in urine (40).

The dosage range is 50-200 mg per day, given in divided daytime doses. Common side effects include dry mouth, tremulousness, restlessness, insomnia, and, infrequently, drug fever (43). In addition, nomifensine, because of its dopaminergic activity, should be used cautiously in bipolar major affective and schizophrenic disorders (24). Exacerbation of both manic episodes and psychotic symptoms has been noted clinically (40).

Studies done in our own clinic in primary depression indicate that nomifensine is an effective antidepressant with greatest effect noted in psychomotor retarded depressions (44). Also, a comparative trial with nomifensine and imipramine in geriatric depression indicates that nomifensine is well tolerated by geriatric patients, with equal efficacy noted between treatment groups (44). This is consistent with international studies (45). Nomifensine has had extensive international utilization since 1977 and should be available in the United States for clinical use late in 1982.

Bupropion is a chloro-propionphenone and is the first of this unique monocyclic amino ketone class of drugs to be used clinically (46). It is different from all other antidepressants in that it has no significant effect on norepinephrine or serotonin and has mild dopaminergic activity, but this is not felt to be clinically significant. Essentially, its mechanism of action is unknown (47). It has no MAO inhibition or direct stimulant effect, and no anticholinergic or antihistaminic effects. It is non-sedating and has no interaction with alcohol (48).

In animal studies, prediction of antidepressant activity with bupropion was positive only on the reversal of tetrabenazine sedation and the potentiation of L-dopa effects (47). In studies on both animals and in man, bupropion has essentially no adverse cardiac effects, as reflected by conduction time, blood pressure, and pulse, nor any tendency for orthostatic hypotension. Bupropion produces a slight reduction of appetite, and there is a tendency for patients on maintenance therapy to lose weight (49). Bupropion has anticonvulsant properties in mice, but like the tricyclic antidepressants, it has slight epileptogenic properties in man (50).

Extensive clinical studies on both inpatients and outpatients with major depressive disorders reveal significant antidepressant activity. Placebo-controlled, double-blind trials on 219 inpatients with marked-to-severe major depressive disorders in four different centers reveal an average significant response for bupropion of 60-70%, and only a 20-30% response for placebo when comparing endpoint clinical efficacy parameters (48). Two double-blind comparisons of amitriptyline with bupropion in 166 depressed outpatients show comparable significant efficacy for both drugs with trends favoring bupropion.

We have recently completed a 28-day double-blind random assignment: bupropion versus placebo study on 67 inpatients with marked-to-severe primary major depressive disorders (51). Standard rating scales for efficacy and adverse effects were done at days 5, 8, 11, 14, 21, and 28. Endpoint data analysis revealed a highly significant ($p<.001$) effect for bupropion over placebo. At endpoint, 63% of bupropion and only 10% of placebo patients had a 50% or greater improvement in HAM-D scores. CGI scores of moderate improvement or better were achieved by 76% of the bupropion patients and only 5% of the placebo patients. This study and others offer substantial evidence that bupropion is an effective antidepressant.

The average dosage range for outpatients is 300-450 mg per day, and for inpatients 450-600 mg per day, usually given in divided doses. Common side effects include restlessness, insomnia, tremor, dizziness, dry mouth, diaphoresis, and nausea. In general, the side effect profile is extremely low for this compound, and in the placebo-controlled trials the placebo patients reported as many side effects as did those on bupropion (48). Also, during both the short-term acute studies and long-term maintenance studies there were considerably less than expected hypomanic or manic episodes, and double-blind controlled trials with lithium and placebo are now underway in bipolar patients.

Because of its low side effect profile and non-sedating properties, bupropion is well suited for geriatric depression, maintenance antidepressant therapy, cardiovascular patients, and patients who are intolerant of the anticholinergic side effects. In addition, data from the double-blind trials indicate that 60% of patients who were previously poor responders to the tricyclic antidepressants demonstrate moderate improvement or better when treated with bupropion (52). This adds further supporting evidence that bupropion has a broad spectrum of clinical application in major depressive disorders.

Alprazolam is a triazolobenzodiazepine and represents a unique class of benzodiazepines by incorporation of a triazole ring in the basic structure resulting in rapid absorption and elimination (53). According to Schatzberg and Cole, who did an extensive literature review in 1978, the classic benzodiazepines are not effective in major depressive disorders (54). Benzodiazepines, however, have a generally low incidence of serious adverse affects with a lack of anticholinergic side effects, low cardiotoxicity, and minimal potential for lethality with overdose (55). Alprazolam was first developed and studied as an anxiolytic by Fabre and was noted in early clinical trials to demonstrate antidepressant effect beyond that accounted for by its anxiolytic and hypnotic properties (56,57). In addition, although alprazolam has a potent GABA-ergic effect similar to other benzodiazepines, it has an effect on REM-sleep in depressed patients similar to the MAO inhibitors and tricyclic antidepressants. Also, it has an effect similar to desipramine on the reserpine-induced model of depression in rats (58,59).

Because of earlier findings suggesting antidepressant activity, we participated in a five-center double-blind, randomized, six-week trial comparing alprazolam with imipramine and placebo in 906 outpatients with unipolar major depressive disorder of at least one-month duration (60). All patients fulfilled the Feighner criteria for depression and in addition were required to have a minimum baseline score of 18 or more on the 21-item HAM-D Scale, 8 or more on the Raskin Depression Scale and a Covi Anxiety Scale less than or equal to the Raskin Score (61).

Of the 906 outpatients enrolled in the study, 183 were not evaluable for a variety of administrative reasons and these patients were evenly distributed within the three treatment groups. Results from the remaining 723 patients revealed that both alprazolam and imipramine were superior to placebo in virtually all efficacy parameters. The effect of alprazolam was comparable to imipramine, and alprazolam demonstrated a faster onset of action ($p < .001$). The efficacy parameters were highly concordant between physician and patient rating scales. These data strongly support antidepressant effect for alprazolam in this patient population.

The dosage range for alprazolam is 0.5–4.0 mg per day given in divided doses with the majority of the dose given at bedtime. Common side effects include drowsiness and lethargy. Alprazolam is generally well tolerated by most patients; clearly, further work is indicated to support the antidepressant effects of alprazolam, and a further analysis of current biochemical mechanisms in major depressive disorders is warranted.

CONCLUSION

Each of the new compounds discussed in this paper represent incremental improvement over existing chemotherapy of major depressive disorders. The stimulant qualities of some of the newer antidepressants still require continued investigation. Further studies should continue to clarify the overall usefulness of these drugs in the long-term treatment of depression in the general population and special groups of patients, such as the elderly. In general, these new compounds are safer, especially if taken in overdose, more specific with fewer clinically significant side effects, and many have a more rapid onset of action

TABLE 1
Pharmacological Profile in Therapeutic Dosage

Drug	Serotonergic	Noradrenergic	Dopaminergic	Anticholinergic effect	Antihistamine effect	Cardiovascular toxicity	Other effects
Trimipramine	4+	1+	0	4+	4+	4+	
Amoxapine	1+	3+	0	2+	2+	3+	7-hydroxymetabolite is a dopamine antagonist with potential for EPS and possible tardive dyskinesia.
Maprotiline	0	4+	0	2+	2+	2+	
Oxaprotiline	0	4+	0	1+	2+	2+	
Mianserin	0	2+	0	0	4+	0	
Trazodone	3+	0	0	0	0	1+	α-adrenergic blocker with potential for sedation and reduced blood pressure.
Zimelidine	4+	0	0	0	0	0	
Fluoxetine	4+	0	0	0	0	0	
Fluvoxamine	4+	0	0	0	0	0	
Nomifensine	0	3+	2+	0	0	1+	
Bupropion	0	0	1+	0	0	0	Mechanism of CNS action essentially unknown.
Alprazolam	0	0	0	0	0	0	GABA-ergic; has a similar effect on REM sleep as tricyclic antidepressants—mechanism of action is unknown.

0 = no significant clinical effect
4+ = marked clinical effect
GABA = γaminobutyric acid

TABLE 2
Clinical Profile

Drug	Chemical Class	Efficacy	Common Side Effects	Dosage
Trimipramine	tricyclic tertiary amine	Similar to standard (std) tricyclic antidepressant (TCA)	atropine-like, weight gain, sedation	50-300 mg; single HS dose or divided dose with major portion HS.
Amoxapine	tricyclic dibenzoxazepine	Similar to std TCA	atropine-like, sedation	100-400 mg; single HS dose or divided dose with major portion HS.
Maprotiline	tetracyclic (bridged tricyclic)	Similar to std TCA	atropine-like	50-300 mg; single HS dose or divided dose with major portion HS.
Oxaprotiline	tetracyclic (bridged tricyclic)	Similar to std TCA	atropine-like	25-200 mg; single HS dose or divided dose with major portion HS.
Mianserin	tetracyclic	Similar to std TCA	sedation, weight gain	30-150 mg; single HS dose.
Trazodone	triazolopyridine	Similar to std TCA. Low propensity to induce mania or exacerbate psychotic symptoms; useful in depressed schizophrenics and bipolar affective disorders.	sedation, lethargy, headaches, gastric distress	50-600 mg; single HS dose or divided dose with major portion HS.
Zimelidine	pyridylallylamine	Similar to std TCA	restlessness, tremulousness, nausea, diarrhea	150-300 mg; single/divided daytime dose.
Fluoxetine	phenylpropylamine	Similar to std TCA	restlessness, tremulousness, nausea, diarrhea, weight loss	20-80 mg; single or divided daytime dose.
Fluvoxamine	aralkylketone oxime ether	Similar to std TCA	restlessness, tremulousness, nausea, diarrhea	150-300 mg; single or divided daytime dose.
Nomifensine	tetrahydroisoquinolone	Greatest effect in psychomotor retarded depression; significant propensity to exacerbate mania and psychotic symptoms; has anticonvulsant effect and useful in depressed epileptics.	restlessness, tremulousness, insomnia, dry mouth	50-200 mg; single or divided daytime dose.
Bupropion	chlorpropiophenone	Similar to std TCA. Low propensity to exacerbate mania; useful in bipolar affective disorders.	restlessness, insomnia, diaphoresis	200-600 mg; divided daytime dose.
Alprazolam	triazolobenzodiazepine	Effective in unipolar anxious depressives—not effective in psychomotor retarded depressives.	sedation, other common benzodiazepine side effects.	0.5-4.0 mg; divided dose with major portion HS.

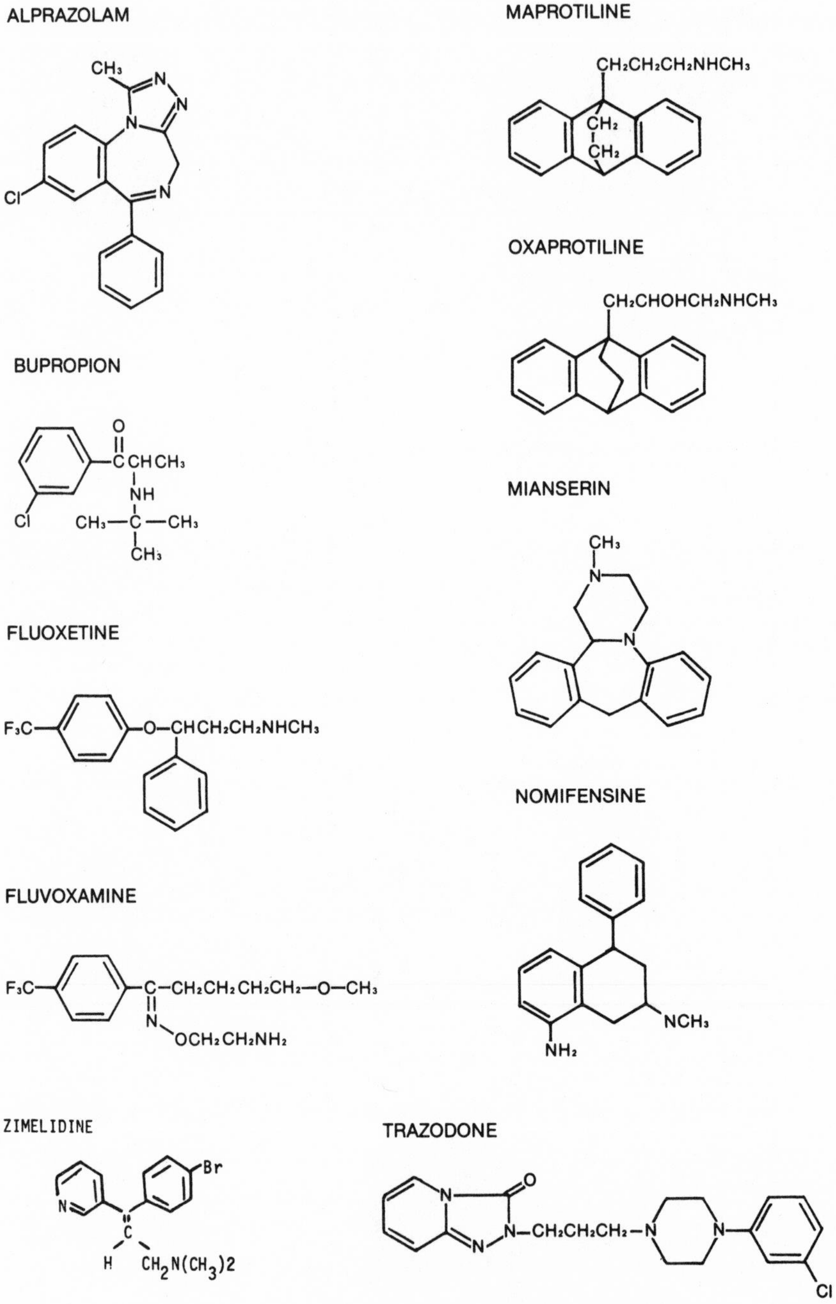

ALPRAZOLAM

MAPROTILINE

BUPROPION

OXAPROTILINE

FLUOXETINE

MIANSERIN

FLUVOXAMINE

NOMIFENSINE

ZIMELIDINE

TRAZODONE

FIGURE 1. Chemical structure of several new antidepressant agents.

than existing antidepressants. In addition, many intractable patients respond favorably to these new compounds, thus enlarging the spectrum of antidepressant activity. It is imperative that the clinician be aware of the optimum clinical usage of these new compounds as they become available over the next several years.

REFERENCES

1. FEIGHNER, J.P.: Clinical efficacy of the newer antidepressants. *J. Clin. Psychopharmacol.*, 6:235-265, 1981.
2. SETTLE, E.C., JR., and AYD, F.J.: Trimipramine: Twenty years' worldwide clinical experience. *J. Clin. Psychiat.*, 41:266-274, 1980.
3. NITTER, L., JR., HARALDSSON, A., and HOLCK, P.: The effect of trimipramine on the healing of peptic ulcer. A double-blind study. *Scand. J. Gastroenterol.*, 11:38, 39-41, 1976.
4. RIFKIN, A., SARAF, K., KANE, J., et al.: Comparison of trimipramine and imipramine: A controlled study. *J. Clin. Psychiat.*, 41:124-129, 1980.
5. GREENBLATT, E.N., HARDY, R.A., and KELLY, R.G.: Amoxapine. *Pharmacological and Biochemical Properties of Drug Substances.* Vol. II, 1979.
6. Data on file, Lederle Laboratories, Wayne, New Jersey.
7. RIESS, W., DUBEY, L., FUNFGELD, E.W., et al.: The pharmakinotic properties of maprotiline in man. *J. Int. Med. Res.*, 3:16-41, 1975.
8. LOGUE, J., SACHAIS, B., and FEIGHNER, J.P.: Comparisons of maprotiline with imipramine in severe depression: A multicenter controlled trial. *J. Clin. Pharmacol.*, 19:64-74, 1979.
9. SELVINI, A., ROSS, C., BELLI, C., et al.: Antidepressant treatment with maprotiline in the management of emotional disturbances in patients with acute myocardial infarction; a controlled study. *J. Int. Med. Res.*, 4:42-46, 1976.
10. Summary for Investigation: Oxaprotiline. Summit, N.J.: CIBA-Geigy Pharmaceutical Research Division, January 1982.
11. FEIGHNER, J.P., and ROFFMAN, M.: An early clinical trial of oxaprotiline in hospitalized patients with primary depression. *Curr. Ther. Res.*, 29(3): 363-369, 1981.
12. ROFFMAN, M., GOULD, E.E., BREWER, S.J., et al.: A double-blind comparative study of oxaprotiline with amitriptyline and placebo in moderate depression. *Curr. Ther. Res.*, in press.
13. BROGDEN, R.N., HEEL, R.C., SPEIGHT, T. M., and AVERY, G.S.: Mianserin: A review of its pharmacological properties and therapeutic efficacy in depressive illness. *Drugs*, 16:273-301, 1978.
14. CONTI, L., CASSANO, G.B., and SARTESCHI, P.: Clinical experience with mianserin. In: Rees, W.L., Drykonigen, G. and Ogara, R.C. (Eds.), *Mianserin Hydrochloride. Progress in the Pharmacotherapy of Depression.* Amsterdam: Excerpta Medica, 1979.
15. COPPEN, A., and KOPERA, H.: Workshop on the clinical pharmacology and efficacy of mianserin. *Br. J. Clin. Pharmacol.*, 5:915-995, 1978.
16. FEIGHNER, J.P., MERIDETH, C.H., HENDRICKSON, G., et al.: A double-blind comparative trial with mianserin and amitriptyline in outpatients with major depressive disorders. *Br. J. Clin. Pharm.*, in press.
17. PEET, M.: Recent clinical and pharmacological studies of the novel antidepressant Org GB94. *Drug. Expl. Clin. Res.*, 1:363-367, 1977.

18. RIBLET, L.A., and TAYLOR, D.P.: Pharmacology and neurochemistry of trazodone. *J. Clin. Psychopharmacol.*, 1:17S-22S, 1981.

19. BROGDEN, R.N., HEEL, R.C., SPEIGHT, T.M., and AVERY, G.S.: Trazodone: A review of its pharmacological properties and therapeutic use in depression and anxiety. *Drugs*, 21:401-429, 1982.

20. AYDE, F.: Trazodone: A unique new broad-spectrum antidepressant. *Int. Drug. Ther. Newsletter*, 14:33-40, 1979.

21. FEIGHNER, J.P.: Trazodone, a triazolopyridine derivative in primary depression. *J. Clin. Psychiat.*, 41:250-255, 1980.

22. SINGH, A.N., and SAXENA, B.: A controlled clinical study of trazodone in chronic schizophrenic patients with pronounced depressive symptomatology. In: F. Antonelli (Ed.), *Therapy in Psychosomatic Medicine*, Vol. III. Rome: L. Puzzi, 1977, pp. 73-82.

23. LAROCHELLE, P., HAMET, P., and ENJALBERT, M.: Responses to tyramine and norepinephrine after imipramine and trazodone. *Clin. Pharmacol. Ther.*, 26:24-30, 1979.

24. FRIEDMAN, E., FANG, F., and GERSHON, S.: Antidepressant drugs and dopamine uptake in different brain regions. *Eur. J. Pharmacol.*, 42:47-51, 1977.

25. GERSHON, S., MANN, J., NEWTON, R., and GUNTHER, B.J.: Evaluation of trazodone in the treatment of endogenous depression: Results of a multi-center double-blind study. *J. Clin. Psychopharmacol.*, 1:39S-44S, 1981.

26. FEIGHNER, J.P., MERIDETH, C.H., and HENDRICKSON, G.: Maintenance antidepressant therapy: A double-blind comparison of trazodone and imipramine. *J. Clin. Psychopharmacol.*, 6:45S-48S, 1981.

27. GERNER, R., ESTABROOK, W., STEUER, J., and JARVIK, L.: Treatment of geriatric depression with trazodone, imipramine and placebo: A double-blind study. *J. Clin. Psychiat.*, 41:216-220, 1980.

28. BERTILSSON, L., TUCK, J.R., and SIEWERS, B.: Biochemical effects of zimelidine in man. *Eur. J. Clin. Pharmacol.*, 18:483-487, 1980.

29. BURGESS, C.D., MONTGOMERY, S., WADSWORTH, J., and TURNER, P.: Cardiovascular effects of amitriptyline, mianserin, zimelidine, and nomifensine in depressed patients. *Postgrad. Med. Journal*, 55:704-708, 1979.

30. COPPEN, A., RAO, V., SWADE, C., and WOOD, K.: Zimelidine: A therapeutic and pharmacokinetic study in depression. *Psychopharmacol.*, 63:199-202, 1979.

31. GEORGOTAS, A., MANN, J., BUSH, D., and GERSHON, S.: A clinical trial of zimelidine in depression. *Comm. Psychopharmacol.*, 4:71-77, 1980.

32. MONTGOMERY, S.A.: Maprotiline, nomifensine, mianserin, zimelidine: A review of antidepressant efficacy in inpatients. *Neuropharmacol.*, 19:1185-1190, 1980.

33. SWIFT, C.G., HAYTHORNE, J.M., CLARKE, P., and STEVENSON, I.H.: Cardiovascular sedative and anticholinergic effects of amitriptyline and zimelidine in young and elderly volunteers. *Acta Psychiat. (Scand.)*, 63:425-432, 1981.

34. WONG, D.T., HORNG, J.S., BYMASTER, E.P., et al.: 3-(p-trifluoromethylphenoxy)-N-methyl-3-phenylpropylamine. *Life Sci.*, 15:471-479, 1974.

35. LEMBERGER, L., et al.: The effect of Lilly compound 94939, a potential antidepressant on biogenic amine uptake in man. *Br. J. Clin. Pharmacol.*, 3:215-218, 1976.

36. FEIGHNER, J.P., FROST, N.R., MERIDETH, C.H., HENDRICKSON, G., and JACOBS, R.S.: A comparative trial of fluoxetine and amitriptyline in outpatients with major depressive disorder. *J. Clin. Psychiat.*, in press.

37. CLAASSEN, V., DAVIES, J.E., HERTTING, G., and PLACHETA, P.: Fluvoxamine a specific 5-hydroxytryptamine uptake inhibitor. *Br. J. Pharmacol.*, 60:505-516, 1977.
38. DOOGAN, D.P.: Fluvoxamine as an antidepressant drug. *Neuropharmacol.*, 19:1215-1216, 1980.
39. SALETU, B., GRUNBERGER, J., RAJNA, P., and KAROBATH, M.: Clovoxamine and fluvoxamine—2 biogenitc amine reuptake inhibiting antidepressants; quantitative EEG, psychometric, and pharmacokinetic studies in man. *J. Neurol. Transmission,* 49:63-86, 1980.
40. BROGDEN, R.N., HEEL, R.C., SPEIGHT, T.M., and AVERY, G.S.: Nomifensine: A review of its pharmacologic properties and therapeutic efficacy in depressive illness. *Drugs,* 18:1-24, 1979.
41. HOFFMAN, I.: A comparative review of the pharmacology of nomifensine. *Br. J. Clin. Pharmacol. (Suppl. 2),* 4:69-78, 1977.
42. BURROWS, G.D., VOHRA, J., DUMOVIC, P., SCOGGINS, B.A., and DAVIES, B.: Cardiological effects of nomifensine, a new antidepressant. *Med. J. Australia,* 1:341-345, 1978.
43. POLDINGER, W., and GAMMEL, G.: Differences in effect between nomifensine and nortriptyline. *Int. Pharmcopsychiat.,* 13:58-62, 1978.
44. FEIGHNER, J.P., MERIDETH, C.H., NASH, R.J., and HENDRICKSON, G.: A comparative double-blind placebo controlled trial of nomifensine vs. imipramine in primary depression. Presentation of the CINP, Jerusalem, 1982.
45. MOIZESZOWICZ, J., and SUBIRA, S.: Controlled trial of nomifensine and viloxazine in the treatment of depression in the elderly. *J. Clin. Pharmacol.,* 17:81-84, 1977.
46. SOROKO, F.E., MEHTA, N.D., MAXWELL, R.A., FERRIS, R.M., and SCHRODER, D.H.: Bupropion hydrochloride: A novel antidepressant agent. *J. Pharm. Pharmacol.,* 29:767-770, 1977.
47. FERRIS, R.M., LOOPER, D.R., and MAXWELL, R.A.: Studies concerning the mechanism of the antidepressant activity of bupropion. *J. Clin. Psychiat.,* in press.
48. Data on file Burroughs Wellcome Company, Research Triangle Park, North Carolina, 1982.
49. HARTO-TRUAX, N., STERN, W., MILLER, L., SOTO, T.I., and CATO, A.E.: The effects of bupropion on body weight. *J. Clin. Psychiat.,* in press.
50. PECK, A.W., STERN, W., and WATKINSON, C.: The incidence of seizures during treatment with tricyclic antidepressant drugs and bupropion. *J. Clin. Psychiat.,* in press.
51. FEIGHNER, J.P., MERIDETH, C.H., HENDRICKSON, G., and STERN, W.: A comparative double-blind study of bupropion and placebo in hospitalized patients with primary depression. (Data to be published).
52. STERN, W.: An overview of bupropion in major depressive disorder. *J. Clin. Psychiat,* in press.
53. GAIL, M., KAMDAR, G.V., and COLLINS, R.J.: Pharmacology of some metabolites of triazolam, alprazolam and diazepam prepared by a simple one-step oxidation of benzodiazepines. *J. Med. Chem.,* 21:1290-1294, 1978.
54. SCHATZBERG, A.F., and COLE, J.O.: Benzodiazepines in depressive disorders. *Arch. Gen. Psychiat.,* 35:1359-1365, 1978.
55. FEIGHNER, J.P.: Benzodiazepines as antidepressants. A triazolobenzodiazepine used to treat depression. In: H. Lehmenn (Ed.), *Modern Problems in Pharmacopsychiatry.* Basel: Karger, in press.

56. FABRE, L.F., and MELENDON, D.M.: A double-blind study comparing the efficacy and safety of alprazolam with diazepam and placebo in anxious outpatients. *Curr. Ther. Res.*, 19:661-668, 1976.

57. FABRE, L.F.: Pilot open-label study with alprazolam (U-31,889) in outpatients with neurotic depression. *Curr. Ther. Res.*, 19:661-668, 1976.

58. SULSER, F.: Pharmacology: Current antidepressants. *Psychiat. Ann.*, 10 (suppl.): 381-387, 1980.

59. SETHY, V.H., and HODGES, D.H.: Role of β-adrenergic receptors in the antidepressant activity of alprazolam. Presented at Benzodiazepine Symposium, National Institute of Health, April 1982.

60. FEIGHNER, J.P., ADEN, G.C., FABRE, L.F., RICKELS, K., and SMITH, W.T.: Multi-center double-blind safety and efficacy comparison of alprazolam, imipramine, and placebo in the treatment of major depressive disorder. JAMA, in press.

61. FEIGHNER, J.P., ROBINS, E., GUZE, S.D., WOODRUFF, R.A., WINOKUR, G., and MUNOZ, R.: Diagnostic criteria for use in psychiatric research. *Arch. Gen. Psychiat.*, 26:57-62, 1972.

Part III

PSYCHOTHERAPEUTIC ISSUES

7

The Evolution of Psychotherapeutic Approaches for Affective and Schizophrenic Disorders

John S. Strauss, M.D.

The final examination in my Introductory History course at college had only one question. It was, "Describe the history of Western Europe." When I was invited to write this chapter on the evolution of psychotherapy for affective and schizophrenic disorders, it felt like much the same kind of challenge. What should be included in the concept of psychotherapy? How can one discuss the psychotherapy of affective disorders and schizophrenia at the same time?

Perhaps the most meaningful way to find an entry point into this challenge is to begin at the end, or what is at least the current "end," with the dominant question: Does psychotherapy work? Is psychotherapy for affective and schizophrenic disorders the definitive treatment, an anachronism, or an imperfect but evolving phenomenon?

Recent research on psychotherapy for these disorders has generated very mixed results. For schizophrenia, the negative findings tend to outweigh the earlier, more optimistic claims. The work of May, Tuma, and Dixon (1), for example, has suggested rather starkly that psychotherapeutic treatments of schizophrenia have little impact at best. A recent review by Mosher and Keith has been more optimistic (2), but another review also by investigators generally sympathetic to psychotherapy (3) has taken a more limited stance regarding the efficacy of

This report was supported in part by NIMH Grants #MH00340, MH34365, and MH35777.

at least traditional psychotherapeutic approaches for schizophrenic disorders. In a recent conference on the psychotherapy of schizophrenia (4), contributors for various backgrounds focusing on both research and practice brought up as many questions regarding the efficacy of psychotherapy for schizophrenia as demonstrations of its value.

Psychotherapy for affective disorders has had more positive but still mixed results. For depression, psychotherapies alone appear to be better at least than no treatment, but not necessarily more effective than medication alone (5). Various combinations of medication and psychotherapy may be still more effective, perhaps with medications having their main impact on symptoms, and psychotherapy its major impact on social function. The value of psychotherapy for more severe ("endogenous" or psychotic) depressions and for mania and bipolar disorders has been strongly questioned, and in many centers it is not used at all in their treatment.

But there has been much criticism of the psychotherapy research itself (6-8). Those criticisms raise questions regarding the findings and their interpretation. To some extent, it is possible that at least some criticisms of psychotherapy research reflect complaining by those who have not liked the results (9). But beyond such a possibility, certain criticisms have been raised that require respectful attention before conclusions can be reached. One might ask the question, "If methodologic details are so important for demonstrating the efficacy of psychotherapy, can the treatment really be very powerful?" The answer may well be yes. Even with a drug as valuable as penicillin, if a treatment is used for an undifferentiated group of disorders or in a less than optimal way, or if complicating factors are not considered, efficacy may be difficult to demonstrate.

To determine what is implied by this welter of findings and criticisms, it may be useful to follow the teachings of Piaget and many others, that if one wants to understand a situation, the best way is to take a developmental perspective, pointing out major themes and trends in the process. For this reason, an historical view of the evolution of psychotherapy for schizophrenic and affective disorders may be especially valuable.

Has there even been such an evolution? Where one starts to explore this question depends on the definition of psychotherapy that is selected and, to a lesser extent, on the definitions used for affective and schizophrenic disorders. Although precise and perhaps even narrow definitions of all these terms may be useful for some purposes, my present goal, that of obtaining a perspective, will be best served by employing an extremely broad definition of psychotherapy and settling, for the time being, for the diagnostic criteria used by those investigators or clinicians whose work will be reviewed. A serviceable definition of psychotherapy, for my purposes, might be "any type of planned human interaction used as treatment for these disorders." Using this broad approach to the topic, the following discussion will describe five main themes highlighted by tracing the evolution of psychotherapeutic approaches for schizophrenic and affective disorders.

1) *The Tendency to Either/Or Reasoning*

With the broad definition described above, I could even begin, as Ehrenwald has (10), with early treatments of mental disorders by the Assyrians and Babylonians. That starting point at the very least suggests that over many centuries some very intelligent people have had the opportunity to struggle with these questions. More specifically, more recently, and more amply documented is the work of Poussin, Pinel, and others at the end of the 18th century (11). The approach that these leaders brought to the treatment of mental illness has its roots in classical history and beyond, and later was termed "moral treatment" as it evolved. This approach focused on providing humane living conditions and considering the person's needs for rest, respect, meaningful activities, and adequate food. It also frequently included the use of didactic methods to teach patients about "mental hygiene."

In more recent times, we have tended to see moral treatment as important for its humanity in stark contrast to the earlier settings that were often provided for the mentally ill. But the moral treatment movement is also often viewed currently as naive in its expectations that even the more severe psychiatric disorders could be influenced by general environmental conditions and didactic input. Any such judgments about moral treatment and about successive treatments on our part might in turn reflect our own naiveté, a naiveté tending to assume that previous efforts were mostly wrong, and that our orientation is mostly right, a naiveté assuming either/or, rather than considering that various approaches might contribute in combination to a treatment regimen. This tendency to either/or thinking is, in fact, the first major theme in the evolution of psychotherapy.

In its current representatives, the moral treatment movement has become fragmented. Some fragments focus on milieu therapy (12-14), others on work (15), and still others on social networks (e.g., 16,17). Although these efforts have provided useful contributions, the precision gained by their fragmentation may have lost the feeling for total life context that was reflected, even though vaguely, in several moral treatment approaches.

2) *The Tendency for Psychotherapy to Evolve from the Interpretive Toward the Reality-oriented*

Toward the end of the 19th century, two phenomena were occurring simultaneously in psychiatric treatment. One of these was the rise of organic orientations based on the advances made in finding specific treatments for specific disorders in the field of medicine. For the followers of this orientation, psychiatric symptoms were seen as reflecting organic diseases (18), and there was the belief, not always implicit, that discovery of the "silver bullet(s)" for mental disorders would sooner or later occur.

At the same time, of course, the notion of psychotherapy that is now considered as traditional was burgeoning. Such treatment (unlike milieu therapy, for example) would meet practically anyone's definition of psychotherapy, focusing as it did on a therapist working with a patient to promote insight by exploring underlying meanings, psychological conflicts, and vulnerabilities.

In the early days of "traditional" individual psychotherapy, a variety of experiences tended to generate several theories suggesting that these types of treatment may be effective for some types of affective disorders, but perhaps not for psychoses, either of an affective or schizophrenic nature. The supposed inability of psychotic or at least schizophrenic persons to form a transference neurosis (19), questions of whether psychotic symptoms had significant meanings (20), and assumptions about organicity in these disorders often discouraged the use of psychotherapies for their treatment. Perhaps the availability of other institutions, theories, and entire academic schools focusing on the more severely disturbed also lessened the pressure to find new and psychological treatments aimed at the care of these patients.

Nevertheless, stimulated by the teachings of Adolf Meyer, several clinicians rejected the idea that psychotherapy was inappropriate for the psychoses. Meyer's view that the environment was important for even the most severe disorders generated many psychotherapeutic efforts. Sullivan, for example, working with schizophrenic patients and others with severe disorders, focused on the interactive aspects of the psychiatric interview and interpersonal concept of psychopathology (20). This approach allowed the psychotherapist to be more active, a characteristic that was often necessary when dealing with disturbed patients. Thus, clinicians such as Fromm-Reichmann and Sullivan viewed the therapist as a participant-observer, and did not deemphasize the participant part of that role. Fromm-Reichmann suggested, for example, that if the therapist was going through a particularly difficult situation in her own life, it might be necessary to mention this to the patient to explain why the therapist may be acting differently (21,22). This type of interaction between the patient and the therapist is explained by the rationale that severely disordered persons, and perhaps especially those with schizophrenia, are extremely sensitive to what appear to be relatively minor changes in the therapist's demeanor. Such a sensitivity requires a corresponding reality-oriented clarification (23-25). This tendency for the psychotherapy of severe disorders to move from more purely interpretive to the more directive and reality-oriented is a second theme in the evolution of psychotherapies for affective and schizophrenic disorders.

Such modification of traditional psychotherapy to meet the needs of severely disturbed patients finds its counterpart today in the work of many therapists. It is especially common in those who have worked at some time in the Baltimore-Washington area, where many of these orientations originated. The treatment orientation of Searles (26), for example, illustrates the interactive and active psychotherapist at work. Others, such as Rosen (27), attempted to extend this activity to the extreme in confronting the patient directly with his unconscious messages and needs, as viewed by the therapist. There is no proof, however, that these more extreme efforts were particularly effective (28). Of course, some of the more modest tendencies toward active interventions were reflected in traditional psychoanalytic circles as well, as in Bibring's description of "parameters" (29).

Conjoint family psychotherapy for affective and schizophrenic disorders arose next, but only after a rather amazingly long interval (30-32). Like individual psychotherapy, family psychotherapy focused at the beginning on the exploration and interpretation of conflicts and meaning, but the family orientation was also a bridge to a broader environmental perspective and so included social concepts such as role and power relationships as well.

Over time, in family psychotherapy, as with individual psychotherapy, more active approaches were explored. These now include such interventions as Minuchin's instructing people to switch chairs in the session or talk to each other in a particular way (33), and Selvini Palazzoli's use of paradoxical interventions, prescribing a particular action or series of actions to be carried out at home (34).

Strikingly, some approaches to family therapy are coming almost full circle back to moral treatment principles. The work of Anderson (35), teaching the families of patients how to deal with various kinds of problems, uses a technique refined, but not entirely different, from that for teaching patients which was often employed earlier in centers of moral treatment.

Group psychotherapy for affective and schizophrenic disorders has had somewhat the same evolution as family psychotherapy, beginning with interpretive approaches and working toward more practical, problem-solving orientations. These latter appear to be particularly effective for persons with severe disturbances (30).

3) *The Tendency of Therapeutic Approaches to Emphasize Their Differences and Ignore Commonalities*

The evolution of psychotherapies does not end here. I will not discuss gestalt, existential, and other approaches, because they have not generally been used with the more severe types of psychopathology. But another evolution in psychotherapy does need to be mentioned, that of the behavior therapies. Many persons, of course, would not consider behavior therapy as psychotherapy. This view is partly a result of the way behavior therapists see themselves, often not emphasizing or even mentioning the relationship aspects of their treatments. This tendency highlights a third theme in the evolution of the psychotherapies, that successive approaches often establish their identity by emphasizing differences and ignoring commonalities. The result is to suggest more discrete differences among psychotherapeutic approaches than actually exist.

4) *The Tendency for Different Conclusions about the Nature of Disorders to Become Associated with Specific Treatment Approaches*

It is particularly important to include behavioral treatments in this review, because they appear to have been more effective with especially disturbed patients than several other approaches. Their inclusion is also important because it throws into relief the tendency to assume that psychotherapy, and perhaps any psychological treatments, must work from the "inside out" (2). Such an assumption implies or states that "real" change (sometimes called "structural") must be generated by changes in the patients' thoughts, perceptions, and feelings. It is believed that these will automatically bring about changes in behavior. This view tends to exclude the possibility that basic changes in the person might also be brought about from the "outside in," that is, by changed behaviors bringing about changes in thinking, feeling, and perception.

The struggles between behavior therapies and more traditional psychotherapies reflect a fourth theme in the evolution of psychotherapy. Different assumptions about the nature of disorder and change are associated with each treatment approach, and these assumptions often come to be viewed as basic truths precluding observations that might suggest the contrary. It is because of this theme that I have taken the broadest view of psychotherapy, to avoid, at least to some extent, assumptions that might keep us from obtaining the kind of perspective that is necessary to help resolve the problems that we are pursuing. The degree of fervor that assumptions about the nature of disorder and change can generate is often seen on those occasions when the various schools do encounter each other. In a recent conference on the psychotherapy of schizophrenia (37), for example, the issue was sometimes stated as who is "really" treating patients.

In describing the evolution of psychotherapeutic treatment approaches for affective and schizophrenic disorders, four evolutionary themes have been noted: the tendency to use an either/or view of treatment methods rather than consider multiple approaches; the tendency of psychotherapies for severe disorders to move from the purely interpretive to the reality-oriented; the tendency for each successive approach to emphasize differences and deemphasize overlap; and the tendency to generate unshakable and conflicting assumptions about the nature of disorder and change. It is important also to notice a fifth and final theme, one that by its very nature is least reflected in writing and research.

5) *The Tendency to Conceptualize Pure Forms of Treatment and to Practice Heterogeneity*

In many centers, and quite commonly in practice generally, rigid adherence to one or another treatment approach may not be maintained. Apparently, many clinicians have had experiences such as the one I had when I began my residency. It was suggested that I run a group psychotherapy for acutely psychotic patients using an approach that was primarily interpretive. After about two sessions, one of the better integrated patients said, "Dr. Strauss, if you don't stop reflecting back to us what we're saying, you're going to drive us all crazy." The behavior of the group suggested that he was, in fact, right, and I modified my technique rapidly.

Psychotherapeutic treatments for affective and schizophrenic disorders seem often in practice to be modified from the conceptual purity of the original or, in some cases, from the second generation purifiers of an originally heterogeneous treatment approach. Because the treatment modifications made in practice do not follow a pure form of any treatment, important double standards may arise (e.g., 38). If practice is not pure, but theory and research continue to adhere to one or another conceptual monolith, a serious split occurs. Research is carried on that does not really provide information about or for practice, and theory is elaborated, increasingly isolated from the preponderant clinical realities. Such an evolution leads to research or theory focused on a single treatment, when most practices may involve a combination of approaches. Or research and theory may focus on pure treatments, when amalgams and modifications or change in approach during the course of treatment are the rule. The admixtures and modifications of treatment as often used in practice may not be as elegant as the purer forms, but their existence, growth, and ubiquity may be trying to tell us that they are not just wayward deviations from an ideal.

There has been an evolution of the psychotherapies for affective and schizophrenic disorders. In fact, there have been several evolutions. The obvious evolutions in pure form and modality have been accompanied by amalgamations, modifications, combinations, and the tendency for research and theory to ignore these.

Considering these evolutions, we can now return to the original question, what is the role of psychotherapy in the treatment of affective and schizophrenic disorders? I would like to suggest that we have not come to grips with how limited our knowledge about this question really is. Until we do so, we may operate on very shaky assumptions, which we presume to reflect truth. Our limited knowledge may be a function partly of not looking sufficiently at the collectivity and evolution of the field, but perhaps we have also hoped to finesse the complexity that such a glance reveals. Maybe patients have various combinations of psychotherapeutic needs. Perhaps the needs for a helping environment (moral treatment), the understanding of conflicts and vulnerabilities (individual psychotherapy) of family relationships (family psychotherapy), and of more general modes of relating socially (group therapy), together with the acquisition of skills (behavior therapy and skills training) may be important for different people in different combinations and different degrees.

Of course, this speculation is not radical at all. But how far behind such a possibility are our patient assessment, clinician training and research procedures? Generally our assessment of patients and their situations does not give us the information needed in these various areas in a systematic way. Frequently we are not even aware of some of the variables that may need attention. In reviewing the literature and many case records as part of our studies on the role of work and social relations in psychiatric disorder, for example, it is amazing how little information is available.

However, the situation with patient assessment may be relatively favorable compared to our conceptualizations and our research. If these do not provide help in understanding and synthesizing the various aspects of people's lives and problems, how can we hope to have an optimally effective psychotherapy (whether we define psychotherapy in a broad or a narrow sense)? Fortunately, contributions to the understanding of interactions between changes from without and within are beginning to be generated (39,40). Research has now been started on the relationship aspects of behavior therapy and the behavioral aspects of relationship therapy (41-43). But the mental health field in many instances still uses a model of disorder that has been so valuable with infectious diseases, and we are still looking for a kind of psychotherapeutic penicillin to treat a mental pneumococcus. Certainly arguments about psychotherapy, pro and con, often assume the form of discussions about penicillin.

The future evolution of psychotherapy and the understanding of psychotherapy or the psychotherapies as treatment modalities may hinge on the further development of a synthesized conceptualization that is more adequate than the tendency to focus on single modalities and rigid implementations. If this is so, and if we do not consider deviation from relatively pure models of treatment or rigid research designs, we may be making a serious mistake. Research that compares one kind of treatment with another for a given diagnostic group may miss the mark widely, if treatments need to be given in various combinations and in "impure" forms, and if patient diagnosis is only one of several equally important variables that reflect patient need and determine therapy effectiveness. If that is so, the clinician modifying treatment approaches and using treatment combinations must be doing so with no sound basis. There is no systematic conception or research helping to organize the realities as he sees them.

What the evolution of the psychotherapies may be trying to tell us is that a single disease, single treatment model, the "silver bullet" concept, is grossly inaccurate, and that much more effort needs to be put into understanding how to combine and modify treatments and how to conceptualize the complexity of disorders and their environmental contexts. Even now, with our limited knowledge, shouldn't we be teaching trainees behavioral and insight psychotherapy techniques and helping them struggle with the problems of integrating these? Shouldn't we also be teaching them about the family, friendship, and work settings, and how to assess and consider these in the treatment matrix? We may be ignorant regarding several of these topics, and even more ignorant about how to consider them together, but training and research need to explore this ignorance, not avoid it.

How can this be accomplished? One possible approach is suggested by our current research (15). We have been studying patterns of patient-environment interaction as they may influence the course of psychopathology. In pursuing this topic, the importance of mapping concurrently several areas of the individual's functioning has been suggested, and the implications of such an approach for studying treatment effects are compelling. The research paradigm employed has involved an intensive follow-up model, using open-ended and semi-structured interviews to assess patients hospitalized for functional psychiatric disorder both at the time of hospitalization and then every two months after discharge for a one-year period. The following example of the schematic course of one subject is presented to illustrate the potential importance of using an intensive multiaxial follow-up model, even to begin identifying the processes that may be involved in treatment impact.

N.E. is a 34-year-old white single woman, who is a skilled factory worker. She has been diagnosed as having schizophrenia (DSM III) and has had delusions and hallucinations intermittently for 16 years. In spite of these symptoms and their duration, most of the time she has worked to support herself, and just seeing her, it would not be possible to tell that she had a psychiatric disorder. Figure 1 represents the change in N. E.'s status measured at two points, admission and one-year follow-up, using her scores on the Global Assessment Scale (GAS)

(44), an overall measure of symptoms and function. This scale and such a time interval are commonly used in treatment studies. Clearly N.E.'s status did not change much over the period measured.

In fact, as with all subjects in our study, we were conducting follow-up assessments every two months with N.E. Adding the intermediate GAS scores to Figure 1 produces Figure 2. The more frequent follow-up data show that N.E.'s course over the one-year period was not as smooth as it appeared in Figure 1, and some major improvements and exacerbations over the 12-month period of treatment have taken place.

If we add to the two-month follow-up data the information being obtained from out multiaxial assessment approach, the picture is enriched considerably, suggesting several important possibilities and negating others (Figure 3). N.E. did not just have ups and downs over the one-year treatment period. She worked at a high level of competence on three occasions during that time. Her symptoms increased precipitously as she reached her peak competence (each time she was offered increased responsibility at her job), and then the symptoms diminished rapidly. N.E.'s social relations remained at an extremely low level until two months before the end of the follow-up period, at which point they began to improve.

Figure 4 identifies various treatments received over the year. Rather than the single constant treatment approach so beloved by traditional treatment research, N.E.'s treatments changed in complex ways over this period. Such an evolution is not rare nor can it be fairly viewed as a clinical aberration. Rather, it might be seen more accurately as the kind of program that may be optimally prescribed as a person's condition and situation changes over time. During the entire period,

Ms NE GENERAL FUNCTIONING

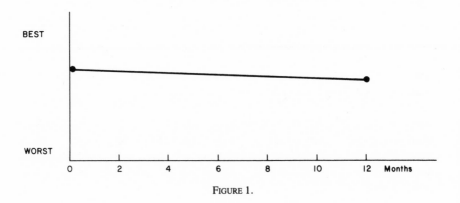

FIGURE 1.

Ms NE GENERAL FUNCTIONING

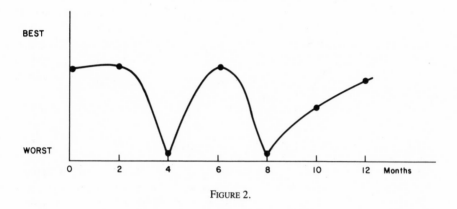

FIGURE 2.

Ms NE AREAS OF FUNCTION

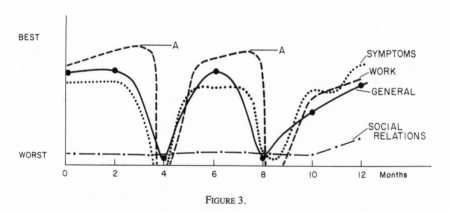

FIGURE 3.

N.E. was being treated with varying but generally relatively high doses of phenothiazines. Weekly reality-oriented individual therapy was begun, and several family sessions were held. After N.E. increased her trust in the individual therapist, she agreed to start group therapy, which she had previously refused. Shortly afterwards she got a new job involving minimal technical skills but providing more personal contact, something she had long desired. N.E. then started vocational rehabilitation. Her social relations functioning began to improve around this time.

Ms NE TREATMENTS & AREAS OF FUNCTION

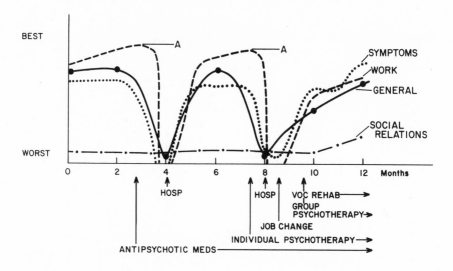

FIGURE 4.

The interactions between the areas of function and apparent relationships to job and other environmental shifts are not necessarily germane here, but relevant to this chapter is the degree to which the relatively frequent follow-up assessments and the multiaxial approach provide a possibility for studying and understanding treatments and their impact in a way that is barely conceivable with the data presented in Figure 1. The model used to study N.E., of course, suggests only one way in which research approaches using complex concepts of disorder and function may shed light on the workings of psychotherapy or other treatment modalities. The clinical implications of this complexity are also considerable. Although they cannot be pursued here, approaches to treatment that consider such complexities have been discussed in detail elsewhere (45).

The evolution of psychotherapeutic approaches for treating affective and schizophrenic disorders has suggested several tendencies. Some of these distort our understanding by either/or reasoning rather than considering multiple approaches, by starting with interpretive approaches which are then modified, sometimes implicitly, to deal with everyday realities, by emphasizing differences among approaches and ignoring their commonalities, by generating different assumptions about the nature of disorder to accompany each of the treatment modalities, and by emphasizing pure forms of treatment rather than the heterogeneous reality. The conceptual approach suggested by our intensive study is not necessarily the only or even the best way to resolve the problems of conceptualizing and understanding combined, modified, individualized, and changing treatments, and the role of psychotherapy among them. Acknowledging the lessons of treatment evolution over time, however, we must explore ways for coping with such complexities in understanding, prescribing, and research, rather than avoiding or ignoring them. Recognition of such needs and the development of attempts to meet them may be an absolute precondition to the further evolution of psychotherapy for affective and schizophrenic disorders.

REFERENCES

1. MAY, P., TUMA, A., and DIXON, W.: Schizophrenia: A follow-up study of the results of five forms of treatment. *Arch. Gen. Psychiat.,* 38:776-784, 1981.
2. MOSHER, L., and KEITH, S.: Psychosocial treatment: Individual, group, family, and community support approaches. *Schiz. Bull.,* 6:10-41, 1981.
3. GUNDERSON, J., and CARROLL, A.: Clinical considerations for empirical research. Presented at the Psychotherapy of Schizophrenia Symposium, Heidelberg, Germany, 1981.
4. STRAUSS, J., BOWERS, M., DOWNEY, T., FLECK, S., JACKSON, S., and LEVINE, I. (Eds.): *The Psychotherapy of Schizophrenia.* New York: Plenum Press, 1980.
5. WEISSMAN, M.: The psychological treatment of depression. *Arch. Gen. Psychiat.,* 36:1261-1269, 1979.
6. FRANK, J.D.: The present status of outcome studies. *J. Cons. Clin. Psychol.,* 47:310-316, 1979.
7. EPSTEIN, N.B., and VLOK, L.A.: Research on the results of psychotherapy: A summary of evidence. *Am. J. Psychiat.,* 138:1027-1035, 1981.
8. KARASU, T.: Impressions from the APA Commission on Psychiatric Therapies. Presented at the Group for the Advancement of Psychiatry, November, 1981.
9. PARLOFF, M.: Discussion: New directions. In: J. Strauss, M. Bowers, T. Downey, S. Fleck, S. Jackson, and I. Levine, (Eds.), *The Psychotherapy of Schizophrenia.* New York: Plenum Press, 1980.
10. EHRENWALD, J. (Ed.): *The History of Psychotherapy.* New York: Jason Aronson, 1976.
11. WEINER, D.: The apprenticeship of Philippe Pinel. *Am. J. Psychiat.,* 136:1128-1134, 1979.
12. ALMOND, R.: *The Healing Community: Dynamics of the Therapeutic Milieu.* New York: Jason Aronson, 1974.
13. MOOS, R., SHELTON, R., and PETTY, C.: Perceived ward climate and treatment outcome. *J. Abn. Psychol.,* 82:291-298, 1973.
14. GUNDERSON, J. (Ed.): *Principles and Practice of Milieu Therapy.* New York: Jason Aronson, 1982.
15. STRAUSS, J., LOEVSKY, L., GLAZER, W., and LEAF, P.: Organizing the complexities of schizophrenia. *J. Nerv. Ment. Dis.,* 169:120-126, 1981.
16. GARRISON, V.: Support systems of schizophrenic and non-schizophrenic Puerto Rican migrant women in New York City. *Schiz. Bull.,* 4:561-596, 1978.

17. BEELS, C.: Social support and schizophrenia. *Schiz. Bull.*, 7:58-71, 1981.
18. GRIESINGER, W.: *Pathology and Treatment of Psychiatric Illnesses* (Robertson, C., trans.). London: New Sydenham Society Publications, 1862.
19. FREUD, S.: The loss of reality in neurosis and psychosis. In: E. Jones, (Ed.), *Collected Papers*, vol. 2, 4th ed. Great Britain: Replika Press, 1946 (orig. 1924).
20. JASPERS, K.: *General Psychopathology*. (Hoenig, J. and Hamilton, M., trans.). Manchester, England: Manchester University Press, 1963.
21. FROMM-REICHMANN, F.: *Principles of Intensive Psychotherapy*. Chicago: University of Chicago Press, 1953.
22. FROMM-REICHMANN, F.: Psychoanalytic psychotherapy with psychotics. *Psychiatry*, 6:277-279, 1943.
23. BULLARD, D.M.: Psychotherapy of paranoid patients. *Arch. Gen. Psychiat.*, 2:137-141, 1960.
24. SCHULTZ, C.: An individualized psychotherapeutic approach with the schizophrenic patient. *Schiz. Bull.*, 1:46-70, 1975.
25. WILL, O.A.: Comments on the "elements" of schizophrenia, psychotherapy, and the schizophrenic person. In: J. Strauss, M. Bowers, T. Downey, S. Fleck, S. Jackson, and I. Levine (Eds.), *The Psychotherapy of Schizophrenia*. New York: Plenum Press, 1980.
26. SEARLES, H.: *Collected Papers on Schizophrenia and Related Subjects*. New York: International Universities Press, 1965.
27. ROSEN, J.: *Direct Psychoanalytic Psychiatry*. New York: Grune & Stratton, 1962.
28. BOOKHAMMER, R., MEYERS, R., SCHOBER, C., and PIOTROWSKI, A.: A five-year follow-up of schizophrenics treated by Rosen's "direct analysis" compared with controls. *Am. J. Psychiat.*, 123:602-604, 1966.
29. BIBRING, E.: Psychoanalysis and the dynamic psychotherapies. *J. Am. Psychoana. Assn.*, 2:745, 1954.
30. WYNNE, L.C.: Family and group treatment of schizophrenics: An interim view. In: R. Cancro, N. Fox, and L. Shapiro (Eds.), *Strategic Intervention in Schizophrenia: Current Developments in Treatment*. New York: Behavioral Publications, 1973.
31. DAVENPORT, Y., EBERT, M., ADLAND, M., and GOODWIN, F.: Couples group therapy as an adjunct to lithium maintenance of the manic patient. *Am. J. Orthopsychiat.*, 47:495-502, 1977.
32. MAYO, J.: Marital therapy with manic-depressive patients treated with lithium. *Compr. Psychiat.*, 20:419-436, 1979.
33. MINUCHIN, S.: *Families and Family Therapy*. Cambridge: Harvard University Press, 1975.
34. SELVINI PALAZZOLI, M., BOSCOLO, L., CECCHIN, G., and PRATA, G.: *Paradox and Counterparadox*. New York: Jason Aronson, 1978.
35. ANDERSON, C.: Family intervention with severely disturbed inpatients. *Arch. Gen. Psychiat.*, 34: 697-702, 1977.
36. PARLOFF, M., and DIES, R.: Group therapy outcome research, 1966-1975. *Int. J. Group Psychother.*, 27:281-319, 1977.
37. STIERLIN, H. (Ed.): *Proceedings of the Psychotherapy of Schizophrenia Symposium, Heidelberg, Germany, 1981*. In press.
38. KLEIN, M., DITTMANN, A.T., PARLOFF, M.G., and GILL, M.M.: Behavior therapy: Observations and reflections. *J. Cons. Clin. Psychol.*, 33:259-266, 1969.
39. WACHTEL, P.L.: *Psychoanalysis and Behavior Therapy: Towards an Integration*. New York: Basic Books, 1977.

40. MASSERMAN, J. and WOODS, S. (Eds.): *The Interface between Psychodynamic and Behavior Therapies*. New York: Plenum Press, 1980.
41. SLOAN, R.B., STAPLES, F.R., CRISTOL, A.H., YORKSTON, M.F., and WHIPPLE, J.L.: *Psychotherapy Versus Behavior Therapy*. Cambridge: Harvard University Press, 1976.
42. GURMAN, A., and RAZIN, A. (Eds.): *Effective Psychotherapy: A Handbook of Research*. Oxford: Pergamon Press, 1977.
43. GOLDFRIED, M.R., and DAVISON, G.C.: *Clinical Behavior Therapy*. New York: Holt, Rinehart & Winston, 1976.
44. ENDICOTT, J., SPITZER, R.L., FLEISS, J.L., and COHEN, J.: The global assessment scale: A procedure for measuring overall severity of psychiatric disturbance. *Arch. Gen. Psychiat.*, 33:766-771, 1976.
45. STRAUSS, J.S., and CARPENTER, W.T.: *Schizophrenia*. New York: Plenum Press, 1981.

8

Cognitive Therapy for Depression

A. John Rush, M.D.

INTRODUCTION

This chapter will review cognitive therapy in its application to patients with major depressive episodes. Specifically, the philosophical basis for this approach, a brief review of cognitive theory (1), and a description of the techniques used in this treatment (2) will be given. The specific indications, contraindications, and adverse effects will be highlighted, and the existing studies of efficacy will be reviewed. Finally, the question of unique effect, prophylaxis, and specific active ingredients will be examined.

Cognitive therapy (2) derives from cognitive theory (1). The treatment is a short-term, active, somewhat directive approach, in which the targets of treatment are symptoms, cognitions (verbal or pictorial mental content), and silent assumptions or schemata.

HISTORICAL BACKGROUND

Cognitive therapy derives from the so-called ''phenomenological'' approaches. The philosophical basis for a phenomenological approach to psychology has been described in detail (3,4). The phenomenological emphasis assigns a central role to an individual's view of himself and the world as determinants of behavior—a notion derived from Stoic philosophers of Greece. Adler (5) emphasized the idea that each person lives in a personal conceptualization or representation of the objective world. The profusion of stimuli that bombard us are immediately organized, conceptualized, and given meaning based upon

178

the individual's personal prior experiences. The term "phenomenal field" refers to this constructed representation of reality.

The "phenomenal field" is a construct that is used to explain why different people respond differently to the same event or series of events. For example, moving to a new city may be seen as a loss by some, while others see the same move as an adventure. Thus, it is not things in themselves, but rather the views that we take of things, that upset or please us.

This phenomenological emphasis appears to have arisen from dissatisfaction with unconscious motivation as a sufficient system to explain and predict behavior. Generally, unconscious motivation is inferred from a behavior or series of behaviors by examining the end products or results of the behaviors. The clinician assumes that the consequences of the behavior express the individual's wishes and desires. If the person denies that he actually desires the end products of the behavior, this testimony may be discounted.

If the consequences of a behavior constitute the *sole* basis for inferring unconscious motivation, diagnostic errors may result. For instance, one may erroneously infer an unconscious desire from a behavioral consequence that the individual actually did not desire. Motivational inferences that *exclusively* rely upon the consequences of a behavior assume that the patient can make anything happen that he wants, that nothing happens that he does not want, and that he can consciously or unconsciously foresee all the consequences of a behavior before undertaking it. These assumptions are rarely applicable to everyday situations.

The cognitive perspective assumes that a person chooses those options that are in his own interest, based upon his particular, often idiosyncratic, view of things. Not only are these views *rarely* objective, they are often highly biased in a stereotyped fashion.

Cognitive therapy first aims at clarifying how the individual views things, that is, how he conceptualizes and gives meaning to specific events. What are the bases for these views? Are they accurate? To what behaviors and feelings do these views lead? For instance, a depressed person often fails to undertake specific measures that might relieve the depression, not because he wants to suffer (one of several possible unconscious motivational assumptions), but rather because he does not conceive of undertaking particular steps to reduce the depression or does not believe that any action will result in relief. On the other hand, the individual may not believe that he can successfully undertake these steps. If a patient is convinced that corrective actions are unavailable or doomed to failure, this anticipation of failure logically leads to a decision not to try.

Recently, ego psychoanalytic (6), neobehavioral (7,8) and cognitive psychological (9,10) movements have added impetus to this emphasis on cognition. Beck (1,11) has emphasized the critical role that cognitions (conscious, verbal or pictorial mental activity) and assumptions or beliefs play in stereotyped repetitive "neurotic" behavior.

A cognitive explanatory system allows for a significant degree of direct empirical testing of many of the presumed determinants of behavior. If the view a patient takes of events leads to particular responses, and if these views are consciously available to him, then the relationship between these views and observed behaviors can be evaluated. Thus, a cognitive perspective appears to permit greater empirical testing than does a strictly unconscious motivational explanation for behavior. Indeed, cognitive theory is supported by various kinds of empirical data (12).

In some instances, however, this empirical attraction may be more apparent than real. People are notorious for making up explanations for what, in fact, they find themselves doing, as evidenced by split-brain studies (13). While they may truthfully report how they conceive of a particular event, this conceptualization may not be formulated until the person is asked to share his view. Thus, some conceptualizations may be retrospectively and inaccurately deduced. In addition, specific conceptualizations may be influenced by the perceived "demands" in specific situations, by what has transpired since the conceptualization occurred, by the relationship between the interviewer and conceptualizer, and so on. These difficulties may be overcome only with improved methods to measure cognitions and beliefs.

DEFINITION

Table 1 shows the various objectives that can be addressed by various forms of psychotherapy (14). Cognitive therapy is designed to provide 1) symptom reduction and 2) prophylaxis. The former objective, according to cognitive theory, is met by identifying and correcting the biased cognitive patterns, the interpretations that are given to note moment-to-moment events by the patient. Prophylaxis is believed to occur as a consequence of identifying and changing maladaptive assumptions or beliefs.

Cognitive therapy is a generic term that refers to a variety of psychotherapeutic techniques that are applied within a theoretical perspective. These techniques are designed to accomplish several specific objectives:

1) The patient is taught to become aware of the views that he takes of various events, particularly upsetting events (i.e., the therapist leads the patient to recognize and examine his "phenomenal" field).
2) The patient learns to assess, reality test, and correct these views (i.e., the patient learns to better match objective reality with particular meanings attributed to specific events), and thus, stereotyped perceptions are identified and corrected.

TABLE 1
Objectives of Psychotherapy (14)

A. Symptom Reduction
    1. Direct symptom change: behavior therapy
        (Example: modify contingencies for bedwetting)
    2. Indirect symptom change: interpersonal therapy
        (Example: clarify patient's response to ongoing role conflict to reduce depression)

B. Prophylaxis—modify factors that contribute to relapse
    1. Behavior therapy: improve social skills
    2. Cognitive therapy: modify silent assumptions or schemata
    3. Supportive therapy: reduce environmental stresses and increase access to resources

C. Reduction of Secondary Consequences of the Disorder
    1. Marital therapy: marital tensions that have resulted from the illness (e.g., manic-depressive illness)
    2. Occupational or skill training to increase employability of previously psychotic patients

D. Increase Compliance with Pharmacotherapy
    1. Provide information about treatment and illness
    2. Provide direct "rewards" for compliance
    3. Change attitudes about medication and/or the disorder
    4. Use a cueing or reminder system for medication taking

The examples provided for each major objective are exemplars. Other techniques or treatments not listed may also accomplish one or more of the above objectives.

3) The patient learns to identify specific silent assumptions or beliefs by inferring these general rules or assumptions from what he says and thinks in various situations. These general rules are not conscious thoughts or behaviors. Rather, these assumptions are the premises by which a person weighs, encodes, and gives meaning to specific events.
4) The patient practices various cognitive and behavioral responses to anticipated and unusual stresses.
5) Finally, new assumptions are generated and applied to actual and anticipated circumstances.

The therapist acts as a guide. The data of therapy consist of cognitions or thoughts, as well as behaviors and feelings, that the patient records or reports. Both experiences within the therapeutic relationship and data provided by the patient from interactions in his ongoing interpersonal relationships are used to teach the patient to recognize and correct steroetyped, biased thinking and self-defeating behavioral patterns.

The relationship between cognitions, schemata, and logical errors—the three critical elements in the cognitive theory—deserves further comment. Cognitions are thoughts or images that are available to consciousness. They are immediate, nearly automatic ideas to which each person is subject when confronted with any stimulus condition. Their content reflects the meaning given to an event by an individual. They are not what a person thinks about a situation; rather, they are what a person thinks to himself *in* a situation. These cognitions are closely tied to and are said to account for both the feelings raised and the behavior(s) displayed in the situation.

Cognitions about self, world, and future are said to be negatively biased by depressed persons (1, 12, 15, 16). Much empirical data support this contention (12, 17). Schemata are assumptions or beliefs derived from early experience that direct the person to attend to certain events, ignore others, and to value or encode these events in particular ways. Thus, schemata account for cognitions. A careful logical analysis of a series of cognitions leads to a rule that can be inferred. This rule is typically an "if. . ., then. . ." statement, a premise that is not thought by the patient but which guides the patient's thinking. For example, "If I am not loved and valued by others, my life has no meaning" might constitute such a rule.

A depressed person is said to endorse a variety of such illogical notions. Thus, when an event occurs that might often lead to transient dysphoria (e.g., breaking up with a loved one or death of a spouse), the person who bases his happiness and self-worth on attention from a single other person will develop a depressive syndrome that exceeds normal dysphoria. As such a schema is activated, it begins to control how the person thinks about other related but less central events (e.g., a friend forgetting to call at a specific time). Notions such as "I am generally unlovable" or "My life has no meaning" begin to enter consciousness. Events that are otherwise neutral in content are construed as further evidence that these negative notions are, in fact, true. For example, being ignored by a salesperson in a department store may stimulate such thoughts as "No one cares about me" or "I'll never get what I want." Silent assumptions both direct the content of cognitions and account for vulnerability to recurrence of depressive episodes.

Logical errors are seen when one examines the logical relationship between cognitions and the associated events. Consider the above case. When the friend does *not* call, although he promised to do so, the event is a non-event (i.e., nothing happened, objectively speaking). However, the patient's thought, "My life has no meaning," is unrelated to the non-event. This *arbitrary inference* is a conclusion drawn on insufficient evidence. The thought, "I'll never get what I want," when ignored by a salesperson, is an *overgeneralization* from the current frustrating circumstance. Other errors include *personalization* (a neutral event is given personal meaning); *magnification;* and *selective attention* (ignoring positive aspects of a situation). These logical errors are consequences, not causes, of negatively biased thinking (15-17).

Table 2 summarizes the relationships between cognitions, assumptions, and logical errors. Table 3 provides examples of cognitions or automatic thoughts taken from the Automatic Thoughts Questionnaire (18). Table 4 provides examples of dysfunctional attitudes derived from the Dysfunctional Attitude Scale (19).

TABLE 2

A Synopsis of Beck's Cognitive Theory (1)

A. Cognitions
   1. Consist of thoughts and images
   2. Reflect unrealistically negative views of self, world, and future
   3. Based on schemata
   4. Reinforced by current interpretations of events
   5. Explain symptoms of depressive syndrome
   6. Co-vary with severity of depression
   7. Logical errors occur in cognitions that are negatively distorted

B. Schemata (silent assumptions)
   1. Consist of unspoken, inflexible assumptions or beliefs
   2. Result from past (early) experience
   3. Form basis for screening, discriminating, weighing, and encoding stimuli
   4. Form basis for categorizing, evaluating experiences and making judgments, and distorting actual experience
   5. Determine the content of cognitions formed in situations and the affective response to them
   6. Increase vulnerability to relapse

TABLE 3

Examples of Cognitions from the Automatic Thoughts Questionnaire (18)

1) I feel like I'm up against the world.
2) I'm no good.
3) Why can't I ever succeed?
4) No one understands me.
5) I've let people down.
6) I don't think I can go on.
7) I wish I were a better person.
8) I'm so weak.
9) My life's not going the way I want it to.
10) I'm so disappointed in myself.
11) Nothing feels good any more.
12) I can't stand this any more.
13) I can't get started.

TABLE 4

Sample Items from Dysfunctional Attitude Scale (19)

It is difficult to be happy unless one is good-looking, intelligent, rich and creative.
Happiness is more a matter of my attitude towards myself than the way other people feel about me.
People will probably think less of me if I make a mistake.
If I do not do well all the time, people will not respect me.
Taking even a small risk is foolish because the loss is likely to be a disaster.
It is possible to gain another person's respect without being especially talented at anything.
I cannot be happy unless most people I know admire me.
If a person asks for help, it is a sign of weakness.

TECHNIQUES OF COGNITIVE THERAPY

The therapist selects specific cognitive techniques depending upon the degree and type of psychopathology present (2, 20, 21). For example, the therapist provides greater structure, direction, and guidance to more severely depressed patients who are less able to think objectively. Typically, therapy begins with techniques that focus on behavioral monitoring and change. These techniques are often very simple. They are designed to provide patients with success experiences. Subsequently, these tasks provide stimuli for the collection and later correction of cognitions.

The homework assignments are critical to treatment. These assignments are created to help the patient to: 1) develop objectivity about situations that otherwise are stereotypically misconstrued; 2) identify underlying assumptions; and 3) develop and test alternative conceptualizations and guiding assumptions. Table 5 lists several of some of the behaviorally oriented techniques. Table 6 lists some of the techniques aimed at changing cognitions or beliefs. This list of techniques is not exhaustive (2). In fact, an experienced cognitive therapist will design homework assignments for each individual patient in each session depending on the cognitive and behavioral targets to be addressed.

To illustrate one technique, consider the Graded Task Assignment (2,15,16). A very depressed woman might state that she is unable to do her housework. The therapist takes this general statement and converts it into a specific series of activities that are encompassed in the patient's version of the term "housework." Let us assume the patient states she cannot vacuum the rooms, empty the wastebaskets, do the wash, and clean the bathrooms. Each component is further broken into stepwise pieces (e.g., plugging in the vacuum cleaner, doing the living room, the stairs, etc.). The therapist then asks the patient to supply evidence to support the notion that she "can't do" each step. The patient is urged to specify precisely what is meant by "I can't do it." Does the patient

TABLE 5
Behavioral Techniques

Activity Scheduling
Mastery and Pleasure Ratings
Graded Task Assignment
Cognitive Rehearsal
Assertive Training/Role Playing
Mood Graph

TABLE 6
Cognitive Techniques

Recording Automatic Thoughts (Cognitions)
Reattribution Techniques
Responding to Negative Cognitions
Counting Automatic Thoughts
Identifying Assumptions
Modifying Shoulds
Pro-Con Refutation of Assumptions
Homework to Test Old Assumptions
Homework to Test New Assumptions

believe that she cannot find the vacuum cleaner, has insufficient energy to vacuum, won't do it as thoroughly as she'd like, etc.?

Next, the patient is encouraged to undertake one step at a time to determine whether the anticipated difficulties are actually encountered and to elicit the specific thoughts that occur while the patient tries to accomplish each step. These thoughts are often self-critical (e.g., "I'm not doing it correctly, fast enough, etc.") or she anticipates failure (e.g., "I'll never do this well enough" or "It will be dirty before I finish the house"). Using a dialogue, the therapist points out partial successes, helps the patient to realize that she is anticipating negative events before they occur, and provides reassurance for undertaking what the patient perceives as a difficult task.

Once the first task is completed, a second more complex task is designed, and the same process is followed. The patient is asked to verbalize her anticipations about each step, her thinking during the task, and her thoughts after she has completed the task. This method provides for repeated identification and correction of negatively biased thinking. Furthermore, a carefully designed hierarchy of tasks that is successfully completed may begin to provide the patient with a series of experiences that contradict her long-held notions about being personally defective, helpless, incompetent, and worthless. The therapist functions as an objective, independent, nonjudgmental source of information. This role is often essential to counteract the depressed patient's tendency to discount, neglect, or minimize successes, or otherwise misjudge herself.

The Graded Task Assignment is only one of many techniques that constitute cognitive therapy. Both behavioral and cognitive techniques can provide methods to elucidate and modify cognitions and assumptions. As the patient reports his thinking patterns in specific situations, the therapist helps him to reappraise objectively each situation, to recognize specific logical errors in his thinking (e.g., personalization, selective attention), to identify recurrent silent assumptions, and to modify these stereotyped thinking patterns and unrealistic or rigid beliefs.

For example, a patient might report that she became very sad when her boyfriend canceled their date at the last minute, thinking at the time, "Nobody loves me, I'll never find anyone who cares about me." These thoughts are global, personalized, and negatively biased. The therapist assists the patient to reassess the specifics of the situation (e.g., "How does a boyfriend canceling a date prove that no one will love you?"). Underlying assumptions are inferred and fed back to the patient (e.g., "You assume that you personally are generally unlovable when one person changed his mind for reasons that are not yet clear. Perhaps you assume that if someone disappoints you, he doesn't care about you"). Thus, the patient-therapist dialogue focuses on evaluating specific cognitions and beliefs. The full treatment program has been detailed elsewhere (2).

The therapeutic relationship must be carefully attended to in this and other short-term approaches (2,21). In fact, cognitive therapy (at least when limited to 20 sessions) is contraindicated in patients who have difficulty forming a working alliance within a short period of time (e.g., borderline patients). The therapist must be both empathetic and objective. He must be able to think like the patient and to understand both the cognitive and emotional responses of the patient, in order to see the world as the patient does. In addition, he must remain objective about the events reported and logical and objective about the patient's thinking. Thus, great tact is required in helping the patient to become objective about his views.

Depressed patients are notorious for overpersonalizing interactions with others. When the therapist identifies and points out negatively biased thinking, many patients may feel as if they are being attacked. As one patient put it, "When I came here, I thought I had just a depression. Now you tell me I can't think straight either."

In order to develop a collaborative alliance, a great deal of time is spent introducing the patient to the rationale for method of treatment. A brief pamphlet, *Coping with Depression* (22), is often used as part of this introduction. Patients are strongly encouraged to point out when they feel criticized or attacked during a session. Each session is reviewed before the patient is dismissed. Each session begins with a review of the patient's responses to the previous session.

Negative transference is dealt with through a cognitive framework (2, 20). The patient's views of the therapist, the therapy, or specific transactions in the session that were associated with increased dysphoria are elicited, evaluated collaboratively, and considered objectively.

One patient who was particularly sensitive to the therapist's behavior reported that she thought, "You don't want to see me," while she waited for me one day when I was a little late for one session. On another occasion when I was a little early, she thought, "I must be especially ill." When I arrived punctually on other occasions, she thought, "You're just running a factory and not taking a personal interest in me." When this pattern was elicited and examined, the patient readily saw that she came out the loser no matter what my behavior was. Careful attention to the therapeutic relationship is essential to insure compliance with homework and to reduce premature termination.

As noted in Tables 5 and 6, the various techniques can be divided conceptually into those with a primary focus of changing behavior and those with a primary focus of changing cognitions and/or assumptions. However, this dichotomy is somewhat artificial, since behavioral assignments are often used to elicit cognitions in specific situations. By recording activities actually undertaken and by rating the sense of mastery (M) and pleasure (P) derived from each, the patient collects data that help the therapist to select particular targets for the following session. The therapist selects activities that sound likely to give a nondepressed person a sense of mastery and pleasure, yet which are not associated with such feelings by the depressed patient. An inquiry into the cognitions surrounding such an activity typically leads to recollection of negatively biased thinking. For example, a patient who wallpapered a neighbor's kitchen reported M-O, P-O. The thoughts surrounding the event focused on how poorly he felt he had done the job and how he had ruined the kitchen as a result. Further discussion with an independent report by his wife about the quality of the work and the neighbor's sense of gratitude finally led to discovering the perfectionistic standards of the patient (for example, "If I don't do the job perfectly, it doesn't count at all") (23).

Similarly, techniques designed to elicit or change cognitions or beliefs often involve carrying out specific behaviors. For example, a shy, insecure, 26-year-old single male reported having difficulty meeting women at various singles bars. His assignment was to engage three different women in conversation that were not to exceed five minutes in length and to record his cognitions prior to the event as well as following it. Only by carrying out the feared behavior could the patient compare his dire predictions with the actual events and, finally, correct his cognitive distortions. In general, experimental testing of cognitions and beliefs, that is, carrying out actual assignments or behaviors, appears to be more powerful in both eliciting and changing cognitions or assumptions than is intellectual, logical discussion. The latter is more useful in preparing and persuading patients to try such experiments.

Members of the social system (spouse, friend, etc.) can be especially useful in certain situations (24). Such persons can be engaged to promote compliance with homework, to provide independent views of events to which the patient is reacting, and eventually to cue the patient when he appears to be making erroneous assumptions or to be coloring new information with a negative bias. Finally, cognitive therapy can be used with groups, couples, or individuals (25).

INDICATIONS

Cognitive therapy has been applied to a variety of psychopathological conditions, including major unipolar recurrent and nonrecurrent depressions, generalized anxiety disorder, phobic disorder, drug dependency, and others. The specific techniques differ depending upon the condition to be treated and upon the phase of therapy. Cognitive theory (1) provides a guide to the kinds of thinking patterns that one might encounter in each disorder. For example, anxious patients frequently perceive danger in situations that are not dangerous, while depressed patients often see evidence for personal defect in situations in which no objective reasons for self-depreciation exist. Paranoid patients may misconstrue situations in terms of being gypped or attacked. Cognitive theory also suggests that specific beliefs are more commonly found in certain disorders. For example, the need for love, approval, and/or success are likely to underlie negatively biased thinking in depression.

Cognitive therapy has been most extensively evaluated in depressed patients. While this therapy has been used with various other disorders, including chronic pain (26,27), research evidence of efficacy is still weak in most of these conditions.

The available outcome studies in depression (17) suggest that patients who are particularly suitable for this approach are mildly/moderately depressed, unipolar, nonpsychotic persons with a capacity for establishing a working alliance in a short period of time. These patients appear most likely to obtain significant symptom reduction in 10 weeks of treatment. Patients with chronic depressions are *not* more responsive and may be less responsive than those with more acute disorders (28).

The response of depressed patients with melancholic symptoms (29) to cognitive therapy has not been systematically evaluated. At this point, such patients should receive chemotherapy or electroconvulsive therapy as a primary treatment.

It is controversial whether those patients with endogenous features according to Research Diagnostic Criteria (30) will respond to cognitive therapy (31,32). While the answer to this question awaits further research data, the clinician is well advised *not* to utilize cognitive therapy alone in such patients in order to obtain symptom reduction. It is important to remember that symptom reduction is *not* the only objective of cognitive or other psychotherapies. The evidence for the prophylactic utility of this method is reviewed below. It is conceivable that some patients may reach a better level of interepisode recovery because of cognitive therapy, even though antidepressant medications may have been essential for symptom reduction.

For example, consider a patient who has endured three episodes of major depression with substantial but not total interepisode recovery. Assume further that the patient has obtained a near full symptomatic remission with amitriptyline. The patient has still experienced a good deal of time in the recent past in a depressed state. Might this experience not have affected his view of himself, his sense of competence, and his view of the world around him? Pharmacotherapy may not be as effective as cognitive psychotherapy in modifying such views, at least in the short run (33). Such a patient might profit from a short course (five to 10 weeks) of cognitive therapy to help him become more objective about both himself and his illness.

Thus, cognitive therapy may be indicated in a patient who requires antidepressants for symptom reduction and/or prophylaxis, and who also needs to relearn or unlearn specific self-defeating views or notions that either preceded or arose in conjunction with the symptomatic manifestation of the depression. A preliminary data analysis suggests that patients with more "chronic" depressions (i.e., those with either longer recent episodes or those with longer total lengths of illness) display greater or more profound negative cognitive distortions than can be explained by severity of the syndrome alone (34).

CONTRAINDICATIONS/ADVERSE REACTIONS

While Beck and coworkers (2) caution that many depressed patients may require medication or may not respond to cognitive therapy, specific *contraindications* to this treatment are yet to be identified. Clinical experience suggests that patients with impaired reality testing (e.g., hallucinations, delusions), impaired reasoning abilities or memory function (e.g., organic brain syndromes), those with borderline personality structures, and those with schizoaffective disorder will not respond to this treatment (2,20,21). It is unclear whether antisocial personalities with major depression or any other secondary depressions will respond to cognitive therapy.

It is my clinical experience that patients with major depression accompanying medical disorders, which is not biologically caused by such disorders (i.e., *not* Organic Affective Disorders by DSM-III [29]), respond rapidly to cognitive therapy, especially patients without history of preexisting psychopathology. For example, patients with their first myocardial infarction, persons with some cancers, and others with physical injuries that require marked psychological readjustments (e.g., blindness, loss of limb) can profit from this approach in very short order (e.g., five weeks). Those with more chronic, disabling, and progressive medical illnesses may profit to some degree but respond more slowly.

The reasons for failure with cognitive therapy have been the subject of a recent review (35). One apparent contraindication has been suggested based on a subtype of depression, namely, endogenous depression with associated dexamethasone nonsuppression (31,36). Most patients who ultimately respond well, in terms of acute symptom reduction, will do so within five to seven weeks of twice-a-week treatment with cognitive therapy alone. While others may have a more gradual response, if 50% symptom reduction by Hamilton Depression Rating Scale (37) or Beck Depression Inventory (38) is *not* achieved by 14 sessions, the treatment plan should be revised.

Three such patients with severe endogenous depressions and dexamethasone nonsuppression who were treated by the author all failed to respond at all to cognitive therapy alone. Perhaps in the future specific biological measures will help to identify responders and non-responders to cognitive or other psychotherapies (31,35).

It is surprising that there are as yet no reports of adverse reactions to cognitive therapy. Adverse reactions may be difficult to differentiate from lack of efficacy. For instance, suicide attempts, as well as premature terminations, may be evidence of either adverse reactions or lack of efficacy. Two studies (39,40) found that cognitive behavioral methods were associated with a significantly lower premature dropout rate than antidepressant pharmacotherapy alone, while a more recent report (32,41) did not replicate these findings. One might suspect that the structured, planned, directive nature of this approach helps retain depressed outpatients. If so, cognitive therapy might be particularly useful in outpatients of low socioeconomic class, whose dropout rate from psychotherapy is particularly high (42).

Lacking research evidence for adverse effects, we must rely on our clinical experience. For example, one patient appeared to misuse the therapy to justify inappropriate behavior. As she came to believe that her need for approval was excessive, she overreacted to this notion and decided to disregard completely her previous overconcern for the feelings and opinions of others, particularly her husband. She began a series of sexual affairs which she readily disclosed to her husband. Additional research into the adverse reactions to cognitive therapy might shed light on either the specific active ingredients or contraindications to this treatment.

FREQUENCY OF TREATMENT

There are few data available that evaluate the relationship between the frequency of treatment sessions and outcome. Only one pilot study (43) has assessed this question. It found that for moderately/severely depressed outpatients, twice-a-week treatment was associated with a lower dropout and better symptom reduction than once-a-week treatment. However, treatment assignment was *not* randomized in this study. This preliminary report and clinical experience suggest that once-a-week treatment may be sufficient for mild/moderately depressed patients, whereas twice-a-week sessions are indicated for the more severely depressed. Severely depressed inpatients may require treatment three times a week or more. More ''behavioral'' techniques are indicated for the more severely depressed, whereas techniques designed to elucidate and change cognitions and silent assumptions are used in mild/moderately depressed patients (2,20).

Maintenance treatment may consist of once- or twice-a-month ''booster'' sessions for six to 12 months after a course of more intensive once- or twice-a-week treatment is completed. The effect of maintenance treatment has not yet been empirically evaluated.

EFFICACY IN DEPRESSED PATIENTS

Cognitive therapy has been most thoroughly assessed in nonpsychotic, nonbipolar depressed outpatients. While many studies have been conducted on ''depressed college student volunteers,'' several recent trials have been carried out on psychiatric patients. Tables 7 and 8 summarize studies with patients treated individually. In one study (40), cognitive therapy exceeded the effects of imipramine. Two more recent studies also contrasted antidepressant medication with behavioral-cognitive therapy (39) or Beck's cognitive therapy (32,41). McLean and Hakstian (39) reported that the behavioral-cognitive approach exceeded the effects of amitriptyline (150 mg/day). In addition, it exceeded the effects of relaxation training and short-term psychotherapy. Blackburn and co-workers (32,41) found that, in general practice depressed outpatients, Beck's cognitive therapy exceeded the effects of antidepressant medication. On the other hand, in psychiatric clinic outpatients, cognitive therapy equalled the effects of antidepressant medication. Yet, by nearly all dependent measures, the combination treatment (cognitive therapy plus antidepressant medication) ex-

TABLE 7
Individual Therapy—Clinic Patients

Study	Measures	Treatment	Sessions No.	Sessions Wks.	Results
Schmickley (45)	BDI, MMPI (N = 11)	1) CM	4	2	Within-sub. Improvement
Rush et al. (40)	BDI, HRSD (N = 41)	1) CT 2) Imipramine	20	11	CT > I
Beck et al. (2)	BDI, HRSD (N = 26)	1) CT 2) CT + A	20	12	CT = CT + A
McLean & Hakstian (39)*	BDI, DACL (N = 154)	1) A 2) RT 3) BC 4) I	10	10	BC > A = RT > I
Blackburn et al. (32)	BDI, HRSD (N = 64)	1) CT 2) med 3) comb	16-17,	12-15	Hospital Clinic: Comb > CT = med; General Practice: CT = comb med

CT = cognitive therapy; BC = behavioral cognitive therapy; CM = cognitive modification; A = amitriptyline; comb = combination; med = medication; RT = relaxation training; I = insight therapy: BDI = Beck Depression Inventory; HRSD = Hamilton Rating Scale for Depression; DACL = Depression Adjective Checklist.
* Included community volunteers and clinic patients.

ceeded either treatment alone in this group. However, a strict replication of the Rush et al. study (40) has yet to be completed.

Tables 9 and 10 summarize studies of cognitive therapy conducted in a group format. Cognitive therapy was more effective than waiting list controls, and behavioral and client-centered therapies in group format (44). Only one study (25) has evaluated the question of whether the format (e.g., group vs. individual) affects the efficacy of cognitive therapy. The group format appeared to be *less* effective than individual therapy (see Table 11). A couples format has not been formally studied, although cognitive therapy is easily adapted to such an approach. One clinical report (24) has suggested specific indications and techniques for involving the couple in cognitive therapy of depression. More studies are needed to evaluate the relationship of format to outcome.

The question of when and whether to combine antidepressant medication with psychotherapy remains unanswered (2,14). Three reports have evaluated the combination of cognitive therapy with medication. Rush and Watkins (25) in a small study found no difference between individual cognitive therapy alone when compared with combination in outpatients. However, the sample size may have precluded detection of significant differences. Recently, Beck and co-workers (2) found that adding amitriptyline did not add to the efficacy of cognitive therapy alone.

TABLE 8
Individual Therapy—College Student Volunteers

Study	Measures	Treatment	Sessions No.	Wks.	Results
Taylor & Marshall (46)	BDI, D-30 (N = 28)	1) CM 2) BM 3) CM & BM 4) WLC	6	3	CM & BM > CM CM & BM > BM CM = BM Each > WLC

Individual Therapy—Community Volunteers

Study	Measures	Treatment	Sessions No.	Wks.	Results
Munoz (47)	MMPI-D	1) CM 2) WLC 3) norm. control 4) High MMP (nondep) control	12	4	Improved CM = WLC
Besyner (48)	BDI (N = 41)	1) CM 2) BT 3) NST 4) WLC	4 (2 hr.)	4	BT > CM CM = WLC BT,CM,WLC>NST
Zeiss, Lewinsohn & Munoz (49)	MMPI-D (N = 44)	1) CM 2) SS 3) PA 4) WLC	12	4	CM = SS = PA>WLC
Carrington (50)	BDI,VAS, HS MMPI-D (N = 30)	1) CT 2) AT 3) WLC	12	12	CT>AT>WLC on BDI,VAS

WLC = waiting list control; VAS = visual analog scale; HS = hopelessness scale; CT = cognitive therapy; BT = behavior therapy; CM = cognitive modification; BM = behavior modification; SS = social skills training; NST = nonspecific therapy; PA = pleasant activities treatment; AT = analytic therapy; BDI = Beck Depression Inventory.

No advantage accrued to the combination over cognitive therapy alone in general practice depressed outpatients, whereas the combination treatment exceeded cognitive therapy alone in psychiatric clinic outpatients (32,41). This study suggests that patient source may influence the probability of response to medication (see Tables 12,13 and 14). Apparently some, but clearly not all, patients are uniquely benefited by the combination treatment. Other patients may benefit from cognitive therapy without medication.

As yet, there are no predictors as to which patients are best suited to cognitive therapy alone, medication alone, or a combination of the two. Endogenous symptoms have *not* been correlated with a poor response to cognitive therapy (32,60). Further studies are needed to identify the specific indications for cognitive therapy or the combined approach.

TABLE 9
Group Therapy—Clinic Patients

Study	Measures	Treatment	Sessions		Results
			No.	Wks.	
Rush & Watkins (25)	BDI, HRSD (N = 39)	1) GC 2) IC 3) IC + medi-cation	10	10-12	GC > IC = IC + meds
McDonald (51)	BDI, DACL (N = 28)	1) CM + DC 2) DC	12	4	Improved but CM + DC = DC
Magers (52)	BDI, MMPI TSCS (N = 18)	1) CB 2) WLC	6	6	CB > WLC
Shaw* (44)	BDI, HRSD (N = 32)	1) CM 2) BM 3) ND 4) WLC	6	3	CM > BM CM > ND BM = ND Each > WLC
Morris (53)	BDI, SRSD (N = 51)	1) CM 2) IG 3) WLC	6	3	CM > Insight Each > WLC

* Student Health Clinic Patients
WLC = waiting list control; CM = cognitive modification; DC = day care; CB = cognitive behavioral therapy; CT = cognitive therapy; GC = group cognitive therapy; IC = individual cognitive therapy; IG = insight group; ND = nondirective treatment; HRSD = Hamilton Rating Scale for Depression; BDI = Beck Depression Inventory.

TABLE 10
Group Therapy—College Students

Study	Measures	Treatment	Sessions		Results
			No.	Wks.	
Kirkpatrick (54)	Self-report Dep./Anx. (N = 46)	1) CM 2) RT 3) AP 4) NT	4	2	CM = RT = AP = NT
Head (55)	BDI, POMS	1) CM 2) AO	11	11	Improved but CM = AO
Hodgson & Urban (56)	Lubin Zung (N = 38)	1) CM 2) BM 3) WLC	8	4	BM > CM Each > WLC
Gioe (57)	BDI (N = 40)	1) CM 2) PGE 3) CM & PGE 4) WLC	5	1	CM & PGE > CM CM & PGE > PGE CM = PGE Each > WLC
Shipley & Fazio (58)	Zung MMPI (N = 38)	1) PS 2) S 3) WLC	3	3	PS > S > WLC

(TABLE 10 continued)
Group Therapy—Community Volunteers

Study	Measures	Treatment	Sessions No.	Wks.	Results
Fuchs & Rehm (59)	BDI MMPI-D (N = 28)	1) SC 2) NS 3) WLC	6	6	SC>NS>WLC

WLC = waiting list control; AO = assess only; CM = cognitive modification; SC = self-control therapy; NS = nonspecific therapy; PGE = positive group experience; BM = behavior modification; AP = attention placebo; NT = no treatment; RT = relaxation training; PS = problem-solving; S = supportive therapy. POMS = Profile of Mood States.

TABLE 11
Mean Beck Depression Inventory Scores at Initiation and Termination of Treatment—Completers Only (25)

Time of Assessment	Group therapy (N = 23)	Individual therapy (N = 8)	Individual therapy plus medication (N = 7)	Full sample (N = 38)
Pretreatment mean	29.2	29.5	31.3	29.6
Standard Deviation	6.2	7.8	9.1	6.9
Posttreatment mean	16.2	8.6	5.9	12.7
Standard Deviation	12.8	6.7	5.1	11.4

TABLE 12
Description of Those Who Completed Therapy (41)

	Hospital Clinic	General Practice
(1) Male/female	10/30	4/20
(2) Age	44.5 ± 11.4	41.3 ± 9.5
(3) Socio-economic[3]	2.4 ± 0.9	3.7 ± 1
(4) Previous depressive episodes[2]	3.1 ± 4.4	0.8 ± 1
(5) Duration of illness (weeks)[1]	86.8 ± 93.7	38.7 ± 39.9
(6) P.S.E. total score[1]	34.1 ± 8.9	29.5 ± 6.6
(7) BDI	24.6 ± 7	23.3 ± 5.3
(8) HRSD	17.3 ± 4.6	19.0 ± 4.5
(9) Suicidal	55%	45%

[1] $p < .05$; [2] $p < 0.01$; [3] $p < 0.001$

TABLE 13
Outcome (41)

	Hospital Clinic			General Practice		
	Responders	Non-Responders	Total	Responders	Non-Responders	Total
Drug	10	3	13	1	6	7
Cognitive therapy	8	6	14	8	0	8
Combination	10	3	13	8	1	9
Total	28	12	40	17	7	24

TABLE 14
Endogenous vs. Non-endogenous by Treatment Outcome (32)

	Endogenous			Non-endogenous		
	Responders	Non-responders	Total	Responders	Non-responders	Total
Drug	9	2	11	9	2	11
Cognitive therapy	5	2	2	11	4	15
Combination	5	4	9	6	5	11

UNIQUE EFFECTS

If unique effects could be found with a particular psychotherapy, we might be able to infer specific indications for employing the intervention. However, few therapeutic approaches have been evaluated to determine if such unique effects actually exist for any psychotherapy. Marital therapy was reported to improve marriages compared to antidepressants (61). Interpersonal therapy improved social adjustment or marital satisfaction (62) and, at first, differentially affected mood, suicidal ideation, guilt, and apathy compared to tricyclic antidepressant medication (63).

With regard to cognitive therapy, Rush and co-workers (64) found that cognitive therapy had a more pervasive and significant impact on self-concept than did amitriptyline by the end of treatment. In addition, cognitive therapy resulted in a greater reduction in hopelessness compared to medication. While chemotherapy did reduce hopelessness by the end of treatment, it had little effect on self-concept dimensions. While these findings require replication, they suggest that cognitive therapy more profoundly improves patients' views of themselves and their future compared to chemotherapy. Furthermore, cognitive therapy differs from imipramine in the timing of its effects on particular symptoms (33). Specifically, views of self and future appear to improve *prior to* other symptom groups (e.g., motivational, vegetative) during cognitive therapy. This finding is consistent with predictions from cognitive theory.

One might speculate that depressions that are characterized by an abundance of negative cognitive distortions are particularly likely to benefit from cognitive therapy. This contention is supported in part by a preliminary report on cognitive therapy with a group of drug-free depressed inpatients. As a group, these patients responded less well and less uniformly than subjects in previously reported depressed outpatients. In addition, those inpatients who evidenced greater cognitive distortions as assessed by a card-sorting task (65) responded better to cognitive therapy than did patients with less negative thinking (66). Further studies to identify unique effects, as well as predictions of response and nonresponse, are needed.

PROPHYLAXIS

Even if psychotherapeutic methods can be shown to be effective, the cost of such treatment must be weighed against the value of the effect obtained. Therapists hope that psychotherapy teaches new, more adaptive behaviors and attitudes. Thus, future symptomatic episodes should be reduced. This hoped-for prophylactic effect of psychotherapy is largely unsupported by available data. Interpersonal therapy did not lead to prophylaxis as contrasted with antidepressant medication (67). However, medication-responsive patients exclusively were selected for this follow-up study.

Does cognitive therapy provide prophylaxis? Only one study has examined this question (60). Subjects treated with cognitive therapy alone (n = 18) or imipramine without cognitive therapy (n = 17) were followed monthly for one year after active treatment was terminated. Both patient groups maintained the overall symptomatic gains made during active treatment throughout the follow-up. The imipramine-treated group had twice the "risk of relapse" during follow-up, although this between-group difference did not reach statistical significance (Table 15). On the other hand, symptom levels by self-report (Beck Depression Inventory [BDI]) continued to distinguish the two groups at the end of the 12-month follow-up (Table 16). Those who had received cognitive therapy reported lower levels of depressive symptomatology. These findings were not confirmed with a smaller sample on which the Hamilton Depression Rating Scale (60) was completed.

The longitudinal course was evaluated in this study by monthly BDI ratings

TABLE 15

Cumulative Relapse in One-Year Follow-up for Patients Who Completed Treatment (60)

Definition of Relapse Met at Any Point During One-Year Follow-up	Follow-up Classification				
	Treatment Assignment	Relapse	No Relapse	X^2	Risk Ratio
Depressed*	Cognitive therapy	7	11	2.33	2.11
	Chemotherapy	11	6		
Received psychiatric-psychological treatment	Cognitive therapy	9	9	2.62	2.09
	Chemotherapy	13	4		
Met either definition	Cognitive therapy	10	8	2.91	2.14
	Chemotherapy	14	3		
Met both definitions	Cognitive therapy	6	12	2.29	2.19
	Chemotherapy	10	7		

* Patient had a score of 16 or greater on the Beck Depression Inventory. The values are based on constant or proportionate risk in each group.

TABLE 16

Clinical Status at End of Treatment and One-year Follow-up of Patients Who Completed Protocol (60)

State of Depression* and Time of Assessment	Protocol Treatment No. of Patients	
	Cognitive Therapy (n = 18)	Chemotherapy (n = 17)
No clinical symptomatology		
End of treatment	15	5
12-mo. follow-up	12	6
Mild symptomatology		
End of treatment	2	7
12-mo. follow-up	4	5
Moderate-severe symptomatology		
End of treatment	1	5
12-mo. follow-up	2	5
Unknown		
End of treatment	0	0
12-mo. follow-up	0	1

* No clinical symptomatology indicates a score of 9 or less on the Beck Depression Inventory (BDI); mild symptomatology, a BDI score between 10 and 15; and moderate-severe symptomatology, a BDI score of 16 or greater.

TABLE 17

One-year Longitudinal Clinical Course of Patients Who Completed Treatment
(60)

Clinical Course of Depression*	No. of Patients	
	Cognitive Therapy (n = 18)	Chemotherapy (n = 17)
Remission	10	6
Intermittently symptomatic	5	5
Chronically symptomatic	3	6

* Remission indicates no Beck Depression Inventory (BDI) score greater than or equal to 16; intermittently symptomatic, less than 50% of the BDI scores were greater than or equal to 16; and chronically symptomatic,50% or more of the BDI scores were greater than or equal to 16.

obtained during the 12-month follow-up period. Fifty-six percent of the cognitive therapy group and 35% of the drug-treated patients remained in remission (no BDI>16) during follow-up (Table 17). This study suggests that some prophylaxis does result for cognitive therapy, at least for a group of depressed patients. Obviously, further studies are needed.

SPECIFIC ACTIVE INGREDIENTS

It is not clear as to which of the various techniques included in the cognitive therapy treatment program account for the effects found with this treatment. What does the relationship itself contribute to the process over and above providing a medium for applying specific techniques? Do the homework assignments actually contribute to efficacy? Only one study (44) has attempted to address these questions. Their findings suggest that both cognitive and behavioral components significantly contribute to a positive outcome. If further research can identify specific "active ingredients," then the treatment package itself might be revised to improve both efficiency and specificity in selected patients.

SELECTING CANDIDATES

While research data provide some general guidelines about subject selection, the clinician is confronted with individualized decisions: when to attempt cognitive therapy; when to discontinue it; and when to supplement it with medication.

I will share my clinical impressions and review some new research data that may help in these complex decisions.

Those patients with the most marked cognitive distortions, as assessed by responses to a card-sorting task, appear to do better with cognitive therapy (66). However, the overall effect of the treatment was less impressive than published outpatient studies.

In a recent study (68), cognitive distortions in the form of dysfunctional attitudes as measured by the Dysfunctional Attitude Scale (DAS) (19) did *not* differentiate endogenous from non-endogenous patients with major depression by Research Diagnostic Criteria. Nor did such attitudes differentiate dexamethasone suppressors from nonsuppressors (Figure 1). Thus, this measure of attitude (the DAS) may not identify responders or non-responders, at least to the symptom-reducing effects of this intevention. Whether those with a more historically chronic course endorse more dysfunctional attitudes is being investigated. If the prophylactic effect of cognitive therapy is substantiated in further studies, then such a cognitive measure may be useful in selecting patients who are candidates for the prophylactic effects of cognitive therapy.

Another recent report (69) suggests that outpatients with unipolar, nonpsychotic major depressions can be subdivided into three groups based on the dexamethasone suppression test (DST) and the sleep EEG: those with neither DST nonsuppression nor reduced REM latency; those with both abnormalities; and those with only reduced REM latency (Figure 2). Whether these groups differ in their responsiveness to cognitive therapy has not yet been fully evaluated. However, with antidepressant pharmacotherapy, those with one or both biological derangements did significantly better than those with neither (31). Furthermore, in an open trial three patients with both biologic derangements failed to respond at all to cognitive therapy alone.

FUTURE DIRECTIONS

While many questions remain for cognitive as well as for other psychotherapies, a growing body of data does suggest that this therapy is effective for some types of depressions. Data of the foregoing type are required to document the efficacy of any psychotherapy. Additional research is needed to clarify the specific indications, contraindications, active ingredients, and adverse reactions to this treatment approach. Most importantly, the prophylactic benefits of this approach deserve extensive investigation in the future.

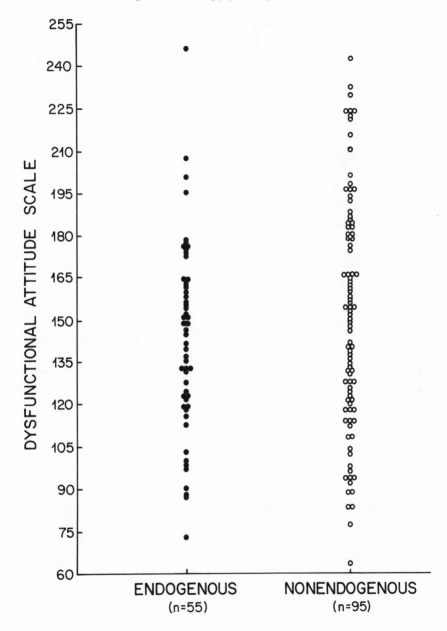

FIGURE 1. Dysfunctional attitudes in endogenous and nonendogenous depressions. From Giles and Rush, submitted to *Biological Psychiatry* for publication.

RELATIONSHIP OF REM LATENCY TO
ENDOGENOUS/NONENDOGENOUS DEPRESSION

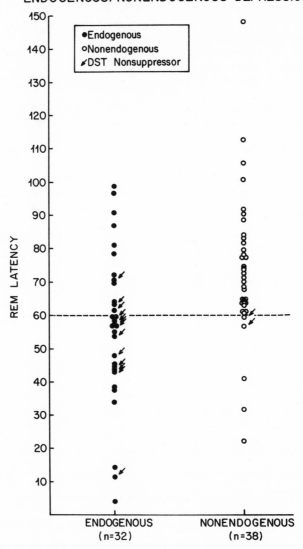

FIGURE 2.

REFERENCES

1. BECK, A.T.: *Cognitive Therapy and the Emotional Disorders*. New York: International Universities Press, 1976.
2. BECK, A.T., RUSH, A.J., SHAW, B.F., and EMERY, G.: *Cognitive Therapy of Depression*. New York: Guilford Press, 1979.
3. SPIEGELBERG, H.: *The Phenomenological Movement* (Vols. 1 and 2). The Hague: Nijhoff, 1971.
4. SPIEGELBERG, H.: *Phenomenology in Psychology and Psychiatry*. Evanston, IL: Northwestern University Press, 1972.
5. ANSBACHER, H.L., and ANSBACHER, R.R. (Eds.): *The Individual Psychology of Alfred Adler: A Systematic Presentation in Selection from His Writings*. New York: Basic Books, 1956.
6. KLEIN, G.S.: *Perception, Motives and Personality*. New York: A. Knopf, 1970.
7. MAHONEY, J.J.: *Cognition and Behavior Modification*. Cambridge, MA: Ballinger Publishing Company, 1974.
8. MEICHENBAUM, D.: *Cognitive Behavior Modification*. New York: Plenum Press, 1977.
9. KELLEY, G.A.: *The Psychology of Personal Constructs*. New York: Norton, 1955.
10. ELLIS, A.: *Reason and Emotion in Psychotherapy*. Secaucus, N.J.: Lyle Stewart, 1962.
11. BECK, A.T.: Thinking and depression: I. Idiosyncratic content and cognitive distortion. *Arch. Gen. Psychiat.*, 9:324-333, 1963.
12. BECK, A.T., and RUSH, A.J.: Cognitive approaches to depression and suicide. In: G. Serban (Ed.), *Cognitive Defects in Development of Mental Illness*. New York: Brunner/Mazel, 1978.
13. GAZZANIGA, M.S., and LEDOUX, J. (Eds.): *The Integrated Mind*. New York: Plenum Press, 1978.
14. RUSH, A.J.: Pharmacotherapy and psychotherapy. In: L. Derogatis (Ed.), *Psychopharmacology in Clinical Practice*, New York: Addison and Wesley, in press.
15. RUSH, A.J., and BECK, A.T.: Cognitive therapy of depression and suicide. *Am. J. Psychother.*, 32:201-219, 1978.
16. RUSH, A.J., and BECK, A.T.: Adults with affective disorders (Chapter 10). In: M. Hersen and A.S. Bellack (Eds.), *Behavioral Therapy in the Psychiatric Setting*. Baltimore: Williams and Wilkins, 1978.
17. RUSH, A.J., and GILES, D.G.: Cognitive therapy: Theory and research. In: A.J. Rush (Ed.), *Short-Term Psychotherapies for Depression*. New York: Guilford Press, 1982.
18. HOLLON, S.D., and KENDALL, P.C.: Cognitive self-statements in depression: Development of an automatic thoughts questionnaire. *Cog. Ther. Res.*, 4:383-395, 1980.
19. WEISSMAN, A.W.: The Dysfunctional Attitude Scale: A validation study. Unpublished dissertation (University of Pennsylvania). *Dissertation Abstracts International*, 40:1389-1390B, 1979. (University Microfilms No. 79-19533.)
20. RUSH, A.J.: Psychotherapy of the affective psychoses. *Am. J. Psychoanal.*, 40:99-123, 1980.
21. RUSH, A.J. (Ed.): *Short-Term Psychotherapies for Depression*. New York: Guilford Press, 1982.

22. BECK, A.T., and GREENBERG, R.L.: *Coping with Depression*. Pennsylvania: Center for Cognitive Therapy, University of Pennsylvania, 1974.
23. RUSH, A.J., KHATAMI, M., and BECK, A.T.: Cognitive and behavior therapy in chronic depression. *Behav. Ther.*, 6:398-404, 1975.
24. RUSH, A.J., SHAW, B., and KHATAMI, M.: Cognitive therapy of depression: Utilizing the couples system. *Cog. Ther. Res.*, 4:103-113, 1980.
25. RUSH, A.J., and WATKINS, J.T.: Group versus individual cognitive therapy: A pilot study. *Cog. Ther. Res.*, 5:95-103, 1981.
26. KHATAMI, M., and RUSH, A.J.: A pilot study of the treatment of outpatients with chronic pain: Symptom control, stimulus control, and social system intervention. *Pain*, 5:163-172, 1978.
27. KHATAMI, M., and RUSH, A.J.: One year follow-up of multimodal treatment of chronic pain. *Pain*, in press.
28. RUSH, A.J., HOLLON, S.D., BECK, A.T., and KOVACS, M.: Depression: Must pharmacotherapy fail for cognitive therapy to succeed? *Cog. Ther. Res.*, 2:199-206, 1978.
29. *Diagnostic and Statistical Manual for Mental Disorders*, 3rd edition. Washington, D.C.: American Psychiatric Association. 1980.
30. SPITZER, R.L., ENDICOTT, J., and ROBINS, E.: Research diagnostic criteria: Rationale and reliability. *Arch. Gen. Psychiat.*, 3:773-782, 1978.
31. RUSH, A.J.: Biological markers and treatment response in affective disorders. *McLean Hospital Bulletin*, in press.
32. BLACKBURN, I., BISHOP, S., GLEN, A.I.M., WHALLEY, L.J., and CHRISTIE, J.E.: The efficacy of cognitive therapy in depression. A treatment trial using cognitive therapy and pharmacotherapy, each alone and in combination. *Br. J. Psychiat.*, 139:181-189, 1981.
33. RUSH, A.J., KOVACS, M., BECK, A.T., WEISSENBURGER, J., and HOLLON, S.D.: Differential effects of cognitive therapy and pharmacotherapy on depressive symptoms. *J. Affect. Dis.*, 3:221-229, 1981.
34. RUSH, A.J., GILES, D.E., KHATAMI, M., and STONE, L.: Biological and cognitive dimensions of chronic depression. Unpublished manuscript.
35. RUSH, A.J., and SHAW, B.F.: Failures in treating depression by cognitive behavioral therapy. In: P.M. Emmelkamp and E.B. Foa (Eds.), *Failures in Behavior Therapy*. New York: Wiley and Sons, in press.
36. CARROLL, B.J., FEINBERG, M., GREDEN, J.F., TARIKA, J., ALBALA, A.A., HASKETT, R.F., JAMES, N. McI., KRONFOL, Z., LOHR, N., STEINER, M., DeVIGNE, J.P., and YOUNG, E.: A specific laboratory test for the diagnosis of melancholia. *Arch. Gen. Psychiat.*, 38:15-22, 1981.
37. HAMILTON, M.: A rating scale for depression. *J. Neurol. Neurosurg. Psychiat.*, 12:56-62, 1960.
38. BECK, A.T., WARD, C.H., MENDELSON, M., MOCK, J.E., and ERBAUGH, J.K.: An inventory for measuring depression, *Arch. Gen. Psychiat.*, 4:561-571, 1961.
39. McLEAN, P.D., and HAKSTIAN, A.R.: Clinical depression: Comparative efficacy of outpatient treatments. *J. Consult. Clin. Psychol.*, 47:818-836, 1979.
40. RUSH, A.J., BECK, A.T., KOVACS, M., and HOLLON, S.: Comparative efficacy of cognitive therapy and pharmacotherapy in the treatment of depressed outpatients. *Cog. Ther. Res.*, 1:17-37, 1977.
41. BLACKBURN, I., and BISHOP, S.: Is there an alternative to drugs in the treatment of

depressed ambulatory patients? *Behav. Psychother.,* 9:96-104, 1981.

42. RUSH, A.J., and WATKINS, J.T.: Cognitive therapy with psychologically naive depressed outpatients. In: G. Emery, S. Hollon and R. Bedrosian (Eds.), *Cognitive Therapy Casebook.* New York: Guilford Press, 1980.

43. RUSH, A.J., BECK, A.T., KOVACS, M., KHATAMI, M., and WOLMAN, T.: A comparison of cognitive and pharmacotherapy in depressed outpatients: A preliminary report. Presented at the Society for Psychotherapy Research, Boston, MA, June, 1975.

44. SHAW, B.F.: Comparison of cognitive therapy and behavior therapy in the treatment of depression. *J. Consult. Clin. Psychol.,* 45:543-551, 1977.

45. SCHMICKLEY, V.G.: The effects of cognitive behavior modification upon depressed outpatients. Unpublished doctoral dissertation, Michigan State University, 1976.

46. TAYLOR, F.G., and MARSHALL, W.L.: Experimental analysis of a cognitive-behavioral therapy for depression. *Cog. Ther. Res.,* 1:59-72, 1977.

47. MUNOZ, R.F.: A cognitive approach to the assessment and treatment of depression. Unpublished doctoral dissertation, University of Oregon, 1977.

48. BESYNER, J.K.: The comparative efficacy of cognitive and behavioral treatments of depression: A multiassessment approach. *Dissertation Abstracts International,* 39:4568-B, 1979. (University Microfilm No. 79-04956.)

49. ZEISS, A.M., LEWINSOHN, P.M., and MUNOZ, R.F.: Nonspecific improvement effects in depression using interpersonal skills training, pleasant activities schedules, or cognitive training. *J. Consult. Clin. Psychol.,* 47:427-439, 1979.

50. CARRINGTON, C.H.: A comparison of cognitive and analytically oriented brief treatment approaches to depression in black women. *Dissertation Abstracts International,* 40:2829B, 1979. (University of Maryland Microfilm No. 79-26513.)

51. McDONALD, A.C.: A cognitive/behavioral treatment for depression with veterans administration outpatients (University of Utah). *Dissertation Abstracts International,* 1978, 39:2944-B, 1978.

52. MAGERS, B.D.: Cognitive-behavioral short-term group therapy with depressed women. (California School of Professional Psychology), *Dissertation Abstracts International,* 38:4468-B. (University Microfilm No. 78-01687.)

53. MORRIS, N.E.: A group self-instruction method for the treatment of depressed outpatients. National Library of Canada, Canadian Theses Division, No. 35272, 1975.

54. KIRKPATRICK, P.W.: The efficacy of cognitive behavior modification in the treatment of depression. *Dissertation Abstracts International,* 38(5), 2370-B, 1977. (University Microfilm No. 77-22661.)

55. HEAD, R.: Cognitive therapy with depressed college students. Unpublished masters thesis, University of Miami, 1978.

56. HODGSON, J.W., and URBAN, H.B.: A comparison of interpersonal training programs in the treatment of depressive states. Unpublished manuscript, Pennsylvania State University, 1975.

57. GIOE, V.J.: Cognitive modification and positive group experience as a treatment for depression. *Dissertation Abstracts International,* 36:3039-3040B, 1975. (University Microfilm No. 75-28219.)

58. SHIPLEY, C.R., and FAZIO, A.F.: Pilot study of a treatment for psychological depression. *J. Abn. Psychol.,* 82:372-376, 1973.

59. FUCHS, C., and REHM, L.P.: A self-control behavior therapy program for depression. *J. Consult. Clin. Psychol.,* 45:206-215, 1977.

60. KOVACS, M., RUSH, A.J., BECK, A.T., and HOLLON, S.D.: Depressed outpatients treated with cognitive therapy or pharmacotherapy. A one-year followup. *Arch. Gen. Psychiat.*, 38:33-39, 1981.

61. FRIEDMAN, A.S.: Interaction of drug therapy with marital therapy in depressive patients. *Arch. Gen. Psychiat.*, 32:619-637, 1975.

62. KLERMAN, G.L., DiMASCIO, A., WEISSMAN, M., et al.: Treatment of depression by drugs and psychotherapy. *Am. J. Psychiat.*, 131:186-191, 1974.

63. DiMASCIO, A., WEISSMAN, M., PRUSOFF, B., NEU, C., ZWILLING, M., and KLERMAN, G.: Differential symptom reduction by drugs and psychotherapy in acute depression. *Arch. Gen. Psychiat.*, 36:1450-1456, 1979.

64. RUSH, A.J., BECK, A.T., KOVACS, M., WEISSENBURGER, J., and HOLLON, S.: Differential effects of cognitive therapy and pharmacotherapy on hopelessness and self-concept. *Am. J. Psychiat.*, in press.

65. LOEB, A., FESHBACH, S., BECK, A.T., and WOLF, A.: Some effects of reward upon the social perception and motivation of psychiatric patients varying in depression. *J. Abn. Soc. Psych.*, 68:609-616, 1964.

66. SHAW, B.: Predictors of successful outcome in cognitive therapy: A pilot study. World Congress on Behavior Therapy, Jerusalem, Israel, 1980.

67. WEISSMAN, M.M., KASL, S.V., and KLERMAN, G.L.: Follow-up of depressed women after maintenance treatment. *Am. J. Psychiat.*, 133:757-760, 1976.

68. GILES, D.E., and RUSH, A.J.: Relationship of dysfunctional attitudes and dexamethasone response in endogenous and nonendogenous depression. *Biolog. Psychiat.*, in press.

69. RUSH, A.J., GILES, D.E., ROFFWARG, H.P., and PARKER, C.R.: Sleep EEG and dexamethasone suppression test findings in outpatients with unipolar major depressive disorders. *Biolog. Psychiat.*, 17:327-341, 1982.

9

Recent Advances in Psychotherapeutic Approaches to Schizophrenic Disorders

John Gunderson, M.D.

Recent empirical studies of psychotherapeutic approaches in the treatment of schizophrenic patients have implications for clinical care. This review of recent research gives selective attention to studies of three treatment approaches:

1) institutional and milieu treatment, which was probably the most productive and informative area of research during the 1970s;
2) family therapy, which is almost certainly the area of the most productive and interesting current body of research; and
3) individual therapy, which is an area of high theoretical and clinical interest and which continues to stimulate controversy.

The review gives little attention to the critical task of evaluating the design or methodology of the various studies.

Institutional and Milieu Treatment

During the past decade, four studies have evaluated the relative merits of brief hospitalization vs. long-term hospitalization for schizophrenic populations (1-8). Although the general conclusion was reached that short-term hospitalization

---

This is a modification of a chapter to be published in *Psychosocial Interventions in Schizophrenia: An International View,* Stierlin, H., and Wynne, L., eds. Heidelberg: Springer, 1982.

offered advantages for most patients, the major exception to this generalization comes with respect to non-chronic schizophrenics. With this group alone, there appeared to be some modest advantages for long-term hospitalizations which were evident in the post-hospital function of discharged patients (4,5).

Another series of studies has shown that patients randomly assigned to day hospital care did as well, if not better, than those assigned to full hospitalization (9-11). In this comparison, schizophrenic patients may be exceptions insofar as full hospitalization appears to have some advantages for them which are not found in other diagnostic groups (12). In an important study which compared day care to outpatient drug management in the aftercare of chronic schizophrenics, Linn et al. found that patients who received day care did considerably better in a variety of ways than those receiving only drugs, and that the more effective day treatment centers were those which had less rapid turnover, that is, longer stays (13). Taken together, these studies of institutional treatment indicate that schizophrenic patients profit more from longer residential stays with gradual transition into the community. In other words, they indicate advantages for patients of moving gradually from initial periods of containment to stable systems of long-term support.

The most impressive evidence for value of any psychosocial treatment in the past decade has come from a series of studies evaluating milieu therapy. These studies have measured the effectiveness of milieu therapy as an addition to, or instead of, drugs, whose effectiveness in treating schizophrenia had been established in the 1960s. This literature indicates that the best milieu therapies for chronic schizophrenics differ from those which are best for non-chronic schizophrenics.

With respect to non-chronic patients, a series of studies by Mosher (14,15), Carpenter et al. (16), and Rappaport et al. (17) has indicated that three- to six-month periods of intensive milieu treatment are as good or even better than drugs in treating comparable non-chronic patients. Although each of these studies has serious methodological limitations, by their cumulative weight they establish a therapeutic potential for intensive milieu therapy with non-chronic schizophrenics which equals or surpasses drug therapy. Parenthetically, they also show that, for a sizable fraction of a sample of schizophrenics, the need for drugs appears to depend upon the milieu context in which the patients are hospitalized.

The results of these outcome studies can be joined with the results of studies that correlate milieu process variables with community tenure (18) to derive a profile for optimal milieu therapy for non-chronic schizophrenics. Such a milieu would have six characteristics, as follows:

1) distribution of power and decision-making authority;
2) the use of peers, with the emphasis on establishing new and corrective relationships;

3) a high sense of involvement obtained through frequent staff/patient interactions and a tight sense of community;
4) an enthusiastic and hopeful attitude on the part of the staff;
5) a view of psychosis as a time-limited experience from which learning can take place, including examination of the interpersonal context in which the psychosis arose, and
6) a high staffing ratio and in small, six- to eight-bed units with a minimum length of stay of three months.

These milieu characteristics emphasize the therapeutic benefits of involvement acceptance, and highly interpersonal interactions, which are typical of effective therapeutic communities. From this description, it is apparent why otherwise effective short-term units may of necessity have qualities which are incompatible with the optimal treatment of schizophrenia insofar as they require an authoritarian system and deemphasize personal attachments.

For the chronic patient, quite different milieu processes are optimal. Paul and Lentz (19) compared two intensive milieu programs, in which drugs were not used, to a single custodial program, in which patients were treated with drugs. In a three-year follow-up, it was found that patients treated in the active milieu programs showed significantly more discharges, less recidivism, and better symptom remissions than the patients who were treated with drugs in the custodial setting.

Of special interest is the comparison between the two intensive milieu programs, one of which used the principles of a therapeutic community and the other of which used a social learning format based on the principles of behavior modification. In comparing the two forms of milieu treatment, the behavior modification or social learning program proved to have substantial advantages over the therapeutic community program in terms of more rapid and greater reduction in psychopathology within the hospital and subsequently in the community. Management of dangerous and aggressive behavior constituted the most obvious failure of the therapeutic community compared to the social learning milieu program. The structure of the social learning program for the chronic patients was useful to the staff in dealing with the angry behavioral disruptions of these patients. It should be noted that the patients in this study were chronically hospitalized and had extremely poor prognoses.

Paul and Lentz (19) state that the social learning program can rehabilitate even the most severely debilitated chronic patients to a point of institutional release into board-and-care facilities after six months and that, if such chronic patients continue for two to three years in a less intensive but still operative social learning aftercare program, a significant number can achieve stable and independent functioning in the community. Such a claim is remarkable. Moving chronic patients out of the hospital is an accomplishment but not necessarily a benefit for the patients; however, moving them out in a way which allows them to function independently in the community is quite remarkable.

The chronic patient seems less able to tolerate an environment which has high interpersonal demands and unpredictability without regressing to disruptive behaviors. Linn et al.'s study (20) of day treatment for chronic schizophrenic patients seems to require a similar conclusion. Of the 10 day-treatment centers that he studied, the most effective had the least active group- and family-intervention programs. What distinguished them were good rehabilitation programs.

These new studies of milieu treatment highlight six ingredients for optimal institutional care of chronic patients. First, active, intensive programs, if well designed, are preferable to passive or custodial care. This recent discovery should be emphasized, because an earlier generation of studies of milieu treatment failed to show any advantages of intensive milieu treatment over custodial care for chronic patients. Thus, the common belief that intense treatment programs are toxic to chronic patients is clearly wrong. Rather, it is the form or type of intervention which determines its effect. Second, the chronic patient's passivity (for example, his attitude that nothing can be done, that he cannot affect his own fate, or that gratification need not be earned) should continually be confronted in an effort to make it ego alien. Third, social interactions should be maximized and have a structured task focus. Fourth, examination and exploration of motives, of historical antecedents, of emotionally charged issues, and of relationships may be contraindicated. Fifth, structure in the form of clarity and predictability of roles, expectations, consequences, and leadership emerges as the most critical process variable in institutional programs which appear to be effective with chronic patients. Finally, continuity of these structures, more than of relationships, should continue into the post-discharge aftercare programs and be tapered gradually.

FAMILY THERAPY

After a wave of enthusiasm for the benefits of ongoing or intensive therapy for families with schizophrenic members, there has been a shift towards more sober claims and more limited therapeutic strategies. The need for family support and the use of time-limited family interventions at critical points have become more frequently recommended. A series of investigations has demonstrated that the family context is an extremely important determinant of relapse (21-25). These studies have raised the question as to whether family intervention can significantly alter families in ways which can diminish relapse rates.

A series of studies has been undertaken to evaluate this question. Goldstein and co-workers studied brief, six-session family therapy in the presence of drugs as an aftercare strategy (26-29). At six weeks, when this limited family intervention ended, the patients in the family therapy sample were significantly less symptomatic and had fewer relapses. By six months, the benefits of the family therapy were just a trend which disappeared altogether in the subsequent follow-ups. These results echo Langsley et al.'s (30) earlier study by showing that crisis-oriented family interventions have effective short-term but not enduring effects.

Another series of studies still in progress is attempting to provide longer-term family interventions designed to decrease the pathological pattern of high "expressed emotion" (EE). EE has two components. One is the degree to which the families are overinvolved with the designated patient. The second is the degree to which they are critical and hostile in their attitudes and comments toward the patients. Families which are overinvolved and critical are referred to as high EE families. Prior work has shown that high EE families enormously increase the likelihood of relapse in discharged patients and that such families are one of the social conditions in which drugs may be effective (24). It may even be that drugs are not necessary for discharged schizophrenic patients who do not live in such high EE social contexts. Preliminary reports show that family interventions can markedly shift high EE families to low EE scoring and that there is a corresponding decrease in relapse rates of patients in the nine months after discharge (31-33). These studies have not yet shown whether the benefits of family interventions endure beyond the period in which the treatment is being given. Nevertheless, these are the first studies of family interventions with schizophrenic patients which have been well designed and have really shown a clear positive effect.

Since these studies show promising results of family interventions, it becomes important to delineate the interventions which have been employed in them. These family interventions, which have been aptly named psychoeducational (34), have four clinical characteristics. First, therapy sessions have focused topics and directive leadership. Transference interpretation is not done. Second, the therapist meets with parents or other significant relatives separately from the designated patient; in fact, it is exceptional for the patient to be included in the meeting. During sessions, the parents are informed about what is known about the etiology and treatment of schizophrenia with emphasis on the long-term nature of the illness and the need for drug compliance. The relatives are directed not to be angry with or critical of the schizophrenic family member. The relatives are asked to identify everyday stressful situations related to living with the schizophrenic person and to develop alternative coping responses. Parents are encouraged to discuss their family situations with other families with schizophrenic members. Third, the illness-producing or sustaining patterns of family relationships are not identified as such. The concept of schizophrenia as one manifestation of a larger family disorder is explicitly not accepted. Fourth, a flexible, pragmatic approach is taken with regard to the composition, scheduling, and location of family meetings.

Now, there are discrepancies between this psychoeducational approach and the traditional approach of family therapists. Stierlin (35), for example, has described the traditional goals of experienced family therapists as follows: to open up dialogue about major conflicts, secrets, and myths within a family; to ally with certain family members and use this alliance as a lever to shift patterns of control and power; to address directly and disrupt the most central distortions in the family's orientation. In contrast, the psychoeducational approach clearly discourages family members from confronting patients with their disturbing behaviors, however maladaptive. Such behaviors are considered symptomatic of illness. Leff (36), for example, has noted in his groups of relatives how

> the low EE relatives show a tolerant, even collusive attitude toward the patient's symptoms and retain a remarkable ability to make light of the most fraught situations. There is no hint of blaming or criticizing the patients.

He closes this description by expressing optimism that high EE relatives can respond to treatment so as to emulate such collusive tolerance.

There is still uncertainty as to how often and when family therapy is indicated. Of that subgroup of schizophrenic patients who have intact and available families, about half of those families will be in the high EE category. There is some suggestion that the psychoeducational approach might also be useful for low EE families. Even when consecutive schizophrenic admissions are evaluated by enthusiasts for family therapy, perhaps 10% or fewer of the cases will be found suitable (37,38), and ongoing conjoint family therapy of more than a few months is unusual. However, parental contacts and supportive crisis-oriented family meetings are common and often considered essential.

No doubt the current wave of studies of psychoeducational family therapy will provide a welcome stimulus to the use of family therapy and to an assessment of techniques of intervention. There is still a need for studies of the benefits and indications for the various forms of family treatment which traditionally have been advocated.

INDIVIDUAL PSYCHOTHERAPY

There has been ongoing debate about the efficacy of individual psychotherapy for schizophrenic patients, and detailed reviews have been published (39). Critics still point to the series of outcome studies of the late 1960s and early 1970s which failed to demonstrate its widely heralded value. Most recently, the complaint has been raised that many of the successfully treated cases in the literature might not be properly diagnosed schizophrenic by modern standards (40). Proponents still point to the limitations of those initial outcome studies and the unexplained but recurrent and still growing number of reports of successful treatment cases under more favorable circumstances.

In the most recent report, which comes from Sweden, a group of schizophrenic patients, selected for individual therapy by a highly invested woman therapist, were compared to a matched group selected by a tolerant but openly skeptical psychopharmacologically-oriented psychiatrist who worked at the same institution (41). To their surprise, in subsequent blind follow-up evaluations of these samples, the investigators found that patients given the individual therapy were significantly better in many areas of function over the following six years.

This and other reports are not convincing of the value of individual psychotherapy for schizophrenic patients. They do underscore the need to recognize more about what can make individual therapy, at least occasionally, therapeutic. Examination of nearly all of the reported successes with this method allow several observations. First, its advantages become evident after patients have been seen for a year and a half or more. Rubins (42) has suggested that the most significant phase of changing growth is in the third year of treatment. Second, individual therapy must be provided within a supportive psychosocial context. Third, successful individual therapy involves at least twice-weekly and generally more frequent meetings. Fourth, therapists must have a long-term commitment and perspective about this work. Fifth, open, active, flexible, and wide-ranging interventions characterize the therapist's activities. Sixth, psychoanalytically-oriented explorations require close supervision by an experienced, personally analyzed therapist.

New evidence is emerging that the early phase of treatment and engagement in individual therapy is important. Studies indicate that, when schizophrenic patients are not selected but are simply assigned to individual therapy, less than 50% will become engaged in it (43). This is so even within a hospital, where voluntary attendance by patients is much less of an issue (44). When consecutive patients are evaluated for individual therapy, approximately 50% will be found suitable (37). In a collaborative outcome study at McLean Hospital and Boston University directed by Stanton, Knapp, and myself, the patients were randomly assigned to either an exploratory or supportive form of therapy. It was found that only one in three non-chronic patients can be expected to continue in their assigned therapy, regardless of the type, for two or more years. That is the time period at which one might expect the benefits of such therapy to become evident.

What are the baseline characteristics of the patients for whom individual therapy is indicated? Stanton has reported from our outcome study that a capacity for adaptive regression (which seems to include such qualities as imagination and capacity for self-observation) and a low degree of denial of illness are important predictors of engagement in therapy (45). When we add to these two characteristics the suggestions from elsewhere that patients should not be highly symptomatic (46) but be poorly functioning (47), we have a list of qualities (with the exception of low denial of illness) which offer a surprising contrast to the usual statements about the patients for whom individual therapy is indicated, that is, that they are bright, young, insightful, and full of conflict.

Three factors within the treatment itself appear to be important determinants of whether, after being assigned to individual therapy, patients will subsequently stay in it or not. One of the possible reasons why longer stays prove beneficial for non-chronic schizophrenics is that they increase the likelihood of patients' having sufficient time to establish attachment to therapists whom they will then continue to see and who will provide needed sustaining functions during the aftercare phase. This premise was recently tested by the author in the collaborative outcome study and was confirmed. Willful discontinuation of psychotherapy is very highly correlated with short hospitalization. It should be added that this is only true up to a point. Thus, after six months of hospitalization, there no longer is a relationship between length of hospitalization and continuation in individual therapy.

Another issue which bears on the likelihood of engagement in psychotherapy by schizophrenic patients is the degree to which the individual therapist imposes demands upon patients for responsible participation or examination of emotionally laden issues under circumstances where this proves intolerable and results in symptomatic exacerbations and relapses. Hence, one can infer both from the May et al. (48,49) and the Hogarty et al. (46,50) studies that initiation of individual therapy at a time when the patients were symptomatically disturbed resulted in subsequent symptomatic relapses. This led those investigators to conclude that individual therapy may be contraindicated under such circumstances. Nevertheless, both the May and Hogarty studies reserve a role for individual therapy, May for the post-hospital phase of treatment and Hogarty for those discharged patients who are not particularly symptomatic.

This conclusion, however, must be tempered by recognition that the therapists in those studies were inexperienced. A recent report from the McLean-Boston University collaborative study by Frosch et al. (51) showed that experienced insight-oriented therapists had a quite different profile of beliefs about techniques and the origins of schizophrenia than those therapists who were providing the supportive therapy. It revealed the intensive insight-oriented therapists to be extremely gentle, supportive, and ego-oriented in their approach in contrast to the confrontative, intrusive, or interpretive methods which might be expected from psychoanalytically-oriented therapists. This raises the question as to whether the relapse problem identified by May and Hogarty is due to the inadvisability of attempts to engage symptomatic schizophrenic patients in individual psychotherapy, as they inferred, or whether it is an issue of the empathic skill with which the interventions are employed under such circumstances that determines whether the effect is going to be harmful or helpful.

A somewhat surprising finding which has emerged from the collaborative project relating to engagement in individual therapy is that unexpectedly strong relationships exist between engagement and the type of match which occurs, not just between the patient and the therapist, but also between the therapist and the milieu program (52). It has been found that an exploratory therapist, working in a control-oriented ward, and a supportive therapist, working on an insight-oriented ward, are sufficiently incompatible that it can be predicted that an ongoing psychotherapy will not occur. This was measured by the frequency of dropouts from an assigned treatment and by the length of time which patients continue in the assigned treatment.

The conclusion can reasonably be inferred from numerous reports that schizophrenic patients who become engaged in long-term individual psychotherapy will do better than comparable patients who do not. Nevertheless, this conclusion is not firmly established. Recent reports suggest that individual treatment is likely to develop meaningfully for one-quarter to one-half of the population of schizophrenic patients seeking treatment. Factors which determine whether engagement in psychotherapy occurs include the amount of support given by the psychotherapists, the length of time in hospital, the attitudes of the hospital staff toward the psychotherapist, and the skill with which the therapist diminishes anxiety during disturbed phases of the treatment.

OVERVIEW

Recent empirical studies indicate that revisions are warranted in general assumptions about the treatment of schizophrenia. One common assumption which these studies call into question is that good quality psychosocial treatments are so expensive that they must, regardless of their benefits, be restricted in practice to only the well-to-do. Studies have now shown that effective psychosocial treatments cost no more than minimal treatment because of their impact on rehospitalization and are far less expensive than equally intensive treatments which are poorly conceived and delivered (19,20,53,54). In addition, milieu programs, such as those of Mosher and Menn (54) and Paul and Lentz (19), which have shown modest increase in the subsequent employment of discharged patients, are potentially far greater money earners in the long run.

Another conception which is challenged by these studies concerns the mechanisms by which change occurs in treatment. The traditional psychodynamic approach has been to modify a patient's inner life and expect that this will bring subsequent changes in his symptoms and relationships to his environment—an "inside-out" strategy. This approach is based on the hope of altering the individual's personality to allow him to adapt successfully to the endless vicissitudes of life. Insight-oriented individual therapy is the purest example of this approach and may explain why, as noted earlier, measurable behavioral change can be expected to occur only after long-term treatment. Gains from this approach are measured by the degree to which they produce enduring changes which go beyond exposure to the therapeutic intervention. This contrasts dramatically to psychopharmacologic therapy, whose effectiveness is measured by whether the patient relapses when drugs are discontinued. Of the studies reviewed here, the milieu studies with non-chronic patients come closest to emphasizing the strategy of attempting to make the schizophrenic person's inner life understandable and acceptable and to clarify and rearrange his views of himself and his prior relationships.

In contrast, most of the studies reviewed have been directed at providing a social context for schizophrenic individuals which makes symptomatic relapses less likely, and only secondarily have they considered that such a favorable environment might bring about internal change. So much has this been the trend that Klein (55) has legitimately questioned whether these studies can be considered to evaluate the treatment of schizophrenia per se, or rather just its social consequences. The principles of this "outside-in" strategy are most clearly found in Paul and Lentz's (19) milieu program for chronic patients, but they are also found in studies with non-chronic patients receiving other forms of therapy, most particularly the psychoeducational approach to family treatment.

Although the results from these studies are impressive, it has long been thought that gains made from supportive and directive techniques will remain highly context-dependent. That is, the question has been whether such learning experiences can be enduringly internalized. In this regard, there are many studies in which schizophrenic patients made gains within various treatment contexts but showed rapid reversals after termination of the treatment. Paul and Lentz's (19) work has shown that social learning experiences, based on behavioral modification techniques, were occasionally internalized to the extent that independent function was achieved after the treatment program was discontinued. This suggested that internal change did occur, secondary to behavioral improvement. In line with this, it has been noted that the family interventions which reduce EE may do more than simply decrease the likelihood of symptomatic relapse. In some instances, they seem to allow improvements or growth to occur (33). The changed home environment may allow schizophrenic persons to experiment with new and more adaptive forms of self-expression. Such signals of successful "outside-in" changes seem to reflect dynamic or psychological growth. Such results are consistent with recent reports of patients treated in short-term therapy who achieve symptomatic improvement without dynamic changes but who, without any further treatment in their follow-up, seem to have acquired dynamic change (56). In any event, these suggestions of internal changes that are a direct or indirect result of treatments aimed primarily at manipulating the social context require an expansion of traditional views of change.

These studies also offer a fresh perspective on the processes within treatments which facilitate change in schizophrenic patients. Many of the studies show that the overt psychopathology of schizophrenic individuals is ameliorated by treatment programs that are stable and emotionally undemanding and which involve structured tasks. Such results have led some reviewers to conclude that schizophrenic patients need de-intensified stimulation. Studies by Silverman et al. (57) have found that hospitalized schizophrenic patients will respond to subliminal stimulations of their symbiotic wishes (a message flashed on and off, such as "Mommy and I are one") with diminished behavioral pathology and thought disorder. On the other hand, subliminal stimulation of themes of aggression or object loss (such as "Mommy is dead") increase cognitive and behavioral symptoms (58). These results are consistent with the explanation that relatively stressless, need-gratifying environments simulate symbiosis in ways which cause remissions in psychotic symptoms. The results are also consistent with the unfortunate frequency with which gains are disrupted at the time of discharge, especially when aftercare programs are discontinuous. If a state of homeostatic symbiosis is responsible for decreasing symptomatic relapses, this helps to explain why added benefits could occur from longer-term treatment programs but can be lost upon discharge, why decreases in EE within toxic family environments may diminish the likelihood of relapses, why conflict between staff members involved in the treatment of the patient can cause schizophrenic patients to regress, and why discontinuities in treatments as diverse as behavioral modification and individual therapy may result in relapse.

If the mechanism of action whereby treatments prevent relapses is via gratification of the illusion of a symbiotic attachment, the obvious question is whether and under what conditions a schizophrenic person can give up a symbiotic attachment once it is established. Searles (59), who helped formulate symbiosis as part of the psychology of schizophrenia, believes that growth out of symbiosis depends upon corrective emotional experiences. Such growth requires considerable therapeutic activity—in his case, interpretations—within the context of a symbiotic attachment. Silverman et al. (57) also found that the potentially harmful effects he anticipated from gratifying symbiotic fantasies by the subliminal stimulation, such as "Mommy and I are one," could be offset by concurrently providing milieu programs having focused tasks which assisted differentiation. This model can be applied to institutional programs when the patients' symbiotic wishes may be gratified, but within which active milieu processes may gradually facilitate the giving up of such attachments.

As we have seen, the critical processes within the milieu programs which are best for non-chronic patients are different from those which are best for chronic patients. For non-chronic patients, in addition to insight, the milieu programs heavily emphasize interpersonal involvement. Paul and Lentz's (19) treatment of chronic patients led some to achieve independent functioning, obviously without the benefit of interpretation but also without reliance on interpersonal involvement. Their work would emphasize the benefits of the affectively bland, interpersonally neutral, but relentless intrusion of progressive expectations as the critical process variables. The psychoeducational approach similarly would emphasize a highly active but detached, "nothing personal," problem-oriented approach, based on clear identification of tasks, roles, behavioral responses, and consequences. The effectiveness of these treatments is consistent with a variety of clinical observations which have shown that very sick schizophrenic patients can respond with dramatically improved function when they do not perceive the requirement to do so as being personal in nature. Thus, when all of the staff in the mental hospital are called away to war or fall ill with some kind of epidemic, patients may rally and rise to such occasions because they do not see the demand to do so under such circumstances as arbitrary or cruel.

It may be critical for success that the therapeutic environment—whether it is an institution or an individual—allows the schizophrenic patient to believe that he is symbiotically attached. The attachment, however, should be only the first step in the treatment process. The more difficult task is to provide interactions within the environment which will allow the attachment to be relinquished. The present evidence supports the idea that there are several ways of doing this—from interpretations to tokens—and they need to be tailored to the individual patient's particular form of schizophrenia.

REFERENCES

1. CAFFEY, E.M., GALBRECHT, C.R., KLETT, C.J., and POINT, P.: Brief hospitalization and aftercare in the treatment of schizophrenia. *Arch. Gen. Psychiat.*, 24(1):81-86, 1971.
2. MATTES, J.A., ROSEN, B., and KLEIN, D.F.: Comparison of the clinical effectiveness of "short" versus "long" stay psychiatric hospitalization: II. Results of a 3-year post-hospital follow-up. *J. Nerv. Ment. Dis.*, 165(6):387-394, 1977.
3. MATTES, J.A., ROSEN, B., KLEIN, D.F., and MILLAN, D.: Comparison of the clinical effectiveness of "short" versus "long" stay psychiatric hospitalization: III. Further results of a 3-year post-hospital follow-up. *J. Nerv. Ment. Dis.*, 165(6):395-402, 1977.
4. MATTES, J.A., KLEIN, D.F., MILLAN, D., and ROSEN, B.: Comparison of the clinical

effectiveness of "short" versus "long" stay psychiatric hospitalization: IV. Predictors of differential benefit. *J. Nerv. Ment. Dis.*, 167(3):175-181, 1979.

5. GLICK, I.D., and HARGREAVES, W.A.: *Psychiatric Hospital Treatment for the 1980s: A Controlled Study of Short vs. Long Hospitalization*, Lexington, MA: Lexington Press, 1979.

6. HERZ, M.I., ENDICOTT, J., and SPITZER, R.L.: Brief hospitalization of patients with families: Initial results. *Am. J. Psychiat.*, 132(4):413-418, 1975.

7. HERZ, M.I., ENDICOTT, J., and SPITZER, R.L.: Brief versus standard hospitalization: The families. *Am. J. Psychiat.*, 133(7):795-801, 1976.

8. HERZ, M.I., ENDICOTT, J., and GIBBON, M.: Brief hospitalization two-year follow-up. *Arch. Gen. Psychiat.*, 36:701-705, 1979.

9. WILDER, J.F., LEVIN, G., and ZWERLING, I.: A two-year follow-up evaluation of acute psychotic patients treated in a day hospital. *Am. J. Psychiat.*, 122:1095-1101, 1966.

10. WASHBURN, S., VANICELLI, M., LONGABAUGH, R., et al.: A controlled comparison of psychiatric day treatment and inpatient hospitalization. *J. Consult. Clin. Psychol.*, 44:665-675, 1976.

11. HERZ, M.I., ENDICOTT, J., and SPITZER, R.L.: Day vs. inpatient hospitalization: A controlled study. *Am. J. Psychiat.*, 127:1371-1381, 1971.

12. MICHAUX, M.H., CHELST, M.R., FOSTER, S.A., et al.: Postrelease adjustment of day and full-time psychiatric patients. *Arch. Gen. Psychiat.*, 29:647-651, 1973.

13. LINN, N.W., CAFFEY, E.M., KLETT, C.J., HOGARTY, G.E., and LAMB, H.R.: Day treatment and psychotropic drugs in the aftercare of schizophrenic patients. *Arch. Gen. Psychiat.*, 36:1055-1072, 1979.

14. MOSHER, L.R.: A research design for evaluating a psychological treatment of schizophrenia. *Hosp. & Comm. Psychiat.*, 23:17-22, 1972.

15. MOSHER, L.R.: Family therapy for schizophrenia: Recent trends. In: L.J. West and D.E. Flinn (Eds.), *Treatment of Schizophrenia Progress and Prospects*. New York: Grune & Stratton, 1976.

16. CARPENTER, W.T., JR., McGLASHAN, T.H., and STRAUSS, J.S.: The treatment of acute schizophrenia without drugs: An investigation of some current assumptions. *Am. J. Psychiat.*, 134(1):14-20, 1977.

17. RAPPAPORT, M., HOPKINS, H.K., HALL, K., BELLEZA, T., and SILVERMAN, J.: Are there schizophrenics for whom drugs may be unnecessary or contraindicated? *Int. Pharmacopsychiat.*, 13:100-110, 1978.

18. GUNDERSON, J.G., and GOMES-SCHWARTZ, B.: The quality of outcome from psychotherapy of schizophrenia. In: J.S. Strauss, M. Bowers, T.W. Downey, J. Fleck, S. Jackson, and I. Levine (Eds.), *The Psychotherapy of Schizophrenia*. New York: Plenum Medical Book Company, 1980.

19. PAUL, G.L., and LENTZ, R.J.: *Psychosocial Treatment of Chronic Mental Patients: Milieu vs. Social-Learning Programs*. Cambridge, MA: Harvard University Press, 1977.

20. LINN, N.W., CAFFEY, E.M., KLETT, C.J., HOGARTY, G.E., and LAMB, H.R.: Day treatment and psychotropic drugs in the aftercare of schizophrenic patients. *Arch. Gen. Psychiat.*, 36:1055-1072, 1979.

21. BROWN, G.W., MONCK, E.J., CARSTAIRS, G.M., and WING, J.K.: The influence of family life on the course of schizophrenic illness. *Br. J. Prev. Soc. Med.*, 16:55-68, 1962.

22. BROWN, G.W., BIRLEY, J.L.T., and WING, J.K.: Influence of family on the course

of schizophrenic disorders: A replication. *Br. J. Psychiat.*, 121:241-258, 1972.

23. SCOTT, R.D.: Cultural frontiers in the mental health service. *Schiz. Bull.*, 10:58-73, 1974.

24. VAUGHN, C.E., and LEFF, J.P.: The influence of family and social factors in the course of psychiatric illness: A comparison of schizophrenic and depressed neurotic patients. *Br. J. Psychiat.*, 129:125-137, 1976.

25. HOGARTY, G.E., SCHOOLER, N.R., ULRICH, R., MUSSARE, F., FERRO, P., and HERRON, E.: Fluphenazine and social therapy in the aftercare of schizophrenic patients. *Arch. Gen. Psychiat.*, 36:1283-1294, 1979.

26. GOLDSTEIN, M.J., RODNICK, E.H., EVANS, J.R., and MAY, P.R.A.: Long-acting phenothiazines and social therapy in community treatment of acute schizophrenics. *Psychopharmacol. Bull.*, 11:37-38, 1975.

27. GOLDSTEIN, M.J., RODNICK, E.H., EVANS, J.R., MAY, P.R.A., and STEINBERG, M.R.: Drug and family therapy in the aftercare of acute schizophrenics. *Arch. Gen. Psychiat.*, 35:1169-1177, 1978.

28. GOLDSTEIN, M.J.: Family therapy during the aftercare treatment of acute schizophrenia. In: J.S. Strauss, M. Bowers, T.W. Downey, S. Fleck, S. Jackson and I. Levine (Eds.), *The Psychotherapy of Schizophrenia*. New York: Plenum Medical Book Company, 1980.

29. GOLDSTEIN, M.J., and KOPEIKIN, H.S.: Short-and long-term effects on a program combining drug and family therapy. Unpublished manuscript.

30. LANGSLEY, D., PITTMAN, F., and SWANK, G.: Family crisis in schizophrenics and other mental patients. *J. Nerv. Men. Dis.*, 149:270-276, 1969.

31. LEFF, J., KUIPERS, L., and BERKOWITZ, R.: Intervention in families and its effect on relapse rate. Unpublished manuscript, 1981.

32. FALLOON, I.R.H., BOYD, J.L., McGILL, C.W., STRANG, J.S., and MOSS, H.B.: Family management training in the community care of schizophrenia. Unpublished manuscript, 1981.

33. FALLOON, I.R.H., LIBERMAN, R.P., LILLIE, F.M., and VAUGH, C.E.: Family therapy of schizophrenics with high risk of relapse. *Family Process*, 20:211-221, 1981.

34. ANDERSON, C.M., HOGARTY, G.E., and REISS, D.J.: Family treatment of adult schizophrenic patients: A psycho-educational approach. *Schiz. Bull.*, 6(3):491-505, 1980.

35. STIERLIN, H.: Psychotherapy and psychotherapists in transformation. Unpublished manuscript, 1980.

36. LEFF, J.P.: Developments in family treatment of schizophrenia. *Psychiat. Q.*, 51(3):216-232, 1979.

37. ALANEN, Y.O., RAKKOLAINEN, V., RASIMUS, R., LAAKSO, J., and JARVI, R.: Developing the treatment of schizophrenia in a community-psychiatric setting: A psychotherapeutic and family-centered approach. Unpublished manuscript.

38. GUNDERSON, J.G.: Engagement of schizophrenic patients in psychotherapy. Unpublished manuscript.

39. GUNDERSON, J.G.: Individual psychotherapy. In: L. Bellak (Ed.), *Disorders of the Schizophrenic Syndrome*. New York: Basic Books, 1979.

40. NORTH, C., and CADORET, R.: Diagnostic discrepancy in personal accounts of patients with "schizophrenia." *Arch. Gen. Psychiat.*, 38:133-137, 1981.

41. SJOSTROM, R., and SANDIN, B.: Effects of psychotherapy in schizophrenia: A retrospective study. Study presented at the 1st European Conference on Psychotherapy Research in Trier, FRG, September, 1981.

42. RUBINS, J.L.: Five-year results of psychoanalytic therapy and day care for acute schizophrenic patients. *Am. J. Psychoanal.*, 36:3-26, 1976.
43. O'BRIEN, C.P., HAMM, K.B., RAY, B.A., PIERCE, J.F., LUBORSKY, L., and MINTZ, J.: Group vs. individual psychotherapy with schizophrenics: A controlled outcome study. *Arch. Gen. Psychiat.*, 27:474-478, 1972.
44. ROGERS, C.R., GENDLIN, E.G., KIESLER, D.J., and TRUAZ, C.B.: *The Therapeutic Relationship and Its Impact: A Study of Psychotherapy with Schizophrenics*. Madison, WI: University of Wisconsin Press, 1967.
45. STANTON, A.H., BOUTELLE, W., GOMES-SCHWARTZ, B., GUNDERSON, J.G., KATZ, H., KNAPP, P., MINTZ, M., SCHNITZER, R., and VANICELLI, M.: An evaluation of individual psychotherapy with schizophrenic patients: Determinants of engagement in therapy. Paper presented at the 132nd Annual Meeting of the American Psychiatric Association, May 1979, Chicago, Illinois.
46. GOLDBERG, S.C., SCHOOLER, N.R., HOGARTY, G.E., and ROPER, M.: Prediction of relapse in schizophrenic outpatients treated by drug and sociotherapy. *Arch. Gen. Psychiat.*, 34:171-184, 1977.
47. BECK, J.C., GOLDEN, S., and ARNOLD, F.: An empirical investigation of psychotherapy with schizophrenic patients. *Schiz. Bull.*, 7(2):241-247, 1981.
48. MAY, P.R.A., and TUMA, A.H.: A follow-up study of the results of treatment. *Arch. Gen. Psychiat.*, 33:474-478, 481-486, 1976.
49. MAY, P.R.A., TUMA, A.H., and DIXON, W.J.: Schizophrenia: A follow-up study of the results of five forms of treatment. *Arch. Gen. Psychiat.*, 38(7):776-784, 1981.
50. HOGARTY, G.E., SCHOOLER, N.R., ULRICH, R., MUSSARE, F., FERRO, P., and HERRON, E.: Fluphenazine and social therapy in the aftercare of schizophrenic patients. *Arch. Gen. Psychiat.*, 36:1283-1294, 1979.
51. FROSCH, J.P., GUNDERSON, J.G., WEISS, R., and FRANK, A.: Therapists who treat schizophrenic patients: Characterization. Unpublished manuscript.
52. FRANK, A., and GUNDERSON, J.G.: Interaction of milieu and individual therapy. Unpublished manuscript.
53. KARON, B.P., and VANDENBOS, G.R.: Treatment costs of psychotherapy versus medication for schizophrenics. *Prof. Psychol.*, 293-298, August 1975.
54. MOSHER, L.R., and MENN, A.Z.: Community residential treatment for schizophrenia: Two-year follow-up. *Hosp. & Comm. Psychiat.*, 29:715-723, 1978.
55. KLEIN, D.F.: Psychosocial treatment of schizophrenia. *Schiz. Bull.*, 6(1):122-130, 1980.
56. MALAN, D.H.: *Individual Psychotherapy and the Science of Psychodynamics*. London: Butterworths Press, 1979.
57. SILVERMAN, L.H., LEVINSON, P., MENDELSOHN, E., UNGARO, R., and BRONSTEIN, A.A.: A clinical application of subliminal psychodynamic activation on the stimulation of symbiotic fantasies as an adjunct in the treatment of hospitalized schizophrenics. *J. Nerv. Men. Dis.*, 161(6):379-392, 1975.
58. LITWACK, T.R., WIEDEMANN, C.F., and YAGER, J.: The fear of object loss, responsiveness to subliminal stimuli, and schizophrenic psychopathology. *J. Nerv. Ment. Dis.*, 167(2):79-89, 1979.
59. SEARLES, H.F.: *Collected Papers on Schizophrenia and Related Subjects*. New York: International Universities Press, 1965.

Part IV

TOWARD UNIFYING APPROACHES

10

Toward a Unified View of Affective Disorders

David J. Kupfer, M.D.

INTRODUCTION

Affective disorders, which include depression and mania, probably constitute the most common psychiatric problem for which people seek help or which they suffer without seeking help (1). Depression has been part of the human condition as long as man has inhabited the earth. Even a brief perusal of early manuscripts or writings reveals descriptions of depression (2). Ancient writers recognized some of the same problems that we are treating 2,000-4,000 years later. A worldwide problem, depression is recognized in all cultures and treated in many ways with varying degrees of success. From 10% to 20% of all Americans will suffer from an affective disorder at some time during their lives. Ten to 14 million people in the United States suffer from depression or mania at any one time. Although the true distribution by sex is not known, epidemiologists currently estimate that about 15% of all women and about 7% of all men will have an episode of affective disorder in their lifetime. Unipolar illness (a depressive episode only) is about twice as common in women as in men; bipolar illness (both manic and depressive episodes) is equally distributed among men and women. Depression has many consequences, the most serious of which is suicide.

An affective disorder can appear at any time from prepubertal years to late life, but it is most prevalent among the middle-aged who are at the peak of job productivity and parental-role demands. It should be stressed, however, that depression does not focus exclusively on middle-aged adults; depression affects people of all ages. Controversy still persists regarding the frequency of childhood

225

and adolescent depression. The need remains for health practitioners to identify these syndromes, because serious impairment of social, family, and school functioning often results from depressive episodes of the young. Similarly, identification of depression in the elderly and separation of the normal aging process from the depressive disease remain an essential medical task.

Depression does not occur in isolation from other psychiatric or medical problems; it contributes to other psychiatric and social problems such as alcoholism and drug dependency. Also, medical and neurological diseases interact with depression, especially in older individuals. Recognition of the depressive syndrome is primary and vital to medical practice because, once it is differentiated from other disease processes, successful treatment is possible. Today the advent of drug therapies and the development of specific forms of psychotherapy have made depression a treatable mental illness.

To understand the progress of the last 10-20 years toward a unified view of affective disorders, it will be necessary to integrate the increasing body of knowledge emerging from different disciplines, ranging from epidemiology to the neurosciences. Elsewhere in this book, chapters have been devoted in detail to biological approaches, the use of clinical laboratory tests in diagnosis and treatment prediction, and the development of newer antidepressants and specific psychotherapies for depressive disorders. Certainly, aspects of issues covered in these chapters are important to appreciating the current state of the art. However, in this overview, more attention will be devoted to diagnostic advances and our increasing level of sophistication in descriptive nosology. Since it is a contention that major sources of confusion have been related to the imprecise use of the term "depression" and the failure to operationalize diagnostic criteria, the first half of this chapter deals with classification. Second, after describing various etiologic theories of depression, a brief overview of certain genetic-familial aspects of depression is covered, followed by some recent epidemiological and psychosocial data. Certain principles of treatment and current treatment approaches are reviewed briefly to provide another important area of inquiry. The final task then becomes the integration of what is currently known about affective disorders from a diagnostic, genetic-familial, and treatment point of view. Indeed, one has more questions to ask now than 10 years ago, but at least one has the sense of considerable progress in diagnosing and treating acute depression.

CLINICAL DESCRIPTION OF AFFECTIVE SYNDROMES

The phrase "I'm depressed" has acquired a certain currency as a shorthand description for feelings of sadness, disappointment, and frustration, which are normal responses to a wide variety of everyday events. However, to the clinical psychiatrist, depression refers specifically to a broad continuum of changes in affective states, ranging from the normal mood fluctuations of everyday life to a severe, even psychotic, melancholia. Depressive syndromes, on the other hand, refer to a group of emotional disorders characterized primarily by a disturbance of mood but also involving a variety of associated features.

The comprehension of depressive syndromes requires an appreciation of the full range of affective disorders, including both depression and mania. The essential features of depression include a persistently sad, depressed, or empty mood, with any or all of the following associated symptoms: loss of interest or pleasure; sleep disturbance; appetite disturbance; decreased energy; feeling of pessimism or guilt; and thoughts of death or suicide. Depression as a clinical disorder is distinguished from everyday ups and downs by the persistence of the mood distrubance, the accompanying symptoms, and the impaired performance in society or at work.

Classification systems that are used to arrive at diagnosis, prognosis, and treatment in depression range from those that describe many distinct disease entities to models that assume a continuum of symptomatology. Still, all clinical descriptions include depressed mood as the characteristic symptom, as reported by over 90% of depressed patients. The patient's self-description includes words such as "sad," "low," "blue," "despondent," "hopeless," "gloomy," or "down in the dumps." Together with this state of inner distress, the clinician often observes changes in posture, speech, facial expression, dress, and grooming consistent with the patient's self-report. Nevertheless, a small percentage of patients do not report the mood disturbance—perhaps because of denial or repression. In these cases of "masked depression" or "smiling depression," the patient manifests other symptoms of depressive syndrome. This diagnostic conclusion is usually supported by a recent loss by the patient, as well as other symptoms consistent with depressive syndrome.

Recently, operational diagnostic criteria for depression have been established in the *Diagnostic and Statistical Manual of Mental Disorders* (DSM-III) (3). The DSM-III represents a multiaxial approach in which the principal diagnosis is given in axis I. In axis II personality disorders (specific personality traits) and specific developmental disorders are described in a fashion similiar to that of physical disorders or conditions which are indicated on axis III. The severity of a psychosocial stressor which is judged to have been a significant contributor to the development or exacerbation of the current disorder is rated in axis IV. Finally, axis V allows the description of the highest level of adaptive functioning within the last year.

According to DSM-III, a major depressive episode is characterized by a dysphoric mood and loss of interest or pleasure in all, or almost all, usual activities. The mood disturbance must be prominent and relatively persistent, but need not necessarily be the most dominant symptom. Momentary shifts from one dysphoric mood to another, e.g., anxiety to depression to anger, that are seen in a state of acute psychotic turmoil do not qualify. In addition, at least four of the symptoms outlined in Table 1 must be present nearly every day for a period of at least two weeks. In this classification schema, associated features may include depressed appearance, tearfulness, feelings of anxiety, irritability, fear, brooding, excessive concern with physical health, panic attacks, and phobias (Figure 1).

When delusions or hallucinations are present, they are usually clearly consistent with the predominant mood (i.e., mood congruent). A common delusion is that the patient is being persecuted because of sinfulness or some inadequacy. There may be nihilistic delusions of world or personal destruction, somatic delusions of cancer or other serious illness, or delusions of poverty. Halluci-

TABLE 1

Diagnostic Criteria for Major Depressive Episode

A. Dysphoric mood or loss of interest or pleasure in all or almost all usual activities and pastimes. The dysphoric mood is characterized by symptoms such as the following: depressed, sad, blue, hopeless, low, down in the dumps, irritable. The mood disturbance must be prominent and relatively persistent.

B. At least four of the following symptoms have each been present nearly every day for a period of at least two weeks:
    1. Poor appetite or significant weight loss (when not dieting) or increased appetite or significant weight gain.
    2. Insomnia or hypersomnia.
    3. Psychomotor agitation or retardation (but not merely subjective feelings of restlessness or being slowed down).
    4. Loss of interest or pleasure in usual activities, or decrease in sexual drive not limited to a period when delusional or hallucinating.
    5. Loss of energy, fatigue.
    6. Feelings of worthlessness, self-reproach, or excessive or inappropriate guilt (either may be delusional).
    7. Complaints or evidence of diminished ability to think or concentrate, such as slowed thinking, or indecisiveness not associated with marked loosening of associations or incoherence.
    8. Recurrent thoughts of death, suicidal ideation, wishes to be dead, or suicide attempts.

C. Neither of the following dominates the clinical picture when an affective syndrome is absent (i.e., symptoms in criteria A and B above):
    1. Preoccupation with a mood-incongruent delusion or hallucination.
    2. Bizarre behavior.

D. Not superimposed on either schizophrenia, schizophreniform disorder, or a paranoid disorder.

E. Not due to any organic mental disorder or uncomplicated bereavement.

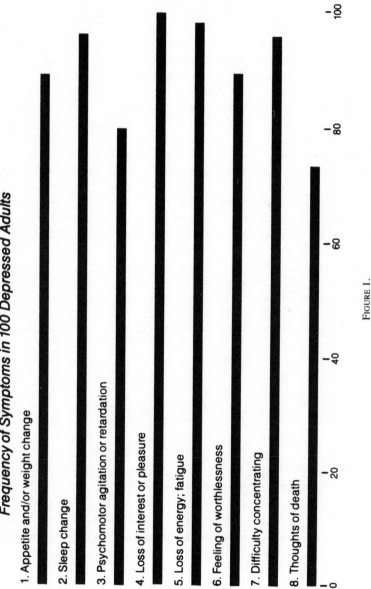

FIGURE 1.

nations, when present, are usually transient and not elaborate and may involve voices that berate patients for their shortcomings or sins. Depressive stupor in which the individual is mute and unresponsive can also be present.

Less commonly, the content of the hallucinations or delusions bears no apparent relationship to the mood disturbance (mood incongruent). For example, in persecutory delusions, the patient cannot explain why he is the object of persecution. Other symptoms such as thought insertion, thought broadcasting, and delusions of control are sometimes reported. The usefulness of the distinction in subsequent treatment between mood-congruent and mood-incongruent psychotic features remains controversial.

Although this classification schema implicitly assumes that the essential features of a major depressive episode are similar in infants, children, adolescents, adults, and the elderly, there are definite differences in the associated features. For example, in prepubertal children, separation anxiety may develop and cause the child to cling, refuse to go to school, and fear that he or his parents will die. Furthermore, a previous history of separation anxiety may intensify the anxiety symptoms with the onset of a major depressive episode. In adolescents, negativisitic or frankly antisocial behavior may appear. Feelings of wanting to leave home, not being understood and approved of, restlessness, grouchiness, aggression, sulkiness, a reluctance to cooperate in family ventures, and withdrawal from social activities with retreat to one's room are common. School difficulties and substance abuse may also develop. Finally, inattention to personal appearance and increased emotionality, with particular sensitivity to rejection in love relationships, can be noted.

In elderly adults, depression may generate symptoms suggesting dementia such as disorientation, memory loss, and distractibility. Loss of interest or pleasure in the individual's usual activities may appear as apathy, difficulty in maintaining concentration, or inattentiveness. These symptoms make the differential diagnosis between "pseudodementia" (due to depression) and true dementia (an organic mental disorder) particularly difficult if based only on clinical symptoms.

Whereas the DSM-III definition of major depressive disorder resembles the older, more general description of depressive syndrome, it improves both the specificity and consistency of diagnosis. The DSM-III sections on affective disorders provide clear-cut categories with unambiguous diagnostic criteria that eliminate terms possessing etiological implications (Figure 2). Furthermore, this new classification collects all types of affective disorders and does not split them into psychoses, neuroses, and personality disorders.

The classification of Affective Disorders in DSM-III differs from many other classifications based on such dichotomous distinctions as neurotic vs. psychotic or endogenous vs. reactive. However, the DSM-III classification explicitly deals

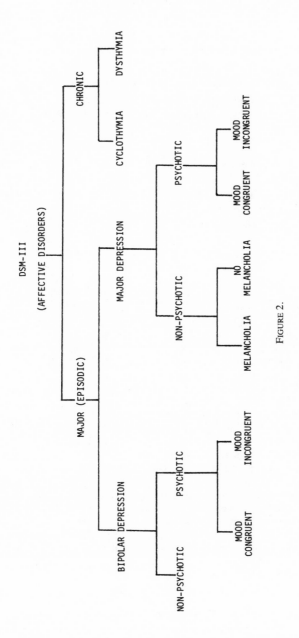

FIGURE 2.

with endogenous (melancholic) states, psychotic depressions, and the unipolar/bipolar distinction. Indeed, only the primary/secondary distinction is not included in axis I, but aspects of secondary disorders could be included in axes II and III descriptions. The class, Affective Disorders, is divided into Major Affective Disorders, in which there is a full affective syndrome; Other Specific Affective Disorders, in which there is only a partial affective syndrome of at least two years' duration; and, finally, Atypical Affective Disorders, a category for those affective disorders that cannot be classified in either of the two specific subclasses.

Major Affective Disorders include bipolar disorder and major depression, which are distinguished by whether or not there has ever been a manic episode. The diagnostic criteria for a manic episode include a predominantly elevated, expansive, or irritable mood which must be prominent and persistent, but could be intermingled with depressive mood. In addition, at least three of the symptoms outlined in Table 2 must be present nearly every day for a minimum duration

TABLE 2
Diagnostic Criteria for Manic Episode

A. One or more distinct periods with a predominantly elevated, expansive, or irritable mood. The elevated or irritable mood must be a prominent part of the illness and relatively persistent, although it may alternate or intermingle with depressive mood.
B. Duration of at least one week (or any duration if hospitalization is necessary), during which, for most of the time, at least three of the following symptoms have persisted (four if the mood is only irritable) and have been present to a significant degree:
   1. Increase in activity (either socially, at work, or sexually) or physical restlessness.
   2. More talkative than usual or pressure to keep talking.
   3. Flight of ideas or subjective experience that thoughts are racing.
   4. Inflated self-esteem (grandiosity, which may be delusional).
   5. Decreased need for sleep.
   6. Distractibility, i.e., attention is easily drawn to unimportant or irrelevant external stimuli.
   7. Excessive involvement in activities that have a high potential for painful consequences which is not recognized, e.g., buying sprees, sexual indiscretions, foolish business investments, reckless driving.
C. Neither of the following dominates the clinical picture when an affective syndrome is absent (i.e., symptoms in criteria A and B above):
   1. Preoccupation with a mood-incongruent delusion or hallucination.*
   2. Bizarre behavior.
D. Not superimposed on either schizophrenia, schizophreniform disorder, or a paranoid disorder.
E. Not due to any organic mental disorder, such as substance intoxication

* A hypomanic episode is a pathological disturbance similar to, but not as severe as, a manic episode.

of at least one week. A category of specific manic disorder is not included in this classification; instead, when there has been one or more manic episodes, with or without a history of a major depressive episode, the category bipolar disorder is used. Bipolar disorder is subclassified as mixed, manic, or depressed; major depression is subclassified as single episode or recurrent. The current episode is further subclassified to reflect certain characteristics such as the presence of psychotic features and, in the case of a major depressive episode, the presence of melancholia.

Other Specific Affective Disorders include cyclothymic disorder and dysthymic disorder. In cyclothymic disorder there are symptoms characteristic of both the depressive and the manic syndromes, but they are not of sufficient severity and duration to meet the criteria for major depressive or manic episodes. In dysthymic disorder (previously associated with depressive neurosis) the essential feature is a chronic disturbance of mood, involving either depressed mood or loss of interest or pleasure in all, or almost all, usual activities and pastimes, associated symptoms, but not of sufficient severity and duration to meet the criteria for a major depressive episode, and no hypomanic periods.

CLASSIFICATION EFFORTS

A specific diagnosis is necessary to establish treatment and to evaluate the progress of treatment. It has long been thought that dichotomous models were particularly useful for the classification of depressive disorders. Of the two most widely accepted dichotomous models of classification, one is based on the endogenous/reactive dichotomy and the other on the psychotic/neurotic dichotomy (Table 3). Endogenous depression occurs most frequently in subjects with obsessive premorbid personality who are 40 years or older and who have had a history of mild "attacks." The onset of symptoms is gradual and characterized by discontinuity of sleep disturbances, early morning awakenings, diurnal fluctuations of mood and activity (both of which tend to be more markedly depressed in the morning than in the evening), decreased libido, impaired appetite, and

TABLE 3
Dichotomous Models of Classification

1. Endogenous/reactive
2. Psychotic/neurotic
3. Unipolar/bipolar
4. Anxious/hyperactive vs.
   Anergic/hypoactive
5. Primary/secondary

weight loss (4). In contrast, non-endogenous or reactive episodes are precipitated by stressful events and occur in subjects under 30 who have a premorbid personality that is characterized by hysteroid features, immaturity, feelings of inadequacy and self-pity, irritability, hypochondriasis, and obsessionality. Symptoms appear suddenly; the course shows great variability with typically little initial insomnia, and, unlike endogenous depression, mood and activity tend to be more depressed in the evening (5,6). Some clinicians feel that this dichotomy reveals differences not only in symptomatology, but also in treatment response and long-term prognosis. Critics of this classification note that even if the relationship between stress and the onset of depression could be documented, the judgment of what constitutes a significant precipitating event is highly subjective, because over 70% of all depression can be linked to some stressful event. Specifically, the terms are misleading because an analysis of the role of life events in the genesis of depressions shows that depressive episodes with ''endogenous'' symptoms are as reactive to circumstances as those with ''reactive'' symptoms.

The considerable controversy surrounding ''endogenous'' depression has led to the resurrection of the term ''melancholia'' to signify a typically severe form of depression that is particularly responsive to somatic therapy. Melancholia signifies a loss of pleasure in all or almost all activities, lack of reactivity to usually pleasurable stimuli (no better feelings, even temporarily, when something good happens), and at least three of the following: 1) distinct quality of depressed mood, i.e., the depressed mood is perceived as distinctly different from the kind of feeling experienced following the death of a loved one; 2) the depression is regularly worse in the morning; 3) early morning awakening (at least two hours before usual time of awakening); 4) marked psychomotor retardation or agitation; 5) significant anorexia or weight loss; and 6) excessive or inappropriate guilt.

The psychotic-neurotic dichotomy, the other well-accepted classification scheme for affective disease, rests on shakier evidence than the endogenous/reactive dichotomy. Although it is generally agreed that ''psychotic'' and ''neurotic'' refer to different degrees of severity, precise definitions of these terms are lacking. The label ''psychotic'' implies an altered ideational process, but when are self-derogatory views held by a depressed patient sufficiently intense to be labeled delusional? As discussed earlier, there has been considerable enthusiasm to characterize delusions or hallucinations as mood congruent or incongruent. The label ''neurotic depression'' is applied to a heterogeneous, non-hospitalized group of patients—including those who are seen early in their illness, others who avoided hospitalization because of an unusually supportive social environment, and still others whose illnesses are mild. A recent review of neurotic depression suggested alternative criteria for depressions that are less socially incapacitating, non-psychotic, non-endogenous, and follow a psychosocially stressful event (7). It was hypothesized that such depressions are consequences of a long-standing, maladaptive personality pattern or of unconscious conflicts. The conclusion of this study was that the value of the term "neurotic" is limited, because various criteria for neurotic depression are not interchangeable, and considerable overlap exists between patient groups.

Despite the weakness of these dichotomizing classification schemes, whenever the terms "endogenous" or "psychotic" are used in their most restrictive senses, they probably segregate depressed patients who will require somatic therapies. In addition, practically all the typologies currently in use differentiate between "retarded" and "agitated" depression. Because thinking, decision-making, and other goal-directed activities are "retarded" in depressed patients, use of this dichotomization is restricted to the level of motor activity, which, like sleep, is notoriously difficult to measure by observation alone.

Perhaps the most satisfactory approach toward classification of depression is rooted in the work of Kraepelin (8) and refined by Leonhard et al. (9), Angst (10), Perris (11), and Winokur et al. (12). These workers distinguished two specific, genetically determined syndromes: recurrent bipolar cyclic disorder with both manic and depressive phases and a unipolar syndrome that, with the rare exception of unipolar manic illness, is usually recurrent depression without mania (11). Because bipolar and unipolar types can be differentiated using genetic and family history, biochemical and psychophysiological factors, and response to certain drugs (13,14), this classification system is eminently suitable for psychobiological studies.

Studies show that the risk of bipolar disorder is 10 times greater among first-degree relatives (parents, siblings, and children) of bipolar patients than in the general population. Although the categories of depressive illness may vary from study to study, a similar morbidity risk occurs among parents, siblings, and children of those individuals identified with bipolar depression (10,11). Specifically, the morbidity risk among first degree relatives is approximately 15% in comparison to the general population's risk of 1% to 2% for bipolar disorder. Furthermore, the genetic evidence supports the use of the bipolar-unipolar classification for patients with affective illness. Bipolar illness carries a higher genetic risk than unipolar illness, a fact supported by data demonstrating an average rate of 6.8% bipolar and 8.3% unipolar illness in first-degree relatives of bipolar patients. Among first-degree relatives of unipolar patients, the incidence drops sharply to 0.4% for bipolar illness and 6.0% for unipolar. Thus, both subgroups of illness are associated with relatives experiencing both types of disorder, but bipolar patients have a greater chance of having affected relatives (15). However, the majority of the ill relatives of bipolar probands (patients) have unipolar rather than bipolar illnesses. Three recent studies of unipolar probands that assess the risk of first-degree relatives having a major depressive disorder (unipolar or bipolar) demonstrate a range of 16.6% to 18.1% (female-male sex ratio, 2:1).

Still, differences between unipolar and bipolar illness are less clear-cut than originally suggested (16). Between 10% and 20% of bipolar patients had three or more episodes of depression before onset of their first manic episode and, up to that point, were classified as unipolar. Comparisons of EEG abnormalities, neuropsychological dysfunction, and prevalence of associated alcoholism have yielded no differences. However, the unipolar/bipolar dichotomy demonstrates that the onset of unipolar depression occurs at a significantly older age and in a greater proportion of females than males.

Another classification system for depression differentiates between two major subtypes of depression: anxious/hyperactive and anergic/hypoactive (17). The anxious/hyperactive type is most frequently encountered in recurrent unipolar depressions and is characterized by increased psychomotor activity, often in the form of pacing or hand-wringing, and by a major sleep continuity disturbance marked by intermittent wakefulness and early morning awakening. On the other hand, the anergic/hypoactive type of depression, which occurs primarily but not exclusively in bipolar disorders, is characterized by profound anergia and significant decrease in psychomotor activity. Sleep, rather than being discontinuous or decreased, tends to be unchanged or even increased, although some difficulty in falling asleep, particularly in younger subjects, may be present. As in the typical anxious/hyperactive group, libido is impaired in the anergic/hypoactive group as well, but not as dramatically. Anorexia, on the other hand, is rarely prominent in the anergic/hypoactive group; indeed, approximately 40% of these patients gain weight while depressed. In approximately one-third of bipolar patients, the depressive phase is often accompanied by hyperactivity and sleep loss rather than anergia/hypoactivity; thus, these groups should be regarded as "pseudo-bipolar," since from a psychobiological point of view there is no true polarity (17).

This method of classification preserves the differentiation between unipolar and bipolar disorder but does away with reactive/endogenous and neurotic/psychotic dichotomizations. The evaluation of severity level depends upon impairment in social functioning and not on the presence or absence of delusions or the need for hospitalization, a feature that has been shown to depend upon a lack of available social support and not the severity of illness.

Finally another classification integrates coexisting medical problems with the depressive disease and uses the terms primary and secondary depression (Figure 3). Robins and Guze (18) and Guze et al. (19), who first proposed this classification, defined a primary affective disorder as one that occurs in individuals with no previous psychiatric disorder (or only episodes of depression or mania) and secondary affective disorder as one that is superimposed on a preexisting psychiatric illness other than depression or mania.

The concept of secondary depression has considerable merit provided the

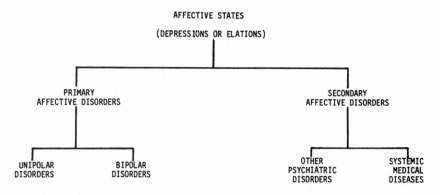

FIGURE 3.

criteria include depressions occurring in association with toxic, infectious, or exhaustive states. The latter are found after the chronic use of, or withdrawal from, alcohol (and other general central nervous system depressants), narcotic analgesics, or stimulants, and after major surgical procedures and other life-threatening medical conditions. The key to the diagnosis of primary versus secondary depression lies in the patient's history.

The symptom picture of secondary depression is almost indistinguishable from primary unipolar depression, although secondary depression is associated with more somatic complaints, anxiety, acting out, suicidal behavior, delusions, and hallucinations. The only symptom that is consistently associated with primary depression is psychomotor retardation.

Nevertheless, this classification schema is ambiguous. For example, after a patient receives a diagnosis of obsessive neurosis, subsequent affective episodes are classified as secondary, even if several years elapse between episodes and the patient is no longer considered obsessive neurotic. Furthermore, the classification does not reveal whether these patients diagnosed as secondary had a proclivity for depressive symptoms in the past, whether future episodes will arise only when provoked by similar causes, and whether the treatment response differs between primary and secondary depression.

In a recent study, the clinical significance of a diagnosis of secondary depression was evaluated (20). A careful comparison of 48 cases of primary and 26 cases of secondary depression showed that patients with secondary depression had a higher familial prevalence of alcoholism. Although the groups differed somewhat in a few demographic, behavioral, and attitudinal variables, they were similar in symptomatology, sex ratio, onset and duration of symptoms, treatment received, and response to treatment. Perhaps the distinction between primary and secondary depression should be retained in psychobiologic research, even though the clinical care of primary and secondary depression is the same.

Many of the advances in classification and diagnostic criteria have been derived from certain implicit biases about the origins and etiology of depressive disorders. However, since recent diagnostic criteria have freed themselves of etiologic "taint," it would be useful to outline briefly some of the major theories of depression, not all of which have been described elsewhere in this volume.

THEORIES OF DEPRESSION

Although the signs and symptoms of depression have been carefully collected, we cannot yet answer the question, "What is the cause of depression?" Currently, both psychological and psychobiological causes of depression are espoused by psychiatrists. The ancient Greek theorists postulated psychologic (literally, arising from the psyche, or soul) origins for depression, believing that certain temperaments or personalities were particularly prone to depression. Even today, the psychological theories outlined below describe factors that make an individual depression-prone. Only in some of these theories is depression-proneness synonymous with depressive personality style characterized by a whiny, "poor me" approach to life. It is not yet demonstrated that such a lifelong style is associated with an increased incidence of depressive disorder. Is the depressive syndrome merely an intensification of a lifelong personality pattern (in this case, chronic-depressive personality), or is there a qualitative difference between chronic depressive personality and a major depressive syndrome (21)?

The first psychological explanations of depression beyond the temperament theory were proposed by the psychoanalytic theorists (22). Analytic theories of the cause of depression posit a fixation (i.e., an arresting of psychological growth) at a highly dependent pregenital phase of development and a real or imagined loss in adult life that triggers the depression. According to Freud, when an actual loss occurs, mourners first "introject" or incorporate the lost person into themselves in an attempt to compensate for the loss. Because mourners harbor both love and unconscious hatred for the lost person, mourners now turn this anger inward against themselves. During healthy grieving, mourners slowly recall memories of the lost individual and use this technique to separate themselves from the lost object. However, highly dependent individuals cannot attain this separation, and the anger and hatred (presumably rooted in unmet dependency needs) remain directed against themselves. Such feelings are manifest in the guilt and self-blame of depression.

Elaborations of Freud's theory broaden the concept of loss to include experiences such as personal rejection. Spitz (23) and Bowlby (24) have provided experimental evidence that loss of an object leads to an altered mood in both primates and human infants. Reformulating psychoanalytic theory to incorporate recent data from a wide range of disciplines, including ethology and experimental psychology, as well as evidence from the clinical sphere, Bowlby has evolved a view that personality depends crucially upon the quality of attachments to caregivers in early life and, in turn, contributes to the individual's ability to mourn healthily when faced with a bereavement in adulthood. This emphasis on psychic structure, however, need not be seen as excluding a more cultural explanation. While Bowlby stresses the critical impact that death or separation from a parent in childhood can have upon psychic maturation, he also argues that a fairly wide range of experiences can lead to "cognitive biases" which will influence later mourning; presumably these vary between cultures.

Attempts have been made to support disruption of cognition and behavior as the cause of depression. The theories of "learned helplessness" (25), reduced reinforcement spiral (26), and cognitive-behavioral theory (27) are the best known. Seligman and his associates based their behavioral model for depression in humans on animal experiments. Seligman found that dogs initially exposed to an inescapable shock had more difficulty learning to avoid an escapable shock than did unexposed animals. Seligman labeled this passive response to an anxiety-producing situation "learned helplessness," implying that the preexposed dogs had learned they had no control over the situation.

Seligman drew a number of parallels between his "helpless" animals and depressed humans (25): Both exhibit passivity and both show weight and appetite loss. Experiments that involved "depressed" and non-depressed college students confirmed his basic hypotheses that outcomes beyond the individual's control elicit depressive-like behaviors in non-depressed persons and that depressed persons are more likely than non-depressed persons to perceive outcomes as independent of their control. It must be remembered, however, that all of these conclusions have been based on "depressed" persons who are fully functioning college students and who score in the "mild" range on a self-report inventory of depression. Despite recent revisions (28), it is not clear whether the learned helplessness model applies to the "depressive personality," proneness to develop depressive syndromes, or the precipitation of the depressive episode.

Lewinsohn, on the other hand, has elaborated another psychologic theory for the etiology of depression (26). He believes that changes in environmental reinforcement schedules first create and then maintain depressive behavior. As with Freud's theory, Lewinsohn's can best be understood by postulating an initial loss such as death. As a result of the loss, the individual loses a source of reinforcement from the environment. Because the pre-loss level of activity was maintained by pre-loss level of reinforcement, the individual's activity level now drops. For a time, this reduced activity level may actually be reinforced by sympathy or extra help from others. This reduced activity means less access to other potential reinforcers and a resultant downward spiral leading to a self-perpetuating condition. Because it is impossible to employ the large-scale naturalistic observation necessary to confirm Lewinsohn's theory, it rests upon analogue studies.

Beck's theory is that the individual's negative and distorted thinking is the basic psychologic problem in depression (27). These distorted perceptions are supported by immature "either-or" rules of conduct or inflexible and unattainable self-expectations. This cognitive behavior pattern is probably acquired early in development and, if uncritically carried into adulthood, predisposes the individual to depression. Since these schemata are long-term, identifiable psychologic patterns that influence attitudes and behavioral responses, they may constitute a cognitive dimension of the depression-prone individual's personality. Contrary to the view that mood alteration is central in depressive syndromes, Beck's cognitive approach focuses on self-castigation, exaggeration of external problems, and hopelessness as the most salient symptoms. The alteration in mood is simply the result of these cognitive errors.

To Beck, the depressed person's aberrant thinking and preoccupation with expectations give distorted views of himself and events (29). As a result, depressed persons are overly sensitive to obstacles to goal-directed activity, interpret trivial impediments as substantial, read disparagement into innocuous statements by others, and at the same time, devalue themselves. The characteristic depressive preoccupations are stereotypical and evident in self-report, fantasy, and dream content. Moreover, the cognitions are frequently irrelevant and inappropriate to the existing situation and reflect a consistent negative bias concerning the self, the world, and the future.

Negative thoughts, even of brief duration, stimulate abnormal physiologic reactions that are experienced as sadness, anxiety, anger, guilt, or a variety of other negative emotions. Excessive negative thoughts inevitably lead to dysphoria, reduced desire to provide for one's own welfare or pleasure, passivity, and, ultimately, resignation. Generally, specific thoughts are "chained" to a particular affect: concern about an anticipated threat is connected with feelings of anxiety; thoughts about being unloved and abandoned are associated with sadness.

Depressive cognitive content is often related to thoughts of loss or perceived loss from what Beck refers to as one's "personal domain." The personal domain includes the individual and his circle of significant others, together with things of value (objects, attributes, ideals, principles, and important goals). For example, if professional accomplishment is a central and cherished goal, a small temporary setback may be magnified out of proportion and may be seen as reflecting one's abilities and one's prospects for future achievement. Such an overgeneralized negative interpretation drives the depressed person into increased dysphoria, dejection, and discouragement.

In the clinical depressions, the patient's perceptions, interpretations, and evaluations do not require outside confirmation; the pervasive negative bias against self thus remains uncorrected. This negative view of self and of the future also prevents the depressed patient from realistic testing of ideas, active problemsolving, and use of appropriate help and advice from others.

Recently, the psychobiologic correlates of depression have assumed importance in the search for etiologic theories, because biologic variables can be measured in the laboratory. Emphasis on psychobiology stresses an understanding of the genetic transmittal of affective disorders and stimulates a search for biologic markers in affective illness. However, regardless of whether depression is caused by psychologic or biologic dysfunction, the diagnosis and treatment of the disease is improved by an understanding of the psychobiology of mood and the biochemical systems that govern it.

Many of the key symptoms in depression reveal a dysfunction of biologic systems: sleep, appetite, weight, psychomotor function, and sexual interest and activity (30). Because these biologic systems have both peripheral and central nervous system connections, it has been hypothesized that these biologic changes in depression are the cause of the illness, not simply the symptoms. Ignoring the longstanding controversy of the psychologic versus the psychobiologic causes of depression, measurement of changes permits objective measurements of the severity of illness, an opportunity to discover correlations between biologic changes and depth of depression, and, perhaps, to establish predictors of clinical response.

The regulatory systems that govern sleep, appetite, motor activity, and sexual activity are regulated by the same hormones and neurotransmitters that probably determine mood. From the viewpoint of a clinician, interest focuses on the changes in these neuroregulatory systems. For example, nearly all depressed patients experience some sleep disturbance. Although the majority of sleep pattern changes favor insomnia, from 15% to 30% of all depressed individuals report hypersomnia. Therefore, because sleep disturbance is one of the earliest and most frequent (90%) symptoms of depression, it is important to characterize the type of sleep change—if only qualitatively (whether they are sleeping more or less than they usually do, having trouble getting to sleep, maintaining their sleep, or getting a restful night's sleep). Recent changes in appetite and weight are equally important: usually appetite is decreased, but, in a considerable percentage of cases, weight increases despite the fact that the depressed patient reports that eating is not pleasurable and that he does not experience "hunger." Changes in weight (usually decreases) are common. Changes in motor activity are also frequent features of depression, with most individuals reporting motor retardation. Some report agitation and a few report both agitation and retardation. Finally, recent changes in sexual interest and activity are areas in which dysfunction can be determined qualitatively.

Considerable evidence supports the notion that a genetic-familial factor is operating in depressive disorders, aside from the unipolar/bipolar data presented earlier. Information derived from twin studies is contributing to such a factor. In monozygotic (MZ) twins, there exists a consistently higher concordance rate (depression in both twins) than in dizygotic (DZ) twins. The overall concordance rate for MZ twins is 70%; the rate for DZ twins is 20% (31). These facts support the presence of a genetic factor. However, the existence of a number of discordant MZ pairs shows that the environment also plays a considerable role. In summary, current investigations support a genetic transmission because there is an increased frequency of illness in relatives of the proband compared to the general population, a greater concordance rate for the disease in MZ twins than in DZ twins, and an increased frequency of psychiatric abnormality in relatives of the affectively ill probands compared to the general population.

Although data are sparse, it appears that depression associated with (or precipitated by) life stresses, including grief, is more frequent in individuals with a family history of depression. Whether such associations are inherited or transmitted by another mechanism is not known, but the search continues for objective markers to detect family members at highest risk for a future subsequent depressive episode.

Several epidemiologic studies in affective disorders have already attempted to clarify key environmental factors associated with depressive illness (32). The New Haven epidemiologic survey suggests that major depression is highest in whites, upper social classes, persons not currently married, persons over age 45, and women (female-male sex ratio, 1.6:1) (33). Are women more prone to depression, or are these observations the results of confounding factors in data collection and analysis? If women are at greater risk for depression, what biologic or psychosocial processes account for the difference? Some question the data and hypothesize that women's perceptions of stress-coping responses, their willingness to express affective symptoms, and the relatively high frequency with which they seek medical help produce such an artifact. Another group of investigators considers that depression can be attributed to an increased female biologic susceptibility or to social causes. Still, Weissman and Klerman argue that women do not have more stressful life events, nor do they judge life events as more stressful (34). Whereas women acknowledge having symptoms and affective distress more frequently, it is not that they feel less stigma or because they wish to win approval. Although women seek help differently from men and make more use of health care, this does not account for the preponderance of depressed women in community surveys, because in such surveys the diagnosis of depression was made from a rating scale and not for a patient in treatment.

Contrary to expectations, the relationship of neuroendocrine systems to the depressed state is inconsistent for both women and men. Presently, little evidence correlates altered mood states with changes in specific hormonal levels or with the balance between several hormones, primarily because no studies have been conducted using "state-of-the-art" endocrinologic methods. Although good data suggest that premenstrual tension and use of oral contraceptives tend to increase rates of depressive disorder, the effects are probably small. Depression does increase in the postpartum period, but depression does not rise during the menopausal period (34).

Factors that create stress in marriage, such as boredom, role restriction, family size, and limited financial resources, have been superficially examined. A key study of the interaction of several of these factors with depression was conducted in a British community survey (35). Studies on the relationship between psychosocial stress and subsequent affective disorders revealed that working married women with young children living at home had the highest rates of depression. Under equivalent levels of stress, working women were five times more likely to become depressed than middle-class women. Loss of a mother in childhood, three or more children under age 14 living at home, and absence of an intimate and confiding relationship with husband or boyfriend were the three most significant factors in producing depression in working women. These studies have received considerable attention and criticism. In a more recent study, Brown et al. (36) postulated four vulnerability factors which in the presence of a provoking agent would make the onset of a depressive episode more likely. These factors were similar to the previous study and, in addition, included lack of employment outside of the home.

All these etiologic theories and factors are, of course, not mutually exclusive and possess several common threads. Prior to integrating material from these theoretical positions, it would be useful to describe briefly some of the treatment approaches used in depressive states, with particular attention to the treatment of the acute depressive episode. (While the treatment of the acute manic episode is certainly appropriate to this task of integration, space permits only a review of the modalities used primarily to treat the depressive episode.)

TREATMENT OF DEPRESSION

Depression varies from a mild but distressing self-limiting change to a severe and disabling psychotic state. Depressed episodes, if they come to medical attention, are treated with techniques ranging from supportive counseling to aggressive pharmacologic intervention. This section emphasizes the treatment of the full-blown depressive episode, which is often seen by the family practitioner or internist rather than by the psychiatrist. I will not deal with the mild episode of depression, although the non-pharmacologic techniques to be discussed are applicable. There are many alternative treatments for the acute depressive episode. I will selectively review the various available biologic modalities, several of the non-pharmacologic techniques, and the use of combined treatment.

Major depression is primarily a recurrent illness (37). Recent studies, using the unipolar/bipolar distinction, demonstrated that on the average unipolar depressions begin at age 45, and a typical episode lasts about six months (38). About one-quarter of the cases will last longer than one year, with 17% lasting more than two years. Future episodes will occur more frequently; phases of the disorder follow one another at shorter and shorter intervals. The depressive disease is thus both chronic and episodic. However, not all patients suffer from relapses; half of the unipolar group show a five-year, episode-free interval.

For the bipolar groups, the onset of the disorder occurs at about 35 years of age, an average episode lasts 4.5 months, less than 20% of the episodes last more than one year, and 14% last longer than two years. Only one-sixth of the bipolar group shows a five-year, episode-free interval. Bipolar disease appears to be less chronic but more episodic; relapse is more likely to occur the older the patient is when the first episode occurs.

Pharmacotherapy

Confronted with a severely depressed patient who requires biologic treatment, the clinician should prescribe tricyclic antidepressants before trying other agents: monoamine oxidase inhibitors or electroconvulsive therapy (ECT). In carefully controlled clinical trials, tricyclics have been shown to be more effective than other modes of treatment (39). Most patients who meet the DSM-III diagnostic criteria for a major depressive syndrome should receive pharmacologic agents to economically reduce suffering and length of functional impairment (17). Of course, there are a number of exceptions—patients with medical conditions in which antidepressant agents are contraindicated and patients previously responsive to other forms of treatment, such as ECT.

Clinicians should make a global assessment of the course of the illness based on their observations and the information received from the patient or the family. Furthermore, to maximize the patient's cooperation, clinicians should manipulate the patient's environment to increase the amount of structure (e.g., insistence on regular mealtimes, bedtime, and waking hour) and decrease the amount of stress (e.g., major decision-making). Regardless of the choice of somatic treatment, clinicians must establish a rapport with the depressed patient and provide reassurance concerning the episodic nature of the illness.

Assuming that the criteria for the diagnosis of depression have been met and that there are no contraindications (e.g., drug sensitivity) to administering a tricyclic antidepressant, treatment begins with 50-75 mg of amitriptyline or imipramine one hour before sleep. Table 4 summarizes the equivalent dosage for the most common tricyclics. Although some clinicians believe that clinical improvement cannot be identified during the initial two to three weeks of drug administration, discrete improvements are noticeable in most patients three to 10 days after treatment begins. Tricyclics will reduce motor activity and increase sleep efficiency beginning with the first night of drug administration. A recent study showed a marked reduction of suicidal feelings, insomnia, and anorexia within one week in depressed outpatients; improvements in ability to work, interests, retardation, pessimism, and hopelessness were more gradual (40). Such changes are worthy of attention especially when treatment other than tricyclics is already in use, or the patient is so agitated or so determined to commit suicide that only a very limited trial is justified before electroconvulsive therapy is considered.

If the patient tolerates the initial dose of 50-75 mg of amitriptyline or imipramine for two days, if there are no complicating medical problems, and if the patient is below the age of 65, the dose of tricyclic can be increased 25 mg daily until the daily dose is 150 mg. If no significant improvement is seen after one week—the usual situation—and the patient continues to tolerate the drug well, the dose should be raised to and kept at the 200 mg dose daily for one week. If there is still little or no improvement, the dose may be raised to 250 mg daily for yet another seven to 14 days before discontinuing the drug. In general,

TABLE 4
Tricyclic Drugs and Their Approximate Effective Dosage Ranges

Generic name	Trade name	Dosage form	Effective dose range (mg/day)
Imipramine	Tofranil	Oral or IM	150-300
Amitriptyline	Elavil	Oral or IM	150-300
Desipramine	Norpramin Pertofrane	Oral	150-300
Nortriptyline	Aventyl, Pamelor	Oral	50-150
Protriptyline	Vivactil	Oral	10-60
Doxepin	Sinequan	Oral	150-300

whenever adverse effects at higher dosage schedules drown out ameliorative effects on mood, it is better to reduce the patient's dosage than to discontinue the drug.

It is questionable whether the dosage schedule for outpatients should be different from that for inpatients. Parenteral administration, although allegedly more rapidly effective, is usually not necessary and should be reserved for patients who cannot cooperate. When tricyclics are administered intramuscularly, the equivalent dose of parenterally administered drugs is 25% lower than the oral dose. Recently, clinicians have advocated that most, if not all, psychotropic medication should be administered in a single dose in the evening near bedtime. This simplified dosage schedule increases compliance without increasing the incidence of orthostatic hypotension or confusional states. Patients suffering from agitation and insomnia may benefit from a substantial bedtime dosage because the drowsiness produced by the drug facilitates sleep without interfering with daytime activities.

The monoamine oxidase inhibitors (MAOIs) are the second line of drug treatment for depressed patients. Although carefully controlled studies are unavailable, clinical observations suggest that the MAOIs have a faster onset of action than do the tricyclics in successfully treated patients. As a result, it is possible to prescribe and evaluate the effectiveness of an MAOI drug regimen in less than the usual three- or four-week treatment period required for tricyclics. MAOIs such as tranylcypromine produce an antidepressant effect in the anergic atypical depression signaled by increased motor activity and decreased sleep time. Most clinicians who are familiar with these drugs recommend initial doses of phenelzine 30-45 mg or tranylcypromine 20-30 mg, and increase these dosages after three or four days to 60-90 mg and 30-60 mg, respectively, until symptoms go into remission (Table 5).

Unlike the tricyclics with bedtime dosage, MAOIs are usually given in divided doses because they tend to precipitate insomnia. Gradual reduction of the duration of sleep, on the other hand, signals a favorable response for anergic depressive patients who complain about sleepiness throughout the day and whose sleep tends to be prolonged or at least unchanged. Reduction of sleepiness is usually

TABLE 5

Monoamine Oxidase Inhibitors and Their Approximate Effective Dose Ranges

Generic name	Trade name	Dosage form	Effective dose range (mg/day)
Tranylcypromine	Parnate	Oral	20-60
Phenelzine	Nardil	Oral	45-75

followed by increased normalization of motor activity (usually increase of daytime motor activity in these anergic patients) and improved mood. After the symptoms have cleared and overall functioning is improved, patients should retain the drug dosage for between three to six months during a period of stabilization.

Whether there are specific indications for MAOIs is still an open question. For instance, amitriptyline has been more effective than phenelzine in depressed outpatients (41), but phenelzine seemed superior to placebo in "anxious" depressive states (42,43). Klein and Davis (44) identified a group of female patients with somewhat similar characteristics who, in their euthymic phase, are flamboyant and histrionic but respond in a catastrophic fashion to stress by sudden depression, hostility, irritability, withdrawal, oversleeping, repeated naps during the day, and overeating. In this study, treatment with MAOI produced prompt improvement in mood, the overeating and oversleeping subsided, and maintenance treatment appeared to have a prophylactic effect against the sudden mood shifts. Results from another uncontrolled clinical trial (45) suggested that the MAOIs are the treatment of choice for depressed patients unresponsive to tricyclics who show marked hypersomnia, decreased levels of psychomotor activity, and frequently excessive eating and weight gain, thus giving some support to the contention that MAOIs are "energizers." Since the majority of these hypersomnic depressive patients who benefit from MAOIs also suffer from bipolar disease (46), it is possible that the unipolar/bipolar differentiation may be relevant not only for choosing the appropriate drug for maintenance therapy, but also for the treatment of the acute episode.

Several points should be made concerning various combinations of psychotropic drugs. In 1982, psychomotor stimulants alone have little role in the treatment of depression. Nevertheless, compounds such as amphetamines are still used as adjunctive measures early in the drug treatment of depression, prior to the onset of antidepressant effect of the tricyclics. Because phenothiazines alone showed activity in some controlled trials, particularly in "agitated" depressions, clinicians used them for some time in combination with antidepressants. However, when tricyclics alone were compared with the combination of phenothiazines and tricyclics, the combination was no more effective than tricyclics alone in the treatment of anxious non-psychotic depression (47,48). It has been suggested that a phenothiazine and a tricyclic should be given in the treatment of psychotic depression to control agitation and diminiish delusional thinking. When the effects of the antidepressants become noticeable after 10 to 14 days, some investigators advocate that the phenothiazine should be gradually tapered, whereas many clinicians continue treatment with the combination. As a result, the use of phenothiazines in the treatment of delusional depression has gained increased acceptance in the last few years.

Electroconvulsive treatment (ECT) is considered by many to be the treatment of choice for the actively suicidal or severely delusional patient, as well as for the patient whose medical condition contraindicates the use of antidepressant drugs (49). Furthermore, ECT may still be the treatment of choice 1) when the patient's response to drug therapy is poor or idiosyncratic, 2) when there are non-psychiatric complications that render administration of drugs hazardous, 3) when the patient is too ill to cooperate, or 4) when manic and depressive symptoms appear simultaneously. The latter, mixed-state, clinical presentation is seen in a number of recurrent, hospitalized, depressed patients as well as in bipolar patients who develop an episode during the immediate postpartum period (50).

Psychotherapy

All psychotherapeutic approaches have, as Weissman points out, two essential features in common: a confiding relationship between patient and therapist and a verbal dialogue aimed at bringing about a change in the patient's current state (51). The psychotherapies for depression are derived from either psychoanalytic theories or from theories relating depression to impaired social and interpersonal circumstances (52). In psychoanalytic psychotherapy, the therapist helps the patient to recognize the sources of his angry feelings and to resolve those feelings. In the process, the anger may be directed toward the psychotherapist. The behavioral and cognitive-behavioral therapies are based on four major conceptual models:

1) The depressive behavior constitutes the disorder and can be modified by suitable manipulation of reinforcers.
2) Depressive behavior is a result of, and is maintained by, a reduced rate of positive reinforcement, and this reinforcement should be reinstated by suitable manipulation of behavior.
3) The depressed individual remains depressed because he feels a lack of control over the environment (treatment demonstrates ability to control).
4) Depression results from an individual with an unrealistically negative view of self and circumstances (treatment corrects these misconceptions).

Other forms of psychotherapy that have been employed in the treatment of depression include interpersonal, marital, and group therapy. Interpersonal therapy is a clearly defined treatment that emphasizes the social and interpersonal context of depression. It is aimed at "enhancing ability to cope with externally and internally induced stress, restoring morale, and helping the patient deal with the interpersonal and social consequences of the disorder" (53). Marital therapy can take many forms, most of which include the patient's spouse in some aspect of the treatment, either with the patient's therapist or a collaborating therapist and often in sessions with the patient (54). Specific techniques for the use of marital therapy in the treatment of depression have not been outlined. Similarly, precise approaches to the group therapy of depression have not been specified (55).

Reviews of psychologic treatments for depression have concluded that, until recently, the lack of controlled trials using psychotherapy for depression prevented the determination of the efficacy of these approaches. In the few controlled trials now concluded on interpersonal psychotherapy (IPT), this treatment is claimed to be more efficacious than the nontreatment control (56). Comparison between psychotherapeutic approaches and psychopharmacologic modalities has generally shown that drugs appear to have a direct effect on symptoms of depression, whereas, not unexpectedly, psychotherapy affects the level of social functioning. In a recent study of IPT, interpersonal function and social adjustment improved, but acute symptomatic relief from the depressive syndrome did not occur, nor did IPT provide a prophylaxis for subsequent episodes in comparison to pharmacotherapy (56). Similarly, a study of marital therapy found that this treatment improved the marital relationship but did not offer symptomatic relief comparable to antidepressants (54).

Consistent with these findings has been one controlled trial where group psychotherapy, as compared to a low-contact supportive control group, had a weak effect on marital relations (55). Marital therapy has been found to be better than a low-contact control group. All three forms of psychotherapy have not improved symptoms as quickly as drug management alone; still, they appear to have additive effects when combined with drug treatment.

Controlled trials that test the efficacy of behavior therapy in treating depression have included a number of approaches: social skills therapy (which teaches the acquisition of verbal skills); assertiveness training; the pleasant events approach (which tries to increase the frequency of such phenomena); and a self-control approach (which attempts, in a manner similar to cognitive therapy, to alter internal attributions of responsibility and negative thoughts). Despite a paucity of good controls, it can be tentatively concluded that teaching self-control is associated with more clinical improvement than membership in waiting-list or low-contact control groups, that self-control may be better than social skills training, and that monitoring increased daily pleasant events is more efficacious than nondirective groups. Still these studies suffer from many of the design problems outlined above: lack of rigorous diagnostic criteria; heterogeneity with respect to severity of illness; inappropriate or absent control groups; variable length of treatment; and weak or absent follow-up data (51).

In contrast to the psychotherapies described above, Beck's cognitive behavior therapy is designed to alter specific symptoms of the depressive syndrome. As discussed earlier, the cognitive model postulates that the patient views himself, his future, and his experiences in an idiosyncratically negative manner. The therapy emphasizes unlearning these dysfunctional cognitive patterns and replacing them with adaptive ones. In one study of about 50 patients treated with either imipramine or cognitive therapy, the results clearly favored cognitive therapy (57). By the end of the treatment, patients treated with cognitive therapy had significantly greater symptomatic improvement than did those treated with imipramine. In addition, therapeutic response was maintained at a three-month follow-up after treatment was completed. Importantly, fewer patients dropped out of treatment in cognitive therapy than with chemotherapy. A follow-up, 12 months after completion of treatment, found that patients initially assigned to cognitive therapy were less symptomatic at one year by self-report than those who received antidepressant medication (58,59). Further, those treated with cognitive therapy had half the risk of relapse compared to those who received the drug therapy.

Given the established efficacy of antidepressant medication, together with a relative lack of demonstrated benefit from psychologic intervention (other than cognitive therapy), it is not surprising that the management of depression has largely become the province of pharmacologic treatments. Furthermore, the treatment of depression is often handled by family practitioners, who feel more comfortable administering medication than conducting psychotherapy. From their viewpoint, intervention with antidepressant drugs associated with a supportive empathic approach saves time. The general failure of psychotherapy to be established on a par with pharmacologic interventions reflects the use of many different, non-operationally defined psychotherapeutic techniques, as well as weak selection criteria, inconsistent outcome criteria, and heterogeneous populations. However, in the past few years, an increasing number of experimental studies have indicated a role for behavioral and, in particular, cognitive-behavioral approaches to the treatment of depression.

Psychotherapy and Pharmacotherapy

The combination of drugs and psychotherapy is frequently prescribed for the milder forms of depression. However, few comparisons have been made among psychotherapy, pharmacotherapy, and the combination. Covi et al. compared "active treatment" consisting of amitriptyline, diazepam, and placebo with two social therapies (weekly group therapy or biweekly supportive contact). He found that the effects of group therapy became evident only after a considerable lag period (55). Friedman compared the effects of amitriptyline and minimal contact, placebo and marital therapy, and placebo and minimal contact (54). In this study, drug effects were superior to the effects of marital therapy when measuring the patient's symptomatic condition. However, marital therapy was superior to drug therapy with regard to the patient's participation in treatment, performance of family-role tasks, and other parameters in the patient-spouse relationship, suggesting that the marital therapy had an additive, rather than a simple interactional effect, with amitriptyline.

Studies have shown that the efficacy of psychotherapy and amitriptyline in overall symptom reduction includes the combination of amitriptyline and short-term interpersonal psychotherapy, either of these treatments alone, or a non-scheduled treatment control group in ambulatory acute, nonbipolar, non-psychotic depressed patients (60). Amitriptyline and psychotherapy were about equal, and the effects of the treatments in combination were additive. The additive effect of combined treatment may be due to the differential effects of the two treatments. Early in treatment and often within the first week, amitriptyline affects mainly the vegetative symptoms of depression, such as sleep and appetite disturbance. Slightly later, at four to eight weeks, psychotherapy affects mainly mood, suicidal ideation, work, and interests.

Maintenance Treatment

The goals of treatment in the acute depressive episode are to reduce the symptoms of depression and to facilitate the patient's return to a premorbid level of functioning. However, the goal of long-term treatment is to prevent relapse of the current episode and the onset of a new episode, which are often manifest by impairment of the patient's social and work performance. In addition, maintanence therapy aims to relieve chronic, low-grade disturbing symptoms, to enhance the patient's social and family adjustment, and to increase satisfaction with life.

Although we do not have the tools for preventing the first episode of primary depression, we can prevent or attenuate future episodes in an already diagnosed patient who has experienced at least one episode of depression. Some argue that patients with recurrent depression of both the bipolar and unipolar types and patients with a chronic depressive disorder often manifested by longstanding depressive, hypochondriacal, neurasthenic, and neurotic symptoms are candidates for maintenance therapy. Such chronic depressions may represent partial resolutions of acute episodes that occurred months or years before, rather than acute episodes superimposed on a chronic depression; or they may be indicative of neurotic patients with tendencies toward fluctuations of their depressive symptoms related to longstanding personality maladjustments and impaired interpersonal relationships.

Two types of drugs with demonstrated efficacy in clinical drug trials have been used for maintenance therapy in unipolar and bipolar patients, namely, lithium carbonate and tricyclic antidepressants, particularly imipramine and amitriptyline (61). Evidence regarding the prophylactic efficacy of maintenance chemotherapy in recurrent affective disorders is convincing, but antidepressants cannot induce remission or prevent recurrence in an absolute sense. Instead, antidepressant drugs mitigate undesirable mood changes. Patients receiving maintenance therapy require less frequent hospitalization and function better at work and with their family. However, antidepressants may not prevent recurrences.

In a collaborative study that compared imipramine and lithium, the relative effectiveness of lithium over imipramine in bipolar patients was largely due to the increased frequency of manic episodes in imipramine-treated patients (61). In unipolar patients, there was no difference in treatment efficacy between imipramine and lithium carbonate. The conclusions are tentative: The number of patients studied was small (less than 100); the syndrome is episodic, with a rather long interval between the episodes (on the average, 30 months between the first and second); and the follow-up period of two years is inadequate. Furthermore, since the majority of relapses in this study occurred in the first four months of treatment, and since the average duration of episodes is approximately 36 months, relapses may have occurred because the patients were put prematurely on a lower maintenance dose and not because the drugs failed to "prevent" the onset of the new episode.

Certain residual symptoms (such as anxiety, mild depression, or feelings of guilt) at discharge predicted failure of "maintenance" treatment. However, this finding was not supported by another study which showed that patients with such residual symptoms derived more benefit than patients who had a full remission prior to entering the maintenance study (62). Still another maintenance study has found that tricyclic antidepressants have an important role in the prevention of relapse in depressed patients of the unipolar type, even when the group contains a significant percentage of "neurotic" patients (63). Placebo-controlled studies, which show amitriptyline to be effective in preventing depressive episodes, have similar shortcomings; none of these trials extend beyond nine months. One of the difficulties inherent in understanding the conclusions to be drawn from these studies is a general failure to separate continuation therapy (treatment up to nine months after the symptomatic remission of the episode has occurred, intended to prevent relapse of the same episode) from maintenance therapy or prophylactic treatment, intended to prevent recurrences (the onset of new episodes). The latter treatment essentially begins at least nine months after symptomatic remission.

In addition to the relatively small sample size and the short duration of almost all published maintenance trials, the problem of compliance was not attacked, although the conventional methods to assure compliance are well documented. Tricyclics can produce a number of somatic symptoms or intensify a preexisting one, thus augmenting the patient's discomfort. Because many of these undesirable effects peak in the first 10 to 14 days of treatment before the beneficial effects are experienced, some patients relapse because they do not take the drug or do not take the drug as prescribed. Longer-term side effects, such as a fine hand tremor or weight gain, can lead to noncompliance. In addition, bipolar patients do not favor maintenance therapy if it deprives them of their periodic "highs." Some patients view continuous treatment as an indication that they have an incurable illness and thus discontinue treatment. If patients were armed with definitive information describing the effectiveness of maintenance treatment, they could weigh the cost and risk of relapse against the cost and risk of prolonged maintenance chemotherapy.

Finally, it is still premature to conclude whether psychotherapy in combination with pharmacotherapy adds to the prophylactic effect. Regardless of whether formal psychotherapy is part of the treatment, however, a level of psychotherapeutic support is mandatory in any continuance treatment strategy. A treatment contract in which the patient and family can communicate abrupt changes in clinical course to the clinician, so that appropriate treatment changes might be made and a new episode avoided is a key ingredient in the overall success of maintenance treatment. Furthermore, important life decisions and events should be discussed openly and as part of a long-term contract with the clinician.

ATTEMPTS AT INTEGRATION

In 1969, a major national meeting on depression called for future research in several directions (64): 1) nosology—the development of a sound, reliable system of classification of the depressive disorders; 2) genetics—the design of studies to permit the definitive test of hypotheses concerning the role of genetics; and 3) pathophysiology—the investigation of the role of specific biochemical, neurophysiological, and endocrine mechanisms implicated in the etiology of depression. Thirteen years later a number of these research efforts have been undertaken, but the results of such studies are not yet available. Nevertheless, the last decade has been highlighted by considerable developments in descriptive nosology. Systematic efforts at examining clinical course have indicated that 40% of patients had not remitted from the index episode six months after initial evaluation. Of those patients who recover, 19% relapse by the time of the six-month follow-up. Index episodes were relatively long with a median duration of 25 weeks from onset to recovery for recovered patients and 67 weeks from onset to follow-up for non-recovered patients (65). Research findings have included new data supporting a genetic predisposition and a quantum leap in information concerning potential neurochemical, neuroendocrine, and neurophysiological factors pointing to psychobiologic "clues"—clues based on studies of central amine neurotransmitters and hypothalamic-pituitary neuroendocrine functioning, as well as data of increased specificity of pharmacotherapies.

During this period several attempts to synthesize the available data have been undertaken. Although numerous efforts have been made to establish a single etiology or cause of depression and then relate it to a specific form of treatment, my own bias is that the current state of knowledge is too limited to propose a single dimensional theory of affective disorders. Rather, I will, in the remainder of this chapter, seek to integrate diverse theories in order to develop a more comprehensive view of affective disorders.

Any theory of affective disorders, independent of its particular basis, ought to lend itself to a series of testable designs. Indeed, regardless of the particular theoretical construct, this theory should not conceptualize affective disorder as a homogeneous disease. Such a restricted view is analogous to assuming that fever represents one disease rather than reflecting a wide variety of acute and/or chronic disease processes. Therefore, a more unified hypothesis must integrate the newer and well-controlled available research data on the varied but systematic presentation of symptoms at different ages, the sex ratio for most depressive subtypes, the emerging genetic-familial data base on depressive subtypes, and the positive treatment response (60-80%) for various modalities for the acute episode, yet a 50% recurrence rate even on maintenance psychotropic medication.

Akiskal and McKinney have argued that depressive illness (especially melancholia) represents a psychobiological final common pathway which is derived from several sources (66): 1) genetic predisposition or vulnerability; 2) developmental events or predisposition; 3) psychosocial events or stressors; 4) physiological stressors; and 5) personality traits. Psychobiological features are present in almost all major and minor depressive episodes. Many new data have been accumulated on the role that neurochemical, neuroendocrine, and neurophysiological factors may play in the pathogenesis of depression. Obviously, however, one can only measure what is measurable, which in turn is contingent on the development of innovative laboratory techniques. Psychobiologic correlates of signs and symptoms such as determinations of 3-methoxy-4-hydroxy phenylglycol (MHPG), a catecholamine metabolite in urine and blood, monoamine oxidase (MAO) in platelets, and various endocrine secretory patterns including opioid and other peptides are now measured at various points in the course of mood disorders.

New hypotheses have been also generated by the use of provocative testing such as the dexamethasone suppression test, induced phase shifting (altering the circadian cycle by changing the individual's entrained 24-hour cycle), examining changes in melatonin secretion associated with alteration of mood by exposure to light, and the use of pharmacologic probes (as, for instance, measuring the effects of tricyclics on sleep). Indeed, one of the interesting questions is whether a new nosology of affective disorders could be based exclusively or almost exclusively on psychobiological data, including those obtained by provocative testing, rather than on psychological symptoms and signs. Are the psychobiologic features primary in that they are responsible for the other clinical features, or do they represent concomitant features similar to dysphoric mood, indecisiveness, etc? In other words, do the changes in central nervous system circuitry precede the behavioral changes, coexist, or occur after the behavioral changes are present?

Since the introduction of antidepressants, compelling arguments have been presented for the biological basis of affective disorders, particularly modeled on notions of neurochemical imbalances or deficit. Such theories have been highlighted by "functional deficit" themes, mostly of a reversible type. Over the years the field has shifted from biogenic amine functional deficit theories to neuroendocrine and neurophysiological alterations in affective disorders with an underlying neurochemical deficit. If these theories were to "explain" the disease, then they need to account for the varying predisposition to disease, initiation of disease, and the course characteristics. While such biological theories depending on regulatory system alterations do account for many of the symptoms, the available data only enable us presently to discuss some of the symptoms and speculate how psychotropic agents may affect these biologic symptoms. Furthermore, none of these theories explains how non-somatic modalities can effect similar changes in depressive states.

Another alternative is not to develop a single "cause" but explore in more detail some of the multiple factors presented by Akiskal and McKinney (66). There are at least four major sets of factors or vulnerabilities which are present to some extent throughout life. The first factor represents the *genetic* component or the biologic equipment with which an individual is born into a particular environment. In addition to biologic and central nervous system circuitry, a number of researchers argue that temperament and even personality style may be determined to some extent by the genetic loading. Second, so-called *developmental* factors, as demonstrated by a variety of investigators from ego psychologists to behaviorists, can play a major role in determining present and future behavioral patterns, response to various environmental stimuli, and in general the level of adaptational deficiency. Third, throughout the life cycle *psychosocial* stressors are present to a varying degree. Different points in the life cycle can be associated with a higher level of vulnerability. Finally, the presence of *physiological* stressors, as defined by the onset of medical illness, the aging process, and accidents can affect the type of physiologic responsivity of an individual. It is our contention that the interrelationship of these four factors and the age of the individual will define the constellation of symptoms at the onset of a depressive episode and their severity (Figure 4). Furthermore, the persistence of these factors (especially with adverse conditions perpetuating a high level of

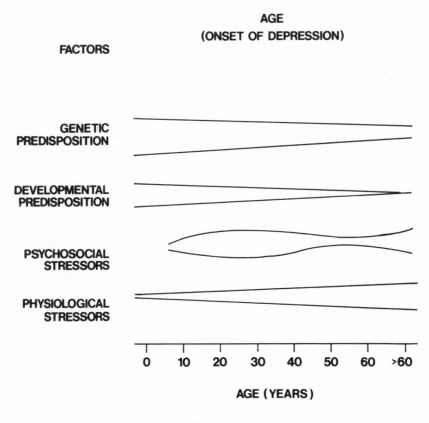

FACTORS

AGE
(ONSET OF DEPRESSION)

GENETIC
PREDISPOSITION

DEVELOPMENTAL
PREDISPOSITION

PSYCHOSOCIAL
STRESSORS

PHYSIOLOGICAL
STRESSORS

0   10   20   30   40   50   60   >60

AGE (YEARS)

FIGURE 4.

vulnerability) will help define chronicity of the illness and the frequency of recurrences.

If one accepts the presence of different types of vulnerabilities, present from birth onward, one can develop an additive model with different weights attached at various age and developmental levels. For example, genetic predisposition may have a major role in the onset and course of bipolar illness if the first episode occurs before age 40. When onset of the illness is after age 40, genetic predisposition may have less importance. A second aspect of the genetic vulnerability factor would be to consider that patients with a heavier weighting of this factor at the onset of their illness are more likely to present with characteristic psychobiologic features of the illness. This does not, of course, rule out the likelihood that the other factors, especially physiological stressors, also "color" the psychobiologic picture.

To further explore this line of thinking, the second and third type of vulnerability—developmental events, especially relating to Bowlby's (24) concepts, and the presence of psychosocial stressors—point the way to a continued vulnerability during the entire life cycle. For example, developmental factors probably have a greater impact up to the age of 30, while psychosocial stressors are present throughout the life cycle and may not exert a major influence until puberty. Brown et al. have argued that social environment plays a crucial role in the etiology in depression, both as a provoking and a predisposing factor (35). They feel that a severe, long-term threatening event, not a short-term stressor, can be important in the onset of the episode. Furthermore, a distinctive feature in the majority of such severe events is the experience of an actual or threatened major loss. (An actual past loss may have an effect on the type and severity of symptom formation.) In short, Brown and colleagues argue that, in the presence of particular background social factors (psychosocial stressors such as lack of intimate ties, loss of mother in childhood, three or more children under age 14 living at home) which increase vulnerability and affect cognitive sets, the presence of a provoking agent (loss, threatened loss, difficulties) may lead to an initial and secondary response in which one major outcome is depression. These events leading to specific illness may be affected differentially by various types of vulnerability, but all can lead to the onset of an affective episode (67).

Finally, in addition to psychosocial or developmental stressors, the presence of physiological stressors (medications, occurrence of medical diseases) may contribute to the onset of illness and may be at the basis of the onset of many secondary affective syndromes. This fourth factor, in a sense the second type of biologic factor (in addition to the genetic one), has probably been underrated as a key issue in precipitating the onset of depressive states. Only recently has the true incidence of medically-associated depressive states been appreciated. Furthermore, the symptom profile and type of somatic/psychologic balance have definite implications for treatment.

We would contend that, given the sufficient presence of different stressors and predispositions, everyone is at risk to develop a depressive episode. The interaction of these stressors in the presence of a provoking agent (real or imagined loss, major work, social and peer difficulties) is responsible for the progressive march of symptomatology leading to the diagnosis of a major depressive episode. With respect to symptomatology, I must point out again that the age and psychosocial development of the individual plays an important role in the presentation of the symptoms. For example, differences in level of psychomotor agitation and retardation, sleep alterations, other biologic symptoms, as well as psychological symptoms of depression, will be influenced immensely by the age of the individual. In summary, then, my model includes the factor of age, especially in terms of symptom presentation, intersecting with several types of specific illness vulnerability which can act singly or in combination. They include the level of genetic vulnerability (be it enzyme deficit, etc.), early developmental vulnerability, followed subsequently by the parallel presence of two types of stressors—psychosocial and physiological. It is the interaction of these biologic and psychosocial factors which clearly affect the timing and characterization of the onset of the depressive illness.

As stated previously, a second set of questions to be addressed by a uniform hypothesis of depression is to explain how different treatments all lead to successful outcomes of most depressions. We also need to account for treatment specificity and severity—e.g., delusions require electroconvulsive treatment (ECT) and/or combined psychotropic treatment, as opposed to chronic minor depressions where medication may not be useful in affecting symptom adjustment. One conclusion would be to argue that there is no treatment specificity and all approaches affect similar symptom complexes, but that potency and onset of action are responsible for the apparent differences. This approach provides a quantitative explanation for the efficacy of both somatic and psychological therapies for depression and suggests that the acute episode can be treated rather nonspecifically as long as any of the treatments is administered correctly and in sufficient "dosage." Another point of view argues for a qualitative difference in treatment whereby individualized treatments have specific target areas, and in some cases combined treatment may be useful.

Interestingly, the first approach negates the simplistic notion that biologic symptoms require somatic intervention and that psychologic symptoms necessitate a psychologic form of treatment. On the other hand, the second approach preserves the "separate but equal" notion of symptom specificity and tends to leave intact various etiology and treatment connections. Thus, psychological (psychosocial or developmental) stressors leading to the onset of a depressed episode marked by mostly psychological symptoms (i.e., inability to concentrate, impaired decision-making, guilt, etc.) will respond best to psychological treatment. A similar case is then made for the so-called biological depression with primarily biologic symptoms (possibly emerging more from genetic and/or physiologic stressors) necessitating somatic intervention. In fact, the resurrection of the term "melancholia" would be a prime example of this approach. However, since evidence is now available that psychologic treatments (e.g., cognitive therapy) can affect both biologic and psychological symptoms, and various treatment trials with tricyclic antidepressants point to changes in the psychological sphere, the first "nonspecific" approach may yet emerge as the most convincing one. If this were the case, then the presentation of symptoms is colored by age, and the relative weights of the various types of vulnerabilities and stressors may affect the overall clinical response rate.

This last point brings me to the final set of issues surrounding chronicity and relapse. Why do 20% of depressed patients continue with a chronic course? Perhaps the most parsimonious explanation is the continued impact of particular vulnerability factors as well as characterologic features. However, one must also explain the onset of recurrent episodes and the various alternative clinical pictures (mania, anergia, excitation, as well as change of symptoms in successive episodes). However, this latter question can be eventually answered if we accept a multivariate hypothesis of affective states. This model implies a multidimensional picture of affective disease. Rather than a final common pathway of psychobiologic features, this alternative approach provides a greater interplay between biologic and psychosocial processes and, by extension, the likelihood that effective treatments can be both somatic and non-somatic. Perhaps, if there is a bias, it is that combined approaches to treatment will eventually be found to be the treatment of choice. Of course, such a conclusion will have to await the acquisition of a large data base on non-somatic treatment and combined psychologic and somatic treatment.

CONCLUSION

As stated in the introduction, depression is a significant health problem affecting individuals of both sexes in all socioeconomic strata. As much as 20% of the population will suffer from an affective disorder at some period in their lives. Depression has been diagnosed for centuries and, although it has been labeled with different names, its devastating effects have been felt throughout recorded history. Beginning in the 19th century and continuing into the 20th century, attempts have been made to determine the cause of and to classify affective disorders. Most nosologic systems have divided depression into dichotomous categories and attempted to identify the most characteristic symptoms of depression. These extensive diagnostic endeavors finally culminated in the DSM-III nomenclature that offered the clinician a level of specificity and consistency not previously available. Aside from DSM-III, there remain many diagnostic dichotomies: endogenous/non-endogenous; psychotic/neurotic; unipolar/bipolar; and primary/secondary. This latter dichotomy is important because a secondary depressive group includes patients with medical problems that may coexist with depressive disease. While depression may coexist with or follow other psychiatric illnesses, the relationship between depression and various medical and neurologic conditions is not completely understood. Regardless of the particular classification scheme used, investigators have sought psychologic or psychobiologic explanations for affective disorders. The psychologic theories have tended to emphasize psychoanalytic notions, although more recent theories based on learned helplessness, reduced reinforcement, and maladaptive cognitive behavior have received attention. From a biologic perspective, depression is thought to represent a disturbance in certain regulatory systems. Such a position has led us to pay more attention to sleep, appetite, and motor and sexual activity changes in patients with affective disorders, so as to improve diagnostic accuracy.

In assessing the various genetic, epidemiological, and familial factors in depression, it is clear that there is a considerable genetic component in affective disorders, especially in bipolar illness. Also, depression seems more common in whites, upper social classes, persons not currently married, individuals over the age of 45, and women. Depressions associated with or precipitated by life stresses, including grief, are more frequent in individuals with a family history of depression. Real and imagined losses, recent or past, may contribute to the overall incidence of affective disorders.

Although depressive disorders may vary from mild to the most disabling psychotic states, treatment is indicated in most cases. Most depressive episodes, if they come to medical attention, are treated with techniques that range from counseling to psychopharmacologic intervention. Presently, various somatic therapies are used alone or in combination with some form of psychotherapy. Most clinicians, confronted with a depressed patient whose illness is severe enough to require biologic intervention, prescribe tricyclic antidepressants before using monoamine oxidase inhibitors or electroconvulsive therapy. A vast array of approaches to treatment has been subsumed under the term "psychotherapy." These approaches have two essential features: establishment of a confiding relationship between patient and therapist and of a dialogue aimed at changing the patient's current state. Several approaches, including behavioral, cognitive/behavioral, interpersonal, marital, and group therapy, as well as psychoanalytic treatment, are used to treat depression. Of course, the combination of drugs and psychotherapy is often prescribed for the milder form of depression; still, little is known about the combination of these treatments. The goal of treatment during the acute depressive episode is to reduce the symptoms and to return the patient to a premorbid level of functioning. However, the goal of long-term or maintenance treatment is to prevent relapse of the current episode and onset of a new episode, or to attentuate a new episode if prevention fails. Finally, our understanding of both diagnosis and treatment, etiology and outcome will be enhanced if we develop testable models to account for the varying presentation of the illness with respect to symptom profile and severity, onset and course of the episode, as well as the factors underlying chronicity and recurrence.

REFERENCES

1. U.S. President's Commission on Mental Health, *Report to the President from the President's Commission on Mental Health,* Washington, DC: Supt. of Documents, U.S. Government Printing Office, 1978.

2. BECK, A.T., BRADY, J.P., and QUEN, J.M.: *The History of Depression*. New York: Insight Communication, 1977.
3. American Psychiatric Association: Committee on Nomenclature and Statistics. *Diagnostic and Statistical Manual of Mental Disorders*. Third edition. Washington: American Psychiatric Assoc., 1980.
4. KILOH, L.G., and GARSIDE, R.F.: The independence of neurotic depression and endogenous depression. *Br. J. Psychiat.*, 109:451-462, 1963.
5. HAMILTON, M., and WHITE, J.M.: Clinical syndromes in depressive states. *J. Ment. Sci.*, 105:985-998, 1959.
6. WATTS, C.A.H.: The mild endogenous depression. *Br. J. Med.*, 1:4-8, 1957.
7. KLERMAN, G.L., ENDICOTT, J., SPITZER, R., and HIRSCHFELD, R.M.A.: Neurotic depressions: A systematic analysis of multiple criteria and meanings. *Am. J. Psychiat.*, 136:57-61, 1979.
8. KRAEPELIN, E.: *Manic Depressive Insanity and Paranoia*. Trans. by R.M. Barclay. Edinburgh: E.S. Livingstone, 1921.
9. LEONHARD, K., KORFF, I., and SCHULZ, H.: Temperament in families with monopolar and bipolar phasic psychoses. *Psychiatr. Neurol.* (Basel), 143:416-434, 1962.
10. ANGST, J.: Zur Atiologie und Nosologic endogener depressiver. *Psychosen Monogr. Neurol. Psychiatr.*, 112:1-118, 1966.
11. PERRIS, C. (Ed.): A study of bipolar (manic-depressive) and unipolar recurrent depressive psychoses. *Acta Psychiatr.* (Scand.) (Suppl. 194), 42:1-188, 1966.
12. WINOKUR, G., CLAYTON, P.J., and REICH, T.: *Manic-Depressive Illness*. St. Louis: C. V. Mosby, 1969.
13. PERRIS, C.: Personality patterns in patients with affective disorders. *Acta Psychiatr.* (Scand.) (Suppl.), 221:43-51, 1971.
14. KUPFER, D.J., FOSTER, F.G., DETRE, T.P., and HIMMELHOCH, J.: Sleep EEG and motor activity as indicators of affective states. *Neuropsychobiol.*, 1:296-303, 1975.
15. GERSHON, E.S.: Genetics of the affective disorders. *Hosp. Pract.*, 14:117-122, 1979.
16. TAYLOR, M.A., ABRAMS, R., and HAYMAN, M.A.: The classification of affective disorders: A reassessment of the bipolar unipolar dichotomy. A clinical, laboratory and family study. *J. Affect. Dis.*, 2:95-109, 1980.
17. KUPFER, D.J., and DETRE, T.P.: Tricyclic and monoamine oxidase inhibitor antidepressants: Clinical use, V. 14. In: L. Iverson, S.D. Iverson, and S. Snyder (Eds.), *Handbook of Psychopharacology*. New York: Plenum Press, 1978, pp. 199-229.
18. ROBINS, E., and GUZE, S.B.: Classification of affective disorders: The primary-secondary, the endogenous-reactive, and the neurotic-psychotic concepts. In: T.A. Williams, M.M. Katz, and J.A. Shield (Eds.), *Recent Advances in the Psychobiology of Depressive Illness*. Washington, DC: U. S. Government Printing Office, 1972, pp. 283-292.
19. GUZE, S.B., WOODRUFF, R.A., and CLAYTON, P.J.: Secondary affective disorder: A study of 95 cases. *Psychol. Med.*, 1:426-428, 1971.
20. ANDREASEN, N.C., and WINOKUR, G.: Secondary depression: Familial, clinical, and research perspectives. *Am. J. Psychiat.*, 136:62-66, 1979.
21. CHODOFF, P.: The depressive personality: A critical review. *Arch. Gen. Psychiat.*, 27:666-673, 1972.
22. FREUD, S.: Mourning and melancholia. In: *Collected Papers*, Vol. I. London: Hogarth Press and the Institute of Psychoanalysis, 1950.
23. SPITZ, R.A.: Anaclitic depression. In: *The Psychoanalytic Study of the Child*, Vol.

II. New York: International Universities Press, 1946, pp. 313-342.

24. BOWLBY, J.: *Attachment and Loss, Vol. 2: Separation, Anxiety and Anger*. London: Hogarth Press and the Institute of Psychoanalysis, 1972.

25. ABRAMSON, L.Y., SELIGMAN, M.E.P., and TEASDALE, J.D.: Learned helplessness in humans: Critique and reformulation. *J. Abnorm. Psychol.*, 87:49-74, 1978.

26. LEWINSOHN, P.M.: A behavioral approach to depression. In: R.J. Friedman and M.M. Katz (Eds.), *The Psychology of Depression: Contemporary Theory and Research*. New York: John Wiley and Sons, 1974, pp. 157-185.

27. BECK, A.T. *Depression: Clinical, Experimental and Theoretical Aspects*. New York: Harper and Row, 1967.

28. SELIGMAN, M.E.P., ABRAMSON, L.Y., and SEMMEL, A.: Depressive attributional style. *J. Abnorm. Psychol.*, 88:242-247, 1979.

29. KOVACS, M., and BECK, A.: Maladaptive cognitive structures in depression. *Am. J. Psychiat.*, 135:525-533, 1978.

30. KUPFER, D.J., FOSTER, F.G., DETRE, T.P., and HIMMELHOCH, J. Sleep EEG and motor activity as indicators of affective states. *Neuropsychobiol.*, 1:296-303, 1975.

31. PERRIS, C.: Frequency and hereditary aspects of depression. In: D.M. Gallant and G.M. Simpson (Eds.), *Depression: Behavioral, Biochemical, Diagnostic and Treatment Concepts*. New York: John Wiley and Sons, 1976, pp. 75-107.

32. WEISSMAN, M.M., and MYERS, J.K.: Rates and risks of depressive symptoms in a United States urban community. *Acta Psychiatr.* (Scand.), 57:219-231, 1978.

33. WEISSMAN, M.M., and MYERS, J.K.: Affective disorders in a United States urban community: The use of research criteria in an epidemiological survey. *Arch. Gen. Psychiat.*, 35:1304-1311, 1978.

34. WEISSMAN, M.M., and KLERMAN, G.L.: Sex differences and the epidemiology of depression. *Arch. Gen. Psychiat.*, 34:98-111, 1972.

35. BROWN, G.W., HARRIS, T., and COPELAND, J.R.: Depression and loss. *Br. J. Psychiat.*, 130:1-18, 1972.

36. BROWN, G.W. and PRUDO, R.: Psychiatric disorder in a rural and an urban population: 1. Aetiology of depression. *Psychol. Med.*, 11:581-599, 1981.

37. ZIS, A.P., and GOODWIN, F.K.: Major affective disorder as a recurrent illness: A critical review. *Arch. Gen. Psychiat.*, 36:835-839, 1979.

38. ANGST, J.: Verlauf unipolar depressiver, bipolar manischdepressiver und schizo-affektiver Erkrankungen und Psychosen. Ergbnisseeiner prospektiven Studie. *Fortschr. Neurol. Psychiatr.*, 48:3-30, 1980.

39. MORRIS, J.B., and BECK, A.T.: The efficacy of antidepressant drugs. *Arch. Gen. Psychiat.*, 30:667-674, 1974.

40. HASKELL, D.S., DiMASCIO, A., and PRUSOFF, B.: Rapidity of symptom reduction in depressions treated with amitriptyline. *J. Nerv. Ment. Dis.*, 160:24-33, 1975.

41. KAY, D.W.K., GARSIDE, R.F., and FAHY, T.J.: A double-blind trial of phenelzine and amitriptyline in depressed outpatients. A possible differential effect of the drugs on symptoms. *Br. J. Psychiat.*, 123:63-67, 1973.

42. ROBINSON, D.S., NIES, A., RAVARIS, C.L., and LAMBORN, K.R.: The monoamine oxidase inhibitor, phenelzine, in the treatment of depressive-anxiety states. *Arch. Gen. Psychiat.*, 29:407-413, 1973.

43. RAVARIS, C.L., NIES, A., ROBINSON, D.S., IVES, J.O., LAMBORN, K.R., and KORSON, L.: A multiple dose, controlled study of phenelzine in depression-anxiety states. *Arch. Gen. Psychiat.*, 33:347-350, 1976.

44. KLEIN, D.F., and DAVIS, J.M.: *Diagnosis and Drug Treatment of Psychiatric Disorders*. Baltimore, MD: Williams and Wilkins, 1969.
45. HIMMELHOCH, J.M., DETRE, T.P., KUPFER, D.J., SWARTZBURG, M., and BYCK, R.: Treatment of previously intractable depressions with tranylcypromine and lithium. *J. Nerv. Ment. Dis.*, 155:216-220, 1972.
46. DETRE, T.P., HIMMELHOCH, J., SCHWARTZBURG, M., ANDERSON, C.M., BYCK, R., and KUPFER, D.J.: Hypersomnia and manic-depressive disease. *Am. J. Psychiat.*, 128:1303-1305, 1972.
47. HOLLISTER, L.E., OVERALL, J.E., JOHNSON, M.H., SHELTON, J., KIMBELL, I. Jr., and BRUSNE, A.: Amitriptyline alone and combined with perphenazine in newly admitted depressed patients. *J. Nerv. Ment. Dis.*, 142:460-469, 1966.
48. PRUSOFF, B.A., and WEISSMAN, M.M.: Pharmacologic treatment of anxiety in depressed outpatients. In: D.S. Klein, and J. Rabkin (Eds.), *Anxiety: New Research and Changing Concepts*. New York: Raven Press, 1981.
49. FINK, M.: *Convulsive Therapy: Theory and Practice*. New York: Raven Press, 1979.
50. HERZOG, A., and DETRE, T.P.: Postpartum psychoses. *Dis. Nerv. Sys.*, 34:231-236, 1974.
51. WEISSMAN, M.M.: The psychological treatment of depression: Evidence for the efficacy of psychotherapy alone, in comparison with and in combination with pharmacotherapy. *Arch. Gen. Psychiat.*, 36:1261-1269, 1979.
52. WHITEHEAD, A.: Psychological treatment of depression: A review. *Behav. Res. Ther.*, 17:495-509, 1979.
53. NEU, C., PRUSOFF, B.A., and KLERMAN, G.L.: Measuring the interventions used in the short-term interpersonal psychotherapy of depression. *Am. J. Orthopsychiat.*, 48:629-636, 1978.
54. FRIEDMAN, A.S.: Interaction of drug therapy with marital therapy in depressive patients. *Arch. Gen. Psychiat.*, 32:619-637, 1975.
55. COVI, L., LIPMAN, R.S., ALARCON, R.D., and SMITH, V.K.: Drug and psychotherapy interaction in depression. *Am. J. Psychiat.*, 135:502-508, 1976.
56. WEISSMAN, M.M., PRUSOFF, B.A., DiMASCIO, A., NEU, C., and GOKLANEY, M.: The efficacy of drugs and psychotherapy in the treatment of acute depressive episodes. *Am. J. Psychiat.*, 136:555-558, 1979.
57. RUSH, A.J., and BECK, A.T.: Cognitive therapy of depression and suicide. *Am. J. Psychother.*, 32:201-219, 1978.
58. RUSH, A.J., BECK, A.T., KOVACS, M., and HOLLON, S.: Comparative efficacy of cognitive therapy and pharmacotherapy in the treatment of depressed outpatients. *Cog. Ther. Res.*, 1:17-37, 1977.
59. KOVACS, M., RUSH, A.J., and BECK, A.T.: Depressed outpatients treated with cognitive therapy or pharmacotherapy: A one-year follow-up. *Arch. Gen. Psychiat.*, 38:33-39, 1981.
60. DiMASCIO, A., WEISSMAN, M.M., PRUSOFF, B.A., NEU, C., and ZWILLING, M.: Differential symptom reduction by drugs and psychotherapy in acute depression. *Arch. Gen. Psychiat.*, 36:1450-1456, 1979.
61. PRIEN, R.J., KLETT, C.J., and CAFFEY, E.M.: Lithium carbonate and imipramine in prevention of affective episodes. *Arch. Gen. Psychiat.*, 29:420-425, 1973.
62. MINDHAM, R.H.S., HOWLAND, C., and SHEPHERD, M.: An evaluation of continuation therapy with tricyclic antidepressants in depressive illness. *Psychol. Med.*, 3: 5-17, 1973.

63. KLERMAN, G.L., DiMASCIO, A., WEISSMAN, M.M., PRUSOFF, B., and PAYKAL, E.S.: Treatment of depression by drugs and psychotherapy. *Am. J. Psychiat.,* 131:186-191, 1974.

64. WILLIAMS, T.A., KATZ, M.M. and SHIELD, J.A. (Eds.): *Recent Advances in the Psychobiology of the Depressive Illness.* Washington, DC: U.S. Government Printing Office, 1972.

65. SHAPIRO, R.W. and KELLER, M.B.: Initial 6-month follow-up of patients with major depressive disorder. *J. Affec. Dis.,* 3:205-220, 1981.

66. AKISKAL, H.A., and McKINNEY, W.T., Jr.: Overview of recent research in depression: Integration of ten conceptual models into a comprehensive clinical frame. *Arch. Gen. Psychiat.,* 32:285-305, 1975.

67. PAYKEL, E.S. Recent life events in the development of the depressive disorders. In: R.A. Depue (Ed.), *The Psychobiology of the Depressive Disorders.* New York: Academic Press, 1979, pp. 245-262.

11

Toward a Unified View
of Schizophrenic Disorders

Robert Cancro, M.D.

The theme of this chapter is an effort toward a unified view of the concept of the schizophrenic disorders. This task obviously is more easily entertained than achieved. I will attempt to present a historical view of what the term "schizophrenia" has meant and how the illness has been diagnosed, some caveats about what is known concerning its etiology and pathogenesis, and finally, the reasons why such a synthesis is premature if it is not to be trivial.

Any history of a particular form of madness must be arbitrary in its choice of a starting point. Madness, undoubtedly, has been with us as long as man. Peculiar and maladaptive behaviors are not restricted to homo sapiens. Yet, because of the sapient nature of the species, madness has been traditionally conceived as including cognitive disturbances. Even severe disturbances of mood, such as are seen in melancholia, are not usually considered madness until the cognitive apparatus breaks down in the form of impaired reality testing, or delusions, or in some similar fashion. It is for this reason that much of the early 19th century psychiatric literature used the term "dementia" so generously. Morel (1) in 1852 used the word dementia to describe the condition of a patient with onset of illness at age 14. Because of the peculiarity of seeing a process of dementia in one so young, he coined the phrase "démence précoce." Morel, although Belgian, was very much in the tradition of French psychiatry and used the words as a descriptive phrase which expressed the salient clinical characteristics of his young patient and not as a nosologic term. He did not presume to be creating a category of disease, but rather to be describing symptoms in an individual.

German psychiatry was much more reflective of a search for disease entities. For example, in 1871, Hecker (2) described the category of hebephrenia and Kahlbaum (3), in 1874, described the category of catatonia. Both authors used nouns to label disease entities which they presumed were being identified and captured in their descriptions. The presentation by Koch (4) of his brilliant experiments on the bacterial transmission of tuberculosis in 1882 was an occasion for the disease entity approach to become even more powerful in continental psychiatry. Within the year after Koch's work received its appropriate scientific recognition, Kraepelin (5) published a small volume in which his lifelong quest for disease entities in psychiatry was already apparent. In the fifth edition (6) of his famous textbook, he placed dementia praecox in a category of disorders characterized by a process of confused and illogical thinking. In 1899, in the sixth edition (7) of this textbook, known to all students of the schizophrenic disorders, he gave up the fourfold classification of the fifth edition and separated dementia praecox from the manic-depressive psychoses. The manic-depressive psychoses shared with dementia praecox cognitive impairment including delusions but tended to have a better prognosis. This division of major mental disorders has remained with us virtually unchanged for more than eight decades. While Kraepelin abandoned his early position about age of onset and the inevitability of dementia, he never abandoned the search for entities.

Bleuler's (8) monograph on dementia praecox appeared in print in 1911, three years after its completion. He intended his book to be, in part, an attempt to apply the ideas of Freud to dementia praecox. Despite this effort to bring psychodynamic and biologic thinking together, the major contribution of this book was in the utilization of a syndrome concept. He rejected dementia praecox as a single disease and saw it as a group of disorders which included several diseases. In a remarkable insight, he argued that they were a group "in the same sense as the organic psychoses." He recognized that the etiologies of the group members could differ as could their courses. They shared in common, according to his formulation, the feature of splitting. This essential feature consisted of a loss of harmony amongst the various groups of mental functions. The unity of the mind was lost. And feelings, ideas, facial expressions, posture, body movement, and emotional tone could be dissociated from each other.

Bleuler made the disorder of association or thought disorder of central importance as a diagnostic criterion. The formal signs of thought disorder are difficult, but not impossible, to quantify in an operational manner (9). Their recognition does require clinical judgment. The presence and the severity of formal signs of thought disorder do not lend themselves readily to the patient's self-assessment but rather require measurement by an observer. The real limitations in applying Bleuler's criteria, coupled with recent trends in scientific fashion, have led to a diminished utilization of these criteria.

MIND VERSUS BODY

Bleuler occupied a position midway between Kraepelin and Meyer. He believed the primary cause of these disorders to be organic but included psychogenic factors as determinants of symptom content and perhaps even symptom form. Meyer (10) placed the schizophrenias exclusively into a reaction mode. They were the reactions of an individual dealing with the vicissitudes of living. Meyer's thinking influenced DSM-I heavily and the official nosology spoke of schizophrenic reactions rather than the schizophrenia of DSM-II or the schizophrenic disorders of DSM-III.

The apparent but almost certainly illusory distinction between organic and psychogenic or endogenous and exogenous etiology has been a recurrent one in nosologic thinking. In the 8th edition of his textbook Kraepelin (11) referred to the endogenous vs. exogenous etiology of mental disorders but credited the distinction to Möbius. Jaspers (12), in 1913, stated that this division was not helpful in the schizophrenias. Bleuler also shared in this general lack of enthusiasm for the approach. In the fourth edition of his textbook (13), published in 1923, he commented on the difference between reactive and process schizophrenia but indicated that "no division can be based on these classes because the two symptomatologies intermingle."

In 1932, Frank (14) returned to this strategy when he spoke of the nuclear group of schizophrenics. He assumed that the population of schizophrenics included a group of true or essential cases which could be distinguished from others who share a similar symptomatology but differ in origin. It is the same model of classification which has been used in epilepsy, hypertension, and alcoholism. It is the same approach taken by Bleuler in classifying the symptoms of the disorder into a fundamental and an accessory group. It is the same strategy utilized by Langfeldt (15) who prefers the terms "true schizophrenia" and "schizophreniform psychoses." All of these observers argue that, although patients may present with similar symptoms, there is a group which tends to have a different premorbid history, a different course, a poorer outcome, and therefore a different illness. This is the kind of thinking that led Sullivan to make a distinction between dementia praecox and schizophrenia. Clearly, the autistic use of language is not restricted to schizophrenics.

DIAGNOSIS

The goal of improving diagnosis by achieving greater reliability has at times achieved near mystical proportions. The most reliable ratings are obtained by asking the patient directly as to the presence or absence of a symptom and immediately recording the response. It is important to understand that this so-called reliability is merely interrater agreement and not a measure of the reliability of the presence of the symptom. The patient who denies hallucinations may not be telling the truth, but the interrater reliability will be superb. This is a frequent source of confusion. Interrater reliability does not equal clinical certainty.

As recently as 1972, an NIMH report (16) indicated that improved diagnosis would help us to understand what schizophrenia is. Improved diagnosis will almost certainly not increase our understanding of the nature of schizophrenia. Our misconceptions can be standardized in such a way that the same patient will be identically mislabeled by an even larger number of colleagues than in the past. A fundamental improvement in diagnostic practice would not be merely improved reliability but a deeper knowledge and understanding of the patient. Improved diagnosis would involve longitudinal rather than cross-sectional study. The very meaning of the word diagnosis expresses the necessity of a thorough knowledge of the patient. This can only occur over a period of time and with repeated observations in a number of different situations and circumstances. The making of a snap judgment based on a cross-sectional assessment of signs and symptoms is in no way compatible with the establishment of a diagnosis. Whatever schizophrenia may be, it is not just a collection of momentary clinical findings. It is both a process which occurs over time and the clinical picture produced by that process. It is important to remember that even though the process and the clinical picture may be given the same name, they are not the same thing. It is also wise to remember Kubie's (17) warning of 1971, in which he stated that a "nosological system which is based on symptom clusters leads to inappropriate diagnostic 'fashions.' "

The development of symptom lists, in which each item on a list has equal diagnostic value, leads to an approach which is not unlike the menu of a Chinese restaurant—one from column A and two from column B. Unfortunately, this tactic leads to increased sample heterogeneity, because the diagnostically equivalent symptoms in fact derive from different genetic and biochemical mechanisms. It may well be wisest to select one clinically identifiable mental system which is believed to reflect biologic differences and use signs of its altered function as the single diagnostic criterion. An initial effort at doing this was published in 1968 (9) and a more elaborate one was published in 1970 (18). It was assumed that a disturbance of thinking paralleled the hypothesized information processing differences between schizophrenics and nonschizophrenics. Thought disorder was, therefore, selected as a good candidate to serve as the diagnostic criterion. Using the classical formal signs of schizophrenic thought disorder, it was shown that sample heterogeneity could be reduced in terms of premorbid social adjustment, rapidity of onset of illness, severity of presenting symptomatology, impairment of abstraction on proverbs, and duration of hospital stay. Obviously, homogeneous groups were not established but homogeneity was significantly increased.

The effort to create meaningful classifications of schizophrenia has always suffered from a persistent tendency toward reification. One cannot help but be reminded of Wordsworth's (19) warning:

> That false secondary power
> By which we multiply distinctions, then
> Deem that our puny boundaries are things
> That we perceive, and not that we have made.

This quotation should be printed on every copy of DSM-III, if not on every page.

Various diagnostic schemata have been developed reflecting the thinking of many of the people cited earlier and others who have not been mentioned. The problem of the extent of overlap amongst different classifications was addressed in a study done by Arthur Sugerman and me and reported initially in 1962 (20) and in more detail in 1968 (21). A consecutive series of patients admitted to a psychiatric hospital with a diagnosis of schizophrenia were rated using the Phillips scale of premorbid adjustment, Langfeldt criteria, and Bleulerian criteria. The intercorrelations amongst these three diagnostic schemata were all moderate to high. The premorbid score correlated with the Langfeldt classification at 0.6 and with Bleuler's classification at 0.7. The Langfeldt and Bleulerian classifications correlated at 0.82. Nevertheless, the amount of variance in one classification accounted for by the second classification ranged from a low of 36% to a high of 67%. In other words, while the intercorrelations between the three classifications were all highly significant, there was a failure of overlap ranging from one-third to two-thirds of the cases. These data remind the observer painfully of Wordsworth's acumen in warning us of the danger of deceiving ourselves into believing "that our puny boundaries are things that we perceive, and not that we have made."

ETIOLOGY

Obviously, when we cannot identify the population suffering from a disorder with reliability let alone with validity, it becomes difficult to speak of etiology with any real confidence. It is in many ways a testimony to the scientific courage of a number of investigators who explored etiologic issues in the schizophrenias when there was little reason to believe that the signal to noise ratio was sufficiently favorable to yield success. The earliest studies on etiology looked at genetic factors while more recent ones have explored both biologic parameters and social factors as well. The literature tends to describe factors as genetic, biochemical, physiologic, psychologic, and social. There is a tendency to think of these as real and separate entities which are independent sources of variance. These so-called factors are nothing more than different levels of abstraction to explain the same observed phenomenon. It is sometimes more convenient, because of the way our cognitive apparatus functions, to think in terms of biochemistry and at other times in terms of physiology. This does not mean that the organism has real biochemical and physiologic levels. The organism functions as a unitary whole, and the observer imposes disciplinary conceptualizations and abstractions on it. It is helpful and productive to think of organismic functions in terms of these disciplines, but as has been observed, there is no evidence to believe that God created the world to correspond to the departmental pattern of a university. It is easier to think in this fashion, but it is necessary to recognize the dangers of both reification and dualism so that they can be reduced if not avoided.

Genetic factors are involved in the transmission of the schizophrenic disorders. This has been statistically demonstrated to the satisfaction of most observers. The studies on which this conclusion is based are clinical and, therefore, not as rigorous as laboratory studies. Nevertheless, the totality of the consanguinity, twin, and adoptive studies which have been published since 1916 compel one to the conclusion that genetic factors are operative in transmission.

Even in the case of the most simple trait, the genotype does not unilaterally nor immutably determine the phenotype. In complex traits there are many more developmental steps between the genotype and the phenotype with still more room for variation. The genotype is only one of the factors which accounts for individual differences. Every gene, be it single or operating in combination, has inherent within it a range of possible phenotypic outcomes. This range is determined by the characteristics of the gene, the environmental factors which activate it, and the timing of the activation. The gene is not an homunculus. It is encoded information. In many ways it is best thought of as a potential instruction. Until that instruction is activated by the environment, the gene has no function. Most genes are never activated during the lifetime of the organism. Different environments will selectively activate different genes. In a very real sense, then, the environment determines which genes are activated and thereby determines the operating or functional genotypic configuration of the organism.

The separation of gene from environment is a semantic convenience. The gene is a real structure, and everything outside that structure is considered the environment. More accurately, the environment is the biochemical "bath" in which the gene sits and which will serve to activate it. That "bath" is influenced by a variety of factors, including psychosocial events. The precise nature of the pathways by which these psychosocial events are translated into biochemical differences in the "bath" are not known.

Every gene inherently contains a range of possible outcomes. If a given gene is activated by a particular environment, it will produce a particular phenotype. A second environment activating the same gene will produce a different phenotype. The number of possibilities within the genotype is finite and the difference in the final characteristic can be small. Conversely, the difference can be of significant proportions, including the presence or absence of a pathologic trait such as audiogenic seizure susceptibility (22). As can be seen from the twin studies, the very genes which contribute to a schizophrenic illness in a given person can contribute to a nonschizophrenic and even a highly adaptive outcome in another. Having the appropriate genes for a schizophrenic illness is not sufficient to produce it.

Just as a knowledge of the genotype does not permit the prediction of the phenotype, a knowledge of the phenotype does not permit the inference of the genotype. Any phenotype can be arrived at from different genotypes. There is no immutable relationship between a phenotype and a genotype. Different environments acting upon different genotypes can produce the identical or different phenotypes. The identical characteristic can be arrived at through different mechanisms in the same individual as well as in different individuals. There is enormous plasticity in every biologic system, and this plasticity results in the rich diversity that characterizes complex organisms. Each member of a species is a unique biologic-environmental experiment never to be perfectly reproduced again. Even identical twins will show differences in phenotypes based on differences in the conditions of the evoking environment and the timing of the activations.

The phenotypes which are necessary but not sufficient for a schizophrenic illness need not be inherently abnormal. They can represent Gaussian variants of the expression of the trait in question. More importantly, they do not have to be immutably pathogenic. There are many steps between a trait and an illness. The expression of the traits which are transmitted genetically does not have to be a disturbance but can be nothing more than a statistically unusual variant in expression. The critical fact is that the phenotypes were present long before the illness emerged. The presence of the phenotype does not explain why only selected individuals decompensate, let alone why a given individual becomes psychotic at age 20 while another waits until age 30. Finally, it does not explain why one individual has long periods of remission and another does not. The identical twin studies demonstrate clearly the insufficiency of the genotype as the single cause of schizophrenia. Similarly, clinical reality demonstrates the insufficiency of the phenotype as the single cause. Behavior genetics can give insights into why the decompensation takes a particular form but does not yet explain why only certain people decompensate rather than others who have similar genetic makeups. Stated more simply, behavior genetics contributes to an understanding of predisposing factors but not of precipitating and/or sustaining factors.

The clinical syndrome of schizophrenia is not invariably associated with any known phenotype. There has been no true genetic marker demonstrated nor any specific chromosome identified which may be involved. While the evidence for the existence of a genetically transmitted phenotypic predisposition is clear, the nature of that trait, the characteristics of the genotype, and the mode of transmission remain obscure. The phenotype can be characterized in a number of ways. This was done traditionally on the basis of a visible characteristic such as color or size. Ideally, the phenotype should be identified at a precise biochemical level. In the behavioral sciences this ideal represents much more of an aspiration than a reality. For the present time, it may be best to conceptualize phenotypes as psychologic traits which can be defined and measured in some operational fashion.

The search for a psychologic phenotype is a reasonable activity but has been conducted at an excessively molar level. The schizophrenic disorders are not phenotypes and should not be so called. The choice of a personality organization such as schizoid to represent the phenotype is only modestly less molar. It is necessary to seek psychologic processes which are more like atoms rather than like complex mixtures of different compounds. The selected process should be one which can be studied both genetically and psychologically. The process must relate to the clinical signs and symptoms of the disorder in a logical fashion. The use of different aspects of attention as the psychologic phenotype in schizophrenia has received increasing interest (23). Attention can be studied genetically, psychologically, and psychophysiologically. It can be related to the clinical picture of the illness, and its careful measurement may serve to reduce the heterogeneity in populations diagnosed as schizophrenic.

Some of my own work may be relevant here. Certain individuals are more oriented toward inner sources of sensory stimulation, while others preferentially attend to outer sources. It was assumed that individuals who differ in preferential attention to the source of stimuli would differ in their form of mental illness. It was also assumed that those who are more inner oriented would develop—during a mental illness—signs more consistent with those used for the diagnosis of schizophrenia, e.g., withdrawal, autism. Through the use of measures of visual fixation and other measures of information processing, it was shown that hospitalized schizophrenics take in fewer bits of information about the visual environment than hospitalized nonschizophrenics and normal controls (24). Schizophrenics behave at their resting level in the way that nonschizophrenics and normals behave when performing a mental task. Once again the differences are *not* qualitative, and schizophrenics behave like nonschizophrenics under different conditions.

While there is only very modest evidence to support the idea of the pre-schizophrenic having an abnormal nervous system, there is good reason to assume that the nervous system will behave differently during illness. The recent development of positron emission tomography (PET) offers a relatively nonintrusive technique to study the metabolic activity of the nervous system. PET is a technique that combines computerized axial tomography (CT) and radioactive isotope tracing. The result of the combination of these two methods is that the technique produces the precise anatomical localization achieved by computerized tomographic imagery construction, with the biochemical assessment made possible through the use of radioactive isotopes. The administration of radioactively labeled substances allows the investigator to follow the fate of that compound through the body using instruments which detect the decay of the isotope. The major limitation of radioactive isotope tracers lies in the fact that the information is available to the investigator only in two dimensions rather than in the three dimensions which exist in the body. CT allows the investigator to reconstruct an image at a specific level of interest and, thereby, adds the third dimension. CT scans alone yield information about tissue density, i.e., structure. Obviously, by the time a pathologic condition advances to the stage of structural change, it is usually quite well advanced and does not permit the investigator the opportunity to study the biochemical processes which have contributed to its development.

In PET, a chemical compound with the desired biologic activity is labeled with a radioactive isotope. This particular isotope emits a positron when it decays. The positron combines almost immediately with an available electron. This combination results in the mutual annihilation of the two particles with the emission of two gamma rays. Because the gamma rays tend to fly off in directions very nearly opposite to each other, the measurement of the gamma ray activity allows the reconstruction of the approximate location of where the positron-electron annihilation took place. One inherent limitation of the technique is that the positron travels a variable distance before it encounters an electron. This is an unavoidable deficiency within the method and limits the localization of the region of interest to a theoretical minimum of several millimeters. Because of a variety of other factors, it is not realistic to believe that the chemical activity can be localized more accurately than approximately 8 to 10 millimeters at this time.

Utilizing a computer, a spatial reconstruction is made of the radioactivity within the subject at a selected plane. The results are displayed either as numerical printouts of activity at regions of interest or as a visual image on a display device.

PET, therefore, gives a relatively noninvasive technique for studying different regions of a given organ in terms of the biochemical processes which the investigator wishes to examine. Most of the compounds that have been used are isotopes of oxygen, nitrogen, and carbon. There is no positron-emitting isotope of hydrogen, but water can be labeled with oxygen[15], and thereby, information on the transport of water becomes available.

There are many problems involved in this technology, not the least of which is the useful half-life of a positron-emitting isotope. It is necessary to be able to produce and handle very short-lived isotopes in a manner that does not do injury to the subject. The PET unit requires not only a cyclotron to accelerate the particles, but also a data acquisition system, a computer, and display devices. The cyclotron must be encased in several feet of concrete. Finally, it is necessary to have a large team of radiochemists and other specialized personnel in order to make such a unit functional. It is not a technology which lends itself to the bedside but rather must be restricted to research centers for the forseeable future.

The principles of imagery construction require that a number of projections be taken at different angles. The accuracy of the reconstruction is proportional to the number of projections. Most PET systems utilize between 100 and 300 projections, which yield a spatial resolution of a few millimeters. The more up-to-date systems can also record up to seven tomographic images of the particular organ simultaneously.

The measurement of regional metabolism is more complex than the measurement of regional blood volume. Nevertheless, it is this quantitative metabolic approach which is particularly exciting to psychiatrists. Quantitative studies of brain metabolism have been conducted with tagged oxygen, with fluorine-tagged glucose, and other compounds as well. These measurements are powerful methods of quantifying and comparing brain activity both within and between subjects.

In 1978 I asked Jonathan Brodie to undertake the development of a program of collaboration between New York University Medical Center and Brookhaven National Laboratories. Under the overall leadership of Alfred Wolf of Brookhaven National Laboratories this collaboration has resulted in a variety of studies. The principle investigator for the schizophrenia section of the collaboration has been Tibor Farkas. Thirteen schizophrenic patients have been studied in the NYU Medical Center-Brookhaven National Laboratory project (25). These patients all met RDC criteria for the diagnosis of schizophrenia and seven were drug-free. Eleven normal volunteers were studied as controls. All subjects were studied with their eyes closed. One tomographic slice was taken at the level of the basal ganglia including the thalamus and lateral ventricles. A second slice was taken at the centrum semiovale level which included the cingulate gyrus. Because 11 of the schizophrenic subjects met Crow Type II criteria, they have been treated as a single group and compared to the 11 normal controls. It was found that there were no significant differences between the normals and schizophrenics in terms of the metabolic activity of the posterior regions of the brain at these two levels. On the other hand, the frontal region showed a significant diminution in both slices at beyond the .05 and the .01 levels. These preliminary data suggest that there is diminished frontal lobe activity relative to the posterior portion of the brain in schizophrenics characterized by negative symptoms.

It is important to stress the preliminary nature of the results of the NYU-Brookhaven collaboration. In many ways, these data are comparable to Rüdin's (26) initial report in 1916 of increased rates of schizophrenia in the relatives of index cases. The finding needs to be replicated and extended. It will be many years before the meaning is clear. Even if the finding of diminished frontal lobe metabolic activity were to be replicable, it is not known at this time whether this antedates or postdates the illness. It is certainly possible that this diminished level of metabolic activity is still within the normal range and that schizophrenia is a disorder of people with low-normal frontal lobe metabolic activity. It is also possible that these people have, for compensatory and/or defensive reasons, withdrawn from contact with the exterior world and, therefore, show lowered activity in the frontal lobes. There is a multiplicity of explanations for the findings, and until they have been replicated and extended in a scientifically vigorous manner, it would be premature to draw any conclusions. It is fair to say, however, that the findings are intriguing and suggestive of altered metabolic activity in the brain of at least certain individuals who meet RDC criteria for the diagnosis of schizophrenia.

THE CONCEPT OF SCHIZOPHRENIA

The repeated intrusions of the healer's ambivalence into the treatment of the mentally ill is a sobering insight. Tragic harm has been done in the name of treatment. If the negatively charged affect elicited by madness is to be reduced, there must be a better understanding of the disorder being treated. To understand schizophrenia fully would yield an understanding of all mental functions—normal and abnormal. The search for a total understanding is futile and destined for frustration. Nevertheless, there is a need for the development of theoretical models or conceptual formulations of the disorder. Yet, the question will arise as to the necessity for such theoretical models. The realities of trying to help people living through the human disaster of the schizophrenic psychosis make many clinicians suspect of what often sounds like useless academic theorizing. This tension between the practice and academic communities is real. Researchers frequently do not treat patients, particularly over prolonged periods of time, and clinicians often do not understand the implications and limitations of research studies. Splitting, too, is not restricted to the schizophrenias.

Clinicians must diagnose and prognosticate and, in order to do so, must have conceptions of the disorder. Restricting our attention exclusively to the so-called practical concerns, such as reliable diagnostic criteria, would be an error. The effort must be made to develop more homogeneous subgroups of schizophrenics, and this requires a better conceptualization of the category. The development of these subgroups is essential if the field is to have any success in identifying the biologic and environmental realities which unite at least some patients who are presently called schizophrenic. There can be little doubt that many patients so labeled in fact do not have the disorder. Yet, there will never be the equivalent of a glucose tolerance test for schizophrenia, until those cases which are clinically similar but biologically different are excluded. The need for an adequate theory is, therefore, obvious.

THEORIES OF SCHIZOPHRENIA

There are almost as many theories of schizophrenia as there are individuals who have thought about the subject. It is very natural to wonder which if any of these formulations is true. Despite the naturalness of this curiosity, it is scientifically unsound. To ask for a platonic or absolutely true theory of schizophrenia is not a scientific request. The theory need not and probably cannot be a perfect representation of the disorder. If we cannot rely on truth as the barometer, then what criteria shall we follow? The theory must be useful. It must be useful in the sense that it leads to testable hypotheses which in turn further our knowledge. Perhaps even more importantly, it must help the student conceptually to organize the data, and thus the theory serves as a cognitive crutch. Every theory will have its own unique array of advantages and disadvantages which must be matched to the requirements of particular situations. It can be anticipated that different theories will be better "fits" for different data. It may even be of value to utilize different theories under different conditions. Not all the criteria, however, relate to the data. An important consideration is personal preference. It is necessary to be comfortable with a particular formulation before it can be utilized effectively. If the theory is to serve as a cognitive crutch, it must fit comfortably with the cognitive style, personality, and values of the person utilizing that crutch. It would be difficult to improve on the logic of Einstein's rejection of the theory of indeterminism when he stated that he chose not to believe it.

Unfortunately, theories, like all other products of human activity, can become hypercathected. Theorists often confuse their speculations with their vital organs. Sadly, they then defend the former with a vigor that would be more appropriate for the latter. These highly partisan positions can be presented as the truth rather than one of many alternative explanations that fit the date equally well. While the only limitations to the number of theoretical formulations that correspond to the data at any given time is the imaginativeness of the available theorists, alternative explanations are often seen as rivals and treated accordingly. The so-called medical model has in recent years suffered the most. Many of the attacks have utilized a hypothetical medical model which is a variant of Koch's postulates and is pre-Kraepelinian in its simplicity. No serious biologic theorist of schizophrenia has advanced such a naive windmill recently, but this has not prevented much needless tilting.

The view being offered here is that the schizophrenic psychoses form a group of disorders which are only moderately homogeneous clinically and share to some degree certain signs and symptoms, but only intermittently. This group of end states has derived from a variety of initial conditions through a variety of pathways. There is no evidence to support the contention that under certain conditions anyone can develop a schizophrenic psychosis and therefore, the number of initial conditions which can lead to this disorder are finite. The initial conditions are conceived of as necessary but not sufficient for the illness. Some of the paths lead from these initial conditions to end states called schizophrenia, while others do not. The initial states need not be pathologic, and even the end states that are labeled "schizophrenia" have important adaptive features. The individual with a capacity for a schizophrenic psychosis may well have a Gaussian variation rather than an abnormal trait as the predisposing factor. The factors that precipitate and/or sustain the illness do not have to be the same as those that predispose. My bias is that biologic differences play a relatively greater role in accounting for individual variance in capacity for the form of the illness, and environmental differences play a relatively greater role in accounting for individual variance in precipitating and sustaining the illness.

It is obvious that any symptom-based nosology cannot be a scientific classification, because it does not identify the consistent differences in etiopathogenesis necessary to establish valid categories. Research efforts should be to move away from a symptom-based nosology toward classification based on stable findings which are more reflective of underlying mechanisms. Increasingly, measures of information processing and metabolic activity in the nervous system offer promise for a numerical taxonomy of the schizophrenias which will be based on the statistical analysis of physiologic differences. These taxonomic efforts will produce a very different nosology than our present ones. At that time a unified view of the schizophrenias may well be possible. In the interim we must use and improve upon symptom-based nosology so as to make it more useful for research and/or clinical purposes. This is a debt we owe to our patients which cannot be postponed.

PERSONAL NOTE

I have treated people labeled "schizophrenic" for the past 26 years and have done research on them for all but the first of those years. Certain impressions emerge from that experience, which may not appear as scientific as an experiment, but which in a very real sense may reflect far greater stability and reproducibility than is the case in much published research. Mental illness as we define it today consists of arbitrary categories. Our categories are hypothetical; the human suffering is real. The schizophrenic disorders range from tragic to catastrophic in their impact on human life. It is true that some patients who have recovered have benefited from the experience. Nevertheless, the cost is excessive, and we must be cautious not to romanticize madness in others, while praying for its absence in those whom we love.

I have been deeply impressed by the integrity of many of these people called schizophrenic who struggle with quiet courage and dignity against an oppressive alien force, which often appears to them neither alien nor oppressive. I have also been impressed by how difficult it often is for the families to live with the consequences of the illness. Professionals frequently are quick to criticize families for excluding such a member when they themselves are more quick to divorce a family member of their own for far less. Why we always expect greater nobility in the damned than in ourselves is an intriguing question deserving more careful study.

The tendency to make schizophrenia the noun remains with us. It is the person who is the noun and not the illness. The shared human experience of the therapist and patient is not significantly diminished by the peculiar form of the patient's anguish. Anguish remains a feeling state with which the psychiatrist can empathize. No matter how devastating the illness, the essential humanity of the patient remains.

Science and medical care suffer from fads and fashions as much as the automobile or fashion industries. Unfortunately, there is more denial operating in mental health and because of our ahistoricality we fail to recognize how arbitrary, if not silly, our current activities may appear in the future. There can be no substitute for the doctor-patient relationship. Egalitarian words about team approaches lend themselves well to after-dinner speeches, particularly if wine has been served with the meal and critical faculties are appropriately dulled. Patients do not want to relate to teams. They want to relate to other people because they—like all of us—are social creatures and need their own kind. The schizophrenic person may need other people more ambivalently but not less intensely. Patients need a stable physician who will assume responsibility for their total care and be available to them as long as they deem necessary.

The schizophrenic patient brings an impaired mind to the therapeutic relationship. This impairment manifests itself in altered modes of communication. In a curious way the schizophrenic is bilingual and the doctor is not. It is useful to try to learn the language of the schizophrenic in the same sense that it is useful to strive to achieve our ego ideal. The process of striving is important, but the goal is never attained. The therapist cannot bridge the communicative gap by learning to speak a version of primary process. The schizophrenic must come to the therapist and will only do so when he feels able and willing. There is no substitute for trust, patience, and hope in this relationship, and these qualities can only emerge in the presence of the doctor's honesty, candor, and willingness to make the patient's needs primary. Trust, particularly, cannot emerge in a relationship which is unilateral. The doctor must learn to trust the patient first.

In an effort to describe the curious relationship that must develop between the doctor and the schizophrenic patient, I used an analogy some years ago which is still helpful. We must let the schizophrenic play Virgil to our Dante, even though we understand no Latin. It is only with this attitude of openness and trusting uncertainty, initially on our part, that we may bridge the gap in communication and find our way through the inferno together.

REFERENCES

1. MOREL, B.A.: *Etudes Cliniques: Traité Théorique et Pratique des Maladies Mentales.* Paris: Masson, 1852-1853.
2. HECKER, E.: Die Hebephrenie. *Arch. Path. Anat. Physiol. Klin. Med.,* 52: 394-429, 1871.
3. KAHLBAUM, K.L.: *Die Katonie oder das Spannungsirresein.* Berlin: Hirschwald, 1874.
4. KOCH, R.: Presentation to the Physiological Society in Berlin, 1882.
5. KRAEPELIN, E.: *Compendium der Psychiatrie.* Leipzig: Abel, 1883.
6. KRAEPELIN, E.: *Psychiatrie. Ein Lehrbuch für Studierende und Ärzte,* 5th ed. Leipzig: Barth, 1896.
7. KRAEPELIN, E.: *Psychiatrie. Ein Lehrbuch für Studierende und Ärzte,* 6th ed. Leipzig: Barth, 1899.
8. BLEULER, E.: Dementia Praecox oder die Gruppe der Schizophrenien. In: G. Aschaffenburg (Ed.), *Handbuch der Psychiatrie.* Leipzig: Deuticke, 1911.
9. CANCRO, R.: Thought disorder and schizophrenia. *Dis. Nerv. Syst.,* 29:846-849, 1968.
10. MEYER, A.: The life chart and the obligation of specifying positive data in psychopathological diagnosis. In: E.E. Winters (Ed.), *The Collected Papers of Adolf Meyer. Vol. III, Medical Teaching.* Baltimore: Johns Hopkins Press, 1951, pp. 52-56.
11. KRAEPELIN, E.: *Psychiatrie. Ein Lehrbuch für Studierende und Ärzte,* 8th ed. Leipzig: Barth, 1909-1915.
12. JASPERS, K.: *Allgemeine Psychopathologie.* Berlin: Springer, 1913.
13. BLEULER, E.: *Lehrbuch der Psychiatrie,* 4th ed. Berlin: Springer, 1923.

14. FRANK, J.: Psychoanalyse und Psychiatrie. *Sammlung Psychoanalytischer Aufsätze,* 99-102, 1932.
15. LANGFELDT, G.: The prognosis in schizophrenia. *Acta Psychiat.* Scand., Suppl. 110, 1956.
16. MOSHER, L., and FEINSILVER, D.: *Special Report on Schizophrenia.* Washington: HEW, 1972.
17. KUBIE, L.S.: Multiple fallacies in the concept of schizophrenia. *J. Nerv. Ment. Dis.,* 153:331-342, 1971.
18. CANCRO, R.: A classificatory principle in schizophrenia. *Am. J. Psychiat.,* 126:1655-1659, 1970.
19. WORDSWORTH, W.: *The Preludes.* Book II. Boston: D.C. Heath and Co., 1899.
20. CANCRO, R.: *A Comparison of Process and Reactive Schizophrenia,* 1962. Ann Arbor: University Microfilms, 69-5166.
21. CANCRO, R., and SUGERMAN, A.A.: Classification and outcome in process-reactive schizophrenia. *Comprehen. Psychiat.,* 9:227-232, 1968.
22. GINSBURG, B.E., COWEN, J.S., MAXSON, S.C., and SZE, P.Y.: Neurochemical effects of gene mutations associated with audiogenic seizures. In: A. Barbeau, and J.R. Brunette (Eds.), *Progress in Neuro-Genetics.* Amsterdam: Excerpta Medica, 1969, pp. 695-701.
23. SPRING, B.J., and ZUBIN, J.: Attention and information processing as indicators of vulnerability to schizophrenic episodes. In: L.C. Wynne, R.L. Cromwell, and S. Matthysse (Eds.), *The Nature of Schizophrenia: New Approaches to Research and Treatment.* New York: Wiley, 1978, pp. 366-375.
24. CANCRO, R., GLAZER, W., and VAN GELDER, P.: Patterns of visual attention in schizophrenia. In: G. Serban (Ed.), *Cognitive Defects in the Development of Mental Illness.* New York: Brunner/Mazel, 1978, pp. 304-313.
25. FARKAS, T., WOLF, A.P., JAEGER, J., BRODIE, J.D., DeLEON, M., DeFINA, P., CHRISTMAN, D.R., FOWLER, J.S., MACGREGOR, R.R., GOLDMAN, A., YONEKURA, Y., BULL, A.B., SCHWARTZ, M., LOGAN J., and CANCRO, R.: Regional brain glucose metabolism in the study of chronic schizophrenia: I. The frontal lobes. In press.
26. RUDIN, E.: *Zur Vererbung und Neuentstehung der Dementia Praecox.* Berlin: Springer, 1916.

SUBJECT INDEX

For information on chemical substances, see drug classes, generic, and trade names, e.g., Tricyclic antidepressants; Trimipramine; Surmontil

281

NAME INDEX

289